Group Psychodynamics
New Paradigms and New Perspectives

Edited by

David A. Halperin, MD

YEAR BOOK MEDICAL PUBLISHERS, INC.
CHICAGO ● LONDON ● BOCA RATON

1 2 3 4 5 6 7 8 9 0 93 92 91 90 89

Library of Congress Cataloging-in-Publication Data

Group psychodynamics.

  Bibliography: p.
  Includes index.
  1. Group psychotherapy.   I. Halperin, David A.
RC488.G692   1989   616.89'152   89-5525
ISBN 0-8151-4051-7

To Gayle, Samara, Ilana, and Maia — my own
support group — with love

Henry Blumfarb, MSW
Faculty and Supervisor
Blanton-Peale Graduate
    Institute
Institutes of Religion and Health
New York, NY

John I. Dintenfass, MD
Assistant Clinical Professor of
    Psychiatry
Mount Sinai School of Medicine
New York, NY
Secretary General
International Society for
    Adolescent Psychiatry

Jeffrey Foster, MD
Assistant Professor of Clinical
    Psychiatry
Director, Geriatric Services and
    Training Program
New York University School of
    Medicine
New York, NY

RoseMarie Perez Foster, PhD
Associate Professor, Adjunct
City College of the City
    University of New York
New York, NY

Theresa Aiello Gerber, MSW
Adjunct Lecturer in Social
    Work
New York University School of
    Social Work
New York, NY

Consulting Supervisor to Pelham
    Family Services of
    Westchester
Consulting Supervisor to Family
    Services of Eastchester

Leslie Hartley Gise, MD
Associate Clinical Professor of
    Psychiatry
Director, The Premenstrual
    Syndromes Program
Mount Sinai School of Medicine
New York, NY

Berney Goodman, MD
Assistant Clinical Professor of
    Psychiatry
Mount Sinai School of Medicine
New York, NY

Hadassah Neiman Gurfein, PhD
Clinical Instructor of Psychiatry
Mount Sinai School of Medicine
New York, NY

Anna Halberstadt, MA. CSW
Psychotherapist
Program for Soviet Russian
    Emigres
Jewish Board of Family and
    Children's Services
New York, NY
Adjunct Professor of Social
    Work,
Columbia University School of
    Social Work,
New York, NY

David A. Halperin, MD
Associate Clinical Professor of
  Psychiatry
Mount Sinai School of Medicine
New York, NY
Director of Group
  Psychotherapy
Roosevelt Hospital of the
  St. Luke's-Roosevelt Hospital
  Center
New York, NY
Consulting Psychiatrist
Cult HotLine and Clinic
Jewish Board of Family and
  Children's Services
New York, NY

Howard D. Kibel, MD
Associate Professor of Clinical
  Psychiatry
Cornell University Medical
  College
Coordinator of Group
  Psychotherapy
New York Hospital — Cornell
  Medical Center, Westchester
  Division
White Plains, NY
Retiring-President
American Group Psychotherapy
  Association

Paul Kymissis, MD
Assistant Professor of Clinical
  Psychiatry
Mount Sinai School of Medicine
New York, NY

Enid A. Lang, MD
Assistant Clinical Professor of
  Psychiatry
Mount Sinai School of Medicine
New York, NY

Lena Mandel, MA, CSW
Psychotherapist
Jewish Board of Family and
  Children's Services of New
  York

Stephen J. Melson, MD
Assistant Clinical Professor of
  Psychiatry
University of Washington
  School of Medicine
Head, Section of Psychiatry and
  Psychology
Virginia Mason Hospital
Seattle, Washington

Peter A. Olsson, MD
Associate Clinical Professor of
  Psychiatry
Baylor College of Medicine
Associate Clinical Professor of
  Psychiatry
University of Texas (Houston)
  School of Medicine
Houston, Texas

Edward K. Rynearson, MD
Associate Clinical Professor of
  Psychiatry
University of Washington
  School of Medicine
Virginia Mason Hospital
Seattle, Washington

Sharon Sageman, MD
Assistant Clinical Professor of
  Psychiatry
New York University School of
  Medicine
New York, NY

Philip Wells Shambaugh, MD
Clinical Instructor in Psychiatry
Harvard Medical School at the
    Cambridge Hospital
Cambridge, Massachusetts

Henry Spitz, MD
Clinical Professor of Psychiatry
Columbia University College of
    Physicians and Surgeons
Director of Group
    Psychotherapy
New York State Psychiatric
    Institute
New York, NY

Susan Spitz, MSW
Coordinator Couples' Treatment
    Program
Columbia-Presbyterian
    Psychiatric Associates

Walter N. Stone, MD
Professor, Department of
    Psychiatry
University of Cincinnati College
    of Medicine
Cincinnati, Ohio

Hillel Swiller, MD
Director, Divison of
    Psychotherapy, Department
    of Psychiatry
Associate Professor of
    Psychiatry
Mount Sinai School of Medicine
New York, NY

Alexander Wolf, MD
Senior Supervisor and Training
    Psychoanalyst
PostGraduate Center for Mental
    Health, Inc.
New York, NY

CONTENTS

ix

This is a splendid book.

When Dr David Halperin asked me if I would be interested in writing a foreword to a volume on group therapy under his auspices, I said I would be honored to do so for I have known him over many years as a gifted psychoanalyst. Surely I would have nothing but pleasure in reading anything he had to say about group psychotherapy.

However, when I saw the titles of the chapters by a number of contributors, I was not so certain that I would be pleased. All my bêtes noires seemed laid out before me: emphasis on group process, group-as-a-whole concepts, short-term group psychotherapy, homogeneous rather than heterogeneous groups, and so on. I reread the title of the volume. Why was I so touchy about it?

After all the book did not claim to be about group therapy. It referred simply to "groups." And why did I need to be so one-sidedly involved with psychoanalysis in groups? There are other kinds of groups that have interest and value. A group may be therapeutic analytically or nonanalytically. A group may be constructive or destructive. A group may be explored for other purposes than treatment. Surely group process may be followed in nonanalytic groups for research purposes without damaging the individual member. Group-as-a-whole emphasis may be explored as long as members are not neglected and submerged in attention to the mass rather than the individual. While in my 50 years of practice of psychoanalysis in groups, I was never able to achieve adequate results in the short term, it did not mean that no one else could do it. Why did I need to be so emphatic about organizing heterogeneous groups when the skilled therapists in this volume were successful with homogeneous groups?

I reread the transcript and shed somewhat (but not altogether) some of my bias. And this time I really enjoyed the volume. It taught me a lot. It is beautifully organized and written. It helped me to see that my way of seeing and doing things is not the only way. It challenged my exclusivity. I am grateful to Dr Halperin and his colleagues for providing me with a wonderful lesson. I believe that others in the field may be equally gratified by the grace with which Dr Halperin and his associates offer us their understanding of the "paradigms and perspectives" of groups.

Alexander Wolf

Contexts and contextualism — this decade has seen a measured redis-
covery of individuals as social beings whose aspirations, arts, and
anxiety are a reflection of their surroundings. Within psychotherapy,
there has been a reappraisal of the manner in which individual psychopathology is an expression of group norms and group dynamics. Thus,
the individual is increasingly seen as the product of his own experiences in growth and development, and as an autonomous being operating within the parameters defined by social status, ethnic identity,
gender roles, and medical stressors. With this heightened appreciation
of the individual in his contexts has come a transformation in which
psychotherapy, hitherto regarded primarily in terms of a dyadic enterprise, is now seen as an area in which group approaches can play a
major role in helping the individual deal with physical illness, social
disability, socially dysfunctional behavior, and in promoting improved
social adaptation.

Group Psychodynamics: New Paradigms and New Perspectives
reflects this changing perspective and the added importance of group
approaches in working with the individual. In a recognition of the
importance of examining all activity within its context, group
psychotherapy itself is placed within its historical context in a historical
memoir by Howard Kibel which incisively discusses the evolution of
group psychotherapy within the United States. His contribution is
more than a historical essay; it is a discussion of the importance of the
mentoring relationship in the development of modern psychoanalytic
perspectives within group psychotherapy.

Group Psychodynamics: New Paradigms and New Perspectives is
divided into three sections. Part I, Historical and Theoretical Perspectives, is designed to provide a survey of significant theoretical aspects
of group psychotherapy. Throughout this section, the focus is on providing the clinician and student with an appreciation of the dynamic
issues that arise in the effort to utilize group approaches in working
with new populations, new problems, and in placing group dynamic
issues within a chronologic context.

The six chapters of part I focus on areas which provide significant
difficulty for the beginning group therapist. Philip Wells Shambaugh's
discussion of group evolution and the role played by myth and fantasy
during a group's evolution provides the student with an appreciation
of the framework in which group activity occurs and evolves. Walter
Stone's chapter on transference is an examination of the central phenomenon of all psychodynamic psychotherapy and its role within
groups and the research approaches which more clearly define its

parameters. Countertransference and its importance within the supervisory process is discussed by David Halperin in the fourth chapter, and forms a central issue in the chapters on coleadership by Enid Lang and David Halperin. Countertransference and its role in the formation of collusive resistances in psychoanalytically oriented group psychotherapy is further examined from a vantage point of the psychology of the self by Henry Blumfarb. Together, these five chapters examine the role of the group leader in the formation of the group and in the evolution of the group. The focus in these chapters remains on the role of the group leader in avoiding the development of therapeutic impasses within the psychoanalytically oriented group and in sponsoring the group's work toward enabling the individual to examine in a meaningful manner those resistances which impede realization of his potential.

Part II, New Populations, is a series of eight chapters in which the principles of psychoanalytically oriented group psychotherapy are examined in the context of their application to the treatment of the medically ill, in the facilitation of self-help groups, and within the educational process. The chapters by Berney Goodman, Sharon Sageman, and Leslie Gise examine the role of group approaches in working with the chronically ill patient in which psychiatric liaison and consultation is an intrinsic aspect of helping the professional caretakers deal with issues of extraordinary concern medically and which resonate deeply within the individual and the community. The remaining chapters of this section examine the extension of group psychotherapy into a wide variety of areas. Henry and Susan Spitz examines the use of group approaches in working with cocaine addiction and abuse. Peter Olsson explores the adaptation of group therapy and psychodrama in working with alexithymia, and Hadassah Gurfein discusses working with the parents of children who are seriously medically ill. There has been a recent and continuing efflorescence in both the self-help movement and in the use of the mental health professional as a facilitator in groups whose primary focus is not formally therapeutic. These extensions of group psychotherapy are presented by David Halperin in his chapter on self-help groups and by Enid Lang, David Halperin, and Hillel Swiller who reflect on their experience in working with process groups in the training of psychiatric residents.

Part III explores the changing face of group psychotherapy during the life cycle and the demands that working with the very young and the very old place on the therapist's sensitivity. Theresa Gerber presents her intriguing work with latency age girls, and Jeffrey and Rose-Marie Perez Foster discuss their work with geriatric patients. Particular emphasis is placed on the use of group modalities in working with adolescents. Paul Kymissis, John Dintenfass, and David Halperin each discuss the use of group psychotherapy and group dynamic principles in understanding the adaptation of group approaches to working with adolescents. Of particular interest is the emphasis of the role of the arts as auxiliaries within the therapeutic discourse. Thus, Edward Rynearson and Stephen Melson examine the use of films and the other plastic arts in intensive group psychotherapy with hospitalized adults. Finally, Anna Halberstadt and Lena Mandel discuss the use of group psychotherapy in working with individuals who have had the experience of living in a malignant grouplike environment. Their chapter on group work with Soviet Russian immigrants provides a necessary reminder that group approaches represent a powerful tool within the therapeutic armamentarium and that group approaches may at times be utilized by the unscrupulous in a society in the service of exploitation and not in the service of the individual.

David A. Halperin

ACKNOWLEDGMENTS

I thank my many friends for their interest, patient support, forbearance, and suggestions which have contributed to this volume. In particular, I express my appreciation to the Department of Psychiatry of the Mount Sinai School of Medicine and especially to the members of the Division of Group Psychotherapy for their constant stimulus. In addition, I owe a debt to both the Department of Psychiatry of the Roosevelt Hospital, of the St Luke's–Roosevelt Hospital Center, and to the Jewish Board of Family and Children's Services of New York City for giving me the opportunity to train and work with the members of their staffs. Finally, I should like to acknowledge the profound debt I feel toward my father, Isaac H. Halperin, MD, and to Aaron Stein, MD, whose compassion and interest in human dilemmas has been a continuing source of guidance in working toward the use of group approaches to meeting individual concerns.

PART I
HISTORICAL AND
THEORETICAL PERSPECTIVES

1

A Historical Memoir on Group Psychotherapy

Howard D. Kibel

The beginnings of group psychotherapy in this country are credited to a Boston internist, Joseph Hershey Pratt. He first applied a group method to the treatment of tuberculosis patients in a class-type setting.[1] His psychological orientation toward medical disease paved the way for his venture into the field of psychotherapy. In 1930, he established a "thought-control class" at the Boston Dispensary for patients with functional nervous disorders.[2] He utilized an inspirational method,[3] first to reassure the medically ill, but later to encourage patients to express their worrisome thoughts and feelings, and admit to their problems.

At the end of World War I, a young, psychoanalytically oriented, staff psychiatrist, Edward W. Lazell, established lecture classes for a group of war veterans confined to the wards for schizophrenics at St Elizabeth's Hospital in Washington, DC.[4] Ten years later, L. Cody Marsh, who was influenced by Lazell, employed a similar method at Worcester State Hospital in Massachusetts.[5] However, his method was more informal. His groups averaged fewer than 20 patients, and he used a variety of (what would be called today) group exercises and activities to promote rehabilitation and re-education. He was committed to the then innovative notion that patients could be supportive to one another.[6] Concurrently, Jacob L. Klapman, unaware of the work of Lazell and Marsh, developed a more didactic and authoritarian approach to both hospitalized and private practice patients.[7] So did Abraham A. Low through his system of group therapy known as willtraining.[8] However, the works of Klapman and Low were reported too late to influence the mainstream of clinical practice.

Trigant L. Burrow was the first American psychoanalyst to study the small group method for treatment purposes. He was a student of Adolf Meyer and Carl Jung, was one of the founding members of the American Psychoanalytic Association, and he later served as its president.[3] He had wanted psychoanalysis to investigate social forces as the origin of neurosis and believed that such research should be carried out in the group setting. Consequently, beginning in 1923 he and his associates — students and patients — analyzed one another in experimental groups of four to 20 members. He first called this method "group-analysis," but later substituted the term "phyloanalysis," to emphasize its investigative nature. His focus was on social research, although he was concerned with clinical applications to a psychotherapeutic group. His work estranged him from the psychoanalytic community and in 1933, when the American Psychoanalytic Association was reorganized, he was dropped from membership. Because of his professional isolation and emphasis on social research to investigate causality, he was separated from the mainstream of development. More central were the works of Paul Schilder and Louis Wender.

Schilder and Wender were the pioneers of psychoanalytic group psychotherapy. Their writings encouraged and directly influenced Alexander Wolf to undertake his first experimental group.[9] Independent of Wender, Schilder began his work in the Outpatient Department of Bellevue Hospital, treating patients with severe neuroses and mild psychoses.[10] He employed psychoanalytic techniques in the group, for which he was later recognized by Slavson.[11] However, because of his emphasis on body image and the exploration of attendant personal ideologies, his method was not adopted or developed by others. Schilder has been said to have been "too cognitive to be therapeutic and too theoretical to be practical."[12]

Wender, on the other hand, was more influential. He directly influenced Aaron Stein, who in turn trained a generation of psychiatrists at the Mount Sinai and Hillside Hospitals in New York City. The latter was this author's mentor. Stein, the student, appears to have influenced and developed the work of his teacher. The same may be said of this author. Tracing the line of development of the works of Wender and Stein maps out the advancement of thought from teacher to student and their reciprocal influences on each other. Hopefully, this chapter can serve as a small contribution to the understanding of the phenomena of mentorship.

LOUIS WENDER

Louis Wender received his early psychiatric training under the aegis of William Alanson White and later completed his analytic training by attending Freud's seminars in Vienna and having an analysis with one of the minor disciples, Ernest Hitchman (P.H. Wender, personal communication, 1988). He was probably the first clinician to conduct psychoanalytically oriented groups.[12] He began in 1929 with inpatients at the Hastings Hillside Hospital in Hastings-on-Hudson, NY, which he helped found (P.H. Wender, personal communication, 1988), and later continued his work at Pinewood Sanitarium, in Katonah, NY.* The treatment was directed at "mild mental patients and psychoneurotics,"[13(p54)] who today would be categorized as being in the upper end of the spectrum of borderline personality organization, that is, those with mild affective and cluster C personality disorders (P.H. Wender, personal communication, 1988). The idea of group psychotherapy was literally a creature of necessity.[14] Having been appointed director of a small psychiatric hospital, he found himself in the impossible position of having to provide intensive psychiatric care to 40 people by himself. Wender was committed to a psychoanalytic orientation. He bemoaned the limitations imposed on psychoanalysis as therapy by the conditions of hospitalization. These included cost, a limited length of stay, the dearth of unsuitable patients, and contamination of the transference in a setting where patients share therapists. He became committed to applying psychoanalytic thinking to this situation. Therefore, he undertook a series of talks with the patients, designed to educate them on current dynamic psychoanalytic theory about how their emotional disorders developed.

Education was welcomed by the patients since it demystified their problems. Wender had the knack of stating psychodynamics in clearly comprehensible terms, with humor and warmth. Very quickly, he observed that the patients provided one another emotional support along with productive feedback. More importantly, he found that "the types of feelings described by patients in analysis, and experienced by them in the transference toward the analyst, came out in full force in the group."[14(p295)]

Later on, Wender[15] reflected on these early experiences. He had noted that group living in a hospital was therapeutic in itself. This too prompted him to consider applying psychoanalytic psychotherapy within a group. In carrying out his early endeavors, Wender was greatly influenced by discussions with his friend and collaborator, Paul

---

* Both facilities have long since closed.

Schilder. Out of their work, psychoanalytic group psychotherapy was born. However, it has been alleged that Schilder credited Wender with devising the method (P.H. Wender, personal communication, 1988).

In the early years, weekly sessions were conducted with six to eight patients. Sessions lasted two to three hours and were closed-ended. However, Wender later experimented with different formats, expanding the attendance to 20 to 30 patients, holding sessions twice weekly, limiting the length to one hour, and inviting the individual therapists to sit in.[16] Eventually, he settled on a once-a-week session with ten to 12 members.[17] His later work, at Pinewood, appears to have resembled the format of today's community meeting, but with a psychotherapeutic focus.

Wender viewed the human individual as a "group animal," a social product whose neurosis or psychosis was motivated by the mores of the group into which he was born, namely the family.[13,18,19] Because that group had traumatized the patient by rejecting, overprotecting, or making him too dependent, the psychotherapy group could be used to afford the patient a corrective emotional experience, in the manner advocated by Alexander et al.[20] As he stated, in the group the individual

> ...learns to understand the problems of others, to associate himself with them, to release his aggressive tendencies, his hates, his loves and his wishes, without accompanying sense of guilt. By working out his difficulties and achieving adjustment in the small group, he becomes able to face the large group (the world) and handle his emotional problems, social or other, on a normal basis.[18(p708)]

These views bear semblance to those of Slavson,[21] but more clearly resemble those of Foulkes.[22]*

Early in his work, Wender began sessions with something akin to lecture material. This consisted of a simple explanation of the psychic apparatus in terms of "primitive instinctual drives, conscious and unconscious elements, significance of dreams, early infantile traumata, reaction formations, repressions, rationalizations, and so on."[13(p57)] This theoretical material was then used to promote a general discussion among the members of basic emotional problems. The context was generic and served "to divert the patients from their immediate problems," while promoting "a feeling of closeness." Wender quickly recognized that individuals entered those discussions in ways that related to their own problems. Therefore, he began to introduce case material that was "sufficiently disguised and modified for the patient not to recognize it as his own."[18(p713)] This gave the patient the

---

* In this regard, it is interesting to note that Stein, like this author, eventually found kinship with the writings of Foulkes and his followers.

opportunity to discuss his difficulties indirectly (or even to request a private interview once he acknowledged the problem as his own). Once drawn into the discussion, the patient talked "freely at times, shedding a great deal of light on his problem, expressing repressed hostilities and frustrations, and producing a great deal of unconscious material."[16(pp52-53)] Wender noted that such a "generic approach minimizes resistance and trauma, since the patient is left free to accept as much as he is ready to accept as applying to him, and to the degree necessary for him is also able to project explanations painful to him on to other patients."[13(p58)]

With time, the lecture format was de-emphasized and the content focused on the individual members, their histories and problems. Members talked about one another's problems in ways that revealed their own. Speaking of oneself indirectly without feeling threatened was found to be an important mechanism in groups, at a deeper level, for overcoming resistance.[17] Sibling rivalry occurred among the patients, so that when one or two talked about their problems, by sheer contagion, others did the same, and the resistances for all were minimized.[18] Additionally, the commonality of problems enabled the patients to identify with one another. Noting that "in the theory of psychoanalysis the idea of transference, rejection [projection] and introjection plays an important role...in group psychotherapy the patient-to-patient transference is capitalized."[18(p711)] In short, Wender was the first to discover that there were group-specific mechanisms that enhanced the therapeutic process.

While the method seemed stereotyped in his early writings, Wender apparently shifted his approach. He reported that when patients were actively encouraged to participate in the discussions, the flow of ideas from one to another resembled free association, with the production of much unconscious material.[16] Ultimately, he advised that there be no set procedure, but that the patients open the sessions spontaneously and participate, each at his own pace. The therapist was directed to deal with the resistance and guide the discussion, but it was the spontaneous productions of the patients which determined the direction and composed the content of sessions.[17] Wender had progressed from the use of a modified lecture format to one in which there was a free-floating discussion.

Wender spoke of four principal dynamics in group psychotherapy. Today, we would refer to these as putative therapeutic factors. These were: intellectualization; patient-to-patient transference; catharsis-in-the-family; and group interaction. In addition, he noted how benefits could be derived from the shifting transferences and identifications of group life.

As a psychoanalyst, Wender was schooled in the notion that only mastery over the unconscious could be mutative. However, he argued that analysts had neglected the conscious too completely as a factor in the healing process. He found that "comprehension of emotional reactions...enables the patient to meet new situations with greater awareness and skill."[13(p58)] He proposed that a special kind of synthesis of intellectual understanding and emotional acceptance in treatment produced insight, which facilitated social adjustment. Perhaps concerned that his analytic colleagues would dismiss the process as being superficial, he acknowledged that it may have had components similar to self-discipline, but stringently argued that "[w]hile group therapy in no way professes or strives to be an intellectual discipline, it does lead to a comprehension of emotional reactions that enables the patient to meet new situations with greater awareness and skill."[19(p139)]

The patient-to-patient transference, Wender noted, contained elements that correspond to the psychoanalytic transference of individual treatment. However, in group psychotherapy this transference was made use of in several ways. It served to facilitate the transference toward the therapist through the identification of one patient with another who had established a transference to the leader. It suited the needs of the patients since they had to abrogate the transference to the therapist for very practical reasons, namely, the necessity to share him. Over time, this relationship between patients took on a meaning of its own, embracing nontransferential areas of personality. Thus, it was deemed to both "afford[s] libidinal outlets and foster[s] more normal socialization."[16(p58)] These notions were developed further by Stein.

Wender described catharsis-in-the-family as perhaps the cornerstone of treatment. He recognized that the group activated a transference of tendencies that were originally directed toward parents and siblings. The therapist became symbolic of the parent and the other patients represented the siblings. This situation permitted the patient to work out conflicts that were not resolved in his own family of origin. In the group, the patient could receive understanding from the "just parent" and was also free to rebel openly, thus averting the repression and guilt feelings engendered in the original experience. Sibling rivalry served as a stimulus for the release of these aggressive tendencies. Emotional release of aggression, Wender believed, gave the patient self-confidence to express himself and removed feelings of guilt and inferiority. In this way, the group served to provide a corrective emotional experience, whereby the original trauma from the family of origin was relieved. Thus, Wender found his own views to be in accord with those set forth by Alexander et al.[20]

Wender viewed group interaction as beneficial in several ways. First, the patient who previous to treatment "regarded his problems as unique...learns through the exchange of the group that many of his fellows have similar...conflicts."[18(p711)] Today, we would refer to this process as universalization. Secondly, in the group the patient learns to evaluate his own experience and problems against those of others. This provides a basis for the patient to readapt himself to social demands and may even give rise to new ego ideals. Third, attendant upon a free flow of ideas in the discussion, resembling free association, unconscious material is released, "frequently without the patient's awareness but to the advantage of treatment when utilized by the therapist."[16(p58)] Fourth, the group possessed certain stimulating properties. In these sessions patients showed attitudes which were very different from those of individual psychotherapy. Particularly, character traits that were often hidden in dyadic sessions frequently became clearly manifest in the group.[17] Lastly, Wender noted, the patient's "drive to become well derives greater impetus from his identification in the group as the sibling rivalry is directed toward constructive instead of destructive channels."[18(p711)]

Early in his work, Wender realized that the rebellion against the father/therapist could also occur against the other patients as siblings and that the patient could obtain therapeutic understanding from his peers, as well as from the therapist.[18] Although not stated as such, he was aware that transference potentials within a group shifted from therapist to patient and back again. He never developed this idea fully. But in later years, he came to recognize thaat the relationship of the patient to the therapist in the group was fundamentally different from that in individual treatment. It was less intense, less threatening, and more real.[17]

Identification with this good parent image enabled the patient to take a therapeutic role with his fellow sufferers.[19] On the other hand, identification with the other patients gave the individual a sense of strength and support to express himself freely. For each individual, similarities with his brethren enabled members to overcome their difficulties in accepting direct interpretations. Acceptance was often achieved "at first as relating only to other people and finally as relating to oneself."[18(p713)]

Wender stressed that these factors in group psychotherapy influenced ongoing individual treatment. This was especially true with those cases where, in individual treatment, the relationship to the therapist was the focus of a great deal of resistance and often insurmountable difficulties. He noted, for example, that in patients with severe character neuroses, so much hostility or competition or anxiety was evoked by the nearness to the therapist that treatment was frequently blocked, while in borderline patients and depressives the transference was frequently threatening or guilt-provoking. However, group psychotherapy helped in a specific way with the transference resistance of individual sessions. The relationship of the patients to the therapist in the group was different from that in individual treatment in that it was much less threatening and was felt less intensely. Additionally, patients felt less anxious expressing disagreement with or aggression toward the therapist, because their mutual identification provided them with a sense of strength and support to express themselves more freely.[17] All this permitted the transference to the individual therapist to be "de-toxified." As Wender stated, "After experience with group treatment, where they learn to regard the therapist more realistically and with less anxiety, patients in individual treatment relate much better to the therapist."[17(p324)]

In a sense, the converse was also true. Wender observed that in a psychotherapeutic group, thinking, and hence verbal production, were censored at first, but that this obstacle was overcome by the private interviews of individual psychotherapy.[18] Thus, throughout his career, Wender used group psychotherapy as an adjunct to individual treatment. The two treatments were conducted by different therapists. Today, this practice would be referred to as conjoint therapy. He advocated this approach for all psychoneuroses, severe character disorders, borderlines, and so-called early schizophrenics. In order words, he saw group as a potentially universal aid to individual psychotherapy, except for severe psychotics "who live completely in a world of unreality."[23(p58)]

Wender never developed a theory of group as such. However, he recognized that groups had unique effects. He worked during an era in which society had been witness to barbaric acts by supposed advanced, civilized nations. This probably caused him to first postulate that "the emotionally immature with weak egos" are prone to be "manipulated by pseudo-leaders within a large social group."[24(p247)] But, he went further to suggest that because "man is born and reared in the group, [and because] he is traumatized in the group,...the desire to be a member of the group for reasons of protection and help remain with him."[15(p384)] He began to speculate, like McDougall, that man needs the group.

Wender was probably the first to use the term "psychoanalytic group psychotherapy."[15] The focus of his interventions was basically toward the individual in the group. However, he was the first to introduce the notion that one should use "psychoanalytic principles in the handling of a group instead of an individual."[25(p346)]

The Use of Groups in Milieu Treatment

In his hospital work, Wender used groups at every level of the organization. As noted, these ranged in size from small therapy groups to the large meeting format. Early in his work, at the Hastings Hillside

Hospital, patient participation in the hospital structure and even governance was encouraged. Through this, Wender developed a kind of therapeutic community which resembled a modern psychosocial rehabilitative model.[26] Patients "were encouraged to participate in all hospital activities on an equal basis with the rest of the staff. Their activities ranged from cleaning their rooms or working on the hospital farm, to planning the meals and helping to organize the recreational activity."[27(p211)] Participation took a concrete form in 1935 when the patients set up an organization of their own, from which self-governing groups emerged. Officers and a policy-making governing board administered all hospital work through the patient community's several committees. Those committees ran the recreational and social treatment programs. Former passive participation by patients in therapeutic activities was soon replaced by spontaneous and quite active participation. Despite the latitude granted to the patients through self-government, the hospital's hierarchy was respected. Suggestions for changing any parts of the hospital program were made by means of letters to the director of the hospital, but the final decisions about these were made by the hospital director.

Wender believed that the miniature society of the hospital reflected, in a small way, all the aspects of reality that the patients would meet when they faced the outside world. The group activity helped the patients to recognize their childish and unrealistic attitudes and to find more adult and realistic ones.

> The patients' group provided a sort of testing place in which the reactions of the patients to the group could be observed and the difficulties in the social adjustment clearly brought out...these difficulties were brought home to the patients in a much more clear-cut and forceful fashion than could have been possible otherwise.[27(p217)]

In this way, the self-governing patient groups helped to facilitate the group psychotherapy proper, that is, by making vivid such aspects of group life as competition, rivalry, reactions to authority, and the need for group support and acceptance.

Wender's milieu treatment, like his small group method, was born of necessity. There were simply too few employees at the hospital to do the work that had to be done. By the same token, the patient government that evolved was concerned with the daily aspects of running the hospital (P.H. Wender, personal communication, 1988). The therapeutic community at Hillside extended beyond the inpatient phase of treatment. Discharged patients were so eager to continue their association that they created a self-help organization analogous to but antedating Recovery, Inc. It was first dubbed, appropriately, "The Wender Welfare League." (Wender had a practice of lending ex-inpatients small amounts of money to help them through difficult times after discharge.) The name was later changed to "The League for

Mental Health." Wender's wife, a social worker by training, was active in its administration. The league and the Wenders helped many ex-patients to function with minimal but continuing contact for periods of up to 30 years (P.H. Wender, personal communication, 1988).

Wender found that both small and large therapeutic groups were an excellent vehicle for teaching residents.[17] In the groups, residents saw individual patients in social interaction. This was used to demon-strate psychopathology. The group method was also used to illustrate the nature of the therapeutic process, specifically transference and resistance.

This early form of milieu treatment appeared to promote, for each patient, identification with the community at large. Wender reported that this bond provided ego support. This notion of identification with the group entity was never developed further by Wender, but proved to be a forerunner of the work of others[28] and was adopted much later by Stein.[29]

THE FIRST MENTORSHIP

Wender and Stein collaborated on three papers. The first consisted of a report of the application of Wender's method to outpatient treatment.[30] A conjoint format was still used and traces of Wender's original method were evident. Lectures were discarded; however, in the first few sessions the group therapist made a few introductory remarks in order to help the patients engage one another. Still, specific elements of the discussion were directed toward patients whom the therapist knew would benefit most from them. Yet, the method had matured. By this time, Wender was advocating minimally structured discussions that resembled the free association of individual analysis. Members were asked to discuss one another's problems and, under the guidance of the therapist, to help one another. Patients were seen to be of assistance to one another indirectly through their identification with one another and by virtue of mutual stimulation.

Although the method was still Wender's, the theory presented showed the influence of Stein. In an earlier work,[16] Wender had referred to Freud's famous monograph on groups.[31] However, in this first Wender-Stein collaboration, they proposed a parallel between Freud's group psychology and the dynamics of group psychotherapy. Specifically, they stated that the essential dynamic forces in the treat-ment emanated from libidinal ties within the group between the mem-bers themselves and between them and the therapist. Like Freud, they considered the relationship to the leader as primary and that the bond between members was based on the shared attachment to the thera-pist, together with the knowledge that they all had a similar type of illness. Up to this point, these theoretical statements were consistent with the previous ones of Wender. However, the writing began to reflect the style of Stein. Then, a new concept was added. It was stated that patient-to-patient identification enabled members "to share their sense of guilt — the largely unconscious guilt arising from the intensified but 'forbidden' instinctual drives underlying their symptoms."[30(p420)] This statement foreshadowed the later notions of Stein as to how groups specifically alleviated superego pressure.[32,33] Additionally, they postulated that dual vector emotional ties (patient-to-therapist and patient-to-patient) "were crystallized into a group-formation, and a unit with an identity and characteristics of its own."[30(p421)]

Here was the seed for Stein's later interest in group dynamics. However, at this point this notion was subordinated to Wender's earlier one of a catharsis-in-the-family, so that a richer re-elaboration of his earlier ideas could be presented in a manner consonant with Freud's theory of groups. Thus, despite the influence of Stein on theory, the practice remained Wender's.

AARON STEIN

Aaron Stein had worked under Wender at the Hillside Hospital and continued his mentor's tradition after the hospital moved to Glen Oaks, NY.[34] There, in 1952, he became Director of Group Psychotherapy, a position he held for 20 years. In 1948, he began to work with groups at The Mount Sinai Hospital in New York City.[35] Then in 1955, he founded the Division of Adult Group Psychotherapy and served as its chief for 25 years. The program he developed there became extensive; it offered treatment to a variety of psychosomatic and psychiatric patients[36] and served as a training ground for graduate clinicians.[37] At these two institutions, he taught a generation of psychiatrists his group-centered method.

Throughout his career, Stein remained committed to a traditional psychoanalytic approach to treatment. Although not an analyst himself, he nevertheless identified himself with analysts with whom he affiliated and collaborated.[38] Accordingly, he referred to his group method as "analytic group psychotherapy" and used intensive individual analytic work as the basis for its comparison. In this regard, he viewed group as contraindicated for those patients with neurotic symptoms who have the capacity to develop a transference neurosis in dyadic treatment, that is, "whose personality and ego strength are relatively intact...these require intensive individual psychotherapy or psychoanalysis."[33] Intensive individual psychotherapy remained for him the more expressive of the two, the more probing and thorough treatment. "In the individual session a more detailed analysis and working out of the transference and resistive manifestations is possible."[39(p87)]

Stein's tutelage by Wender influenced his entire career. His first groups were conducted in the fashion of Wender.[35,40] In his early writings, one sees an elaboration of his mentor's thinking and its enrichment. Stein applied to group therapy the postulates that Freud had offered in his classic monograph. He described a collective resistance of the group members that emanates from their mutual transference to the leader[41] and showed how the group experience facilitates the correction of faulty superego attitudes.[32]

His work at Hillside and Mount Sinai exposed him to a wide variety of hospitalized[36,42] and psychosomatic patients.[43–45] These experiences caused him to recognize the advantage of group psychotherapy for patients with impaired ego structures. In this regard, he was influenced by the work of Freedman and Sweet[46] (H.S. Alpert, personal communication, 1988) who viewed group treatment as a specific modality for selected patients in that spectrum. Likewise, Stein produced his own inclusion criteria for group psychotherapy.[33] This was his first departure from Wender's position.

The second divergence came when he advocated that group be used as a primary or solo modality for these patients to the exclusion of individual treatment.[47,48] At Mount Sinai there were many clinic patients who had proved resistant for years to individual treatment with several therapists.[35] All had developed dependent, nonproductive, anaclitic transferences to their therapists.[49] Yet each had a strong, positive transference to the clinic (H.S. Alpert, personal communication, 1988). Putting them in a group dispelled their ambivalent dependency on the therapist by changing the nature of their relationship to him. The group interaction, in contrast, opened up new channels for expression of transference attitudes in a fashion that had not been possible before. These patients' improvement continued even after their individual sessions had been terminated.[49] Earlier work with unselected patients had produced variable results.[35] Consequently, whereas Wender had advocated combined therapy for most patients, Stein came to the conclusion that group could be used alone, in a specific way for selected individuals, that is, there existed "valid criteria for using group psychotherapy as a selective form of treatment."[37(p563)] However, near the end of his career he modified his position on combined treatment.

Retrospectively, it appears that Stein's work was influenced initially by Wender and the analytic tradition, but then by other workers of his time, notably Slavson. With the latter he shared crucial notions of the vicissitudes of transference in groups[50] and the relevance of specific selection criteria for membership.[51] However, the technique he employed appeared to be uniquely his own. This was something he taught extensively, but only mentioned in late[39,52] and then final publication.[29] An outline of his contributions is worth presenting.

The Group's Internal Dynamics

Well before his acquaintanceship with the British group dynamicists,[47] Stein considered such concepts. Early in his work, he noted that members regarded the group as something particular, namely "as though it represented the superego...a strict, critical and judging body."[32(p498)] He postulated that they identified with the group entity in such a way that there developed a "group ego" which provided them emotional support.[44] He extended this notion to the hospital clinic itself[36] in accord with the traditional concept of the "transference to the hospital,"[44(p50)] and reported that the view of the hospital, as if it represented some emotionally important figure, correlated directly with and influenced the work of the group often to a surprising degree.[35,44]

Stein also reported what today would be viewed in terms of projective identification, that members used selective individuals as spokesman or scapegoat by projecting forbidden ideas and feelings onto them and then identifying with them.[53] Moreover, when describing group resistance as a function of the members' negative transference to the therapist, he stated: "A new group formation occurs and the resistance...is, therefore, more than the 'sum of the parts'; it is a distinctive expression of a group formation functioning as such, rather than as a collection of individuals."[41(p80)]

Stein's interest in group dynamics was further spurred by a visit to the Menninger Clinic (L. Horwitz, personal communication, 1987) in the mid 1960s, where a Tavistock method had been employed. However, those early ideas remained in embryonic form until his collaboration with the present author, late in his career. Then he began to explore further the notion that group members have a relationship to the group as an entity, in which the group itself functions as a fantasied, need-gratifying object.[28,39] However, for the most part he tended to view group-as-a-whole responses in a limited way, namely either as a form of transference resistance[39,54] or as a source of ego support.[39] It was not until the final collaboration[29] that holistic group reactions were considered to facilitate the exposure of unconscious conflicts.

For most of his career, Stein focused on the manner by which the individual's dynamics, that is, those normally observed in dyadic treatment, were modified by the group experience. He believed that these "dynamic factors that operate in group psychotherapy differ in many important respects from those in individual psychotherapy... [and that there are] different dynamic processes occurring...[and] at a different level, than in individual psychotherapy."[32(p495)] More specifically, he claimed that the group altered and modified the expression of transference and superego manifestations so as to make it a more suitable treatment for certain patients, as a variant from traditional psychoanalytic psychotherapy. Many of his ideas evolved during work with psychosomatic patients who had done poorly in individual treatment but improved remarkably in group.[45]

Following the work he began with Wender, Stein elaborated on the nature of the transference in groups in accordance with the ideas formulated by Freud in his famed monograph and noted how deflection of the original ties to the therapist led to group formation. He repeatedly stated that: "(1) the intensity of the transference directed toward the therapist is lessened (diluted, diminished, etc.), and (2) the transference is split (diverted, fragmented, etc.) since it is directed toward the other patients in the group as well as toward the therapist."[36(p93),47(p416),52(p156)] He expanded Wender's notion that group psychotherapy facilitates treatment for those cases where the transference is a focus of resistance. With certain patients, Stein noted, "the transference to the therapist has more primitive characteristics...necessitating special treatment techniques."[47(p416)] They feel too threatened by a close relationship with an individual therapist. For their treatment, a less regressive transference is required.[33] He concluded, therefore, that group psychotherapy was suitable for all those patients who lacked the ability to develop a transference neurosis in intensive dyadic psychoanalytic therapy, such as borderline and narcissistic conditions and character neurosis where defenses have been incorporated into the personality in an ego-syntonic fashion. Here group was deemed the treatment of choice.

Inhibition of the transference to the leader, he noted, caused it to be deflected from the leader onto the group members producing an increase in intragroup tension. "Patients utilize roles in the group, based upon unconscious fantasies, to act out and to try to get the other patients to act out transference roles and conflicts."[47(p420),52(p157)] These are expressed through "group member interactions which can be designated as a therapeutic type of acting out in the group session."[52(p157)] As a result, opportunities for transference manifestations are augmented in group; they constitute what other authors have labeled multiple transferences in which members view one another as one parent or the other, a spouse, a sibling, or a son or daughter, etc. In contrast to most other theorists who view this sort of group interaction either as a product of members' interpersonal needs or as a manifestation of autonomous, organic group forces, Stein continued to view "the intragroup tension as a derivative of the inhibited transference to the leader."[47(p419),52(p156)] In fact, he viewed the latter as the driving force behind all group processes; it is "the fundamental relationship which holds the group together."[53,p270] He recognized that the members' own interpersonal needs caused them to identify with one another and hence bond together, but he considered such "partial identifications" to be transient and less lasting.

Alterations of superego manifestations are a second major consequence of being in a group, according to Stein. The group itself symbolically represents the standards of society, and often its harsh, critical aspects, as for example in scapegoating. However, the leader modifies this effect. He is seen by the patients as an idealized father figure. Again, paraphrasing Freud, Stein claimed that once the libidinal ties that bind the group are established, the members "set up the leader in place of their own ego ideal or superego."[32(p497)] By this he meant that:

> By virtue of their identification with the idealized figure of the therapist, patients are enabled to adopt more tolerant, flexible and realistic attitudes far more quickly than is possible in individual therapy. In this way, group psychotherapy is particularly useful for patients with archaic, harsh superegos who have little or no awareness of their underlying coinflicts[33(p148)]

such as those with psychosomatic conditions, obsessive-compulsive, depressed and masochistic characters, and rigid personalities. Put in another way, there is a sharing of guilt and members provide one another support in defiance of their own superegos.

Stein viewed superego alterations in the group as a regressive phenomenon. Faced with the necessity to share the leader and because he cannot be possessed as an object, patients identify with and incorporate his values and attitudes. This process is "expressed by the formula 'If I cannot have him, I will be like him'"[32(p501)]; "this is similar to what occurs at the time of the passing of the Oedipal complex in that there has been a regressive change in the relationship to the leader from object choice to identification."[52(p155)] More properly, since this idealization of the leader as an ego ideal stood in contrast to the more punitive view of the group itself, it would be correct to speak of these change as the "splitting up or degradation of the superego." This phenomenon was considered intrinsic to the therapeutic process. It permitted a "controlled 'regression' that makes accessible the underlying thoughts and feelings that are the source of conflict."[53(p271)] Fundamental to Stein's position was the notion that the therapeutic group altered the dynamics of the patient's treatment but that being in the group did not, in itself, change the nature of his conflicts. It merely made them available to therapeutic scrutiny. Rather, it was the interpretation of those conflicts (usually by other group members) and the working through that was mutative.

The Practice and Method of Treatment

Most of the early leading figures in the field practiced group before having formulated their theoretical underpinnings. With the advantage of training by Wender, Stein could work within his mentor's framework first before developing his own theoretical structure. The latter, in turn, became the basis for his technique. His methodical nature lent itself to this process, namely the development of theory as an antecedent to practice. The method he devised had two notable characteristics: the use of group as a selective modality for specific conditions, and a definite set of guidelines for or restrictions on the therapist's behavior.

Stein recognized that the group psychotherapies constituted a gamut of treatments in which techniques could be modified to fit the treatment setting for a given patient population. But he believed that the analytically oriented, small-group type stood as an expressive mode alongside individual treatment, and that patients should be evaluated as to whether they would gain greater benefit in one or the other.

His recommendations for group were precise and detailed.[33] Their specifics are beyond the scope of this chapter, but will be summarized. They are based on the aforementioned dynamic effects that Stein postulated the group had on personality and treatment variables. He claimed, in one sense, "that participation in a group may effect all three structures of the personality: the id, the ego and the super-ego."[33(p146)] In another sense, he stated its uniqueness derived from its specific effect in altering the transference, providing emotional support, strengthening reality testing and impaired identity, alleviating unconscious guilt, exposing character defenses, and loosening the repression of intrapsychic conflicts. In this regard, he recommended group for many who could not tolerate the transference of intensive dyadic treatment because of their severe ego deficits; for borderline patients and selected chronic psychotics; for those with characterologic depression and who were masochistic[48]; in most personality disorders, especially those with severe character pathology; and for neurotic patients with underlying character defects; and for all those who had little awareness of their underlying conflicts, such as psychosomatic patients and those with related medical illness.[55] In contrast, he believed that group psychotherapy was contraindicated for most neurotic patients, those with mild personality disorders, and all unstable patients with defective ego boundaries, or in other words the least disturbed and the sickest. These required individual treatment, that is, intensive analytic psychotherapy or psychoanalysis for the former two groups and supportive psychotherapy for the latter.

For much of his career, Stein used group as the solo psychotherapeutic modality for indicated patients. Patients were initially seen a few times individually prior to placement in a group. Extensive individual contacts were avoided so as to preclude the development of regressive transference reactions (A. Stein, unpublished data, March 1965). Yet, several preparatory sessions were advised in order to allow for careful clinical evaluation, to make a treatment recommendation, to discuss the workings of group, to make the treatment contract (A. Stein, unpublished data, March 1965), to educate those new to therapy as to the nature of introspection, to establish the transference to the leader (H.S. Alpert, personal communication, 1988), and for some to lessen the impact of its loss.[48] The number of such sessions varied, depending on the clinical resources available and the patients' needs (A. Stein, unpublished data, March 1965).

The group met once weekly for 75- or 90-minute sessions. It had an upper limit of eight patients (A. Stein, unpublished data, November 1962). In select cases, group was combined with individual treatment. Stein claimed that many fragile, narcissistic patients needed group but had difficulty tolerating the tensions arising from its interactions. For them, he recommended concomitant individual treatment for purposes of providing support through transference gratification. Some rigidly defended patients who were candidates for intensive dyadic treatment were thought to benefit initially from group as a consequence of universalization. At the other end, those who had difficulty terminating from individual psychotherapy were deemed to need "the group in helping the patient deal with his unresolved transference to the individual therapist...[and] in helping him work through the necessary separation."[39(p86)] Notice how in each of these instances one modality was used as an adjunct to the other.

For most patients, Stein opposed the use of combined therapy on theoretical grounds. He noted that the transferences evoked by each modality were different. Consequently

> ...at least in relation to the transference to the leader, the concurrent use of intensive individual analytic therapy and group psychotherapy would set up conditions in which the patient would respond in two different and opposing fashions. Such a state of affairs would seem, on the face of it, to cause confusion to the patient and to be unnecessary and undesirable.[47(p420)]

In a similar vein, he advised against extramural socialization and opposed the use of alternate sessions or other meetings of patients without the therapist, fearing that these would promote acting out of transference needs outside the purview of analytic investigation, thereby rendering them unavailable for treatment[36,48,52] (A. Stein, unpublished data, November 1962 and March 1965). By and large, with respect to the management of transference in treatment, Stein was a purist.

Later in his career, Stein modified his admonition against a combined treatment approach.[39] He qualified his earlier warning that the transferences of individual and group therapy opposed each other with "the caution:... unless care is taken by the therapist to analyze, interpret and integrate the transference manifestations in both forms of treatments."[39(p80)] He then proceeded to recommend a dual approach for some of the same kinds of patients he had earlier recommended for group alone. He had come to believe that, for borderline patients, most severe character disorders, and rigid personalities, a combined approach was better than the use of one modality alone. Still, he remained committed to the notion that each form of treatment has specific effects. Thus he continued to view group as the medium for resolving intractable and primitive transferences, exposing character defenses, and in general mitigating resistances to individual treatment. Given their specificity when both modalities are used, one must serve the other, one is primary and the other adjunctive.

Stein evolved a method that fostered member-to-member interaction. During the group's initial phase of development, the therapist was advised to play an active role in promoting group discussion. All the patients were to be treated equally so that no special attention or any other form of gratification was given to one patient more than to another. The therapist indicated to the group members that they were expected to discuss their problems and here-and-now reactions with one another and evaluate one another. While they well might attempt to seduce the therapist into becoming an advice giver, a suggestion maker or an information provider, he was not to give in. He was to continue to direct the discussion away from himself and toward the members of the patient group. In other words, the therapist's task was to help the patients move from a therapist-centered position to a group-centered one. The process was as though the therapist moved from the center of the group to a position somewhat outside of it (A. Stein, unpublished data, March 1965). The analogy can be seen here between Stein's position and that of Foulkes.[22]

Stein's approach to treatment was precise and defined. Even after the group coalesced, the therapist's role continued to be prescribed. It was as follows:

> The leader must limit his interactions with the individuals and direct all his comments, be they questions, observations, clarifications, confrontations, or interpretations, to the entire membership. When members'

actions, verbalizations, or behavior are considered noteworthy, they are called to the attention of the entire group for scrutiny. For example, interventions which draw attention to the behavior of one or several members, should include an invitation to the membership to further investigate and speculate on its meaning.[29(p327)]

The therapist's behavior was designed "to frustrate individual members' persistent efforts to interact with him and thus gratify unconscious [leader] transference wishes. In this way the leader facilitates the development of intragroup tension and member-to-member interactions...and sets in motion the phases of the group's interactional pattern."[39(p82)] Only by this method did Stein believe that the group's internal dynamics would be optimized and the richness of multiple transference phenomena unfold. Short of this, that is, by reacting to or with one member, the therapist would merely be conducting individual treatment in a group setting; the group method would be deprived of its uniqueness.

Stein advised the leader merely to shepherd the interaction until a crescendo was reached, where its nature and the contributing members' characteristics became clear. Then, "unless a group member does it, the therapist intervenes, again in a group-centered fashion"[29(p327)] and halts the action. After that the members, under the guidance of the therapist, were to describe and explore what happened. This phase of the session included members' discussion of their own and one another's character defenses and transference patterns. The entire procedure was somewhat stylized.

With proper tutelage, Stein believed, patients are able to reveal the meaning they see behind one another's behavior, that is, they can and do function as adjunct therapists. Their abilities are enhanced by the group's internal dynamics which causes them to identify with the leader as an idealized figure and incorporate his attributes. "In effect, then, in a psychotherapy group, the patients through this incorporation of and identification with the therapist become the therapist in the group or, more accurately, assume the role of the therapist in the group."[56(p465)] This leaves to the leader the task of attending to the group's overall functioning and its resistances.

Late in his career, when his interest in group dynamics took hold, Stein added the following suggestion for the therapist: "He must maintain a group-centered orientation for comprehension of all material; that is, he must consider how each group event, no matter how seemingly insignificant, relates to the group as a whole."[29(p327)] At that point, he also advised that the exploration phase of the session begin with a description of the group formations that were erected during the interactional phase. This, he came to believe, enriched each member's understanding of his participation in the overall therapeutic process.

The Mechanisms of Change

Throughout his papers, Stein wrote about the healing effects of group psychotherapy. He considered members' interpretations of one another's transference patterns to be beneficial. However, he never presented his observations in an organized fashion as Wender did. This will be done here using material scattered throughout his texts. Before proceeding, it will be necessary to outline the ways in which members identify with various aspects of the group, since these identifications form the basis of its mutative effects.

To begin with, members identify with one another because they are mutually in psychic pain and sense similarities in one another's symptoms, attitudes, and conflicts. This is the well-known phenomenon of universalization.[33] Next, they share the same relationship to the therapist.[57] Quoting Freud, Stein agreed that members "identified themselves with one another in their ego."[52(p155)] Through these new relationships in the group, the patients develop a special kind of "identification with the self-investigative tendencies with the other members of the group and the therapeutic approach of the therapist."[55(p239)] This permits them to function as adjunct therapists for one another. Lastly, they identify with the significant objects in one another's lives so that they function as transference objects for one another.[49,52] In this way, members reenact unconscious transference roles with one another, making these available for therapeutic scrutiny.

Change occurs in the group in four basic ways. First, the group experience serves a supportive function in several ways. Members receive acceptance, sympathy, approval, encouragement, advice, and guidance from one another. Universalization also provides ego support, the group diminishes internal superego demands, repression is alleviated, and object relatedness is encouraged through the interactions. The latter is the means for patients to directly "provide support and gratification for each other in terms of the infantile needs of the transference,"[52(p160)] that is, through transference gratification.

Second, members' transference patterns toward one another are exposed, explored, and discussed. They interpret the unseen meaning behind one another's transference manifestations. While Stein did speak of members becoming aware of their unconscious significance,[52] he always considered the work in group to be less intensive than could be found in individual analytic psychotherapy. He probably would have agreed that interpretations in group promote ego mastery over internal conflicts.

Third, because of the many group identifications noted above, members replace conflicted object ties with new ones. Thus, they relinquish pathologic identifications, which are superseded by more mature, adult, realistic relationships in the group.[49] Faulty attitudes are corrected "by a process of substitution, identification, and ego and defence strengthening *rather than by a basic alteration in dynamic structure*" (italics mine).[32(p504)] In this way, the group experience provides a corrective emotional experience. At once we see here how Stein's view continued to parallel that of Wender.

Lastly, all these changes in the ego, the superego, and the id produce "a more useful realignment of intrapsychic forces,"[45(p599),55(p242)] so that it is no longer necessary for the patient to express conflict in a regressive fashion through symptom formation. Here Stein was differentiating analytic group psychotherapy from its intensive, dyadic counterpart. Treatment with the latter produces restructuring of personality components, whereas group psychotherapy yields a new alignment of internal structures, so that premorbid symptoms are no longer necessary to maintain one's sense of inner equilibrium.[44] Change of this sort can be lasting. In short, group is one kind of analytic treatment which produces substantive modifications of character.

THE SECOND MENTORSHIP

Stein's major contribution to theory lay in the realm of the group's effect on the individual member, specifically of altering transference, superego manifestations, and resistance. This has more to do with the member's relationship to the group than his being a part of a group entity. Considering the latter, that is, thinking of the group itself as an organic unit, takes one beyond the domain of individual psychology into group dynamics. As noted earlier, Stein was interested in group dynamics but restricted himself to the application of traditional psychoanalytic concepts to group psychotherapy. Yet he eventually came to believe "that the study of the group as an entity (group-as-a-whole) reveals the functioning of the individual member in his full complexity and should be the basis of therapeutic intervention."[54(p410)]

Collaboration with this author paved the way for the incorporation of group dynamic theories into his writings. Agreement developed with Bion's[58] "contention that group-as-a-whole experiences stir developmentally early layers of psychic functioning even in relatively well-integrated patients."[29(p318)] This meant that coexistent within collective group reactions lay multiple transference layers, comprised of both advanced and primitive object relationships.[59] If one assumes, as Stein did, that his technique promoted group cohesion, then the group should be an excellent medium for the expression of primitive object relationships. Viewed in another way, partial primitivization of the ego can be deemed to feed the interactive process.

The implications of group dynamics for theory and technique are important. Stein had originally viewed members' relationships to each other to be the product of their mutually frustrated transference to the leader. Other authors have considered peer relationships in groups to be relatively autonomous,[60] deriving strength from members' inherent needs for interpersonal relationships and mutual defense complementation.[61] It now appears that they are also precipitants of the common experience of being in and part of a group. In sum, group members' "interactions function as a condenser, a final common pathway for the expression of a gamut of internal psychological processes that are activated by group life."[29(p317)]

The therapist can still be seen as the group's prime mover, so to speak, who has created this entity and fostered its cohesion. But once established, the bonds between members have a driving force of their own; they are relatively autonomous. Under such conditions it would be difficult to imagine how anyone, even the therapist, could easily disrupt these bonds. For this reason, the therapist need not be so cautious that by intervening in a cohesive group he will foster a regressive leader transference. He can deal with one member for the moment without abandoning his group-as-a-whole orientation. After all, interventions at one level of the group will have effects (often unpredictable ones) at all other levels.[59] This is because the group *always* functions as a holistic, multidimensional system.

With the incorporation of object relations theory and group dynamics, it now becomes clear that the therapist's method and the treatment procedure need not be so stylized as Stein had advocated. Of course treatment strategy will vary according to the nature of the particular patient population and the group's phase of development. However, it appears that a group-centered approach is more relevant to the overall method and style of conducting the treatment rather than it dictating a precise technique. In short, a group-centered orientation is more germane than any specific procedure.

This evolution in thinking is consistent with the currents within the field. Earlier the literature was replete with arguments supporting the relative merits of each of the differing approaches to treatment, the individualistic, the interactional, and the group-as-a-whole.[62] However, recently there have been notable attempts to integrate the theories of group dynamics and individual psychology.[63,64] General systems theory was the forerunner of this trend. In a recent text on psychodynamic group psychotherapy, Rutan and Stone[65] came close to adopting an integrated approach. These trends are nudging the field toward the position held by Foulkes,[66] namely, that each of these three perspectives merely defines different ways of looking at facets of a gestalt, that is, each is part of the larger whole of the field or system of the group. If this is so, then a group-centered orientation is always applicable since unitary group functioning is present at all times. A group-centered method remains necessary to build and maintain cohesion. But once the latter is operative, the therapist can use greater latitude in designing his interventions.

CONCLUSION

The mentorships described in this chapter have historical significance. In one sense they demonstrate classic teacher-pupil influences which are both reciprocal and evolutionary. However, in another sense they are prototypical of development in any field. The pioneers are the innovators who break new ground. For them, practice precedes the development of theory. The second generation of workers stake out their claims to orthodoxy. Consequently, divergence of theory is characteristic of their era. The third generation is less invested in guarding its turf. These theorists are receptive to mutual influences and opened to integration of variant perspectives. For them, the challenge is to synthesize the body of knowledge so as to make the work coherent, teachable, and functional.

REFERENCES

1. Pratt JH: The class method of treating consumption in the homes of the poor. *AMA J* 1907;49:755–759.
2. Spotnitz H: *The Couch and The Circle*. New York, Knopf, 1961.
3. Rosenbaum M, Berger M: *Group Psychotherapy And Group Function: Selected Readings*. New York, Basic Books, 1963.
4. Lazell EW: The group treatment of dementia praecox. *Psychoanal Rev* 1921;8:168–179.
5. Marsh LC: Group treatment by the psychological equivalent of the revival. *Ment Hyg* 1931;15:328–349.
6. Marsh LC: Group therapy in the psychiatric clinic. *J Nerv Ment Dis* 1935;82:381–392.
7. Klapman JW: *Group Psychotherapy: Theory and Practice*. New York, Grune & Stratton, 1946.
8. Low AA: *The Technique of Self-Help In Psychiatric After-Care*. Chicago, Recovery, 1943.
9. Wolf A: The psychoanalysis of groups. *Am J Psychother* 1949;3:16–50.
10. Schilder P: Results and problems in group psychotherapy in severe neuroses. *Ment Hyg* 1939;23:87–98.
11. Slavson SR: *A Textbook in Analytic Group Psychotherapy*. New York, International Universities Press, 1964.
12. Anthony EJ: The history of group psychotherapy, in Kaplan HI, Sadock BJ (eds): *Comprehensive Group Psychotherapy*. Baltimore, Williams & Wilkins, 1971, pp 4–31.
13. Wender L: The dynamics of group psychotherapy and its application. *J Nerv Ment Dis* 1936;84:54–60.

26

14. Wender PH, Klein DF: *Mind, Mood, and Medicine*. New York, Farrar, Straus, Giroux, 1981.
15. Wender L: Current trends in group psychotherapy. *Am J Psychother* 1951;5:381–404.
16. Wender L: Group psychotherapy within the psychiatric hospital, in Glueck B (ed): *Current Therapies of Personality Disorders*. New York, Grune & Stratton, 1946, pp 46–58.
17. Wender L, Stein A: The utilization of group psychotherapy in the social integration of patients. *Int J Group Psychother* 1953;3:320–329.
18. Wender L: Group psychotherapy: a study of its application. *Psychiatr Q* 1940;14:708–718.
19. Wender L: The psychodynamics of group psychotherapy. *J Hillside Hosp* 1963;12:134–139.
20. Alexander F, French TM, et al: *Psychoanalytic Therapy: Principles and Application*. New York, Ronald Press, 1946.
21. Ekstein R: The search and yearning for and the rebellion against the father — a group dilemma. *Int J Group Psychother* 1978;28:435–444.
22. Foulkes SH: *Therapeutic Group Analysis*. New York, International Universities Press, 1964.
23. Wender L: Selection of patients for group psychotherapy. *Int J Group Psychother* 1951;1:55–58.
24. Wender L: Reflections on group psychotherapy. *Q Rev Psychiatry Neurol* 1951;6:246–248.
25. Wender L: Group Psychotherapy. *Sociometry* 1945;8:346–349.
26. Appelbaum A, Munich R: Reinventing moral treatment: and the effects upon patients and staff members of a program of psychosocial rehabilitation. *Psychiatr Hosp* 1986;17(1):11–19.
27. Wender L, Stein A: The utilization of group psychotherapy in the social integration of patients: an extension of the method to self-governing patient groups. *Int J Group Psychother* 1953;3:210–218.
28. Scheidlinger S: On the concept of the "mother group". *Int J Group Psychother* 1974;24:417–428.
29. Stein A, Kibel HD: A group dynamic–peer interaction approach to group psychotherapy. *Int J Group Psychother* 1984;34:315–333.
30. Wender L, Stein A: Group psychotherapy as an aid to out-patient treatment in a psychiatric clinic. *Psychiatr Q* 1949;23:415–424.
31. Freud S: *Group Psychology and the Analysis of the Ego*. London, Hogarth Press, 1940.
32. Stein A: The superego and group interaction in group psychotherapy. *J Hillside Hosp* 1956;5:495–504.
33. Stein A: Indications for group psychotherapy and the selection of patients. *J Hillside Hosp* 1963;12:145–155.
34. Stein A: Hillside hospital and group psychotherapy. *J Hillside Hosp* 1963;12:131–133.
35. Stein A, Lipshutz DM, Rosen SR: Experiential and specific types of group psychotherapy in a general hospital. *Int J Group Psychother* 1952;2:10–23.
36. Stein A: Group interaction and group psychotherapy in a general hospital. *Mt Sinai J Med* 1971;38:89–100.
37. Stein A: The training of the group psychotherapist, in Rosenbaum M, Berger M (eds): *Group Psychotherapy and Group Function*. New York, Basic Books, 1963, pp 558–576.
38. Tarachow S, Stein A: Psychoanalytic psychotherapy, in Wolman BB (ed):

Psychoanalytic Techniques: A Handbook for the Practicing Psychoanalyst. New York, Basic Books, 1968, pp 471–510.

39. Stein A: Indications for concurrent (combined and conjoint) individual and group psychotherapy, in Wolberg LR, Aronson ML (eds): *Group and Family Therapy 1981.* New York, Brunner/Mazel, 1981, pp 78–91.
40. Miller JSA, Kwalwasser S, Stein A: Observations concerning the use of group psychotherapy in a voluntary mental hospital. *Int J Group Psychother* 1954;4:86–94.
41. Stein A: Some aspects of resistance to group psychotherapy. *J Hillside Hosp* 1952;1:79–88.
42. Stein A, Solomon I: Group psychotherapy as an aid to patients upon discharge from the hospital. *J Hillside Hosp* 1953;2:72–79.
43. Stein A: Group psychotherapy in patients with peptic ulcer. *Arch Neurol Psychiatry* 1955;73:580.
44. Stein A: Psychosomatic disorders, in Slavson SR (ed): *The Fields of Group Psychotherapy.* New York, International Universities Press, 1956, pp 40–58.
45. Stein A: Group therapy with psychosomatically ill patients, in Kaplan HI, Sadock BJ (eds): *Comprehensive Group Psychotherapy.* Baltimore, Williams & Wilkins, 1971, pp 581–601.
46. Freedman MB, Sweet BC: Some specific features of group psychotherapy and their implications for the selection of patients. *Int J Group Psychother* 1954;4:355–368.
47. Stein A: The nature of transference in combined therapy. *Int J Group Psychother* 1964;14:413–424.
48. Stein A: Group psychotherapy in the treatment of depression, in Flach FF, Draghi SC (eds): *The Nature and Treatment of Depression.* New York, Wiley, 1975, pp 183–196.
49. Belinkoff J, Bross R, Stein A: The effect of group psychotherapy on anaclitic transference. *Int J Group Psychother* 1964;14:474–481.
50. Slavson SR: A contribution to a systemic theory of group psychotherapy. *Int J Group Psychother* 1954;3:3–29.
51. Slavson SR: Criteria for selection and rejection of patients for various types of group psychotherapy. *Int J Group Psychother* 1955;5:3–30.
52. Stein A: The nature and significance of interaction in group psychotherapy. *Int J Group Psychother* 1970;20:153–162.
53. Stein A: Some aspects of the dynamics of group therapy with special reference to the function of patient leaders and spokesmen. *J Hillside Hosp* 1961;10:267–274.
54. Kibel HD, Stein A: The group-as-a-whole approach: an appraisal. *Int J Group Psychother* 1981;31:409–427.
55. Stein A, Wiener S: Group therapy with medically ill patients, in Karasu TB, Steinmuller RI (eds): *Psychotherapeutics in Medicine.* New York, Grune & Stratton, 1978, pp 223–242.
56. Belinkoff J, Resnick EV, Stein A, et al: The effect of a change of therapist on the group psychotherapy in an outpatient clinic. *Int J Group Psychother* 1962;12:456–466.
57. Stein A, Steinhardt RW, Cutler SI: Group psychotherapy in patients with peptic ulcer. *Bull NY Acad Med* 1955;31:583–591.
58. Bion WR: *Experiences in Groups.* London, Tavistock, 1959.
59. Kernberg OF: A systems approach to priority setting of interventions in groups. *Int J Group Psychother* 1975;25:251–275.
60. Grunebaum H, Solomon L: Towards a theory of peer relationships, II:

On the stages of social development and their relationship to group psychotherapy. *Int J Group Psychother* 1982;32:283–307.

61. Fried E: Some aspects of group dynamics and the analysis of transference and defenses. *Int J Group Psychother* 1965;15:44–56.

62. Parloff MB: Analytic group psychotherapy, in Marmor J (ed): *Modern Psychoanalysis*. New York, Basic Books, 1968, pp 492–531.

63. Tuttman S: Theoretical and technical elements which characterize the American approaches to psychoanalytic group psychotherapy. *Int J Group Psychother* 1986;36:499–515.

64. Horwitz L: An integrated, group-centered approach, in Kutash IL, Wolf A (eds): *Psychotherapist's Casebook*. San Francisco, Jossey-Bass, 1968, pp 353–363.

65. Rutan JS, Stone WN: *Psychodynamic Group Psychotherapy*. Lexington, Mass, Collamore Press, 1984.

66. Foulkes SH: The group as matrix of the individual's mental life, in Wolberg LR, Schwartz, EK (eds): *Group Therapy 1973*. New York, Stratton Intercontinental Medical Book, 1973, pp 211–220.

2

The Cultural Theory of Small Group Development

Philip Wells Shambaugh

"Would you tell me, please, which way I ought to go from here?"
"That depends a good deal on where you want to get to," said the Cat.
"I don't much care where —" said Alice.
"Then it doesn't matter which way you go," said the Cat.
"— so long as I get *somewhere*," Alice added as an explanation.
"Oh, you're sure to do that," said that Cat, "if you only walk long enough."

Alice in Wonderland[1]

A vast literature shows that small groups follow a remarkably consistent pattern as they evolve from a collection of individuals to an integrated whole,[2] yet it is theoretically inconclusive. In this chapter we propose that small group development is modeled by a sequence of covert, shared fantasies and shaped by the leader's professional ideology.

Most theories of development can be clustered around Freud's three approaches in *Group Psychology and the Analysis of the Ego*.[3] The first is his observation that ephemeral groups are deficient in social structure and intellectual ability compared to stable, long-lived groups. The most prominent example is Tuckman's[4,5] first major review of the literature in which he offers the fundamental pattern of four (later expanded to five) stages of group structure and task activity. The recent contributions of Beck[6] and of MacKenzie and Livesley[7] detail the stages from social psychological, and general systems perspectives, but their functional analyses are more descriptive than explanatory.

Freud's best known formulation is psychological. Members of long-lasting groups supplement leader superego identification with ego identification and peer identification with object love. They may even replace the leader by an abstraction. In their classic study Bennis and Shepard[8] argue that groups move from preoccupation with authority relations to preoccupation with personal relations. Saravay[9] synthesizes the psychoanalytic theories. He characterizes the phases of development by increasingly mature transferences to the leader or by shared unconscious fantasies, but resolving the fantasies into the individual members' reactions obscures their group-wide functions.

Freud's third approach is symbolic or cultural. All groups, he postulates, are revivals of the primal horde, a prehistoric band of brothers that rose up, slew their despotic father, and replaced him by the totemic law. Although neither the content nor the lamarckianism was ever widely accepted, the notion that covert, shared symbols model group interaction and development is the foundation of a small literature.

Bion[10] is the most influential advocate. He states that in every group there are two simultaneous mental activities, the "work group" and one of the "basic assumption groups." The former is that aspect of functioning and social organization which relates to the task for which the group has come together. It includes the members' cooperative interaction and the image of a rigidly organized, authoritarian group. At its apex sits the terrifying, sphinxlike leader, who embodies the task and articulates the group's reality. Beneath him the members rationally work, each slotted according to his capabilities.[11] The latter are tacit, irrational basic assumptions or fantasies about the aim of the group that obstruct or occasionally support work group activity, the dependency, fight-flight, and pairing assumptions. All three are "formations secondary to an extremely early primal scene,"[10(p164)] have specific leadership roles for which they draft susceptible individuals,[12] and can be detected in large groups and societies as well. Forceful interpretation does not cause them to progress, but rather to cycle from one to another starting and ending with dependency while the work group is becoming dominant.[13(p236)] After publishing a collection of his articles, Bion vacated the field. His rationalistic theory and harsh technique have been perpetuated in the Tavistock study group.

A number of authors contend that shared fantasies or myths model developmental processes. In early studies, Thelen and Dickerman[14] write that stereotypes characterize the phases, and Kaplan and Roman[15] offer mythical models. Invoking Malinowski, Dunphy[16] hypothesizes that an indigenous myth or "overarching symbol system"[17(p289)] justifies each phase. Starting from the conscious developmental fantasies of the members, Slater[18] deduces unconscious images of the group and the leader to which he links Bion's basic groups and draws many mythical parallels. Hartman and Gibbard[19] suggest a developmental sequence of fantasies. Usandivaras[20] adduces as a model the myth of the voyage of the Argonauts, and Hall[21] the Garden of Eden. Shambaugh[11] details the modeling and homologizes Bion's early basic groups to myths of paradise and the Fall. Goodman[22] demonstrates that bionian fantasies induce specific counter-transference reactions in the leader. Although we cannot agree with all the details, evidently a sequence of covert, shared fantasies shapes and portrays the stages of development.

It is not always appreciated that the leader's ideology molds a group's evolution. Haskell[23] observes that developmental processes are not natural regularities, but artifacts of implicit value structures, specific techniques, and ideological premises. There are many sources of a group's values, society at large, the organizational context, the members, and their interaction, but the leader is paramount.[24] It is he who selects the goals, monitors progress, and supplies whatever is needed for effective performance.[25(pp133,134)] Transcending his explicit goals are his professional values or "meta-goals,"[26(pp30–35)] and central to his values is his ideology.[27(p344)] Societal ideologies are templates for understanding and manipulating the social world.[28] They identify one group as the residence of virtue, another as the source of evil, and urge a utopian fulfillment.[29] The many small group ideologies (Lieberman[30] estimates that there are as many as 216 self-help organizations) are similar. The leader pursues his ideology's utopian aim for the group-as-a-whole and for the individual members[31] by means of his design of the event and by his interventions. The interaction continually activates his professional and his personal ethical values and his personal integration of the leader role. His behavior communicates the value systems.[24,32]

The classic developmental scheme appears to connote a democratic, humanistic ideology. Later reviewers[23,34] have confirmed and refined Tuckman's[4,5] pattern of stages. Lacoursiere[34(pp195–196)] attributes its maximal visibility in training and therapy groups to their increased group-formative regression. However, Bion's[10] groups are profoundly regressed, but do not develop. The critical difference seems to be ideological. Most of Lacoursiere's training groups are T-groups conducted in the tradition of the National Training Laboratory or self-analytic classroom groups, and most of his therapy groups are freudian. The meta-goals of the T-group trainer are democratic, humanistic, and broadly scientific,[26] his utopia is an efficient, freely interacting working group in which he plays a member role,[35(pp103–109)] and his ideal behavior is unassertive, socially sensitive, and supportive.[36] The ideologies of his other leaders are homologous. Bion's autocracy and collectivism, dystopian work group image, and rigorous methodology are quite different.

As Bion's experience suggests, other ideologies seem to modify the classic paradigm. Haskell[23] reasons that encounter groups exhibit few of the usual regularities because their leaders operate from different ideological premises. On the other hand, Lacoursiere[34(p142)] finds that their development is in "considerable agreement" with the scheme. Rosenbaum's[37] analysis is more discriminating. He points out that Carl Rogers'[38] benign pursuit of a trusting, cohesive basic encounter group and spontaneous, intimate members tones down what we will term the stage of dissatisfaction and arrests development at the stage of enchantment. Lacoursiere[34(p184)] writes that authoritarian, rigidly structured groups tend not to develop, whereas democratic, loosely structured groups do. Schroder and Harvey[39] reason that progress along the classic line depends on the leader's approach. Autocratic, collectivist values and external controls arrest development at the first phase. Democratic, individualistic values and freedom to explore allow full development. Conditions related to the members, the task, the leader, the temporal and spatial boundaries, and the external environment also modify the paradigm.[34]

In sum, it is apparent that a sequence of covert, shared fantasies models the pattern of development. There is considerable evidence that the leader's ideology shapes it. We now outline the cultural theory. We will summarize the classic developmental paradigm and the origin and functions of the associated images, offer a progression of fantasies pointing out pitfalls and challenges for the leader, and contrast development shaped by a democratic, humanistic ideology with the Tavistock ideology.

PATTERNS OF DEVELOPMENT

The classic scheme has alternative beginnings. Nonvoluntary groups frequently begin in an atmosphere of fear, resistance, and rebellious hostility, Lacoursiere's[34] negative orientation stage. In contrast, willing members usually orient themselves positively and turn to the leader for guidance. Dissatisfaction with his performance ensues, and hostility emerges. As they resolve their aggressive conflicts, groups become cohesive and harmonious, elaborate norms and roles, and improve their task performance. Bennis and Shepard[8] call this the stage of enchantment. Disenchantment and hostility supervene en route to the stage of production, which is characterized by a positive atmosphere, functional role-relatedness, and attempts at task completion. As termination approaches, the members attempt to deal with the loss and integrate the experience.

If the paradigm begins with positive orientation, there are three stable, harmonious phases separated by two periods of hostility and threatened disintegration.[40,41] Regular variations include the absence of enchantment and disenchantment, the relative absence of termination,[34(pp170–173)] and the occurrence of pairing in any stage. Negative orientation is occasionally followed by dissatisfaction and then the remainder of the scheme.[34(pp128–137)]

We will follow the full arrangement, negative orientation or positive orientation and dissatisfaction, enchantment, disenchantment, production, and termination, and discuss pairing throughout.

IMAGES AND COUNTERTRANSFERENCES

The initial situation is ambiguous.[35(p105)] The loss of ordinary social structure, the suspension of customary social roles, and the simultaneous presentation of multiple objects severely threaten the individuals' personal identity and activate primitive impulses, defenses, and internalized object relations.[42–44] The members externalize certain object relations units and act them out, eliciting further projections.[16] The fantasies converge into shared images, discursive arguments, and knowledge structures,[45] which are internalized and shape behavior during the stage. Given the nature of human development, the repertoire of images stimulated by the situation is very limited and easily shared.

Two sorts of fantasies model each phase, large controlling images or myths of the leader and the group, and sets of role-images tied together by lines of communication.[45] By combining views of the here-and-now with distinctive moods, motivations, and sets of values, the myths organize the experience and activate behavior.[11] They render meaningful the enigmas of group life, prescribe its social structure and task approach, and precipitate distinctive psychological conflicts. They include a statement of cause and effect, for example, the possibility of receiving solutions without effort. Only those justifying the stage of production have progress built in. The others are static and timeless. They are symbolic quasi-realities and resemble other worlds of fantasy, such as those of dreams, the fantasy chains of self-analytic groups, organizational cultures, and societal myths.[11] Throughout a phase, the members test the prevailing myth against reality. If disconfirmed, they replace it with another and move on.

The sets of role-images are complementary. In the democratic, humanistic tradition and in the Tavistock as well, the leader's observing ego stands on the psychological boundary of the group, in touch with the emotional forces yet able to stand aside, monitor them, and guide them. His influence stems from his emotional position and his unique perspective.[32,46,47] The members project powerful role-images onto him and one another. Performance may occur when a projection (or projective identification) resonates with one of the recipient's personal role-images.[48,49] The members' projections create a suction for the leader's countertransferences, which he may have difficulty handling effectively. Although "'a group can only develop as far as the neurosis of the therapist,'"[50(p300)] successful movement through a phase depends on "a dynamic blend of the patient's transferences and the therapist countertransferences."[22(p480)] To illustrate, the personal needs of three of O'Day's[51] T-group trainers impelled them to arrest development by acting out the role-images of the orientations; those of the fourth allowed him to accept, encourage, and analyze the expression of counterdependent hostility.

A PROGRESSION OF FANTASIES

Occasionally the initial chaos is prolonged. The image is a confused, anxious, aggressive, out-of-control group with a weak, ineffectual, indifferent leader.[16(p294)] To maintain the group's existence and curb anxiety and destructive acting out, he may apply controls.[52,53] Alternatively, the members may resort to denial, often supported by intellectual discussions.[54]

Negative Orientation

The images justifying the phase of negative orientation are hostile, even macabre. The leader is viewed as strong, malevolent, and manipulative.[16] Some groups alternately overvalue and undervalue him[55] or ask him to speak authoritatively and then attack whatever he suggests.[56] Others see him as devious, uninterested, withholding, or punitively authoritarian.[54,57–59] A group of juvenile delinquents[52] imagined that their male coleader would physically attack them, resulting in the loss of limb or death. Paradoxically some groups visualize him as inadequate and noncontributory.[60,61]

The group is pictured as icy, rejecting, secretive, and dog-eat-dog.[16,62] One subgroup derided another that was exploring feelings,[56] and several groups of institutionalized delinquents were contemptuous of other inmates.[58] Members may seek to define simplistic roles for themselves[63] and imagine that the group is a complicated, malevolent experiment.[18] At times they displace their hostile imagery onto the surrounding institution or society.[58,64]

The group's attention may be riveted on a desperately intense, highly ambivalent pairing relationship.[62] According to Slater[18(p189)] the members are fantasying that they are watching their heroic leader fighting or copulating with the group-mother and that their separation and differentiation will result from her dismemberment or impregnation.

The leader may arrest development by trying to explain away his actions, defending the host institution, making premature interpretations, or reacting with open hostility and cold withdrawal.[51,58,64] He may push the group into believing it cannot perform without him or frighten it by a hostile, dominant stance.[51,55] For the members to give up the image of a persecutory tyrant, he must be a beneficient and benevolent authority[52] and display an evocative curiosity about their attacks.[58,65]

Positive Orientation

Voluntary groups imagine that the leader is omniscient and omnipotent and will take care of all their needs. Bion's[10] dependency group depends on their deified leader in a fearful, immature fashion, certain that he will provide security, protection, solutions for their problems, and material and spiritual nourishment. They are opposed to working and ask questions or silently wait for him to produce the answers. Hall[21] homologizes pairing to the myth of Adam and Eve in the Garden of Eden. Some leaders of groups of hospitalized chronic schizophrenics enact the role-image by making interpretations that are warm and accepting, but condescending and hopeless.[66] Ideally, the leader should be dependable, confident, competent, and task-oriented.[67–69]

The image of a paternalistic group is somewhat less regressive. Its benevolent leader is imagined to structure the group and tell the members exactly what to do.[39] Endeavoring to actualize the fantasy, they look to him for structure and direction and test to discover what interpersonal behaviors are acceptable.[4] He may impede development by employing active direction,[70] a nurturant, authoritative style,[51] controlling, oracular interpretations,[71(p308)] and collusive authoritarianism masquerading as participatory democracy.[72] He should define the group's general purposes, initiate and support facilitative group norms, and maintain an open peer leadership structure.[69]

Lacoursiere[34(p41)] observes that in practice every group starts with a mixture of participants along a continuum from negative to positive orientation. Their clustering toward one pole or the other accounts for the two phases.

Dissatisfaction

The leader's failure to meet the members' extravagant demands precipitates the release of primitive rage and fears of group dissolution, abandonment, and death.[18(pp24,134)] Some members' images of the leader and of the group change to those of negative orientation, and they destructively attack. Others retain their idealizations and denigrate the attackers. The group may split into reciprocally projecting subgroups advocating the opposing images.[8] The negative picture of the leader usually prevails, and the group revolts.[18(p44),73] If the positive triumphs, intermember confrontation ensues.[74] Pairing is another mode of rebellion.[18,21,60] The leader may act out his countertransference, take sides, and exacerbate the schism. He should provide a model of responsible authority by bringing both subgroups back to the primary task.[75]

Enchantment

Groups considering a revolt often imagine that a hero or messiah will arise from the membership, overthrow the leader, and inaugurate an idealized, utopian group.[16] Its values include love, trust, closeness, and harmony.[76] Hostility has no place. The members may elaborate commemorative poems or songs[8] and are skillful at playing conciliatory, manipulative, and integrative roles.[14,39] Strong social controls press for uniformity, consensus, and equal treatment for all.[69] The leader is fantasied to be a benevolent despot and miraculous savior who can be counted on to guide the group, take care of it, and protect it.[39,54,77] All decisions are unanimous, but the issues are inconsequential.[8] Thelen and Dickerman[14(p314)] call the fantasy "the institutionalization of complacency."

Pairing is an alternate route to enchantment. Bion[10] states that its purpose is reproduction. The members look on hopefully, imagining that two of them (of the same or opposite sex) are getting together to create a messiah, a person, idea, or utopia. Later investigators write that the idealized pair is a grandiose member confirmed by a mirroring individual,[78] either a mirror relationship in the narrower sense or a twinship or partnering.[78,79] The narcissist may be taking care of his protective mirror,[54] who is often borderline or schizophrenic,[80] yet he may harbor antinomian, even murderous sexual fantasies.[22] Rogers[38] describes extraordinarily close, deeply accepting, sexually tinged I-Thou relationships. The pairing image of enchantment has links to the Adamite utopia of Bion's dependency group,[10(p166)] to the relatively undistorted pairing of the stage of production,[9] and to adolescent romantic love.[81]

The leader may misuse the idealizing transference. He may debunk it, leaving the members confused and regressed.[78] Some narcissistic, authoritarian therapists sexually abuse their female patients and encourage submission, obedience, and adoration with totalistic, paranoid patterns of thought.[82] Before intervening, the leader should accept the idealization and allow it fully to develop.[78,83] Within appropriate limits he should encourage member self-revelation and be open about himself.[6,68] He should support the emerging structure, assist members to fulfill roles, encourage more facilitative and effective operating procedures, and mediate group sanctions.[69]

Disenchantment

With a sense of failure the utopian images of enchantment give way to the dystopian images of disenchantment. The group is imagined to demand immaturity, excessive closeness, and sacrifice of personal identity.[8,84] The leader appears to be the authoritarian defender of a rigid and suffocating structure.[85] Some members disparage the group, attend irregularly, and resist further involvement. An opposing subgroup defends the utopia and advocates unconditional love.[8] Hostile individual confrontation, critical introspection, and ambivalent and vacillating role acceptance occur[7,68,86] and modify the normative structure in the direction of increasing individual and group autonomy.[7,84] On occasion the leader is attacked and even asked to leave.[40] Pairing is another assertion of individuality, with sexual attraction and competition, oedipal leader transferences, and conflicts about intimacy.[6,9,76]

The leader is pressured to respond by tightening controls and defending the utopian norms or by overthrowing the structure altogether.[85] He should endeavor to maintain cohesion equilibrium and task commitment.[69]

Production

In the stage of production the members actualize the democratic, humanistic images which by now they have negotiated and internalized.[40] They deal with one another as unique individuals with strengths and weaknesses while respecting their own dignity and integrity.[87,88] Roles are fluid,[4] and communication is open, honest, and frank.[68] The members combine and recombine according to the demands of the task.[6] Interpersonal responsibility and group commitment allow for idiosyncratic behavior; to break a norm constructively is the norm.[68] Heterosexual pairing is based on realistic appraisal and normal affective ties.[9] The members use the leader primarily as a resource person or for emergencies,[68] while viewing him more realistically and relating to him as an internal object and as an equal partner.[6,9,89] They tackle their problems in a cooperative, experimental, and creative fashion, selecting their goals and pacing their achievement.[90]

This is a utopian phase,[32,90] and groups may not consistently operate on this level. Bion[10(pp57,60)] gives two very transitory examples. The members and the leader have contributed to their group's unique version of this widespread fantasy,[91] and they collaborate in its actualization.

Termination

Two sets of images model the sessions prior to termination. The first consists of a mourning role-image and the fading picture of the production group. After a period of denial, the members begin to confront their sadness and grief over the loss. Oral themes are common, and food may be brought to the meetings.[92] They review their time together, incorporate it as a personally important experience,[7] and attempt to extrapolate its meaning to outside relationships.[6] They may insist that the group will never die because each of them will carry it away inside,[18(p111)] but gradually they come to terms with the impending change.[92] The group often rearranges itself so that various pairings can deal with unfinished business[6] while the leader handles individual issues outside.[93] When the end comes, the members can take away the memory of a place where feeling, thought, and behavior were faced with increasing honesty.[94] Subsequently, some model themselves on group patterns and create groups in which they can enact the leader's role.[95]

The counterpoint is an ancient theme which denies the finality and asserts that the end is but a new beginning. At the same time it helps the members rethink and assess the meaning and value of the experience.[96] Referring to traditional societies, Eliade[97] calls it the "regeneration of time." Its essentials are the abolition of the experience, sometimes by means of scapegoating, the restoration of the initial chaos, and the reactualization of the generative fantasies of the orientations. Some members attempt to recapture the *status quo ante* by expelling the worthless thoughts and judgments which they have internalized and asserting that the experience was one long process of brainwashing and poisoning.[98(p180)] They may exhibit various rejecting and rejection-provoking behaviors[96] and repeat or review past episodes of scapegoating.[98,99]

Fantasies are expressed that the last session will be an orgy,[18(p133)] and acts such as stealing and drinking may occur, even overt psychosis.[96,100] The members may physically cluster together[96] and be elated or manically euphoric.[98,99] Pairing fantasies are bacchanalian, in one instance ranging over "group marriage," incest, pedophilia, necrophilia, homosexuality, and polygamy.[18(p134)] A male dreamed of turning into a woman and being enjoyably raped by a gigantic black man.[101]

Members may beg the leader to provide "the word" and total absolution and love and to admit that the whole group was an experiment[89,95,98] Sometimes they imagine that they and the leader have created a progeny that is immortal and uniquely valuable to the world beyond. Some females stake out a special role as its carrier.[98] Members may fantasy scattering pieces of the group corpse on the ground and engendering little groups all over the land.[18(p74)] Some relive, reenact, review, and evaluate the events of the beginning.[96] Afterward, individuals may fantasy a reunion.[95]

The leader should eschew denial and facilitate open discussion of termination. He should share his own feelings[71(p374)] and show the members how to look back on collective accomplishments while relinquishing attachment.[93]

DISCUSSION

More than 35 years ago Foulkes[102] summarized the development of a group conducted by a democratic, humanistic leader. His words are as cogent now as they were then. A group-analytic group, he writes, functions on two levels, the manifest and the latent. The leader is a participant observer. On the manifest level he keeps in the background. He treats the group as if they were mature adults on his own level and sets an example of desirable adult behavior. He addresses them as if they were, or were to become, an integrated whole, and promotes independence, appreciation of individual differences, frankness, and reason. On the latent level the group members unconsciously fantasy that he is omniscient and omnipotent and expect magical help. He passively accepts this role and does not deny it or exploit it for his own needs. Playing God would fix the group at an intermediate stage of development. He lets them in stages bring him down to earth and change him from a leader *of* the group to a leader *in* the group. On the manifest level there is a crescendo move in the maturity of the group, and on the latent a decrescendo move in the authority of the leader. The group-analytic experience, Foulkes concludes, is a means of democratic education, and the leader's qualifications correspond to a desirable type of leader in a democratic community.[102]

To compare development under a different ideology, we analyzed 11 histories of Tavistock study groups.[103–113] All 11 begin with negative orientation. A counterdependent revolt follows in six. Ten progress to a brief phase of enchantment, which also actualizes the softened, Tavistock version of Bion's work group image[47,67]: an affectionate, cohesive atmosphere; a helpful, caring leader; self-disclosing, mutually supportive members; the elaboration of functional norms and roles; and a mature approach to the task. Two proceed to disenchantment, but none go on to production. Eight deal with termination.

The negative beginning and the unusual interpolation of dissatisfaction parallel the Tavistock emphasis on the tragic and paradoxical elements in group life, problems of leadership and authority, and the extreme difficulty in forming a work group.[35(p116),114] The leader (or consultant as he is called) approximates the role-images of negative orientation and dissatisfaction. He is depriving, distant, powerful, and authoritarian.[115] His interpretations are narcissistically assaultive, leader- and group-centered, unsupportive, and prescriptive.[116–118]

The arrest at enchantment reflects a millenarian trend in the ideology. Rioch[114,119] glowingly contrasts the relatively rare and immensely valuable work group to pathologic groups dominated by fanaticism or illusion. In some Tavistock conferences a "moral rhetoric, sometimes with an almost evangelical fervor" is heard.[120] A center of the A.K. Rice Institute failed because it was a "covert quasi-religious organization" whose conferences were a "kind of 'secular sacrament'" dedicated to making converts and helping people experience a transcendent vision.[121] Consultants resist the strong temptation to become cultists with "the answer,"[122(p101)] but are not always successful. Sometimes they are arrogant and contemptuous, magnified by fancy interpretation, fascinated by their enormous, secret power, and spiritually fulfilled by psychological merger with the work group.[123,124] Some collude with their members to actualize the good Tavistock group, with deviants scapegoated along the way.[111] Setting up the work group as an icon and then trying to will it into existence by trenchant interpretation is quite different from collaborative "working through" along the road to the production image.[124] Popper's[125(pp157–168)] distinction between utopian and piecemeal social engineering is homologous.

The cultural theory is very powerful. It furnishes the practitioner with an approach to leadership and a map of the social terrain. It offers the theoretician a way to organize a large mass of data and a number of theories of development. It urges further study of covert fantasies, values, and ideologies and of the complex relationships between leadership behaviors, professional philosophies, and personal needs. It transcends the field of the small group. Developmental fantasies and processes can be located on a hierarchy that has at least four levels: individual, small group, organizational, and societal. Following the homologous images across and between the levels enriches their meanings, which become more profound as one rises in the hierarchy.[11] For example, the individual fantasy of the good small group[91] leads to the shared image of the production group, McGregor's[126] theory Y of management, and the diffuse utopia of modern Western democracy.[127] The cultural theory realizes Foulkes's[102] vision of the small group as a meeting ground of the sciences of the human collectivity.

If a leader were to ask us how he ought to conduct his group, we would paraphrase the Cheshire cat and tell him that it depends on where he wants to get to. He may arrive at a different place than he thought, and along the way he may find some dreams, dreams shared by many others.

REFERENCES

1. Caroll L: *Alice in Wonderland and Other Favorities*. New York, Washington Square Press, 1960, p 56.
2. Anderson JD: Working with groups. Little-known facts that challenge well-known myths. *Small Group Behav* 1985;16:267–283.
3. Freud S (1921): *Group Psychology and the Analysis of the Ego*. Standard Edition, vol 18, Strachey J (trans-ed). London, Hogarth Press, 1955.
4. Tuckman BW: Developmental sequence in small groups. *Psychol Bull* 1965;63:384–399.
5. Tuckman BW, Jensen MAC: Stages of small-group development revisited. *Group Organ Stud* 1977;2:419–427.
6. Beck AP: Phases in the development of structure in therapy and encounter groups, in Wexler DA, Rice LN (eds): *Innovations in Client-Centered Therapy*. New York, Wiley, 1974, pp 421–463.
7. MacKenzie KR, Livesley WJ: Developmental stages: An integrating theory of group psychotherapy. *Can J Psychiatry* 1984;29:247–251.
8. Bennis WG, Shepard HA: A theory of group development. *Hum Relat* 1956;9:415–437.
9. Saravay SM: A psychoanalytic theory of group development. *Int J Group Psychother* 1978;28:481–507.
10. Bion WR: *Experiences in Groups*. New York, Basic Books, 1961.
11. Shambaugh PW: The mythic structure of Bion's groups. *Hum Relat* 1985;38:937–951.
12. Sherwood M: Bion's *Experiences in Groups*. A critical evaluation. *Hum Relat* 1964;17:113–130.
13. Bion WR: Group dynamics: A re-view. *Int J Psychoanal* 1952;33:235–247.
14. Thelen H, Dickerman W: Stereotypes and the growth of groups. *Educ Leadership* 1949;6:309–316.
15. Kaplan SR, Roman M: Phases of development in an adult therapy group. *Int J Group Psychother* 1963;13:10–26.
16. Dunphy DC: *Social Change in Self-Analytic Groups*, thesis. Harvard University, Cambridge, Mass, 1964.
17. Dunphy DC: Social change in self-analytic groups, in Stone PJ, Dunphy DC, Smith MS, et al: *The General Inquirer: A Computer Approach to Content Analysis*. Cambridge, Mass, MIT, 1966, pp 287–340.
18. Slater PE: *Microcosm. Structural, Psychological and Religious Evolution in Groups*. New York, Wiley, 1966.
19. Hartman JJ, Gibbard GS: A note on fantasy themes in the evolution of

group culture, in Gibbard GS, Hartman JJ, Mann RD (eds): *Analysis of Groups.* San Francisco, Jossey-Bass, 1974, pp 315–335.

20. Usandivaras RJ: The Argonauts' expedition and groups, in Wolberg LR, Aronson ML (eds): *Group Therapy 1975: An Overview.* New York, Stratton Intercontinental Medical Books, 1975, pp 21–35.

21. Hall JM: Revolt in the Garden of Eden: An alternative group model. *Group* 1984;8:29–40.

22. Goodman M: Group phases and induced countertransference. *Psychother: Theory Res Pract* 1981;18:478–486.

23. Haskell RE: Presumptions of group work. A value analysis. *Small Group Behav* 1975;6:469–486.

24. Cooper CL, Levine N: Implicit values in experiential learning groups: Their functional and dysfunctional consequences, in Cooper CL, Aldercer CP (eds): *Advances in Experiential Social Processes*, Chichester, England, Wiley, 1978, vol 1, pp 1–27.

25. Schein EH: *Organizational Psychology*, ed 3. Englewood Cliffs, NJ, Prentice-Hall, 1980.

26. Schein EH, Bennis WG: *Personal and Organization Change Through Group Methods: The Laboratory Approach.* New York, Wiley, 1965.

27. Gibbard GS, Hartman JJ, Mann RD: The dynamics of leadership, in Gibbard GS, Hartman JJ, Mann RD (eds): *Analysis of Groups.* San Francisco, Jossey-Bass, 1974, pp 337–348.

28. Geertz C: Ideology as a cultural system, in Geetrz C: *The Interpretation of Cultures.* New York, Basic Books, 1973, pp 192–233.

29. Shils E: Ideology and civility: On the politics of the intellectual. *Sewanee Review* 1958;66:450–480.

30. Lieberman MA: Group therapy beyond the therapy group. *Group Anal* 1980;13(suppl):1–14.

31. Tillich P: Critique and justification of utopia, in Manuel FE (ed): *Utopias and Utopian Thought.* Boston, Beacon Press, 1967, pp 296–309.

32. Kernberg OF: A systems approach to priority setting of interventions in groups. *Int J Group Psychother* 1975;25:251–275.

33. Hare AP: Theories of group development and categories for interaction analysis. *Small Group Behav* 1973;4:259–304.

34. Lacoursiere RB: *The Life Cycle of Groups. Group Developmental Stage Theory.* New York, Human Sciences Press, 1980.

35. Back KW: *Beyond Words. The Story of Sensitivity Training and the Encounter Movement.* New York, Russell Sage Foundation, 1972.

36. Deutsch M, Pepitone A, Zander A: Leadership in the small group. *J Soc Issues* 1948;4:31–40.

37. Rosenbaum M: The leader and cultural change, in Liff ZA (ed): *The Leader in the Group.* New York, Jason Aronson, 1975, pp 271–282.

38. Rogers CR: The process of the basic encounter group, in Bugental JFT (ed): *Challenges of Humanistic Psychology.* New York, McGraw-Hill, 1967, pp 260–276.

39. Schroder HM, Harvey OJ: Conceptual organization and group structure, in Harvey OJ (ed): *Motivation and Social Interaction. Cognitive Determinants.* New York, Ronald Press, 1963, pp 134–166.

40. Farrell MP: Patterns in the development of self-analytic groups. *J Appl Behav Sci* 1976;12:523–542.

41. Shambaugh PW: The development of the small group. *Hum Relat* 1978; 31:283–295.

42. Kernberg OF: *Object–Relations Theory and Clinical Psychoanalysis.* New York, Jason Aronson, 1976.
43. Kernberg OF: *Internal World and External Reality. Object Relations Theory Applied.* New York, Jason Aronson, 1980.
44. Kernberg OF: The couch at sea: Psychoanalytic studies of group and organizational leadership. *Int J Group Psychother* 1984;34:5–23.
45. Boulding KE: *The Image. Knowledge in Life and Society.* Ann Arbor, Mich, University of Michigan, 1961.
46. Whitaker DS, Lieberman MA: *Psychotherapy Through the Group Process.* New York, Atherton Press, 1964.
47. Turquet, PM: Leadership: The individual and the group, in Gibbard GS, Hartman JJ, Mann RD (eds): *Analysis of Groups.* San Francisco, Jossey-Bass, 1974, pp 349–371.
48. Astigueta FD: Bion, Tavistock, the Argentine School and psychoanalytic group psychotherapy. *Int Ment Health Res Newsletter* 1974;16:6–9.
49. Borriello JF: Leadership in the therapist-centered group-as-a-whole psychotherapy approach. *Int J Group Psychother* 1976;26:149–162.
50. Anthony EJ: Reflections on twenty-five years of group psychotherapy. *Int J Group Psychother* 1968;18:277–301.
51. O'Day R: Individual training styles. An empirically derived typology. *Small Group Behav* 1976;7:147–182.
52. Kimsey LR: Out-patient group psychotherapy with juvenile delinquents. *Dis Nerv Syst* 1969;30:472–477.
53. Khantzian EJ, Kates WW: Group treatment of unwilling addicted patients: Programmatic and clinical aspects. *Int J Group Psychother* 1978; 28:81–94.
54. Shambaugh PW, Kanter SS: Spouses under stress: Group meetings with spouses of patients on hemodialysis. *Am J Psychiatry* 1969;125:928–936.
55. Berkowitz B: Stages of group development in a mental health team. *Psychiatr Q* 1974;48:309–319.
56. Flach FF: Group approaches in medical education, in Kaplan HI, Sadock BJ (eds): *Comprehensive Group Psychotherapy.* Baltimore, Williams & Wilkins, 1971, pp 799–820.
57. Austin DM: Goals for gang workers. *Soc Work* 1957;2:43–50.
58. Shellow RS, Ward JL, Rubenfeld S: Group therapy and the institutionalized delinquent. *Int J Group Psychother* 1958;8:365–375.
59. Mathis JL, Collins M: Progressive phases in the group therapy of exhibitionists. *Int J Group Psychother* 1970;20:163–169.
60. Roth BE: Understanding the development of a homogeneous, identity-impaired group through countertransference phenomena. *Int J Group Psychother* 1980;30:405–426.
61. Berger DM: The multidiscipline patient care conference. *Can Psychiatr Assoc J* 1976;21:135–139.
62. Wong N: Combined group and individual treatment of borderline and narcissistic patients: Heterogeneous versus homogeneous groups. *Int J Group Psychother* 1980;30:389–404.
63. Ammon G, Ament A: The terminal phase of the dynamic process of a group-dynamic teaching group. *Int J Group Psychother* 1967;17:35–43.
64. Thorpe JJ, Smith B: Phases in group development in the treatment of drug addicts. *Int J Group Psychother* 1953;3:66–78.
65. Horowitz L: Training groups for psychiatric residents. *Int J Group Psychother* 1967;17:421–435.

44

66. Papanek H: Group psychotherapy interminable. *Int J Group Psychother* 1970;20:219–223.
67. Rioch MJ: The work of Wilfred Bion on groups. *Psychiatry* 1970;33:56–66.
68. Bonney WC: Group counseling and developmental processes, in Gazda GM (ed): *Theories and Methods of Group Counseling in the Schools.* Springfield, Ill, Thomas, 1969, pp 157–180.
69. Sarri RC, Galinsky MJ: A conceptual framework for group development, in Glasser P, Sarri R, Vinter R (eds): *Individual Change Through Small Groups.* New York, Free Press, 1974, pp 71–88.
70. Lundgren DC: Trainer style and patterns of group development. *J Appl Behav Sci* 1971;7:689–709.
71. Yalom ID: *The Theory and Practice of Group Psychotherapy*, ed 3. New York, Basic Books, 1985.
72. O'Day R: The T-group trainer: A study of conflict in the exercise of authority, in Gibbard GS, Hartman JJ, Mann RD (eds): *Analysis of Groups.* San Francisco, Jossey-Bass, 1974, pp 387–410.
73. Hartman JJ, Gibbard GS: Anxiety, boundary evolution, and social change, in Gibbard GS, Hartman JJ, Mann RD (eds): *Analysis of Groups.* San Francisco, Jossey-Bass, 1974, pp 154–176.
74. Lundgren DC, Knight DJ: Sequential stages of development in sensitivity training groups. *J Appl Behav Sci* 1978;14:204–222.
75. Gustafson JP: Schismatic groups. *Hum Relat* 1978;31:139–154.
76. Gibbard GS, Hartman JJ: The significance of utopian fantasies in small groups. *Int J Group Psychother* 1973;23:125–147.
77. Boris HN: The medium, the message, and the good group dream. *Int J Group Psychother* 1970;20:91–98.
78. Stone WN, Whitman RM: Contributions of the psychology of the self to group process and group therapy. *Int J Group Psychother* 1977;27:343–359.
79. Bacal HA: Object-relations in the group from the perspective of self psychology. *Int J Group Psychother* 1985;35:483–501.
80. Fried E: Combined group and individual therapy with passive-narcissistic patients. *Int J Group Psychother* 1955;5:194–203.
81. Kernberg OF: Adolescent sexuality in the light of group processes. *Psychoanal Q* 1980;49:27–47.
82. Temerlin MK, Temerlin JW: Psychotherapy cults: An iatrogenic perversion. *Psychother: Theory Res Pract* 1982;19:131–141.
83. Kriegman D, Solomon L: Cult groups and the narcissistic personality: The offer to heal defects in the self. *Int J Group Psychother* 1985;35:239–261.
84. Sadock BJ, Kaplan HI: Group psychotherapy with psychiatric residents. *Int J Group Psychother* 1969;19:475–486.
85. Crabtree LH, Cox JLD: The overthrow of a therapeutic community. *Int J Group Psychother* 1972;22:31–41.
86. Tulane Studies in Social Welfare: *Use of Group Methods in Social Welfare Settings.* New Orleans, Tulane University School of Social Work, 1957.
87. Papanek H: Change of ethical values in group psychotherapy. *Int J Group Psychother* 1958;8:435–444.
88. Spotnitz H: The concept of goals in group psychotherapy. *Int J Group Psychother* 1960;10:383–393.

89. Mann RD: The development of the member-trainer relationship in self-analytic groups. *Hum Relat* 1966;19:85–115.
90. Martin EA Jr, Hill WF: Toward a theory of group development: Six phases of therapy group development. *Int J Group Psychother* 1957;7: 20–30.
91. Cloyd JS: Small group as social institution. *Am Sociol Rev* 1965;30:394–402.
92. Husband D, Scheunemann HR: The use of group process in teaching termination. *Child Welfare* 1972;51:505–513.
93. Winter SK: Developmental stages in the roles and concerns of group co-leaders. *Small Group Behav* 1976;7:349–362.
94. Semrad EV, Kanter S, Shapiro D, et al: The field of group psychotherapy. *Int J Group Psychother* 1963;13:452–475.
95. Mills TM: *Group Transformation. An Analysis of a Learning Group.* Englewood Cliffs, NJ, Prentice-Hall, 1964.
96. Garland JA, Jones HE, Kolodny RL: A model for stages of development in social work groups, in Bernstein S (ed): *Explorations in Group Work: Essays in Theory and Practice.* Boston, Charles River Books, 1976, pp 17–71.
97. Eliade M: *The Myth of the Eternal Return* or, *Cosmos and History*, Trask WR (trans). Princeton, NJ, Princeton, 1965.
98. Mann RD, Gibbard GS, Hartman JJ: *Interpersonal Styles and Group Development. An Analysis of the Member-Leader Relationship.* New York, Wiley, 1967.
99. Lewis BF: An examination of the final phase of a group development theory. *Small Group Behav* 1978;9:507–517.
100. Johnson D, Geller J, Gordon J, et al: Group psychotherapy with schizophrenic patients: The pairing group. *Int J Group Psychother* 1986;36: 75–96.
101. Kline FM: Terminating a leaderless group. *Int J Group Psychother* 1974;24:452–459.
102. Foulkes SH: Concerning leadership in group-analytic psychotherapy. *Int J Group Psychother* 1951;1:319–329.
103. Rice AK: *Learning for Leadership. Interpersonal and Intergroup Relations.* London, Tavistock, 1965.
104. Musto DF, Astrachan BM: Strange encounter: The use of study groups with graduate students in history. *Psychiatry* 1968;31:264–276.
105. Astrachan BM, Redlich FC: Leadership ambiguity and its effect on residents' study groups. *Int J Group Psychother* 1969;19:487–494.
106. Klein EB, Astrachan BM: Learning in groups: A comparison of study groups and T groups. *J Appl Behav Sci* 1971;7:659–683.
107. Bunker BB: The Tavistock approach to the study of group process: Reactions of a private investigator, in Milman S, Goldman GD (eds): *Group Process Today: Evaluation and Perspective.* Springfield, Ill, Thomas, 1974, pp 63–77.
108. Astrachan BM: The Tavistock model of laboratory training, in Benne K, Bradford L, Gibb J, et al (eds): *The Laboratory Method of Changing and Learning.* Palo Alto, Calif, Science & Behavior Books, 1975, pp 326–340.
109. King PD: Life cycle in the "Tavistock" study group. *Perspect Psychiatr Care* 1975;13:180–184.
110. Klein EB: Transference in training groups. *J Pers Soc Syst* 1977;1:53–63.

46

111. Eagle J, Newton PM: Scapegoating in small groups: An organizational approach. *Hum Relat* 1981;34:283–301.
112. Burton MV: *Regression in Tavistock Groups as a Function of Size of Group, Sex of Consultant, and Stage of Group Development*, thesis. George Washington University, Washington, DC, 1983.
113. Rugel RP, Meyer DJ: The Tavistock group. Empirical findings and implications for group therapy. *Small Group Behav* 1984;15:361–374.
114. Rioch MJ: Group relations: Rationale and technique. *Int J Group Psychother* 1970;20:340–355.
115. Harrow M, Astrachan BM, Tucker GJ, et al: The T-group and study group laboratory experiences. *J Soc Psychol* 1971;85:225–237.
116. Gustafson JP, Hartman JJ: Self-esteem in group therapy. *Contemp Psychoanal* 1978;14:311–329.
117. Kibel HD, Stein A: The group-as-a-whole approach: An appraisal. *Int J Group Psychother* 1981;31:409–427.
118. Gustafson JP, Cooper L: Collaboration in small groups: Theory and technique for the study of small-group processes. *Hum Relat* 1978;31:155–171.
119. Rioch MJ: "All we like sheep —" (Isaiah 53:6): Followers and leaders. *Psychiatry* 1971;34:258–273.
120. Lawrence G, Barham P: Some notes on Tavistock working conferences. *Group Anal* 1974;7:92–102.
121. Maguire TV, Hirson S, Schachtel Z, et al: Organizational dynamics of an institution whose primary task is "group relations" work: The case of a center of the A.K. Rice Institute. *J Pers Soc Syst* 1980;2:77–87.
122. O'Connor G: The Tavistock method of group study. *Sci Psychoanal* 1971;18:100–115.
123. Rioch MJ: Why I work as a consultant in the conferences of the A.K. Rice Institute. *J Pers Soc Syst* 1978;1:32–50.
124. Gustafson JP, Cooper L: Toward the study of society in microcosm: Critical problems of group relations conferences. *Hum Relat* 1978;31:843–862.
125. Popper KR: *The Open Society and Its Enemies*, vol 1, *The Spell of Plato*. Princeton, NJ, Princeton, 1966.
126. McGregor D: *The Human Side of Enterprise*. New York, McGraw-Hill, 1960.
127. Brinton C: Utopia and democracy. *Daedalus* 1965;94:348–366.

3

Transferences in Groups: Theory and Research

Walter N. Stone

The concept of transference has been an object of considerable attention from the perspective of both theory and research. Indeed, the entire notion has expanded well beyond the original formulation of more than eight decades ago. During the past two decades a number of studies have appeared that specifically addressed this concept as it has been applied to patients in group psychotherapy. It is the purpose of this chapter to provide a selected review of the notion of transference in both dyadic and group psychotherapy. Following this review the slowly increasing volume of research on transferences in groups is surveyed. The conclusion points to further directions that may provide a firmer basis for understanding this complex phenomenon in groups.

EVOLVING CONCEPTS OF TRANSFERENCE

Among Freud's many seminal discoveries was that of transference. His genius was expressed not only in his creativity, but also in the capacity to reexamine his initial formulations. In the postscript to the Dora case, Freud[1] belatedly recognized the impact of Dora's transference on the outcome of treatment. He wrote:

> What are transferences? They are new editions or facsimiles of the impulses and fantasies which are aroused and made conscious during the progress of the analysis; but they have this peculiarity, which is characteristic for their species, that they replace some earlier person by the person of the physician [p 116]....Psychoanalytic treatment does not

create transferences, it merely brings them to light like so many other hidden psychical factors [p 117]. . . . In this way the transference took me unaware and because of the unknown quantity in me which reminded Dora of Herr K, she took revenge on me as she wanted to take revenge on him, and deserted me as she believed herself to have been deceived and deserted by him [p 119].

The three elements — the past brought into the present, the context of the analysis bringing transferences into the open, and the person of Freud which evoked the responses — laid the groundwork for conceptualizing transference and provided a starting place in the evolution of this concept. As Freud observed, transference is not created in psychoanalysis. What is specific and peculiar to the analytic situation is the therapist's assumption of an unobtrusive stance. By focusing on the needs and wishes of the patient, the analyst does not interfere in the development of transferences.

Two major trends in the concept have emerged. The first is the historical, drive model in which transference is determined almost exclusively by the patient's developmental history. In this tradition Greenson[2] lists two criteria for determining the presence of transference: (1) "It is an indiscriminant non-selective repetition of the past," and (2) "it ignores or distorts reality and hence is an inappropriate reaction." Drives, affects, and defenses from past relationships are considered to be part of all current relationships. They are determined by developmental experiences that have been gratifying or frustrating and become grafted onto the relationships in the present. These distortions generally are outside of the individual's awareness. The "blank screen" analyst creates conditions in which the analysand's central conflicts gradually unfold in a coherent pattern which facilitates interpretation and working through. In this model the impact of the analyst is minimal. The focus is on the past, with the therapeutic efforts centered on uncovering childhood experiences or fantasies as the source of present distortions.

The modernist model emphasizes the contribution of the patient's perceptions of the analyst based on reciprocal interactions in the present. This approach searches for and focuses upon the meaning of the here-and-now patient-therapist interaction.[3,4] Additionally it assumes the omnipresence of transferences, which includes habitual reactions to others, and therefore, at times, the model conceptually overlaps with that of character formation.[5] For instance, the manner in which a patient enters treatment, reacts to strangers, or deals with a break in the routine all might be considered part of the transference, but also may be characterologic. In the analytic situation that which is initially considered character may, at a different point in treatment, be formulated as transference.

In everyday life, multiple transferential needs are stimulated but simultaneously inhibited by the reality testing provided by the presence of others. Nevertheless, transferences may persist or become intensified because they are not dealt with in a therapeutic or salutary fashion. Stated another way, fragments of the transferences emerge at times with considerable intensity, but are experienced as reality.

With the advent of self-psychology the notion of transferences acquired an additional dimension. Kohut emphasized the narcissistic individual's need to establish a self-object transference in order to restore a disrupted or fragmenting self.[6] The self-object was required to fulfill a function that was insufficiently developed, and the "other" was not experienced as a separate, autonomous individual. The formulation that the self-object needs were a continuation of the past into the present placed these concepts within the psychoanalytic tradition. Additionally, self-object transferences were perceived to indicate the individual's efforts to reestablish growth, whch highlighted a dimension of the transference beyond that of repetition-compulsion.[7]

Concomitant with the evolving formulations of transference was the recognition of defenses against and resistances to transferences. Concepts such as "defense transference" and "defense against the transference" were efforts to clarify the complexity of the therapeutic encounter. Daniels noted that *defense transference* deals with the habitual character style which protects the individual from experiencing the more threatening, anxiety-provoking encounter with the therapist. In contrast, *defense against the transference* is an effort to ward off any feelings about, or experiences with, the therapist.[8]

The confusion between the interpersonal and intrapsychic aspects of these formulations may be diminished by assuming that the intrapsychic structures become manifest in interpersonal relations. In any interpersonal relationship there will be a combination of the transferential wishes and resistances to awareness emerging as character defenses or "emergency" responses. In a therapeutic session, resistances are evident in allusions to extratherapeutic events or other behaviors. The latter may include acting outside of the session as a way of diminishing the inner tension evoked by feelings during the therapeutic hour.

With this brief and necessarily incomplete summary of some of the major trends in the notions of transference, we now turn to transferences in group psychotherapy.

TRANSFERENCES IN THE GROUP SETTING

The historical formulations of transferences in group psychotherapy has paralleled those in dyadic treatment. The early practitioners, in making the transition from individual to group treatment, relied heavily on concepts derived from the dyadic setting. They were particularly influenced by the drive model in which the therapist was considered the central figure on whom the therapeutically significant transferences would be invested. The presence of others, in this view, would interfere with the consistent elaboration of the transference. Trigant Burrow, a pioneer group therapist, succinctly stated this attitude: "What would be the individual transference in a private analysis becomes neutralized in the social participation of many individuals in their common analysis."[9(p170)]

In place of a cohesive unfolding transference, the group therapist had several therapeutically useful alternative manifestations of transference. These include dilution of the parental transference where such feelings were experienced as too intense with the displacement of affects onto other patients; and the opportunity for sibling transference evoked by the familylike atmosphere of the group.

These ideas became enmeshed in the formulations of indications for and treatment advantages of group therapy. Patients who developed "nonverbal" defensive dependency or idealizing transferences in dyadic treatment might be more amenable to therapeutic change in groups.[10,11] It was reasoned that in heterogeneous groups some members would be less afraid to express their negative transference, and through identification and rehearsal, these "stuck" members would be able to forego their defensive positive transference and allow negative feelings to emerge.[12] For patients with major resistances, the multi-person setting would enable them either through imitation or identification to recognize their affects in relationship to the therapist or others.

Transposition of the dyadic model to the group situation carried with it the therapist's efforts to maintain a blank-screen, relatively noninteractive stance in order to promote transference. The austerity of this position, however, produced only limited therapeutic gains primarily in individuals who had prior dyadic treatment and could tolerate the approach.[13] A proposed solution to this problem was the inclusion of a regularly scheduled session without the therapist present — the so-called alternate session. Wolf provided the rationale for this arrangement, telling prospective group members that "one of our objectives in treatment is to resolve your need for me. I believe you can function effectively with your peers."[14(p327)] The alternate session has not achieved widespread acceptance, but the model attests to the concern that the dilution of transference to the therapist was not as complete as anticipated.[15]

In place of the exclusive focus on transferences to the therapist was the recognition of repetitive interactional patterns as transference responses. These patterns, parsimoniously labeled roles, describe behaviors in which the individual assumes stances characterized as the helper, good child, joker, perfect host (hostess), rebel, etc. Presuming that these behaviors were a product of both the individual and group pressures, the individual's contribution to the transferential situation could be explored.[16]* Feelings and attitudes directed toward members not only were possible displacements from parental figures but were considered to represent sibling transferences as well. The argument held both for patients who had grown up with one or more siblings in which the group would recreate the competitive, destructive, tender, or loving feelings, and for those who were an only child, with the inevitable fantasies and wishes regarding siblings. These formulations were consistent with the drive model.

In concert with the modernist concepts, groups provided an opportunity to explore the contributions of the object of the transference to the quality and intensity of the interaction. Examination of the interpersonal responses, which optimally becomes a major focus of the advanced, cohesive group, creates a setting in which a member gains awareness of his contribution to the interpersonal transactions. With that starting point the patient may proceed to explore the childhood sources of these interactions. Achieving this developmental process may require extended treatment periods.

The perspective provided by self-psychology is particularly pertinent in gaining such an understanding. In the self-psychology paradigm the "other," a self-object, fulfills certain functions which are insufficiently developed. Mirroring, idealizing, or twinship self-objects fulfill developmental needs required to establish and maintain inner equilibrium or help restart growth. The therapist or members may fulfill these functions in a silent, self–self-object relationship. The transferential nature becomes apparent when the needed functions are thwarted; then affect displays, withdrawal, or self-soothing responses are activated and signal that the self has been injured and the transference disrupted.[17] These formulations bring into sharp relief the interpersonal nature of the intrapsychic needs. Moreover this model provides an avenue to exploring the responses evoked in the "other" when he or she is needed as a self-object. Often considerable discomfort is evoked when a person is placed in the "role" of the idealized object or is required to mirror others. Responses to these pressures may represent other specific transferences on the part of the self-object or may be an expectable response to the experience.

---

* In some instances, the pressures within the group "require" that a certain function be fulfilled and under these circumstances an individual may be pulled into a particular role (the process has been labeled "role suction").

A significant addition to the dyadic model was achieved with recognition of the members' transferences to the group-as-a-whole. Although some saw group-as-a-whole dynamics as an interference with the analytic work,[18] this became a minority view as expressions of the members' image of the group were more thoroughly explored. At times the group seems to become reified in members' minds. Therapists and members alike make reference to what the group is thinking or feeling, which adds to the mystique. The dynamic basis for these remarks is that members responded "as if" the totality of the members formed a distinct entity.

Bion, in his description of basic assumption life, was describing transferences to the leader.[19] Heath and Bacal summarized the position of the British school of object relations in the following fashion:

> ...disconnected thoughts, affects, and actions of an individual at any particular time during the psychotherapy session belong together dynamically, i.e. they are meaningfully related from an unconscious source....A remark made by a member 'clicks', i.e. some aspect of it is relevant to and can fit into the ongoing dominant unconscious fantasy of the rest, then it is taken in by others and becomes the unconsciously determined topic of the group.[20(p23)]

A view of transference as expressed to the group-as-a-whole was described by Whitaker and Lieberman.[21] The here-and-now focus of their group focal conflict theory shifts emphasis to the activation of derivatives of members' core conflicts through interpersonal stimulation of belonging to a group. The formulations take into account both realistic and distorted assessment of reactions and personalities of other group members.

Group-as-a-whole observations led to a variety of models of development.[22–25] The forces engendered by a group going about the business of accomplishing its goal were observed to follow predictable sequences. The members, as a consequence, would be caught up in these forces and would re-experience their personal developmental stages and re-evoke transferences from those periods. Frequently, theorists did not express their ideas in transferential terms, but their formulations clearly suggested the presence of the concept.

In early developmental stages members might experience a personal, intimate attachment to their image of the group and attempt to construct the reality to fit their inner transferential needs. At times the group may be experienced as frightening, controlling, or devouring.[16] On other occasions it is warm, nurturing, caring, and loving.[26] These affects can be expressed toward one individual as representative of the entire group as in idealization or scapegoating. Under these circumstances, generally the entire membership is caught up in a common intense affect and little diversity is allowed and reality testing is impaired. This lack of flexibility and general intensity is a hallmark of group-wide transference.

In an advanced group where some of the group-as-a-whole transferences have been worked through and the group composition is such that individual conflicts and developmental arrests have been resolved, allowing for recognition of others as separate and autonomous individuals, then more triangular(oedipal)-level conflicts can be consistently explored and worked through.[27,28] Regression with reinstitution of developmentally earlier defenses and transferences are stimulated by breaks in the therapeutic framework, that is, vacations, terminations, new members. The result is another opportunity to experience and therapeutically gain from these transferences.

A significant contribution, highlighting the resistance to recognition of transference, is the work of Gustafson and Cooper.[29] These authors propose that patients enter a group and quickly activate an unconscious plan which they attempt to implement with the hope of forestalling anticipated traumatization as they had experienced in childhood. Through a series of tests, members try to negotiate a new experience. The therapist's interventions exposing the interacting defenses among members, stimulated by the group process, brings the transferences into awareness.

RESEARCH FINDINGS

Research into the manifestations of transferences in groups can be categorized into four areas: (1) examination of members' repetition of feelings and attitudes from the past as expressed toward the leader/therapist; (2) examination of the transferences to the therapist in the here-and-now without specific linkages to the past; (3) measurement of transferential feelings toward the image of the group-as-a-whole; and (4) exploration of transferences over time — a developmental perspective.

Chance,[30] studying one group, asked patients to respond to the general question, "How descriptive are these statements of the way you feel toward me or the way you think I feel toward you?"* An identical questionnaire was administered with statements directed toward the members' self-selected important parent. Responses were recorded on a Likert-type scale. Five of the eight patients expressed attitudes and feelings directed to the therapist that were similar to those directed to the important parent. For two of these five individuals, the important parent was father. For the other three, it was

---

* This group had two prior therapists. Data were collected following the 15th session in which Dr Chance assumed leadership.

mother. Chance concluded: "It seems that the correspondence between the treatment relationship and the parental relationship is not a function of facts about these two people, but rather of the manner in which the patient sees them."[30(p46)]

Burrows studied a 15-member self-analytic group meeting four days a week during summer school.[31] A scale assessed affective orientation toward the coleaders (male and female) utilizing 13 categories of positive and negative acts (ie, challenging, hostile, complying) plus a more subjective evaluation of nonverbal behavior. The composite rating was a summation of positive feelings toward the leader of one gender and negative feelings toward the other leader, that is, positive toward the female plus negative to the male. Ratings were made following the fourth session. Members also recorded their early memories. Independent judges rated the members' relation to authority as revealed in the memories and derived a final rating parallel to that of the member-to-leader affect orientation. Correlation between the two variables was significant ($P < .005$). The author concluded that "members' initial interactions with a male and female leader tend to reflect early childhood feelings towards male and female authority figures."[31(p10)]*

Burrows refined this study with a report of a male-led self-analytic group which met one hour 3 times weekly during a university semester.[32] Seventeen of the 19 members were male. At the end of the semester members filled out a parent orientation scale (separately for each parent) from which it was determined which parent was the greater source of emotional support. During the first 5 weeks of the group, positive member-to-leader ratings correlated with "father-oriented" members as determined from the parent orientation scale ($P < .025$). Although no additional data were reported, the author stated, "after the first 5 weeks, members were shown to exhibit more here-and-now, rather than transferred, affective responses to the leader, who at that point was becoming more active but less salient in the group."[32(p190)] These observations speak to the developmental processes in groups.

An extension of this study explored two additional components of group transferences. The first examined ratings of members' interpersonal style of dominance-submission and an overall intensity score of early parental relationships. The positive correlation ($P < .005$) suggested a strong relationship between the intensity of the early inter-

---

* The author addressed the question of the scoring methodology, arguing that the procedure was necessary because both interactional cues and memories lacked sufficient data about the two genders and alternate scoring methods would have limited interpretations.

action with parents and "prominence" within the group. A second element showed that member-member attraction and affiliation (derived from a sociometric exercise) tended ($P < .10$) to be greater for those individuals who had similar parental orientation and provided some data for the transferential basis of peer relationships.

Greene et al explored the nature of transferences in co-led homogeneous groups of borderline patients meeting twice weekly in a day treatment setting.[33] The research strategy was to measure splitting (a construct related to the type of transferences established by borderline individuals) and correlate that with measures of the patient's "borderlineness," patients rated each cotherapist separately. The divergence in patients' perceptions of the cotherapists was taken as an enactment of the split-off transference. Borderline pathology was assessed using measures of self-representation, object relations, and self-object boundary. Forty-two patients from five groups were studied.

Seven of the 12 borderlineness subscales correlated positively with the patient's degree of splitting of cotherapists, thereby supporting the hypothesis that borderline patients would repeat their pathologic object relations (splitting) within the group context.

A second report by the same research group assessed the cotherapists' independently rated severity of patients' complaints.[34] The differences between the cotherapists were assumed to measure disagreement. The degree of cotherapist difference was positively correlated with the measure of patient splitting. The authors suggested that these findings lend preliminary support to the notion that patients who split their therapists are more likely to evoke differing assessments of the severity of their complaints, suggestive of a countertransference response.

These studies measure transference and countertransference by linking character style with interactions in the group. The underlying assumption is that character solutions and defenses originating in childhood are reenacted in the group and are likely to be reflected back on the patients by the therapist.

An ahistorical approach to measuring transferences assumes that a wide variation in members' perception of the leader represents transferences. Yalom asked group members to rank order peers and therapists for activity according to the total number of words spoken during a group session.[35] He found intermember reliability in members' rankings of their peers but not of the therapists. Members might rate the therapist either most or least active in the same meeting. Yalom concluded that "the powerful and unrealistic feelings of the members towards the therapists prevented an accurate appraisal, even on this relatively objective dimension."[35(p92)]

Klein,[36] examining standard deviations of members' ratings of their leader during a training conference in which the members participated both in a study group (Tavistock) model and a human relations (T-group) approach, assumed that larger standard deviations (as a measure of diversity) signaled greater transference reactions.* The findings were concordant with the hypothesis that the more opaque study group leader would evoke greater variability (ie, transferences) in participants' responses. The initial finding from two groups was replicated in six additional groups.

The difference in variability between the study and human relations groups was greater in the beginning meetings, converged during the middle sessions, and diverged again prior to the termination. In keeping with theories of group process, Klein speculated that during the opening and closing phases more individual, leader-directed transferences were present.[36]

Stone et al examined standard deviations of patient ratings of both the leaders and the group-as-a-whole in five newly formed outpatient groups.[37] Data were collected 2, 4, 6, and 8 months following the beginning of treatment. At all four time periods the variability of ratings directed to the leader was greater than that directed to the group. At two of the four times the difference reached statistical significance ($P < .05$) and at a third time approached significance ($P < .10$). The results suggest that members exhibited greater transferential responses to the leaders than to the group. In addition, the levels of variability did not change during the period of study, which contrasted with the finding that direct ratings of both group and leaders significantly increased during the period of study, suggesting that transference is not related to the levels of evaluation.†

One further report provides an additional measure of transferences. A study of 53 groups at the American Group Psychotherapy Association Annual Institute was reported by MacKenzie et al.[38] Evaluations of the training were obtained immediately following the two-day experience. The authors report that "seven percent of members of groups rated as most successful evaluated their groups quite poorly. Similarly, four percent of the members of the least successful groups rated their groups in the most successful category."[38] These ratings of

---

* The study group paralleled the drive-related transference paradigm in which the consultant remains relatively opaque and restricts interventions primarily to interpretations in the here-and-now. In contrast, the T-group leader is more interactive, using his position of authority to demonstrate useful behaviors, including self-revelation and giving and receiving feedback.

† The Klein (1977) study[36] did not report the levels of variability. What was reported was the changes in difference in variability *between* the study and human relations groups.

most and least successful are subjective and they may represent group-as-a-whole transferences rather than actual success. In addition, since these groups were on the extreme ends of the evaluation, there may have actually been an underreporting of the variability.

DISCUSSION

The rich and continuing developments in the concept of transference reflecting its centrality in psychodynamic theory have spawned relatively sparse research efforts. Perhaps this is so because of the problems inherent in finding satisfactory research methodologies. Nevertheless, some creative studies have provided valuable data confirming some of the theory and pointing the way to further research.

Groups have provided an excellent opportunity to examine transferences both because of the number of subjects available at a given time as well as the potential for diversity or similarity in viewpoints. Several of the studies confirmed the hypothesis that group members are prone to repeat perceptions and feelings from childhood with the leader/therapist. The various methodologies which tap both conscious and preconscious (via early memories) attitudes, affects, or defense patterns established in childhood lend support to the belief that these elements will be repeated in members' affective and attitudinal responses directed to the therapist. The gender of the therapist was not specifically the focus of the transference, but verbal or nonverbal interactions appeared to be the stimulus that elicited the transference. These studies are concordant with the drive-related model of transference which emphasizes the role of childhood experiences with the significant parent as the organizer of emotionally laden relationships in the present.

However, the research also demonstrates that patients rapidly enact their habitual character defenses and attitudes within the group setting. Repetition of interpersonal styles in groups occurred along a dominance-submission axis in a student self-analytic group and in the use of splitting operations in borderline patient groups. Of particular clinical significance is the report of Greene et al demonstrating the therapists' response to patients who utilize splitting defenses.[34] It is unclear whether or not the therapists actually acted on their feeling response, but the ability of the patients to evoke such responses is evident and highlights the interactional nature of treatment. This was further emphasized by the findings comparing responses to study and T-group leaders. The more opaque interpretative leader evoked greater transferential responses, which is concordant with the drive model but at the same time confirms the relationalist model in that the stance of the therapist/leader has a significant impact on the nature of the interactions.

Only the study by Stone et al has directly explored the nature of transferences to the group-as-a-whole.[37] The finding that across the 8 months of the study the variability of ratings to the group was smaller than those to the leader pointed to the continued focus by the members on their leaders rather than intermember transactions. In contrast, the report of Burrows describes an apparent decrease in member orientation to the leader and greater interest in peers, which is in concordance with theories of group development.[32] Similarly, Klein's report supports the notion that transferences vary over time.[36] Both the latter two studies were time-limited educational experiences in contrast to the open-ended treatment groups reported by Stone et al.[37] This may account in part for the reported differences. In addition, the findings are confounded by the presence of neophyte cotherapists in the patient groups, whereas the training groups were conducted by experienced leaders. Thus these studies are only the first phase of a much needed effort to confirm hypotheses about shifting transferences within the group.

Many methodologic issues are raised by these data in using variability as a measure of transference. As Stone et al have pointed out, two situations must be taken into account.[37] First, a wide variability appears to measure individual responses, and second, a very narrow variability may measure group-as-a-whole transferences when intense group pressures require members to respond with unanimity. Such a circumstance would fit a basic assumption group as described by Bion.[19]

Therefore, transferences might be conceptualized along a continuum with one end represented by a wide variability in member perception indicating individual transferences and the other end marked by great uniformity indicating group-as-a-whole transference. In the middle area there would be a modicum of agreement, a condition which might be analogous to Bion's concept of a work group. A basic assumption group would be characterized by little variability in either the ratings of group or the leader, depending on which basic assumption was mobilized.

An additional interesting area of exploration is the nature of peer ties in groups. One strategy individuals adopt to ease their entry into groups or to manage other anxieties is to "pair" with other members. It is possible that this pairing can take place across a continuum from conscious to unconscious forces. Burrows' data suggest that peer attractions, in part, are determined by the pair harboring similar feelings about a same-gender parent.[32] This research strategy could be utilized in examining twinship transferences as described as the framework of self-psychology.

Finally, these studies despite their limitations point to the need for further exploration to transference phenomena. The complex task of measuring and differentiating group-as-a-whole, leader, and peer transferences has barely been touched upon. There is only a beginning examining of the development of transferences over time. Certainly notions of group development suggest activation of different transference constellations at different stages and data exploring these concepts would add considerably to our understanding of our theories of group development.

SUMMARY

This chapter reviews the evolution of theories of transference, both in individual and group psychotherapy. Against this background, research studies of transferences in groups have been examined. The findings, although preliminary, support the idea that affects, attitudes, and defenses from childhood experiences become activated toward the therapist/leader in the group. Additionally, a model for exploring individual transference directed toward the therapist(s) or the group-as-a-whole provides an important starting point to explore questions of the evolution of transference over time, the relationship between transferences and group development, and transferences directed to the leader or the "group-as-a-whole." This research opens a wide door of opportunity to further examine the nature of transferences, which stand as one of the fundamental bases of psychodynamic theory.

REFERENCES

1. Freud S (1905): *Fragment of an Analysis of a Case of Hysteria*. Standard Edition, vol 7, Strachey J (trans-ed). London, Hogarth Press, 1953.
2. Greenson RR: *The Technique and Practice of Psychoanalysis*. New York, International Universities Press, 1967.
3. Cooper AM: Changes in psychoanalytic ideas: Transference interpretation. *J Am Psychoanal Assoc* 1987;35:77–98.
4. Greenberg JR, Mitchell JA: *Object Relations in Psychoanalytic Theory*. Cambridge, Mass, Harvard, 1983.
5. Sandler J, Dare C, Holder A: *The Patient and the Analyst*. New York, International Universities Press, 1973.
6. Kohut H: *The Analysis of the Self*. New York, International Universities Press, 1971.
7. Ornstein A: The dread to repeat and the new beginning: A contribution to the psychoanalysis of narcissistic personality disorders. *Annu Psychoanal* 1974;2:231–248.

60

8. Daniels RS: Some early manifestations of transference: Their implications for the first phase of psychoanalysis. *J Am Psychoanal Assoc* 1969;17:995–1014.
9. Burrow T: The group method of analysis (1936), in Rosenbaum M, Berger MM (eds): *Group Psychotherapy and Group Function*, New York, Basic Books, 1975, pp 163–173.
10. Fried E: Some aspects of group dynamics and the analysis of transference and defenses. *Int J Group Psychother* 1965;15:44–56.
11. Block SL: Some notes on transference in group psychotherapy. *Compr Psychiatry* 1966;7:31–38.
12. Glatzer HT: Aspects of transference in group psychotherapy. *Int J Group Psychother* 1965;15:167–176.
13. Malan DH, Belfour FHG, Hood VG, et al: Group psychotherapy: A long-term follow-up study. *Arch Gen Psychiatry* 1976;33:1303–1315.
14. Wolf A: Psychoanalysis in groups, in Rosenbaum M, Berger MM (eds): *Group Psychotherapy and Group Function*. New York, Basic Books, 1975, pp 321–335.
15. Ethan S: The question of the dilution of transference in group psychotherapy. *Psychoanal Rev* 1978;65:569–578.
16. Durkin HE: *The Group in Depth*. New York, International Universities Press, 1964.
17. Stone WN, Whitman RM: Contribution of psychology of the self to group process and group therapy. *Int J Group Psychother* 1977;27:343–359.
18. Slavson SR: Are there group dynamics in therapy groups? *Int J Group Psychother* 1957;7:131–154.
19. Bion WR: *Experiences in Groups*. New York, Basic Books, 1961.
20. Heath ES, Bacal HA: A method of group psychotherapy at the Tavistock clinic. *Int J Group Psychother* 1968;18:21–30.
21. Whitaker DS, Lieberman MA: *Psychotherapy Through the Group Process*. New York, Atherton Press, 1964.
22. Bennis WG, Shepard HA: A theory of group development. *Hum Relat* 1956;9:415–437.
23. Tuckman BW: Developmental sequence in small groups. *Psychol Bull* 1965;63:384–399.
24. Saravay SM: A psychoanalytic theory of group development. *Int J Group Psychother* 1978;28:481–507.
25. MacKenzie KR, Livesley WJ: A developmental model for brief group therapy, in Dies RR, MacKenzie KR (eds): *Advances in Group Psychotherapy: Integrating Research and Practice*. New York, International Universities Press, 1982, pp 101–116.
26. Scheidlinger S: On the concept of the "mother-group." *Int J Group Psychother* 1974;24:417–428.
27. Kernberg OF: A systems approach to priority setting of interventions in groups. *Int J Group Psychother* 1975;25:251–275.
28. Stone WN, Gustafson JP: Technique in group psychotherapy of narcissistic and borderline patients. *Int J Group Psychother* 1982;32:29–47.
29. Gustafson JP, Cooper L: Unconscious planning in small groups. *Hum Relat* 1979;32:1039–1064.
30. Chance E: A study of transference in group psychotherapy. *Int J Group Psychother* 1952;2:40–53.
31. Burrows PB: The family connection: Early memories as a measure of transference in a group. *Int J Group Psychother* 1981a;31:3–23.

32. Burrows PB: Parent orientation and member-leader behavior: A measure of transference in groups. *Int J Group Psychother* 1981b;31:175–191.
33. Greene LR, Rosenkrantz J, Muth DY: Splitting dynamics, self-representations and boundary phenomena in the group psychotherapy of borderline personality disorders. *Psychiatry* 1985;48:234–245.
34. Greene LR, Rosenkrantz J, Muth DY: Borderline defenses and countertransference: Research findings and implications. *Psychiatry* 1986;49:253–264.
35. Yalom ID: *The Theory and Practice of Group Psychotherapy*. New York, Basic Books, 1970.
36. Klein EB: Transferences in training groups. *J Pers Soc Syst* 1977;1:53–64.
37. Stone WN, Green BL, Grace M, et al: Transference in groups. Presented at American Academy of Psychoanalysis Annual Meeting, New York, 1987.
38. MacKenzie KR, Dies RR, Coche E, et al: An analysis of AGPA institute groups. *Int J Group Psychother* 1987;37:55–74.

4

Countertransference and Group Psychotherapy: The Role of Supervision

David A. Halperin

There is an increasing awareness that the effectiveness of the group psychotherapeutic process is dependent on the character and quality of the skills that the group leader brings to his task. This heightened recognition of the interactive nature of the group psychotherapeutic enterprise has led to an increasing examination of the role played by countertransference. This chapter examines the manner in which countertransference affects the group's therapeutic effectiveness and the role of the supervisor in helping the inexperienced group therapist to mature into competence.

Countertransference is an ambiguous term. Freud narrowly defined countertransference as the therapist's responses to the patient's transference. It was seen primarily as a contaminant of the therapeutic relationship. Recent work has adopted a more inclusive definition. Kernberg[1] defines countertransference as the totality of the therapist's conscious and unconscious responses within the therapeutic situation. The countertransference issues discussed in this chapter, and which are the subject of supervision of group psychotherapy, approach countertransference primarily within this more inclusive totalistic framework. But it cannot be overemphasized that the problems encountered by the beginning group psychotherapist cannot and should not always be ascribed to countertransference. The supervisor who approaches supervision from a perspective that attributes all the problems encountered by the group psychotherapist to countertransference and overlooks the realistic technical problems that arise when an individual works with in groups is not helping his supervisees and may be counterproductive.

The supervisory process is a delicate relationship. The contract between supervisor and supervisee is limited. The supervisee will legitimately experience the supervisor as being intrusive and invasive if the supervisor's primary activity is to probe for dynamic material ostensibly to help the supervisee deal with his countertransference. A respect for the supervisee's privacy should preclude the supervisor from attempting to explore the underlying dynamics which express themselves in countertransference. Even when the supervisor is able to appreciate the origin of countertransference reactions, he must respect the reality that the supervisee's commitment is to participating in supervision rather than therapy. Of course, when substantial countertransference issues arise, a referral to a therapist is appropriately in order. But the boundary between supervisory and therapeutic relationships should be maintained.

Supervision is most effective when it deals with countertransference problems as they are reflected in the actual process of the group. The supervisor is often most helpful when he encourages the group leader/supervisee to speculate about how a group leader might feel about the process within the group at a particular point. By using hypotheticals and encouraging the supervisee to approach the group on an "as if" basis, a climate of openness is created within the supervisory situation. By emphasizing the concrete interactions — the actual details — the possibility of "therapizing" is decreased and the "normative" anxiety of supervision is diluted. Above all, the supervisor should structure supervision in a manner which increases the supervisee's sense of competence.

The group presents to the beginning group therapist a rich and confusing field of activity. So much is happening, has happened, and appears to impend. By using anecdotal material and presenting clinical vignettes during the course of supervision, the supervisor decreases the supervisee's anxiety and confusion. It is often particularly helpful if the supervisor presents himself as an individual who has faced problems comparable to those currently afflicting the supervisee (and who has presumably learned to effectively cope with them). Such material also supports the supervisee by its provisioning supervision with "cookbook recipes" to help the supervisee deal with the events that always seem to present themselves with a peculiar immediacy during the course of a group interaction. Approaching the supervisee in an open and nurturing fashion re-enforces the beginner by demonstrating that the problems he is currently experiencing are neither unique nor necessarily the product of his personal inadequacy or incompetence. Supervision within a group setting often permits the supervisees to share from one another's growth and serves to negate any sense of incompetence and the supervisee's sense of isolation. Supervision within a group also permits the supervisor to explore the parallel processes that develop within the supervisory group — an opportunity which often richly illustrates the development of countertransference.

Focusing on the development of themes and the evolution of group dynamics provides a useful vantage point from which to examine group processes. When the supervisee is encouraged to examine the process within his group utilizing the schema of group dynamics, the superficially confusing becomes clarified and the role of the group leader is demystified.

Certain stages of group formation and development as well as certain types of patients are unusually evocative of intense counter-transference reactions. Effective supervision focuses on these contexts and on these patients. An obvious point of departure is the reluctance of the would-be group psychotherapist to form a group.

The reluctance to form a group may express itself in a variety of ways. The therapist may express a fear of "diluting and diffusing" his analytic relationship with the patient. Or he may express his fear of losing the patient to the group (and group leader). On closer examina-tion, these fears of "contaminating" the individual relationship often reflect the beginning group psychotherapist's fear of placing his patient in a therapeutic context in which he fears he has less control over the process of treatment. On another level, it translates into a fear of the group as an entity capable of uniting and unanimously expressing rage and hostility toward the group therapist. The beginning group therapist may sense the group, in an ill-concealed manner, as a "primordial horde" ready to unite in the destruction of their leader. When the supervisee's fears and the group's actual potential for the expression of anger are discussed in an open and supportive manner, they disappear. It is remarkable how readily group supervisees are reassured when they are reminded that the group's need to preserve its leader consti-tutes a most important group dynamic.

The formation of a group is a complex matter. Groups should be formed which encourage the active participation of all their members. For the beginner, the group's ability to foster participation may evoke the fear that participation within the group may be so traumatic an experience to the individual patient that the patient will promptly leave treatment as an expression of anger at having been coerced into par-ticipation in the group. Or the beginning group therapist may fear the individual's active participation in the group will become so all-consuming that it will drain off any significance from the individual sessions. Supervisees should be encouraged to consider that group and individual treatment can (and usually do) act synergistically and that participation in a group often stimulates the progress of individual treatment.

In the formation of a group, leaders usually attempt to strike a balance among age, educational level, sex, the ability to articulate feelings, and ego strength. Heterogeneity is usually preferred except when the group task leads the group leader to intentionally form a homogeneous group. In the formation of groups, the group leader articulates the group tasks. Thus group leaders will characterize a group as "supportive," that is, consisting primarily of schizophrenic or relatively dysfunctional characterologic patients, or "insight-oriented," that is, groups with neurotic and higher-functioning characterologic patients.

Unfortunately, these characterizations may more realistically reflect the group leader's aspirations rather than a realistic assessment of the member's strengths. Moreover, such characterizations tend to remain static. Thus, the inexperienced group leader aspiring to work with an insight-oriented group may tend to exclude all schizophrenic patients (regardless of their current level of functioning) without recognizing that groups of neurotic and higher-functioning borderline patients can comfortably tolerate a single schizophrenic patient[2] to their mutual benefit. Their unwillingness to introduce members to groups on a more flexible basis may also reflect conditions within the institutional setting in which the supervisees work primarily with schizophrenic or severely borderline patients. Thus, the beginning group leader may be very resistant to seeing the more insight-oriented group's being "polluted" by a more dysfunctional patient. The supervisor can help the beginner recognize that his need for "achievement" or "success" may be operative in his restricting the membership of a group, as the following illustrates:

Oscar S, a 32-year-old male, was referred for group psychotherapy primarily because nothing else had been helpful. For the past 3 years, Oscar had been unemployed. Weighing over 270 lb and bizarrely dressed, Oscar typified his diagnosis of schizophrenic, chronic undifferentiated type (in partial remission). The initial recommendation had been to place Oscar in a supportive group with comparably dysfunctional individuals. But then it was noted that he had previously been a member of comparable groups without any benefit. Thus the decision was made to introduce Oscar into a group of articulate, insight-oriented, high-functioning patients.

The decision to introduce Oscar was made with great trepidation. Initially the trepidation appeared to be justified. The group's initial response was very negative. The group members questioned the group leader's judgment — wondering at his motives for introducing so inappropriate a member to their group. The group leader began to identify with the group members and to question his own decision. However, during the course of supervision, the supervisor and supervisee explored the supervisee's need to preserve his group as an "analytic" group — a need which had led him to overidentify with the group members, and more explicitly their need to deny their own pathology. He began to recognize that even though Oscar's dependency needs were great, they were similar to the dependency needs of other group members (needs which they had denied even while projecting them onto the group's most obviously dependent member). Thus, the group therapist became much more comfortable with his initial decision.

Ultimately, he was able to help the group members increase their awareness that their attacks on Oscar reflected their own unwillingness to confront their own passivity. As the group leader reflected on his countertransference toward Oscar, he was able to help Oscar join the group in a meaningful manner. Oscar was then able to utilize the group constructively — he lost a substantial amount of weight and was ultimately able to leave his home to live in a long-term residential setting and accept placement in a sheltered workshop. The presence of a significantly less functional member did not interfere with other insight-oriented activity within the group. Indeed, Oscar's progress provided the other group members with a sense of accomplishment and achievement.

The aspiration of the group leader may lead to impatience with the actual level of group activity. A group will pause as the members exchange ideas and realistic concerns about future business ventures. The group leader impatiently interrupts this activity to observe that the members are not dealing with "important" issues and that the cooperative character of their interactions conceals their unwillingness to deal with another, "darker" agenda. During supervision, the supervisor commented that the group is, above all, a human experience and that a pause is part of the human experience and was not the group leader trying to fit all interchanges prematurely into a procrustean analytic bed? During the course of further work, the supervisee reflected that he had been acting out of his own need to make this group conform to his own preconceived schedule — that his countertransference had encouraged him toward approaching the group from his own rigidly conceptualized framework which led to his "working too hard."

Conversely, the inexperienced group leader may impose an intrusive homogeneity on a "supportive" group. Here, the group leader becomes so overprotective of his more fragile patients that he unnecessarily dampens or controls the group's activity. During supervision, the supervisor can help the group leader recognize that his rationalized overcontrol may reflect his fear of losing control of the group and his fear of criticism for potentiating the decompensation of such poorly defended individuals. The following vignette illustrates these issues:

> A member of an inpatient group began to complain about the staff's inability to provide a continuous round of ward activities. As the discussion continued, another patient began to express her anger at the staff for her dependency on them. She was joined by another group member who was voluble in comparing the inattentive staff to her unconcerned and neglectful family. The resident psychiatrist intervened by discussing the scheduling problem faced by the unit's staff and answered the patients' complaints on a point-for-point basis dealing exclusively with reality issues.

The group had begun to deal with its ambivalence on its dependency toward significant authority figures. But the inexperienced group leader had viewed these fragile psychotic patients as being totally resourceless — without any potential for insight or growth. Indeed, in his interactions with them, he had been unusually dedicated to providing support for them precisely because he saw them as being so irrevocably fragile. During supervision, he began to discuss his fear of what might happen if these patients began to express their anger toward their caretakers (himself included). His need to control as a means of avoiding their rage was examined. Eventually, he was able to accept that the process or reintegration might proceed without his making heroic sacrifices to provide a supportive environment for his group members.

Countertransference may express itself in more global terms. Bion has described the "basic assumptions" group with its "dependent," "flight/fight," and "pairing" assumptions that develop with the "breakdown of the task group."[3] The group leader's activity is a most significant factor in the formation of the task-oriented group. However, leader activity that reflects countertransference may contribute to the breakdown of the task-oriented group and lead to the formation of the basic assumptions group. Of particular importance in this context is the group leader who under the pressure of intense countertransference acts in an inappropriate manner and through his self-aggrandizement or self-denigration sponsors regression with the group and its members.

The group leader who becomes a group guru represents a particularly blatant example of this process. During the course of his "apotheosis," the potential guru acts out his countertransference by uncritically accepting the members' idealization and overvaluation, and by his uncritically accepting their devaluation of themselves as individuals who are incapable of acting autonomously and who require constant nurture.[4] He may subtly encourage sexual intimacy between group members because so "beneficial" an experience should perpetuate itself. Gradually, the boundaries between group leader and group member become blurred with the leader feeling that his patients are incapable of functioning or working through their dependence without his continuing and often continuous intervention.[5] Inevitably, the group guru exacerbates the members' sense of helplessness by his re-enforcing the group's dependent and flight-fight assumptions.

The members' need to rely on the leader may be further re-enforced by creating conditions of isolation and pointing to broader social conditions which "require" members to limit their contact with the outside world. For example, members of a "therapeutic cult" were discouraged from contact with the outside world by focusing on the AIDS epidemic or the need for group cohesiveness in the event of an impending nuclear catastrophe. During the formation of a "therapeutic cult," group members are actively discouraged from constructive or even skeptical intragroup contact. The group remains totally leader-centered. Ultimately, the guru-controlled group may act out the pairing assumption among the members or encourage the group leader to engage in sexual activity with individual group members.

The basic assumptions group is both the product and fosters the development of an authoritarian style of group leadership. Within the basic assumptions group, the group leader operates as a benevolent if infantilizing parent, but his "benevolence" conceals his own inability to tolerate anger either within himself or when expressed by others. His pseudo-benevolence feeds on itself because his style is one in which he chooses to fulfill the demands of the group members rather than explore their demands. This is a process doomed to frustration and increasing anger. Kernberg's description[6] of the appropriate parameters of group leadership is particularly relevant in this context. He describes the ideal group leader as one who will:

1. Systematically elaborate the negative transference
2. Interpret the defensive constellations of the patients as they enter the transference
3. Provide limit-setting in order to block acting out of the transference
4. Systematically verify the patient's perceptions

Supervision should help the supervisee to approximate these ideals. By encouraging the nascent group guru to examine his need for his highly directive style of group leadership, and by encouraging him to examine his perception that his patients require such continuous and intrusive input, the supervisor renders a service to both group and group leader.

The group therapist in training may attempt to control his group most frequently through the exercise of self-denial and self-denigration. Thus he will avoid interpreting manifestations of negative transference as they appear within the group. Or he will avoid setting limits in order to gain the group's approval. He directs the group's process toward avoiding the expression of anger. And he intervenes to provide "fragile" group members with unnecessary support. Thus, he may extend sessions, emphasize the importance of additional sessions (either individual or group), allow group members to avoid payment, or even limit or otherwise interrupt his own vacations in order to "reassure" the group of his "concern." In a more subtle effort to defuse group anger, the group leader may disavow his role as group leader by inappropriately sharing personal matters with the group.

The group supervisor should adopt a supportive role in helping the leader who deals with his fear of group anger by self-denigration and self-abasement. Thus he should encourage the group therapist who has been reluctant to take adequate vacation time to do so. In addition, he should explore with the student practices such as "making up time" through additional sessions. This examination should not be conducted in judgmental terms, even when confronting the supervisee with his having attempted to limit group interaction through the use of self-denial, which carries the implicit message of "How could the group be angry with such a nice leader whose concern for it is so great that he gives up fulfilling his own legitimate needs?" The group leader's need to relate to the group members as an omnipotent, omnipresent parent may be such that it requires examination in another setting.

Training often occurs in settings where the supervisee either does not collect the fee or where the fee is set at an arbitrarily low figure. Thus, setting limits as reflected in the demand for payment for services rendered often does not arise as an overt issue during the course of group therapy conducted in such a setting. Nonetheless, the supervisor should help the supervisee examine his refusal to raise the issue of nonpayment with his clinic patients. This refusal often reflects his overidentification with his patients (is not a resident by definition deprived?). Or his reluctance may reflect his devaluing of his work — his acceptance of the relatively low status often accorded group modalities within the hospital hierarchy — or his need to evade his patient's anger.[7] The supervisee should be encouraged to develop an awareness of how payment may be used to suppress the expression of angry feelings within the group.

Certain issues evoke intense transference and countertransference. The expression of racial or religious slurs within a group is such an issue. Supervision can be very helpful it focuses on this particularly delicate problem, as the following vignette illustrates:

> Zelda, a holocaust survivor, was speaking in her characteristically monotonous and obsessive manner about her employer's inability to tolerate her rigid and compulsive style. Suddenly, Katherine (a non-Jewish group

member) burst out with, "I wish you'd gone up in smoke." The group paused. The instantaneous reaction of the Jewish group members was dramatic. The Jewish group leader was totally nonplussed by this dramatic turn of events. The group appeared to be on the verge of sudden dissolution as a majority of the group talked about their refusal to remain in a group with a rabid anti-Semite and demanded her immediate exclusion from the group. Indeed, the group leader himself wondered if he could continue to work with Katherine. Fortunately, at that point the group session ended.

The group leader's initial response was an amalgam of anger and confusion. But on reflection during the course of supervision, he remembered that Katherine had visited Israel numerous times, had worked exclusively within Jewish institutions, and had chosen to be in treatment with a Jewish therapist. All of this pointed to her comment as being something more than just the unalloyed product of prejudice. He was then able to analyze his "totalistic" countertransference toward Katherine which comprised his anger at her racial slur and his anger at her for having provoked the possible dissolution of the group. In the light of his reflection, Katherine was no longer the omnipotent anti-Semite but rather a woman who was extremely ambivalent about her right to express anger. Moreover, in her expressing anger toward Zelda she was on some level expressing the group's rage toward a controlling obsessive woman. She had expressed her anger (and the group's) in a masochistic manner calculated to displace the anger the group felt toward Zelda (and the group leader for his passivity toward Zelda) onto herself.

After examining his countertransference, the group leader was able to help Katherine deal with her inability to express anger more openly and effectively. Then, other group members were able to deal with their own sense of passivity and helplessness in relation to the issue of anti-Semitism, and with their anger toward Zelda which they had previously denied because of their feelings about her traumatic past. Provocative remarks about Jewish avarice, Italian criminality, Black indolence, or Hispanic promiscuity may provide comparable countertransference problems for the beginning (and even more experienced) group therapist. These remarks also will provide similar opportunities for conflict resolution with the exploration of the anger that is so often expressed in this inherently unacceptable manner. The use of these slurs should be considered as markers of pathology and not dismissed because they appear to form part of the common coin of communication (pace Archie Bunker) in our society.

When scapegoating or the overprotection of a group member occurs, it may reflect either the group leader's own attitudes or his activity. During the course of supervision, the group leader should always monitor his activity for the possibility that it is eliciting group responses that may, in turn, evoke intense countertransference. For example, the beginning group therapist may be very ambivalent about assuming an actively interpretive role toward the overly helpful patient and thereby accord this patient a special, cotherapist status, as the following illustrates:

> The group therapist was going on vacation. The group spent an entire session angrily discussing his impending desertion. Other issues such as the expense of therapy, the brevity of the sessions, the leader's disinterest, and even the discomfort of the clinic chairs were raised. Terry remained silent throughout. Then, in an authoritative fashion, she announced that the other group members were acting like children. At once, the other group members denounced her for her arrogance and contempt. The group leader ineffectually intervened to protect Terry from the group's onslaught.

The group leader's attitude toward Terry was complex. She was a strikingly attractive woman who presented a veneer of sophistication and control. Moreover, he felt gratitude toward her as a helpful, ostensibly objective member of the group. However, his sense of gratitude had prevented him from seeing that her "objective" observations reflected her need to form a coupling alliance with the group leader, and to dissociate herself from the group. Thus, the group leader had protected Terry in her expressions of disdain for the other group members. His protection had shielded Terry from being confronted with her arrogance. The group leader was effectively in collusion with this attractive woman in her use of objectivity and intellectualization as defenses in denying her feelings of anger toward significant figures, including the group leader who was deserting her as well. By protecting Terry, the group leader had managed to focus group activity onto her and away from himself, shielding himself from the group's anger. His "gratitude" toward the "helpful" group member was discussed in supervision. Subsequently, he was able to help his "cotherapist" join the group.

The supervisor recognized that the beginning group therapist had faced a painful dilemma. Because the beginner frequently works in clinic settings with relatively inarticulate and unresponsive patients, he often begins to feel that he needs all the help he can get irrespective of the quarter from whence it comes. He is, therefore, uncomfortable in examining his underlying motivation. Supervision can help the supervisee realize that the exploration of overprotection is not a study of the therapist's pathologic dependency on a patient, but constitutes an attempt to open up all aspects of group activity to examination and resolution.

Borderline patients often present particularly difficult problems within the group.[8] Their regression to a more primitive level of object relations may mobilize all the anger present within the group and lead to their being scapegoated. The group leader must intervene early and effectively to prevent this denouement:

> Nancy L, a mental health professional, entered group therapy to explore her sense of isolation. Initially, a withdrawn nonparticipant, she became visibly tremulous during sessions. Finally, the group members questioned her about her obviously increasing anxiety. She protested volubly that her refusal to talk about her problems was caused only by her not wanting to take up the group's time with a discussion of her trivial problems, and that the other group members' difficulties were more urgent than hers. This response rapidly mobilized the group's rage. As a self-denying, guilt-invoking mother (she was indeed older than the other group members), Nancy presented an inviting target.

The group leader was in a dilemma. Nancy was a productive, creative, successful mental health professional. Her history of volatility and rapid enthusiasms with equally rapid withdrawals did suggest an underlying borderline personality structure. Yet how could the group leader have so misjudged her potential for regressive behavior? Or how could a woman who had realized so much professionally function in so self-destructive a fashion within the group? Conjoint treatment was discussed. Nancy's difficulties presumably would resolve after a brief period of conjoint therapy. And recent literature has emphasized the advantages of working with the patient with borderline personality structure in conjoint treatment, although Wong[9] has noted that even when undertaken early in the group experience it is not a panacea. Eventually, the group leader had to accept that the depth of regression and the pervasiveness of her fragility made it inadvisable for Nancy to continue in group therapy.

During supervision, the group leader reviewed his therapeutic experience with Nancy. He was able to accept that his initial misperception of Nancy's suitability for group therapy reflected his overidentification with her as a creative, successful mental health professional. Significantly, he was able to appreciate that therapeutic overoptimism is not unavoidable and that it did not reflect on his competence as a professional. He accepted the reality that therapeutic zeal and its occasional disappointment form part of the universal experience of the training process — that no group leader, irrespective of his experience, is totally immune from rescue fantasies — but that in retrospect he should have been alert to the possibility of overidentification with Nancy because of the particularly positive terms in which he had described her to the other group members prior to her entry into the group.

Similarly, the supervisor should alert the supervisee to the possibility that his need for success may lead him to continue a chronically ill patient in a group when it is clearly in neither the patient's nor the group's interest to do so:

> Kenneth L had functioned well after his discharge from the hospital. He was employed and talked about marrying the woman with whom he had initiated what appeared to be a stable and satisfying relationship. He appeared to be coping with his difficulties with major problems, although he presented himself within the group as a help-rejecting complainer. Suddenly, he became obsessive about his girlfriend's interest in marriage. Despite a rapid increase in his medication, he became more and more obsessive. Finally, he entered a group session, sat down, rolled up his shirt sleeves, and displayed to the other group members (who had been supportive to him during the previous sessions) numbers he had written up and down his arm to show them that "his girlfriend's demands made him feel like a concentration camp inmate." He was obviously very confused and disturbed. The group leader then escorted him from the group.

The group leader had developed an obvious pride in Kenneth's apparent rehabilitation. His stake in Kenneth's recovery had allowed him to gloss over Kenneth's increasing anxiety and obsessiveness. His sense of accomplishment as the leader of a group of schizophrenic patients (all of whom had had the experience of a lengthy hospitalization) who were now successfully autonomous and functional had been challenged by Kenneth's increasingly obvious decompensation. In supervision, the group leader discussed his sense of failure over Kenneth's rehospitalization. But eventually he was able to appreciate that the rehospitalization simply indicated that Kenneth's successes had been too threatening and that the group had become too intensely involving an experience. Above all, he accepted that it was a species of machismo for him to assume that either he or the group could help Kenneth deal with this degree of anxiety and repair his fragile ego. The supervisee was able to continue leadership of the group, albeit with a chastened and more humble view of his and the group's ability to deal with acute illness.

The area of sexual orientation and gender role identification may evoke intense countertransference. The beginning group therapist may feel the need to be overprotective, gratuitously supportive, or reassuring when patients discuss their profound anxiety about being sexually active in a world constrained by the reality (and fear) of AIDS. In this case, he closes off the issue of sexual orientation and its complexities as an appropriate topic for group exploration. Ultimately, the group leader's role is not to control his patient's sexual expression, as the following illustrates:

> Seymour G entered group therapy with the goal of exploring heterosexuality. Exclusively homosexual, he had become increasingly disinterested

in his relationship with his long-term (10 years) partner. During the year prior to his entry into group therapy, he had experienced an increasing interest in sexual experience with women. During the course of treatment, he became actively heterosexual and detached himself from the homosexual milieu. He was contemplating marriage. At this juncture, a lesbian member of the group challenged him about the possibility of his having further homosexual liaisons. Seymour became exceedingly anxious, murmuring that he did not know what would happen after marriage. He looked to the group leader for reassurance. The other group members then challenged the group leader about Seymour's apparent vacillation.

Seymour's profound change during treatment had given the group leader a genuine sense of accomplishment. He was initially tempted to reply to the question/challenge by being gratuitously supportive and reassuring to Seymour. He resisted that temptation and simply replied that he could not and would not exercise control over Seymour — that it was up to Seymour to assume this control. With this, the group continued with its members reassured that the group was indeed a place to explore their sexual feelings without constraint or judgment.

SUMMARY

This chapter describes the role of supervision in helping the group therapist deal with countertransference issues. Areas of difficulty include the formation of the group, stereotyping group activity, and the role that the group leader should play in facilitating group interaction. Other problematic areas which evoke intense countertransference include ethnicity, the pseudo-cotherapist, working with patients with a borderline personality structure, and the area of sexual orientation. The role of supervision in equipping the group therapist to deal with these issues is discussed in detail.

Acknowledgments

The author thanks the late Aaron Stein, MD, and other members of the Division of Group Psychotherapy of the Department of Psychiatry of the Mount Sinai School of Medicine for their suggests and critique. An earlier version of this chapter appeared in *Group* 1981;5:24–33.

REFERENCES

1. Kernberg O: *Borderline Conditions and Pathological Narcissism.* New York, Jason Aronson, 1976.
2. Day M: Psychoanalytic group therapy in clinic and private practice. *Am J Psychiatry* 1981;138:64–69.
3. Ezriel H: Notes on psychoanalytic group psychotherapy (II): Interpretation and research. *Psychiatry* 1952;15:119–126.

4. Wolf A, Schwartz E: *Psychoanalysis in Groups*. New York, Grune & Stratton, 1962.
5. Halperin D: Psychiatric approaches to cults: Therapeutic and legal parameters, in Schetky D, Benedek EP (eds): *Emerging Issues in Child Psychiatry and the Law*. New York, Brunner/Mazel, 1986, pp 150–166.
6. Kernberg O: Psychoanalytic object-relations theory, group processes, and administration: Toward an integrative theory of hospital treatment. *Ann Psychoanal* 1973;1:363–388.
7. Halperin D, Hoyt M: Psychiatrists and group psychotherapy: The reluctant marriage. *Group* 1975;5:53–57.
8. Wong N: Clinical considerations in group treatment of narcissistic disorder. *Int J Group Psychother* 1979;29:325–347.
9. Wong N: Combined group and individual treatment of borderline and narcissistic patients: Heterogeneous versus homogeneous groups. *Int J Group Psychother* 1980;30:389–404.

5

Coleadership in Groups: Marriage à la Mode?

Enid Lang
David A. Halperin

Coleadership of groups, like other pairings, may be a response to institutional pressure, social custom, or a conscious decision on the part of two therapists to work in conjunction with each other. Like all pairings, coleadership possesses its own inherent internal dynamics which impact on the interactions of the group leaders and through them on the evolution and the development of the group. Coleadership of a group enhances leadership experience because it allows the coleaders to lend support to each other. Specifically, coleaders can aid each other in the observation of group process, especially in the recognition and exploration of group defenses and resistances. The pair can monitor each other's behavior and countertransference, as well as the transference of the group to each of the leaders. Coleaders serve as role models in their behavior toward each other and the group, as well as recreating the family unit. In addition, the diffusion of the intensity of group transference allows each of the two leaders to make interpretations to the group that are difficult to make alone.

One of the inherent difficulties of coleadership is the wish to impress the other with the "rightness," appropriateness, and sensitivity of one's intervention. This is particularly true in the early phases of coleading a group. It is a pressure on each of the two coleaders that is a combination of courtship and competition. Coleaders tend to be more abstinent and more confronting of the group than either leader would be alone. They also are less gratifying than they would be in running a group alone. The "peer supervision" effect of doing cotherapy is frequently beneficial to each of the leaders, perhaps leading them to question the effect of overgratification on their patients when they are working alone.

This chapter discusses this complex interaction with the caveat that not all pairings are made in heaven, that divorce may be not only inevitable but desirable, but also with the recognition that the process of divorce is time-consuming and may for practical purposes be (either) so complex as to render it an unrealistic solution to the very human problems that people experience as they attempt to work together. Moreover, the very fact of two therapists working together within a group setting, like other working relationships in which the partners join their individual strengths and distinctive approaches to the enhancement of the process of individuation and the development of autonomy, often enhances the experience of group leadership for the leaders and for the group members alike. The issues that arise during the process of group evolution affect the interaction of the group leaders. Thus it is useful to examine the interactions between group leaders from the vantage point of the inevitable changes that occur as a group evolves and develops.

COLEADERSHIP AND GROUP FORMATION

The decision to colead a group may occur as the result of a conscious decision on the part of two therapists to join forces — to pool their patients and their talents to work together. Or, coleadership may arise in an institutional or educational context in which a decision is made that the educational opportunities will be enhanced by giving a junior therapist the opportunity to work with a therapist of greater experience and presumed sophistication. Within an institutional framework, coleadership of groups may be encouraged because of a paucity of patients which requires therapists to work together if either is to have the experience of leading a group, or it may reflect an institutional policy to maintain a continuity of patient care. Thus the group may be inherited by generations of residents, each one of which may have in turn worked under a more experienced therapist. Whatever the initial reason that the cotherapists have chosen to work together, certain basic approaches are necessary if it is to be a productive and therapeutic (for both patients and leaders) relationship.

Coleadership can be successful only if it occurs in an atmosphere of mutual respect and understanding between the leaders. The prospective coleaders should meet in advance and discuss with all the insight that they possess their approach toward working with patients in group. At this early stage, it is important that prospective cotherapists share with each other their theoretical perspectives on the role of the group leader, and most especially their attitudes toward the appropriate level of group intervention, their degree of comfort or discomfort with the expression of anger within the group, the degree to which the gratification of group demands is an appropriate part of the treatment process, and the extent of comfort with therapist self-disclosure. In addition to a discussion of technical issues, this pregroup contact should be one in which both parties feel comfortable in discussing personal areas of character traits which they experience as provocative. For example, if one potential group leader rarely takes vacations and anticipates being present throughout the year, it is extremely important for that group leader to discuss his feelings about a partner whose lifestyle permits him to travel. Similarly, if one partner anticipates absences to meet family responsibilities, for example, school holidays, it is important to directly confront the feelings that absences over school vacations will arouse. Other areas, such as the importance of punctuality, smoking or eating during sessions, promptness in ending sessions, in which group leaders can differ, should be discussed, since these can elicit intense responses that should be anticipated and worked out.

A central issue in working as a cotherapist is the degree to which the leaders will feel comfortable in disagreeing both privately and in front of the group. The cotherapists stand in statu parentis and the manner of expressing their disagreements and the substance of disagreements in some sense will inevitably parallel the comparable familial situation. However, for the coleader, the opportunity to learn from another professional about style and to receive feedback about his or her own therapeutic style is one of the most valuable aspects of participating as a group coleader. For this educational process to take place, it is extremely important for both cotherapists to make provision for regular and often lengthy postgroup sessions. Only through such sessions can an atmosphere of mutual respect be maintained and task orientation fostered. A willingness to attend such postgroup sessions is a sine qua non of coleadership, and it is difficult to envisage how it would be possible for coleadership to be a meaningful enterprise without this commitment. During such sessions, the coleaders should feel free to discuss their transference toward the cotherapist and any countertransferential distortions they they experience during the conduct of the group. The range of topics to be discussed in these sessions should extend from the therapist's initial fear of forming a group to their anxieties about the group's expression of anger, to their sense that the cotherapist may be colluding with the group in scapegoating the other group leader.

Cotherapy is often used as an educational tool in which a younger, less experienced therapist is given the opportunity to work with a therapist of greater experience. Frequently, there may be other related disparities, that is, the older therapist is a male (reflecting the demographics of his period of training) and the younger therapist is female (reflecting the demographics of her period of training), or the therapist may differ in terms of profession, for example, psychiatric resident and psychiatric nurse. These disparities may be exaggerated in the group setting in which the younger cotherapist may begin to experience the older therapist as a parental figure, and, on a less conscious basis, the more experienced therapist may relate to his cotherapist as if she were a student rather than a colleague and an equal. As noted, these perceptions may be intensified by the cotherapist's sensitivity to denigration on account of gender or professional status.

On a different level, when the cotherapists differ in gender, the potentiality for their being stereotyped into playing a particular role within the group is ever-present. Thus when the coleaders constitute a nuclear family, the male psychiatrist may be perceived as the distant authoritarian father while the female psychiatrist may stereotypically be perceived as a nurturing maternal figure. This stereotypical experience of the group leaders may express itself in a wide variety of ways such as the assumption that the male cotherapist is necessarily the more experienced group therapist. Such transferential distortions can be confronted by a "Why does the group always turn to Ms X for the expression of feelings?" Yalom has noted that coleaders are usually split with one leader being perceived as being attuned to the group's affect and the other leader as being attuned to dealing with the group process.[1] However, the division of roles between the coleaders is highly volatile and shifts from session to session, and even fluctuates within a session, particularly when working with a group of relatively healthy patients. A pathologic stalemate can develop in which the roles become stereotyped and fixed. In such a stalemate, splitting becomes normative and one leader may form an alliance with the group against the other leader. While this can happen in any group, if there is an inequality between the leaders in training or status, the splitting may become much more fixed and divisive.

When forming a group in which one cotherapist is significantly senior or more experienced than the other cotherapist, the potential for the expression of this difference within the group should be considered in any examination of the group process. For example, if the less experienced therapist is a woman and during the course of the group adopts a submissive stance, the women within the group may act in concert and adopt a deferential and submissive stance both in relationship to the senior therapist and to other male members of the group. Indeed, this submissiveness may express itself in the formation of a group whose degree of premature cohesion and superficial adoption of a task orientation may mask the existence of unresolved covert anger at having to adopt a quietistic stance. Even if the senior (male) group leader is aware of this secondary agenda, it is often exceedingly difficult for the junior (female) member to confront what she may experience as a limitation on her role as coleader. Not surprisingly, the impulse to openly disagree with the senior coleader often seems to arise when the coleader is seen as joining in a group resistance. When such disagreements are openly confronted, the response of the group members is often reminiscent of children who wonder if parents can continue together after having engaged in an acrimonious argument. Nonetheless, such confrontations and disagreements among the coleaders ("parents") often permit the group members to express themselves in a more authentic fashion and allows them to dissolve what may have been an unduly cohesive group and deal more openly with competition among themselves.

Differences between group leaders, particularly when they have unequal experience, may manifest themselves nonverbally and may even be resolved nonverbally within the group. However, such issues should be resolved on a more conscious level between group leaders. For example, in one group the senior coleader would look at his watch at the beginning and end of every session thus stating to the group that he is the primary keeper of the group's boundaries. Moreover, he not only moved his chair from a tangent to the head of the table, but he would also move the chair of the coleader to an equal position of authority, thus establishing his identity as a senior but not authoritarian leader and announcing some discomfort on his part with being the sole authority. Over time, and with careful attention to these nonverbal cues, each leader assumed equality in maintaining the boundary of time.

The composition of the pair of coleaders is often reflected in the actual process of the group. If both coleaders are of the same sex, the group content may reflect a fear of the homosexual valence and speak exclusively about heterosexual fantasies of conquest and openly pair off heterosexually within the group. Or the group may regress in tandem with the same sex compositions of the coleaders and divide into male and female subgroups, behaving as a latency age group. Such defensive responses to the homosexual connotation of a same-sex pair should be examined within the group. However, many group issues will remain the same irrespective of the genders of the leaders and one leader will inevitably be seen as nurturant and the other as the distant, process-oriented leader.

Leaders may differ in terms of their involvement wth the group members. This occurs most frequently when a group is formed by two therapists pooling their private patients to form a single group. Not surprisingly, the group members will tend to maintain a more intense emotional tie with the therapist they have seen in individual treatment and initially will relate to the other group leader and his patients as a stepfamily. Patients will consider themselves to be "his/hers." This subgrouping should be discussed within the group, and between the group leaders who may rationalize their overinvolvement with "their" patient as being the product of their "knowing" the individual rather than their acting out their countertransference.

COTHERAPY AND GROUP EVOLUTION

The relationship between cotherapists determines the nature of the interactions within the group.[2–4] But it can extend to determining the manner in which basic assumptions[5] will be expressed within the group's evolution from a basic assumption. For example, if there is an inequality in the status of the cotherapists, this may be reflected in a prolongation of the dependency phase within the group. The prolongation occurs because the group responds to the unconscious wishes of both junior and senior cotherapists to maintain the junior cotherapist in a dependent status.

If the relationship between the cotherapists is primarily competitive (as contrasted with nurturing or sexual), this also is reflected in the group process. Competitive pairing of therapists often occurs when two presumably equally experienced and qualified therapists decide to work together ostensibly because their particular skills are complementary. Often such pairs are selected in teaching facilities by the director of training. In such pairs, the therapists compete to win the approbation of the director. Thus, if one of the leaders has extensive psychoanalytic training and approaches groups from a psychoanalysis-in-group approach, while the other coleader (with comparable experience) approaches groups from a group-as-a-whole perspective, the coleaders may compete within the group in which they will utilize their differences in perspective in the service of their individual competition with each other. This competitive relationship between the coleaders may be manifested in the expression of a prolonged "fight-flight" basic assumption within the group. Thus, group members may flee into the formation of subgroups either within or outside the group. Flight may also express itself in the form of absences or tardiness by group members, or in an unusually high dropout rate.

While competition between coleaders may be the expression of theoretical differences or the differences that inevitably arise when two people who share the competitive strivings that encouraged each individually to work as mental health professionals attempt to work together, these differences should be acknowledged and openly discussed. Severe difficulties can frequently be avoided if both coleaders participate in peer supervision. The question arises as to the extent that these differences should be acknowledged before the group. It has been the experience of the authors that when differences in style or theoretical perspective are openly but professionally acknowledged with an "I see this rather differently...," this open acknowledgment of differences provides the group members with a useful demonstration that individual disagreement is not lethal nor does it interfere with the task orientation. Indeed, it provides a vivid role model of social interaction.

McMahon[7] has noted that the expression of the "pairing" assumption that occurs within the group is influenced by the manner in which pairing occurs within the cotherapy relationship. Indeed, McMahon suggests that coleadership is more desirable in group therapy precisely because it encourages pairing among group members.[7] While the desirability of pairing and subgroup formation is debatable, there is little question that the pairing that does occur is a reflection of comparable processes between the coleaders. When pairing is acknowledged by both group and leaders without the exclusion of other group members, pairing may enhance the group's knowledge of group dynamics. However, if the pairing entails the formation of an opposite-sex pair, a pair which sees itself as a "revolutionary" pair, dedicated to the disintegration of the group, then the formation of this pair should be examined as an expression of the entire group's need to defy or undermine the group leaders. In insight-oriented groups, the oedipal implications of the group's responses to pairing among the group leaders and within the group may be fruitfully explored.

One aspect of the pairing assumption is the development of a "messiah" assumption. This messiah is a new group leader who will magically prolong the group and rescue it from the intense anxiety which accompanies the threatened termination of the group. This assumption may be expressed in several forms. In one variant, the messiah is a group member whose authority arises from the displacement of the charisma of one or both group leaders onto a group member. This occurs most frequently when one of the coleaders is being scapegoated, often in the context of an unacknowledged competitive relationship between the coleaders. The competition may be a struggle for the affection of the group members, particularly when one leader is less comfortable in dealing with the group's expression of hostility. In this context, one leader may consciously or unconsciously relate to the group in a seductive fashion, leading to an impasse in which one leader can do nothing right and the other leader is inevitably "wrong." Such splitting certainly is uncomfortable and if it is neither acknowledged nor explored may become a permanent fixture of the group's dynamics. Under such conditions, the group messiah is created to heal the split between the leaders and to prevent the termination which often impends. However, the messiah may even take the reality of the birth of an actual baby. While it is certainly speculative to suggest that the birth of a child occurred in response to group demands, it is intriguing to note that when the child's mother has brought the child to the group session, the child appears to inaugurate the reign of peace within the group.

When scapegoating occurs between coleaders, peer supervision presents the optimal approach for dealing with an issue which otherwise may destroy a group or adversely impact upon a group leader who introjects his sense of failure as a group leader. The value of peer supervision is illustrated in the following:

> Drs X (the scapegoated coleader) and Y attended a meeting of their peer supervision group. Dr Y invited Dr X to present the recent events of the group. Despite the anxiety which most coleaders experience when presenting a group, Dr X leapt with alacrity at the opportunity. The peer group then commented that again Dr X was being manipulated into standing before the firing line. During the course of the supervisory session, other members of the peer group wondered about Dr Y's discomfort with the affect of anger and whether or not she had not affectively seduced the group into directing its anger toward the coleader. During the course of their work together Drs X and Y were able to work out a more viable relationship.

The actual process of the group had been affected by the split between the group leaders. However, because of Dr X's capacity to constructively deal with the aggression directed toward him, the group retained its ability to express anger. Had he, for example, apologized to the group or modified his interpretive stance in order to mollify the group, the group would have felt that through its expression of hostility, it had destroyed one of the group leaders. This oedipal victory would have seriously inhibited the future expression of anger.

Fantasies about the Cotherapists

The fantasies that the group develops about the relationship between the cotherapists is an integral aspect of group process. The actual character of the fantasies is a reflection of the developmental level of the group. The group's fantasies may be based on their accurate perception of the actual feelings that the cotherapists have for each other such as rivalry and competition, idealization or contempt, and sexual attraction. In most instances, the group's fantasies about the coleaders are not grounded in reality but are based on the interactions between group members and the projections by pivotal members of the group onto the cotherapists. These aspects of fantasy development are illustrated in the following vignette:

> After a group meeting, several group members saw Dr Y get into Dr X's car and drive away. During the next session, the members appeared to be more guarded during the session. Eventually, the coleaders asked the group about their response to seeing the coleaders drive off together. Both leaders assumed that any group fantasies would be sexual in nature. But since the group had just formed and the nature of the group transference toward the leaders was dependent and preoedipal, the group revealed that they had assumed the leaders had driven off to discuss the group, and particularly to assess the emotional stability of the group members.

This fantasy reflected the wishes of this newly formed group, still acting on the basis of the dependency basic assumption, to be cared for, albeit with a certain phase-appropriate ambivalence expressed in their suspiciousness of the leaders' bona fides. As the group evolved, fantasies that were appropriate to this later oedipal phase were expressed, for example, when the coleaders were seen eating together in a restaurant, in an aftergroup meeting, the group members discussed their fantasy that this lunch was a preliminary to a sexual liaison. Finally, when one of the coleaders became pregnant, the group members expressed the fantasy that the other coleader was the actual father of the child.

Not all the fantasies expressed relate to the sexual-social relationship of the group leaders. Members will discuss their fantasy that one of the coleaders is vastly more experienced than the other, or that their decision to work together was imposed on them, leading one leader to regard the other as an incompetent, whose disappearance would be welcomed. Like all fantasies, these fantasies should be examined, but the underlying reality should not be disclosed. While the group leaders may agree at the beginning to openly agree or disagree in front of the group to provide them with appropriate models for identification, even at the termination of the group, questions such as "How do you feel about each other?" or "Will you ever lead a group together, again?" should be dealt with as expressions of the group's feelings about termination and not as a specific inquiry about the coleaders. Underlying such questions is a group fantasy that their aggression had ripped apart a parental pair causing a divorce, rather than the expression of good wishes (though they may be present as well) that attend a task well done.

Group Communication between Coleaders

The key to effective coleadership is constant and continual communication between coleaders at regularly scheduled meetings. At such meetings, the leaders must discuss not only the group process but their feelings about each other as they have evolved during the group itself. Tardiness, differences in style, or the nature of interventions should be examined. If a coleader cannot attend meetings, comes late, leaves early, or otherwise avoids such meetings on a regular basis, it is clearly a resistance and should be directly confronted. When such resistances are characterologic, they should be monitored by both leaders. These discussions may be particularly fruitful on a personal basis as the following illustrates:

> Dr Y intervened in the group process. Dr X became visibly perturbed and proceeded to put her down. When confronted by his actions in postgroup meeting, he angrily said that he experienced Dr Y's interventions as obtuse and so "dense" as to be infuriating. But why had this "obtuseness" elicited so intense a response? Eventually, during the course of discussion, Dr X appreciated that he felt "taken care of" by his partner only when there was total agreement between them about his perception of the group process, and that the alternative to being taken care of was total abandonment. With this new self-knowledge, Dr X was more comfortable in tolerating differences.

A similar situation arose when Dr B (a young female) was coleading a group with Dr C (senior, male, and vastly experienced). Here, Dr B noted that whenever she would intervene, Dr C would soon follow with a remark which neither affirmed nor negated Dr B's intervention but instead entirely ignored or disregarded it. In the course of postgroup meetings, Dr C began to understand his long-standing need to devalue the intellectual importance of women and to deny his emotional dependence on them. Both cases illustrate a willingness to accept confrontation in a nondefensive manner and a willingness to work with another professional whose observations are of dynamic importance although they are being advanced in a nontreatment context.

While aftergroup meetings are not therapy, their result may certainly be therapeutic. Thus coleaders should optimally share a certain modicum of personal data with each other. Issues that are particularly important revolve around marriage and divorce and siblings and competitive strivings. Of particular importance is whether or not they are parents and their feelings about their relationship with their children. Thus the following:

> Dr D (a female with young children) and Dr E (father of older adolescents) were coleading a group. Dr D made numerous unnecessary interventions. Finally, in exasperation, Dr E said to her, in front of the group. "Dr D, let the group alone." After the group meeting, they (not surprisingly) discussed the unconscious determinants of the interaction. Dr D began to discuss her relationship with her small children who were in the process of starting elementary school. On the other hand, Dr E was faced with the task of helping his wife accept that their children had become young adults. The discussion helped him to get more in touch

with the resentment he felt toward his wife who inhibited their relationship because of her inability "to let the children go."

While not therapy, this discussion was both therapeutic and facilitated his working through his transference toward his cotherapist. Obviously, the course of group leadership will go smoother if the coleaders are able to meet before starting work with the group and share any awareness of issues or behavioral patterns that may well provide for intercurrent provocations. Finally, it is equally important for the coleaders to meet after the termination of the group to discuss their respective roles, to enumerate the qualities that each brought to the group that made it work, and the obstacles they would try to avoid if they were to work together again.

SUMMARY

Coleadership of groups provides a challenging and occasionally traumatic experience for a group therapist. The presence of coleaders recreates for the group the initial nuclear family. However, as in other families, the leaders must develop a degree of self-knowledge and acknowledge a degree of respect for the other leader if the coleadership/parenting experience is to provide both group members and group leaders alike with a viable forum in which issues of intimacy, autonomy, and role development are to be explored. This chapter discusses these issues with particular reference to psychoanalytically oriented group psychotherapy.

REFERENCES

1. Yalom I: *Theory and Practice of Group Psychotherapy*. New York, Basic Books, 1975, p 320.
2. Fallon I: Interpersonal variables in behavioral group therapy. *Brit J Med Psychol* 1981;6:133–141.
3. Hellwig K: Partners in therapy: using the cotherapists' relationship in a group. *J Psychiatr Nurs* 1978;4:41–44.
4. Levine C: The group within the group: Dilemma of cotherapy. *Int J Group Psychother* 1979;4:175–184.
5. Bion WR: *Experience in Groups*. London, Tavistock, 1981.
6. Stein A: The training of the group psychotherapist, in Rosenbaum M, Berger M (eds): *Group Psychotherapy and Group Function*. New York, Basic Books, 1983, pp 558–574.
7. McMahon N: Cotherapy: The need for positive pairing. *Can J Psychol* 1984;8:385–389.

6

Collusive Projective Processes in Group Psychotherapy: A Mode of Resistance and a Vehicle for Change

Henry Blumfarb

The existence of collusive projective processes represents an important aspect of individual and group resistances. Such collusive group processes serve to "relieve intrapsychic and interpersonal pain,"[1] enable group members to maintain self-cohesion, and promote "reenactment and repair of the early traumatic holding environment."[2] This chapter examines the operation of collusive projective processes in therapy groups. Unless such processes are experienced and understood by the therapist, they impede the development of the growth-promoting work of the group.

A brief review of the literature which focuses on primitive communications in the group and the regressive forces that contribute to this phenomenon will add to our understanding of collusive projective processes. It should be noted that this mechanism is related to the concept of projective identification which constitutes the mutual projective processes within the group. The concept of projective identification is clarified later in this chapter.

THE DEFINITION

Collusive projective processes are a mechanism that is the product of the interaction between "collective group phenomenon"[3] and projective and introjective mechanisms. They involve multiple projective identifications (along with denial and splitting) used collectively and repeatedly by the group members and the therapist to protect against "intrapsychic and interpersonal pain,"[1] maintain self-cohesion through the creation and maintenance of an environment that permits the group members and the therapist to support ego-syntonic character defenses, and to "reenact and repair the early traumatic or defective holding environment."[2] A familiarity with the operation of collusive projective processes provides the group therapist with a focus which enables him to understand primitive emotional communications in the psychotherapy group. These communications involve the individuals' unconscious attempts in words and action to influence the internal states of the other group members and the therapist. It should be noted that collusive projection processes represent an aspect of regressive phenomena which occur in groups where projective identification is the driving force.

REVIEW OF THE LITERATURE

Freud[4] introduced the notion of "collective mental life in the group." He suggested that "affective contagion was one of the primary characteristics of the psychology of the group." He described several other characteristics of the psychology of the group: "...individuals become more susceptible to suggestion, individuals acquire an unconscious sense of invincible power, and repressions of unconscious instinctual material are thrown off."[4] Modell summarized Freud's conceptions by noting that "affective experience in groups tends to become intensified, and in a certain sense archaic. The individual members in the group are subject through its influence to what is often a profound alteration in their mental activity."[5]

Horwitz,[6] following the observations of Bion, characterized these communications as involving "oscillating transfers of mental contents in a setting of blurred ego boundaries." He further elaborated on some additional characteristics of regression in groups. These involve "the prevalence of envy, rivalry, competition, and the threat of loss of one's individuality and autonomy."[6]

Stein and Kibel[3] described the "partial primitivization which feeds the interactive process...it is a form of nonpathological regression in the service of the ego." They also refer to the operation of "identifications rather than transference in the group since they reflect primitive modes of object relations which in the psychoanalytic hierarchy of object relations precede real object ties." They posit the operation of projective identification since it is "the mechanism by which members defend against the anxiety induced by the partial primitivization of the ego...." They further note that "group interactions that stem from unconscious resonation, can be seen as the vehicle for expression of primitive object relationships."[3]

Scheidlinger[7] elaborated on this phenomenon in the following manner. He stated that "regressive emotional pulls...tend to loosen the individual self boundaries and reactivate primitive wishes and modes of early object relations, including identifications...." He added: "Such regressive patterns are not necessarily pathological insofar as even in the most mature personalities, the infantile need satisfying modes of relating persist, and are subject to reactivation at moments of threat and anxiety." Scheidlinger went on to describe

> ...group emotionality as entailing each member's regression to earlier stages of object ties, i.e. to identifications...in particular the projective and introjective mechanisms, which are defenses brought into play in response to the marked anxiety engendered by intrapsychic conflicts, with what the Kleinians' term "internal objects" and "part objects," and by the threat of losing one's personal identity in the group.[7]

In order to maintain a broader perspective of the operations in a psychotherapy group, it should be noted that in addition to the operation of regressive forces, group life is also characterized by positive and nontransferential identifications which "mitigate regression,"[3] and contribute to group cohesiveness. Thus an essential ingredient to the successful operation of the group is the positive identifications which are analogous to the working alliance in individual psychotherapy and psychoanalysis. These positive identifications permit the therapist to enlist the collective observing egos of the group members to study the operation of individual and group resistances, in particular the operation of collusive projective processes, and enable the therapist to reenforce positive identifications that occur between group members.

THE CURATIVE WISH

Patients enter group therapy with both the conscious and unconscious wish to change or to be cured. Scheidlinger has described the curative wish as involving "a covert wish to restore an earlier state of unconflicted being inherent in the child's exclusive union with the mother, which is represented by the group entity."[7] However, this wish also brings with it some complications. Feinsilver's thinking enables us to understand the *paradoxical nature of the curative wish*.[2] He stated that it takes the form of the "wish for the emergence of the good parent from the state of rejection." This unconscious quest is simply described by him as: "If only I can be rejected the way I once was by my parents, then I will refind the parents, and he/she will make everything good, and prove once and for all that I am not the bad seed I am afraid I am."[2]

It is crucial for the therapist to remain aware of this paradox. He must keep in mind that the member's shared wish to be loved, cared for, and understood is often overshadowed by the shared wish to stay connected to the bad object — the rejecting, neglectful, disappointing, ignoring, or hateful environment. This paradox influences the interpersonal interactions in the group so that the members and at times even the therapist unwittingly cooperate to create and maintain an environment that will support existing character defenses. This collective group activity is one major source of individual and group resistances. It operates primarily to protect against the emergence of the original pain, and the unconscious expectation of being overwhelmed by it. Secondarily, it functions in the here-and-now to prevent the possibility of experiencing injuries that would reactivate the pain associated with the original trauma. In this case, the collusive projective processes operate to impede the work of the group. Bion has described the work of the group as "mental activity directed to the solution of the problems for which individuals seek help."[8]

The group therapist works in a unique environment, especially during the formative phases of group development. He works at the point at which every group member tries to protect himself, and colludes to support each member's character defenses, thus reproducing an environment which is a reasonable facsimile of the members' and often the group therapist's originally traumatic environment. In other words, the group members help one another relive one another's internal self and object worlds in the present. What follows is an illustration of a therapy group which has reproduced such an environment.

"THE GROUP THAT LACKED CURIOSITY"

The group to be discussed here is composed of six members, four men and two women, ranging in age from the early 30s to the late 50s. They have been meeting for 18 months. Diagnostically, the members reflect various personality disorders including schizoid, borderline, avoidant, and narcissistic personality organization. No one has had a history of psychotic breaks or hospitalizations, or suicide attempts. Several of the members have used antianxiety or antidepressant medication during some difficult periods in their lives. All of the group members except for one man have been regularly employed; the one man has only worked periodically, and is supported by his family. Except for this one man, all the other members have either been married or lived with someone. The same man has had no love relationships at all. One member is a parent. The two women are heterosexual; the majority of the men are heterosexual. All but one of the members have completed college degrees, and this one is in the process of doing so. All of the patients are seen by the same therapist in individual treatment, either once or twice a week.

The group members share a similar unconscious concern and belief about the self; that is, that the self is defective in one fashion or another. Their early caretaking environments have been characterized by parental attitudes of overt or covert hatred, sexual abuse, rejection, ignoring of the child's natural strivings, or using the child as a "self-object" or caretaker, for unconscious, unmet needs.

The atmosphere that pervaded the group during its formative phase of development for the first 18 months could best be characterized as that of "the group that lacked curiosity." Member-to-member interactions were typically cautious and careful. Minimal information about the self was voluntarily provided and minimal spontaneous curiosity was shown. Members displayed intense dependence on the leader to be curious and attentive. Right from the outset, the members collectively disowned their assertiveness, curiosity, and aggression in relation to one another. They collectively presented themselves as vulnerable, emotionally inaccessible, dependent, or victimized. Each of the members appeared to protect a precarious self-representation, characterized by a self-experience of feeling defective. Thus, sessions were characterized by topical chitchat, banter, descriptions of their problems, mutual problem solving, teasing, and playfulness. This pleasant setting permitted the group to establish and maintain their usual defensive positions while getting to know one another and the leader in a safe way.

In order to more vividly appreciate group processes, a brief characterization of the group members is in order. One member, a male with a schizoid personality disorder, can be characterized as "the skunk." Preoccupied with the belief that he "repels" others, his group-mates, and especially women he finds attractive, he is convinced that there is something pervasively unappealing about him. In actuality, he is a bright, witty, and playful man who is physically and emotionally attractive. A highly gifted man, he is well-read, good with his hands, and has generated a vivid fantasy life, especially about women. He maintains an intense conscious wish to be special, and refuses to be involved in any kind of work which is not of the highest status. The thought of any other kind of work immediately stimulates feelings of inferiority. This overcompensatory wish to be special protects him from intense self-hatred. In his day-to-day world, he keeps interpersonal contact to a minimum.

One of the women in the group with a borderline personality disorder can be characterized as the "frightened tigress." She is an attractive, soft-spoken, caring, and talented young woman. A gifted artist, she has begun to study the martial arts as an expression of using her strength and asserting herself. She alternates between two ego states. Either she feels extremely sensitive and easily overwhelmed and overpowered by others, or angry and lethal when hurt or disappointed. When walking down the street, she says she hates everyone she sees, and envies what they have. At other times she is afraid of being liked; she anticipates that others will discover that there is no substance to her. Her experience of herself in part serves to maintain a self-boundary and buttress her self-cohesion. At the same time, she is involved in a passive-aggressive effort to defeat the therapist. Thus she denies herself in the present what her early caretakers could not adequately provide in the past.

Another man in the group with a narcissistic personality disorder may be characterized as the "entertainer–lone wolf." He keeps the group, including the therapist, laughing and charmed by his well-told stories. He becomes the center of attention. While keeping them laughing he distracts everyone, including himself, from crying. He covers up the tragedy he and the others share. He is a fun-loving individual, self-taught and proud of it. He has a love of nature, and enthusiasm for sex. He is multitalented in the fine arts. Unfortunately, he is extremely self-defeating and, beneath all this enthusiasm, he is not sure there is either love or caring for him or anyone else. He states, "Even if I could show my vulnerable side, I'm not sure it would get me anywhere. It never has."

Another man with a narcissistic personality disorder may be characterized as the "pretender." He is handsome, charming, and chatty. Because his capacity to feel is underdeveloped, he play-acts at feeling good. He is a gifted man academically. He is knowledgeable in engineering, both theoretically and practically. A natural athlete, he has both agility and endurance. He enjoys people, and they enjoy him. He presents himself as always eager to be involved with everyone in the group, to share his feelings and encourage the others to be as open as he feels he is. He often assumes the role of cotherapist and caretaker. Yet he complains that the group is not moving at his pace, and does not help him. Internally, he prefers to be anonymous, and keep his "true self"[9] in cold storage. Although liked by most of the members, they are also annoyed, as they experience him as "elusive and unknowable."

The second woman in the group has an avoidant personality disorder with dependent features; she may be characterized as the "invisible woman." She is an attractive older woman, well cared for, and slightly overweight. She is culturally knowledgeable and well-traveled. She is a fine cook of continental cuisine. Nevertheless, this woman at times blends into the woodwork. This occurs particularly when she is empty and depleted within. She perceives herself as someone who finds it difficult to initiate conversations, and to contribute something meaningful. She forgets information and details all the time

— whether at work, with friends, with her lover, and in therapy. She doubts much can be done about this and jokingly comments, "maybe it's Alzheimer's disease." In group, she usually waits for someone to speak to her. Often, this is the leader. In her own shorthand she says as little as possible. She is pleased to be asked to speak, yet cannot wait to get it over with. Her style enables the members and the therapist to forget her. Her desire for anomie represents her unconscious wish to be forgotten by her malevolent mother who abused her, and to be forgotten by the envious and dependent mother who failed to notice her positive qualities, or quickly forgot them.

The sixth member of the group is a male with a borderline personality organization. He occupies the role of the "frightened sulker." However, he is the most real and available member in the group in responsiveness to others. He is well-liked, playful, and funny. His perceptions of others are astute and communicative. He is a well-respected manager, known for his interpersonal skills. In the group, he is protective of others as well as himself. Although others like him and encourage him to be involved, he insists that he is afraid of them, and fears being ignored. As a child he felt like a "puppet." His mother used him as a self-object to comfort herself sexually and emotionally. She rarely listened to him. In his interpersonal relations, he has a history of sadomasochistic homosexual activities. Thus, he places himself in dangerous situations in which he has the illusion of control. Most often, he believes he has no control over how he is treated by others.

During the initial phase of the group, each member acts out in terms of the roles and interpersonal styles just described. Each in his or her own way contributes to the absence of authentic contact, contributing to an unconscious shared group belief that it is unsafe to reveal any aspect of the "true self." At this time, the group colludes to keep their "primary object love"[10] longings to a minimum, as well as to maintain existing defenses and unconscious belief systems. Thus, at the outset, the members create an environment that minimizes need and contact. As long as the "skunk" believes that he is repulsive, he does not have to confront his intense object hunger, nor the associated dread of intimacy. As long as the "pretender" maintains the belief that he wants to be involved intimately with others he can avoid the recognition that his feelings are painful, and maintain the illusion that he experiences pleasure and optimism. As long as the "entertainer-lone wolf" is able to charm everyone, he can maintain the belief that he can nurture himself, and avoid the risk of needing help from others. As long as the "frightened tigress" can maintain the belief that she is lethal and has no substance, she can avoid knowing and communicating her needs with all the "separation guilt" that is evoked. As long as the "frightened sulker" maintains the belief that no one is interested in him, he can avoid the anxiety involved in wanting more for himself, which his superego does not permit. Finally, while the "invisible woman" maintains the belief that she cannot help forgetting and has little of value to say, she is able to forget her positive qualities and her intense need and fear of seeking nurturance from others.

During this formative phase of group development, the therapist's countertransference responses were varied. At times, the therapist felt isolated. Sometimes he felt alone with no one to help do the work of the therapy. This was an objective countertransference response, identifying with the shared self-representations of abandonment. He experienced the rejection that the patients experienced as children in relation to their primary caretakers. At other times, the therapist experienced a sense of impatience and anger in response to the minimal contact among members and their demand for caretaking by him. His feelings represented his identifications with the shared object representations of the group members. In other words, the therapist experienced himself as the rejecting, angry caretaker. Collusive projective processes which the therapist examined within himself enabled him to make various trial identifications with the shared internal worlds of the group members. Initially, the therapist was the only consistently curious individual in a group of people who had minimal curiosity about themselves and others — a not uncharacteristic position during the early phases of group development. During this phase, the group alternated between the "dependency and fight-flight basic assumption groups."[8] Splitting predominated, the therapist being seen as the only individual with whom it was safe to express dependency strivings, or the therapist would be attacked for inquiring about what the members thought was going on in the group, because his inquiry was seen as alienating.

THE MECHANISM OF PROJECTIVE IDENTIFICATION

To enable the therapist to observe how the group members unwittingly use each other to externalize internal conflicts, he must be familiar with the mechanism of projective identification. This provides him with an in-depth understanding of group interactions and permits him to observe how he unwittingly participates in the group collusive process.

A number of writers, including Bion,[11,12] Money-Kyrle,[13] Racker,[14,15] Heiman,[16] Ogden,[17] Langs,[18] Feinsilver,[2] Horwitz,[6] and Gorkin,[19] suggest that projective identification is a universal phenomenon which is part of normal mental activity. It is utilized by individuals at all diagnostic levels, and occurs when there is a blurring of boundaries between two or more people.

Gorkin[19] summarizes this perspective quite well. He states:

> ...the clear-edged differentiation between self and others may give way to temporary blurring of boundaries in situations of deep interpersonal contact....I believe this to happen rather commonly even among neurotic and normal people, although less commonly than among more disturbed individuals. One need not — and with healthy individuals, one seldom does — lose an *overall* sense of differentiation between oneself and the other. The blurring takes place in the one sector of the self that is engaged in the interaction.[19]

A number of other theorists have contributed to our understanding of projective identification.

Main states: "...projective identification along with denial and splitting is a common defense against mental pain. It is a primitive form of relatedness, and involves unconscious attempts to relieve pains by externalizing them, and assigning or requiring another to contain aspects of the self."[1]

According to Feinsilver, what is externalized or gotten rid of are "unwanted dangerous or endangered aspects of the self and object world."[2] The externalization process involves unconscious "attempts, subtle or blatant to manipulate the therapist's (other person's) internal experience."[17] This involves forcing thoughts, feelings, sensations, and abilities into another. Kernberg elaborates on this. He states that the other functions to receive and contain the projections. This enables the projector "to maintain a sense of empathy with what is projected" and maintain a primitive attachment to the receiver (O. Kernberg, MD, unpublished data, May 1984).

It should be noted that while projective identification is a universal phenomenon and part of normal mental activity, there may be pathologic consequences for both the projector and the receiver. Main suggests that the consequences for the projector are twofold: "the self of the projector is deplenished by the projective loss of important aspects of the self, and the individual becomes less aware of its whole."[1] Thus the projector pays a high price. Even though one kind of pain is diminished, the self is left depleted, depressed, anxious, and fragmented. Thus, further defenses are erected to cope with emptiness, anxiety, and depression.

The consequences for the recipient are dependent on the recipient's "role comfort or discomfort" with the projections. For example, if the receiver of the projective identification has the character traits or qualities that match the projections, the receiver will experience little discomfort. Then, the collusion will go on smoothly, and the potential for reenactment is higher. However, if the qualities of the receiver do not sufficiently match the projections, the receiver will experience varying degrees of discomfort; for example, he will not feel like himself, he will feel taken over, he will resent what is going on.[1] He will, therefore, be in a position to disrupt the collusive process.

Given this understanding of projective identification, the therapist's ability to help the group members recognize how and with whom they recreate their traumatic internal self and object world is fortified. He can assist the group members in recognizing when they are attempting to solve problems, and develop solutions which reflect the operation of the repetition compulsion rather than the reality principle. The therapist is thus in the position to help the group identify when its responses are of a rigid, overdetermined, and self-depriving nature. In doing this, he can assist the group members in turning the energy invested in staying connected to the bad object into effectively separating themselves from it. Members can begin to give themselves what their original caretakers were unable to provide. "Separation guilt" is the glue that keeps the individual tied to the bad object.[5]

Following is an illustration of how the group members collude to disown their mutual competence, in order to avoid separation guilt. During the early phase of treatment, the members operated collectively from two alternating "basic assumption groups." One was the "dependent" position, where the capacity to give to oneself and to the other was disowned. The other was the "fight-flight/counterdependent position" where the members believed they had to protect themselves from being dominated or overpowered by the leader. These restrictive solutions to dealing with the anxiety about giving and taking enabled the group members to maintain unconscious ties to their bad objects and in the process to avoid separation guilt.

In one session, the group interaction focused on the members' concerns that the group was a dull and boring place. How cautious and timid they all were! They could not imagine ever getting anywhere. The members recognized that they were being polite. They were uncomfortable about inquiring about each other. The "entertainer" and the "frightened sulker" complained that the therapist was not doing enough. The two were acting as spokespersons for the group's resistance to owning their competence, and taking risks. These two members voiced concern about possible misunderstandings and injuries that could arise from more forthright interaction. At this point in treatment, the group was in the position only to receive, and only from the therapist. The therapist asked the group what they thought he should do. The "pretender" suggested that he add new members to the group. The "entertainer" suggested that he ask more questions, since the group could not be counted on to do the job. The other members agreed.

The dependency basic assumption group served the purpose of

enabling the group to collectively disown their capable, curious, and nurturing qualities, and to project these qualities into people outside the group, that is, potential members, or the group therapist. Thus, the group was able to store its capacity to be nurtured in a safe place so when ready to repossess this it would be available. The time was not yet right. The therapist then asked the group to consider why they all believed that he was the only one with the ability and skill to make things happen in the group. The "entertainer" jokingly said, "Because you are the one with the professional training; we tell you our problems, and you give us the solutions." The "frightened sulker" and the "frightened tigress" said that the therapist was the only one in the group that each felt safe to be less cautious with. He was the only one to be trusted not to be too vulnerable or too aggressive. He was the one least capable of being hurt, and would be best able to deal with aggression if it were directed toward him.

A salient factor which must be kept in mind, considering the early phase of the group's development, is that the therapist in reality was probably the safest object to demand nurturance from, as well as the safest target for agression. This placed the group members in a precarious position in relation to the therapist. Considering the dependent position they collectively placed themselves in, the therapist could easily expose or injure any one of them.

This collective group activity left the group members depleted of the capacity to protect themselves against the power the therapist was unconsciously experienced to have over them. This became the source of anxiety for the group as a whole, and some solution had to be found. The "entertainer" began to take the leadership position for the collective counterdependent position of the group by devaluing the therapist. In an anxious and joking manner, he began talking about how he had been thinking that maybe the therapist was not doing his job well. Perhaps that was why the group was not getting anywhere. The "pretender" joined in, and in a nervously playful manner said that he had been thinking for a while that his individual therapy was not getting anywhere either. The "frightened tigress" and the "frightened sulker" resonated to this, and wondered aloud if they were with the right therapist. The "invisible woman" in her own mild way stated that she remembered reading an article about the unreliability of psychotherapy and therapists. The "skunk" added that he had not doubted the therapist's competence, but wondered about his ability to help him.

The therapist asked the group what it was like for them to experience him as the only one who might possibly be able to help them, at the same time questioning that. He went on to comment that they experienced themselves as unable to provide much at all. What a dilemma they were in! After some silence, the "frightened tigress" began to talk about how afraid she was of her hateful feelings. She expressed concern that if she were more spontaneous, she would say the wrong thing and hurt someone. She experienced the individuals in the group as easily hurt. The "frightened sulker" said that he really had a good relationship with the therapist in his individual sessions, and liked the therapist. It was being in the group that frightened him; there were just too many people. The "skunk" indicated that he experienced the therapist differently in group. In individual sessions he felt better liked. In group, he felt ignored by the therapist. The "pretender" stated that he felt more at ease in the group than in his private sessions; he felt more understood by the members. The "entertainer" said that he was only kidding earlier. He felt he had been helped by the therapist. He said they were a difficult group of people to get to talk spontaneously. The "invisible woman" said that she felt more at ease in her private sessions, and thought it would take a miracle to get her to be more spontaneous.

The above intervention interfered with the collusive projective processes. It enabled the group members to question some of their projections into the therapist, and to notice how they rid themselves of their competence. The therapist asked the group what they should do under the circumstances. There was some laughter and a brief silence. The "pretender" asked that the therapist let them know when they were being "resistant." The others agreed, stating that the therapist was the best one to do this, since he was more aware of these things than they were. The therapist asked if they would be interested in assisting him in this task. Everyone laughed. The "frightened tigress" said in a lighthearted fashion that she did not think the group was ready for this yet. The others, including the therapist, laughed. After a brief silence, the therapist asked the group when they thought they would be ready to help him identify when they were being too timid and cautious, thus going around in circles. There was a consensus that they would have to wait and see how they would respond to the therapist doing this more often. They were not sure they would be able to tolerate more direct interchanges among themselves at this point in treatment.

In this case, the group members were collectively re-creating an atmosphere where it was not safe to be oneself nor take the risk of spontaneously interacting with one another. This involved their re-creation of an environment where they felt that their natural life-affirming inclinations would destroy rather than foster positive affirmation of their separate and individual qualities. At this point in treatment, the collusive projective processes served the purpose of protecting the group members from experiencing the superego retaliation that is evoked when the wish to change, and the capacity to accept one's own competence, is activated. Moreover, during this early phase of the group's development, sufficient collective ego strength was not yet available for tolerating, experiencing, and studying their shared self-hate.

TWO SUBTYPES OF PROJECTIVE IDENTIFICATION

Familiarity with the distinction between the two subtypes of projective identification enables the therapist to accomplish the task of tracking the complicated interactions in the group. This allows him to assess the individual, subgroup, and group-as-a-whole resistances. It enables him to determine the group members' accessibility to reality testing. This information is available to be utilized in the interventions that can promote insight within the group. Thus, he can identify the individuals who demonstrate role comfort or discomfort with particular projections, and observe the process of externalization. The therapist's familiarity with these distinctions is particularly useful in allowing him to work with the group around issues of "benign or trial projective identification," and "malignant projective identification."[1]

BENIGN OR TRIAL PROJECTIVE IDENTIFICATION

The Impact on the Projector

When benign projective identification is in operation, the individual's capacity to understand himself and others is preserved. This capacity remains readily available. The projections are not forceful, and reality testing is minimally impaired. The present is tested against the past. External events are tested against internal ones. The projector maintains his individuality as he learns about who he is or is not, and who others are, and so forth. When reality testing confirms the benign projective identification, that is, if it conforms to the other person's characteristics, the projector learns positively about the other, and positively about his ability to appreciate the other. If the projection does not conform to the other's characteristics, the projector should, hopefully, own his projection, thereby clarifying some aspect of his identity, or the identity of the other.[1]

The Impact on the Recipient

In this climate, the recipient may experience a mild to moderate internal sense of discomfort. Something is being inaccurately attributed to him. He feels invaded with an experience of himself that does not fit, or that seems exaggerated or distorted. In this context, the recipient may be left to feel either idealized or devalued, either very clever or very incompetent, or very nurturing or very denying.[1]

Trial or benign projective identification is illustrated by the following vignette: For a long period of malignant projective identification, the therapist was the recipient of intense devaluation by the "frightened tigress," who had a history of unmet dependency needs. Her mother, a good mother of symbiosis, had been unable to tolerate the patient's strivings for autonomy and individuation. When these strivings emerged phase-appropriately, the mother alternated in abandoning the patient, or submerging the patient's feelings within her own. Thus, the patient would devalue the therapist in order to protect herself from the transferential responses she anticipated from the therapist. The "frightened tigress" could not imagine being close to another person while maintaining a separate identity. In more than one session, she hesitantly told group members that she was frightened and reluctant to attend because she anticipated that she could not count on the therapist to care about her. She feared that if a new patient paying a higher fee came along, the therapist would immediately drop her. The "frightened tigress" seemed sad and fearful. The group members were silent.

The therapist, hearing this week after week, could not help but wonder silently if he were not doing something wrong. He asked the group if they agreed or differed with the "frightened tigress'" perception of him. The "entertainer" wondered if she were overreacting, and if maybe, beneath her fears, she was in love with the therapist. The "skunk" agreed with the "entertainer." He added that she seemed to want to be special to the therapist. He wished she were interested in him instead. The "frightened sulker" identified with the "frightened tigress," stating that he sensed that she wanted the therapist's love, but was pushing him away. He commented that he sometimes gets scared of wanting the therapist's attention, and pushes him away the way she was doing. The "frightened tigress" visibly relaxed and smiled. She said that she saw the therapist as fatherly and paternal, that he was a very nice man, but did not see him in a romantic light, as some of the other members suggested. She recognized that she treated the therapist the way she treated other men she met, that she tried to frighten them away as soon as they got to know her. She recalled how close she had been to her own father until age 6, when he lost his business and became seriously depressed. She remembered that she could find no way to get through to him after that, even if she were nasty to him. She also shared with the group how lonely she felt in life, and that she really liked the therapist. She said that she was afraid to depend on him because of this, since she feared that she would have to give up her identity just like she had with her last boyfriend. She had allowed this boyfriend to take care of her but as a result seemed to lose a sense of herself. That the only way she could stand up to him was to yell at him and berate him. After a few years, the relationship became torturous.

MALIGNANT PROJECTIVE IDENTIFICATION

The Impact on the Projector

In a climate of malignant projective identification the individual demonstrates minimal capacity to understand himself and others. The projective process is massive and forceful. It leads to a loss of a major part of the self, and to impoverishment of the ego. Reality testing is diminished to the degree that the projector's ability to test her judgment about herself or others is restricted. The other person is therefore not recognized for what he is, and remains a container of the disowned aspects of the self. "Interpersonal relations may become unreal, narcissistically intense, up to a point of insanity."[1]

The Impact on the Recipient

In a climate of malignant projective identification the recipient may experience a severe sense of internal discomfort. He may feel he is losing a grip on his identity. He may end up joining the projector in ignoring aspects of himself other than what is being projected.[1] For example, the chronic and persistent complaints of the "frightened tigress" that the therapist did not care about her and would let her down created a hostile and rejecting atmosphere. The therapist was left with an internal experience of himself that he, like the patient's mother, had nothing to offer her when her separation-individuation strivings came to the forefront. The therapist would regularly be left with the feeling that he could not be of help to her when she wanted to be her own person. At times he would forget that he understood the patient, and that she had made quite a bit of progress while in treatment with him.

The mild form of malignant projective identification is further illustrated by this vignette: The "skunk" in the group emitted an odor which was chronic, persistent, and just strong enough to keep people at a safe distance. This odor consisted of repeated self-devaluation — "I repel women, and I'm inferior to men," — as well as complaints about the group and the therapist finding him unappealing, especially in the face of their attempts to give to him. This behavior achieved its unconscious goal, that is, it frustrated and angered the other group members, and at times the therapist. The group often expressed annoyance at the "skunk's" lack of appreciation, and at times retaliated. On one occasion, the "pretender" became overwhelmed with this rejecting style, and angrily pointed to the "skunk's" poor adjustment to life. He criticized him for not having the guts to get a job or to be involved in relationships. This then infuriated the "skunk" and served to validate his unconscious expectation that he would be rejected.

By keeping the atmosphere hostile and rejecting much of the time, he avoided the danger of ever having to reveal his wish to attract people and to be loved. Through his complaints he was able to get the group members and the therapist to feel inadequate, since he repeatedly rejected what they offered. This "help-rejecting complainer" was able to rid himself of some of his own self-hatred which manifested itself as the aspect of the self that could not see the good in him. His behavior was a repetition of his interaction with his father who could only see what was wrong with him. The "pretender" was most sensitive to the "skunk's" style. He demonstrated the greatest role comfort with the projections. These projections constantly reminded him of his own sense of inadequacy which he tries to disown and hide through his cheerful false self-representation. The "pretender" was the most invested in keeping up a façade of adequacy and, therefore, the most deeply wounded by the "skunk's" complaints that the group was not good enough. Their mutual arguing, or mutual emitting of odors, involved a collusion between them to deny their wishes to expose vulnerability, and to be cared for.

Thus they were able to rid themselves of their shared and feared dependency wishes. Intervention consisted of commenting to the group that as long as the two of them continued to argue, the atmosphere would remain tense and unhelpful. The "pretender" said that he felt picked on by the therapist who he experienced as trying to shut him up. The "skunk," also annoyed at the therapist, said that he enjoyed taking on the "pretender." It made him feel strong. In this case, the two patients indicated that they were not yet ready to own their projections, nor tolerate the closeness that might be overwhelming at this stage of the group's development.

SUMMARY

The understanding of collusive projective processes can be of great assistance to the group therapist in identifying and resolving individual and group resistances to work and intimacy in the psychotherapy group. Collusive projective processes consist of multiple transferences driven by the mechanism of projective identification. These transferences essentially constitute the repetition compulsion, in which each patient relives his early traumatic experiences with the therapist and members in the group. This reenactment, which is initially a mode of resistance, permits an understanding of the intrapsychic and interpersonal world of each patient. Thus, the therapist utilizes this material in the service of the group's growth and change. The collusive projective processes initially deplenish the group members' and therapist's feelings of strength and integrity. As these processes are experienced, understood, and interpreted, the members and the therapist emerge and are recognized as individuals who experience themselves as acknowledged and fortified.

REFERENCES

1. Main T: Some psychodynamics of large groups, in Kreeger L (ed): *The Large Group — Dynamics and Therapy*. London, Constable, 1975, pp 57–86.
2. Feinsilver D: Reality, transitional relatedness and containment in the borderline. *Contemp Psychoanal* 1983;19:537–569.
3. Stein A, Kibel H: A group dynamic — Peer interaction approach to group psychotherapy. *Int J Group Psychother* 1984;34:315–333.
4. Freud S (1921): *Group Psychology and the Analysis of the Ego*. Standard Edition, vol 18, Strachey J (trans-ed). London, Hogart Press, 1955.
5. Modell A: *Psychoanalysis in a New Context*. New York, International Universities Press, 1984.
6. Horwitz L: Projective identification in dyads and groups. *Int J Group Psychother* 1983;33:259–279.
7. Scheidlinger S: On the concept of the mother group. *Int J Group Psychother* 1974;24:417–428.
8. Bion WR: Group dynamics: A re-view, in Klein M, Heiman A, Money-Kyrle RE (eds): *New directions in Psychoanalysis*. London, Tavistock, 1955, pp 440–477.
9. Winnicott DW: *The Maturational Process and the Facilitating Environment*. New York, International Universities Press, 1965.
10. Balint M: *Primary Love and Psychoanalytic Technique*. New York, Liveright, 1953.
11. Bion WR: *Elements of Psychoanalysis*. New York, Basic Books, 1963.
12. Bion WR: *Attention and Interpretation*. London, Tavistock, 1970.
13. Money-Kyrle RE: Normal countertransference and some of its deviations. *Int J Psychoanal* 1956;37:360–366.
14. Racker H: A contribution to the problem of countertransference. *Int J Psychoanal* 1953;34:313–324.
15. Racker H: The meanings and uses of countertransference. *Psychoanal* 1957;26:303–357.
16. Heiman P: On countertransference. *Int J Psychoanal* 1950;31:81–84.
17. Ogden TH: *Projective Identification and Psychotherapeutic Technique*. New York, Jason Aronson, 1982.
18. Langs R: Therapeutic misalliances. *Int J Psychoanal Psychother* 1975;4:77–105.
19. Gorkin M: *Uses of Countertransference*. New York, Jason Aronson, 1987.

PART II
NEW POPULATIONS

7

Group Therapy for Medically Ill Patients

Berney Goodman

I. OVERVIEW

Group therapy for the medically ill differs in many ways from traditional group psychotherapy. Although its practice has a long history, its benefits have not yet been fully recorded, understood, or recognized.

The amorphousness of medical groups with differing compositions, durations, processes, and styles of group interventions; the number of medical illnesses; the different phases of any medical illness; and the relative lack of involvement of psychiatric physicians in this field contribute to ignorance of the benefits of group therapy for these patients. However, there are enough common themes to suggest an emerging field with the potential for a major contribution to the health and quality of life for the medically ill.

History

The field of group psychotherapy was founded in this country in 1905 by a nonpsychiatric physician, J.H. Pratt of Boston.[1] His approach, not widely used now in traditional group psychotherapy situations, is still of importance in group work with the medically ill.

Pratt introduced what he called "mass instruction" in the treatment of tubercular patients and noted the improvement in those who attended his "clinic classes."[2] He later applied his techniques to diabetic and heart patients[3] and others followed his practices.[4-6] The patients appeared to benefit significantly.[7] The early practitioners were instructional, inspirational, and repressive.[1] "Pull yourself together and find an interest in life" were the implied bywords of these often authoritarian therapists who exploited group transference. Significantly, these group procedures were considered highly efficient, and of special importance for poorer populations.

For the purposes of this study, 90 literature references dating from 1966 were surveyed. There were 19 studies of groups for obese patients; 13 for postmyocardial infarction; 13 for bronchial asthma; nine for chronic pain; six for cancer; six for diabetes mellitus; four for poststroke; three each for hypertension, chronic lung disease, and rheumatoid arthritis; two each for amputees, multiple sclerosis, and death and dying; and one each for acquired immunodeficiency syndrome (AIDS), myasthenia gravis, hemodialysis, irritable bowel syndrome, and hemophilia.

In an attempt to present such a heterogeneous subject coherently, a series of questions and answers is considered. In addition, a personal experience with a weekly group for ostomy patients in a hospital setting is described to further elucidate some of the principles of medical group work.

What Is Group Therapy?

Group therapy involves the use of the group process to alleviate illness or distress. To accomplish this a group should meet regularly, be small, face to face, and have a leader to encourage free discussion and interaction. An atmosphere should be created in which members can get to know themselves better, feel sufficiently confident to disclose their concerns, and, hopefully, improve the way in which they cope with their disabilities and lives in general. Ideally, the patient should not be told what to do, but rather encouraged to deal with the problems himself.

What Makes Group Therapy Effective?

As conceptualized by Yalom,[8] 12 factors contribute to the promotion of group effectiveness. They are:

1. Interpersonal learning, that is, feedback from others.
2. Catharsis or ventilation.
3. Group cohesiveness. The feeling that the group is worthwhile and the appreciation of the members for one another may increase self-esteem and diminish social isolation.

4. Insight.
5. The development of socializing techniques through feedback about behavior and reactions to it can provide a powerful incentive for change.
6. Existential factors. For instance, finding a new meaning to life.
7. Universality. This involves the realization that one is not the only person in the world who has problems.
8. Instillation of hope.
9. Altruism.
10. Corrective recapitulation of the family of origin. Here the leader is used to correct distortions of authority figures gathered from childhood and often resulting in personal devaluation.
11. Imparting information.
12. Imitative behavior. The role model effect of the leader and other members.

What Is Group Therapy with Medical Patients?

Group therapy with medical patients conforms to the definitions just outlined, but it is the approach that distinguishes it from traditional group psychotherapy, and makes it more like Pratt's model. Numerous factors make a different approach essential. Medically ill patients rarely want psychiatric involvement because therapy is seen as something for "crazy people." Group therapy with psychiatric patients usually explores personal feelings *ab initio*. However, medically ill patients rarely want to participate in this self-exploration, indeed they may abhor it. Group therapy with medical patients almost always contains a strong didactic, technical element.

Since the goals of group psychotherapy include self-learning with a minimum amount of directiveness by the leader, this strong educative element in group psychotherapy with medical patients may appear anomalous. But emotional self-learning should not be confused with technical learning. In fact, the didactic approach is often the path to emotional growth for patients unable to tolerate the stresses of emotional probing. Medical groups may be inpatient- or outpatient-based. Most of those described have been held in the hospital.

How Should Medical Groups Be Led?

While there are advocates of both the directive and nonstructured approaches, the majority of authors of the papers surveyed noted better patient response with a directed, structured approach.[9–17]

Stern et al started their group of postmyocardial patients with a nondirective approach.[9] Patients were encouraged to talk freely about any topic they wished. Patients would frequently interrupt to ask questions about their medical condition, medical procedures, and medications, disrupting the group. When a more structured educational and behavioral methodology was introduced for the first five of 12 sessions, the remaining seven sessions could be more process-oriented and better tolerated at this stage by the patients.

Bucher et al, working with stroke patients, compared three group settings.[12] In the first, the leaders were nondirective, whereas in the second and third the leaders were more directive and the groups more structured. The third group spent a longer time on initial induction when the patients were verbally given basic information about the group and also a simple typed description. The third group was less directive than the second but the informational aspects were most emphasized in the third group. It was the third group that was evaluated as most successful.

A fine example of structured group therapy is given in work by Baider et al.[11] Thirty-one women postmastectomy were seen in two groups for 12 sessions each. The group intervention comprised 12 structured sessions. Each had a specific thematic subject, which the leader presented to the group without focusing on any particular member but rather as a "working" assumption to the entire group. The subjects brought up for discussion were divided into four basic categories: (1) definitions and assumptions; (2) perception of self; (3) reallocation of roles; and (4) mourning and adaptation.

Each basic category was further subdivided for discussion. Included in definitions and assumptions were sociodemographic data, information related to surgery (discovering the lump; reaction to surgery; fantasies before and after surgery), and treatment modalities.

Discussions of "perception of self" encompassed before-and-after body images, asymmetry, sexuality, self-perception as a woman, mechanisms of adjustment, sexual relationship with partner, and re-adjustment to sexual behavior.

"Reallocation of roles" discussions centered on change and re-adjustment in the context of the family; patterns of sharing and communication with health teams, that is physicians, etc; and views of the past and wishes for the future.

"Mourning and adaptations" sessions brought up fear of new occurrences; the dichotomy between certainty and uncertainty; the anticipation of mourning; fear of loss, separation, and death; group separation; and sharing of symbolic gifts. Clearly there was considerable overlapping and no topic was brought up in a formal sequential pattern.

Some writers have recommended insight-oriented groups for

medical patients. Crawford and McIver favored such an approach in multiple sclerosis patients and found significantly less depression in their patients after 50 group sessions.[18] In 1966, Schoenberg and Senescu described analytically oriented group psychotherapy for patients with chronic and multiple chronic complaints.[19] 5-year-follow-up showed a significant decrease in somatic complaints and clinic visits after 18 months of group therapy. However, neither of the insight-oriented groups can be considered to be time-limited, each requiring in excess of a year of weekly meetings to achieve its results.

Group behavior modification over 5 weeks was used in obese adolescents with resultant weight loss.[20] This approach has also been found useful in chronic low back pain patients[21] who attended only ten weekly sessions. It may be that the behavioral approach is particularly useful when a particular medical symptom is the target for relief in group therapy. Basler et al divided 107 obese patients with hypertension into four groups.[22] Each was subjected to 12 weekly sessions of different informational or behavioral and relaxation programs. No differential effect between the various therapy procedures could be demonstrated.

The consensus emerging from these studies is that a structured and directive approach has been found more useful in time-limited group therapy with medical patients. Informational sessions have been associated with more successful outcomes. Behavioral and insight-oriented approaches may be of value but they appear to be most useful when preceded by or combined with informational sessions. Flexibility in approach seems to be the byword of most experienced group leaders.

Who Should Lead Medical Groups?

Groups for the medically ill are led by a large variety of people, trained and untrained. Often these groups are organized by societies such as the Ileostomy Society or cancer organizations. Volunteers who themselves have experienced the illness lead the sessions. Others may be run by charismatic leaders purporting to have a special psychological approach related to the etiology, and therefore outcome, of the medical illness. These groups are commonly seen with cancer patients.

Psychiatrists have led many of the groups reported in the literature, particularly where a statistical assessment of the groups' effectiveness has been made. Some authors have maintained that groups for the medically ill do not necessarily need a psychiatrist as leader or participant. A study with a diabetes group revealed a higher rate of absenteeism when a psychiatrist was leader than when a nonpsychiatrist led the group. This may have been related to the psychiatrist's inability to answer technical questions or the perception of the psychiatrist as an outsider and as not belonging to the primary treatment team. Additionally, it was thought that a psychiatrist's presence may be inhibiting to some patients.

While questions can be raised as to the necessity of a psychiatrist-leader, it *is* stressed that a trained leader is necessary.[23] Nurses and technicians who were subjected to a 6-month training program did not feel compelled to provide answers constantly and were able to encourage interaction. Untrained leaders were often seen as putting patients on the "hot seat" or they tended to become "amateur psychoanalysts," emphasizing the sexual. Spiegel et al have suggested that the treatment process is more important than the professional background of the leader.[24]

The issue of coleadership appears to be nowhere near as controversial in medical groups as it is in traditional groups. The presence of a technically skilled staff at group meetings where the dissemination of instructional material is of the essence seems essential. A psychiatrist or indeed any mental health professional or lay person leading the group might not be able to fulfill the function of imparting detailed technical information alone.

On the other hand, a psychiatrist as a physician would have greater familiarity with medical illness, procedures, treatments, and physician-patient relationships than a nonpsychiatrist leader.[15] Together with skills as therapist and group leader as well as the ability to objectively rate changes in the medical and emotional condition of the patients, the psychiatrist's physician status puts him in a preferred position to lead such groups when specialized technically trained staff is present to provide needed information.

Should a Medical Group Be Homogeneous?

Homogeneity in terms of diagnosis or symptomatology is a virtual common denominator for all medical groups described. This is not surprising since most of these groups had a strong informational component.

Homogeneity for age has not been stressed in the reports surveyed except in groups for adolescents. Attempting to bring a higher degree of homogeneity to a medical group by assigning patients of the same sex and weight base to different obesity groups bore no greater fruit than the mixed obesity group.[25]

For How Many Sessions Should Medical Groups Meet?

Duration of the medical groups surveyed varied from 6 weeks to years. Most were short-term and met weekly for six to 12 sessions. Inpatient groups might meet daily while the patients were hospitalized.[26] Some authors have suggested that very short-term groups, that is, six sessions, did not allow for sufficient understanding of the patients.[12] Others found six sessions sufficient for noticeable benefit.[27,28]

Thus no clear-cut number of sessions or duration of the group experience is recommended. Although short-term groups have been favored, they, themselves, have differed markedly in scope and duration. In many described medical groups patients were informed at the outset that a limited number of sessions would be provided.[11,12,28] Despite this, in some cases patients were able to continue voluntarily in the group following this for much longer periods of time.[11,16,29]

What Is the Optimum Number of Patients for Medical Groups?

As with number of sessions, there was great variability in the number of patients in each group in the papers surveyed. Bucher et al[12] advocated an optimum number of eight patients, but as few as three[26] and as many as 14[18] patients have been included.

Should Medical Groups Be Open or Closed?

Again, there has been much variability reported on the question of closed-vs-open groups. Closed groups could be converted to open ones and vice versa. Clearly no rigid format is indicated.

Should Significant Others Be Invited To Attend?

Zakus et al have recommended the presence of family members where the patient showed low levels of independence and internal controls.[20] In pain patients, this has been highly recommended because of the often disturbed family relationships seen as a result of the medical illness and as a predictor of a negative outcome.[26] Groups have been described where family members have been invited to the same or different group sessions.[20,26,30]

Should Certain Patients Be Excluded from Medical Groups?

It has been observed that patients with high levels of hypochondriasis[26] and low levels of perceived internal controls[20] may do poorly in medical groups. It has been suggested that these patients not be admitted to such groups. Patients who do poorly in medical groups may adversely affect the outcome for the remaining patients.[26] Thus it has been recommended that patients who do not benefit after a short period be excluded so as not to negatively influence the treatment for others.

Conversely, it has been recommended that patients benefiting from the group experience be included with newcomers to provide a positive influence on the latter's treatment.

Do Medical Groups Help?

The consensus of the published articles would indicate positive results from medical groups. Improvements in compliance,[15,20,22,31–33] attitude and coping,[9,16,22,24,26,33] medical condition, morbidity, and mortality,[15,22,26,28,34–36] emotional state,[11,18,24,26,36–38] and cost benefits[39,40] have all been reported.

Spiegel et al reported on a weekly supportive group for metastatic breast cancer patients over a 1-year period.[24] In his randomized prospective outcome study the treatment group had significantly lower mood disturbance scores, and maladaptive coping responses, and they were less phobic than the control group. Contrary to predictions, changes were not found for denial, self-esteem, or sense of control. Other studies had reported the latter as positive results of such groups.[37]

Groen and Pelser found improvements in both medical condition (asthma) and attitudes in their patients.[10]

Rahe et al examined the effects of six group meetings on 44 postmyocardial infarction patients. A 4-year follow-up was possible.[28] There was significantly less morbidity and mortality in the treated patients. Return to work and rehabilitation was improved compared to the control group. There was no change in depression, anxiety, or sexual activity compared to the control group, again contradicting other reports of emotional change in medical group patients.[28]

Deter reported on a significant reduction in lost working days in 22 asthmatic patients after group therapy for 1 year.[39]

Basler et al treated obese hypertensives and compared them to a nontreated control group.[22] The treated group lost weight and lowered their blood pressures after 6 months and maintained improvement for 4 more months of follow-up.

In a study of 24 postmastectomy patients, 11 (46%) reported being helped significantly, 9(37%) were helped moderately, and 4(17%) were not helped at all. These findings were objectively confirmed by comparing pre- and postgroup psychological scales. The findings of lessened psychological distress reached statistical significance in those who said they were helped. Those not helped seemed to have started out with a higher level of psychological distress. All in all, it was unclear what made the difference, but it should be noted that those helped were nearer the time of surgery.

Thus, both controlled studies and impressionistic ones have indicated a positive effect of medical groups for patients with a wide variety of medical disorders. In fact there have been striking findings in some of the controlled experiments. The significant lowering of morbidity and mortality in the postmyocardial infarct group subjected to group therapy is particularly encouraging, given the six-session duration. The 4-year follow-up in part eliminated a prominent objection to many such studies, namely, insufficient follow-up. It is also important that assessments of outcome not only include physician and staff assessment, but also include patient input and objective medical findings. The latter makes the evaluation of studies with medical patients potentially more accurate than those involving psychiatric patients.

How Do Medical Groups Help?

Stern et al treated 26 postmyocardial infarction patients in a 12-session group therapy program.[9] The patients completed self-rating measures before and after therapy. The measures ranked group process variables. Most valued by the patients were learning positive qualities; experimenting with new behavior; receiving advice; and gaining positive insight by learning how their life-styles played a role in the development and management of their coronary condition. These variables fell into the category of guidance factors. Lowest ranked were interpersonal learning, catharsis, and the testing of group acceptance by revealing embarrassing things about themselves. Altruism and instilling of hope were secondary. A dependent relationship with the therapist was universal. Patients avoided being confronted and challenged, experiencing negative feelings, or becoming anxious and depressed in the course of working through such issues as early object loss or narcissistic entitlement.

These findings underscore the vast difference between medical patients and most other client groups in ranking therapeutic factors. Traditional group therapy patients expect to gain insight from understanding the past, seeing undesirable things about themselves, experiencing negative feelings (as measured on the Lieberman questionnaire), and value interpersonal learning, catharsis, cohesiveness, and self-understanding as important to their therapeutic success. With the exception of self-understanding, all these factors were ranked low in the cardiac patients of Stern et al. Maxmen has shown that hospitalized patients rank instilling of hope, cohesiveness, altruism, and universality of greatest use to them following short-term therapy.[41] What appears to be highly counterproductive in medical patients is the encouragement of catharsis and interpersonal confrontation. Education and learning positive-oriented behaviors would seem to be most therapeutically beneficial.

Rahe et al,[28] however, reported that while their groups of post-myocardial infarction patients were all educationally directed, and the patients were thought to have been helped by this approach, the patients themselves forgot the educational aspects of the group over the long-term 4-year follow-up. He concluded that the supportive aspects of the group were paramount even though the educational were initially regarded as helpful.[28] What is initially seen to be therapeutic by patients is therefore not always the case. In the group of Bucher et al, sharing of information was assessed as particularly helpful because it lessened isolation.[12] Diminished isolation through transferring and expressing of negative feelings and concerns to a group rather than the patient's own family has been cited as useful by other authors.[24]

The patient-physician relationship, often difficult or impaired, was commonly discussed in medical groups. Help with this thorny problem was seen as very useful. Some studies have referred to lower depression and anxiety scores in medical patients following group therapy, but the controlled studies have not, by and large, borne this out. Interestingly, Crawford and McIver recorded such changes in the emotional status of their patients in an insight-oriented group.[18] Certain factors have been noted to predict better outcomes with medically oriented groups. Zakus et al reported that in their group of obese adolescent girls, those with a perception of greater internal control stayed longer with the group and benefited most from it.[20] Moore et al noted that their pain patients who had lower hypochondriasis scores and higher hypomanic scores on the Minnesota Multiphasic Personality Inventory (MMPI) benefited most.[26]

Bucher et al warned against the negative effects of changing leaders during the life of such groups, emphasizing the importance of the leader in the therapeutic process.[12] Patients doing well can help the therapeutic process, while those doing poorly can hinder it.

Can a Medical Group Do Harm?

This question of whether a medical group can do harm remains a common one, and is posed most frequently by nonpsychiatric physicians. There is often allusion to harm caused by psychiatric interventions on an individual basis. These experiences are cited to justify caution with group interventions. Most often these concerns are related to reported confrontations and the breakdown of defensive operations, particularly denial.

As with individual psychotherapy, the perceptions of patients and physicians in a group are influenced by personal feelings and commonly held views. The perception of group therapy adds to the fears that the patient will be exposed. Indeed, in probing groups, the patient's experiences may well be negative. Given the short-term nature of most groups for the medically ill, no opportunity for further working through and subsequent relief may be offered. The result is that the patient (and physician) does not perceive the group as beneficial and may see its results as harmful.

A commonly asked question is whether the presence of patients in the late (or terminal) phases of illness will negatively influence (harm) patients with the same disease but who are less seriously ill. No clear answer is possible at this time although it can be said that groups may even have to be relatively homogeneous with respect to phase of illness, particularly in cancer patients, to avoid any such possibilities.

Overdependency may develop in medical groups and the patients may use the group indefinitely (if the group is continuous and open-ended). In some patients this could tend to be psychologically harmful. On the other hand, the evidence suggests that group therapy for the medically ill is not harmful as long as caution is exercised in not unearthing unconscious material prematurely, confrontation is held to a minimum, and the early phases of the group experience lean toward instruction rather than insight. Perhaps the availability of an involved staff group member at times between group sessions would be helpful if it were deemed necessary to discuss deeper material during the group. In essence, the same precautions would be adhered to in any constructive group therapy.

II. AN INPATIENT GROUP FOR ENTEROSTOMY PATIENTS

The second section of this chapter is devoted to a description of a 2½-year experience leading a medical group for patients with ileostomies and colostomies who were seen in the group postsurgery in the hospital. The experience bears out much of what has been described in the literature with respect to how such groups should be led, who should lead them, optimum number of patients, inclusion of significant others, exclusion of certain patients, effectiveness, reasons for effectiveness, and potential harm. The discussion approximates the sequence of the question-and-answer format used in the first section where applicable.

History

The group was started approximately 8 years ago in a major urban teaching hospital to "provide a forum for these patients to discuss their emotional reactions to their diseases and to the medical plan of treatment." The stresses of having an ileostomy or colostomy were considered relatively unique because of the loss of control over normal bodily functions. It was observed that ostomy patients shared information, anxieties, and conflicts with one another while on the ward, with positive effect. However, without a structure they often tended to impart incorrect information, thereby increasing anxiety.

Attendance was voluntary, the patients being referred by private physicians, nursing staff, or resident staff. Both pre- and postoperative patients were included. The group met once a week for one hour. It was led by the enterostomy clinicians (RNs) in conjunction with the liaison psychiatrist, nursing supervisor, social worker, one staff nurse, and one surgical resident. The group has evolved considerably over the years.

Current Organization and Makeup

The group's leadership is now in the hands of a liaison psychiatrist. The enterostomy therapist remains the pivotal staff person imparting technical information, but the rest of the staff have become very familiar with most of the medical aspects of ileostomies and colostomies. Two volunteers, one from the Ileostomy Foundation, the other from the Colostomy Society, attend regularly, serving as models for identification and sharing their personal experiences. Both have lived for over 7 years with their ostomies; one after cancer, the other after many years of ulcerative colitis. The social worker on the colorectal service who is familiar with most of the patients attends; and the nursing supervisor on that service comes intermittently. Surgical residents do not attend. I took over the leadership about 2 years ago replacing the original psychiatrist who resigned.

The patients come from the colorectal service and from other beds in the hospital. They are asked by the enterostomy therapist whether they wish to attend. Most patients attend; some who refuse initially often change their minds. Because hospital stays have become progressively shorter over the years, and a period of postoperative recovery is necessary before patients are well enough to attend the group, most patients can only come to one meeting. A few come 2 to 3 times. A small number return after discharge; some do this frequently. Between two and eight patients usually attend, although four to five is the average. Some patients are so ill they can only attend a part of the group. Patients' families and close friends are welcome to attend.

The majority of ileostomy patients have had chronic long-standing ulcerative colitis; multiple polyposis patients are not rare. Most of the colostomy patients have had carcinoma of the colon or rectum; they are usually older than the ileostomy patients and their disease has been more acute, unexpected, and overwhelming. The group is not homogeneous in terms of illness, age, or stage of illness; the unifying common denominator is a bowel ostomy in one form or another.

Experience with Style of Leadership

My initial experience with the group soon proved what has been discussed in the literature. Given a plethora of depressed and anxious patients with carcinoma, I elicited their feelings about their conditions. The enterostomy therapists told me that the patients were dissatisfied with this approach, although it was clear the therapists were too. They reminded me that the group had a theme, ostomies, and it was matters related to this that we were there to discuss. After that the group was always introduced as the "ostomy group," to which patients came to talk about this subject. This focus eased patient and staff anxieties considerably. A series of group meetings which were highly focused and structured were then attempted. The group meetings were introduced with patients asking questions about their ostomies. If the questions did not cover certain topics, subjects for discussion were offered. The topics introduced included diet, clothes, food, smells, reaction to the ostomy and its appearance, and its effects on spouses, lovers, friends, and family. While this approach did not produce too much anxiety, the overstructuring proved inhibiting. The patients were satisfied with the information and the opportunity to see others who have ostomies flourishing but little spontaneous emotional work took place.

A more flexible approach has proved most satisfactory. After a brief introductory period, the patients are invited to talk about their concerns and ask questions. Themes are not routinely introduced but are brought up more naturally when they do not arise spontaneously. The experience with this group bears out what has been written about styles of medical group leadership. A directive, nonstructured approach emphasizing common themes and the imparting of information from staff and more experienced patients seems to provide a good balance.

Experience and Problems with Leadership

Although the enterostomal therapists were originally supposed to lead the group, the psychiatrist assumed this role from the inception. This has evoked ambivalent feelings among staff. They seemed to feel my presence is comforting if any psychiatric event expresses itself during the group and they turn to me when a patient asks a question about psychopathology (eg, a patient asked whether his feelings of "paranoia" were normal now that he was no longer taking steroids). Similarly, they depend on me to identify hidden, serious psychopathology and prevent rambling and intrusions.

While I was encouraged to set the leadership style, the staff made it clear that the style had to be one which allowed them to be comfortable. In practice, this proved restrictive. The staff continually stressed the theme of universality. While this aspect of the group experience was one of the most helpful, the group was often pictured as rewarding *only* when the patients shared particular anxieties about adjustment to their new lives, and could realize that their concerns were shared and appropriate. In reality, together with information sharing, this may have been all that could be expected from a "one-time" group experience. At times, however, the patients indicated that they would be amenable to more profound expressions of conflict. In a group where patients with ulcerative colitis were the majority, angry feelings were easily discernible, but usually swamped by an atmosphere of reassurance.

On occasion, staff members expressed anger toward me when they felt that I had been too confrontational or too structured. At these times, during the postgroup meeting, I attempted to arrive with them at a consensus supporting the use of different models and observing their effect. On one occasion, this evoked from the staff the angry response that "we were here to discuss patients." In retrospect, some staff complaints were reasonable, but others were apparent displacements from other areas of conflict within a stressful environment. What was and remains particularly inhibiting is the absence of a mandate to deal with staff interaction at a psychological level, as one might attempt to do in a psychiatric setting.

A physician-leader may bring certain advantages to the group. As a physician, it is easy to become acquainted with the medical aspects of the context. To increase my awareness, I attended a set of lectures on enterostomies and observed a patient cleaning and changing appliances. And because I was available for psychiatric consultations on the service, the group could provide valuable psychiatric information about the patients and the need for further psychiatric intervention. In addition, the rest of the staff was in frequent contact with the patients and was able to provide support and encouragement outside of the group. Theoretically, the presence of a physician-leader allowed for greater exploration on all levels within the group. Thus, the patients would not be asked to express their conflicts and be left without follow-up after a single meeting. As a result, no patient objected to the presence of a psychiatrist and questions were often directed toward the psychiatrist-leader *ab initio*.

Group Effectiveness

Even with such a short-term group the criteria for group therapy were met. All of the features that contribute to group effectiveness were observed in the compressed time frame. Some factors were more in evidence: universality, instillation of hope, altruism, imparting information, imitative behavior, interpersonal learning, and catharsis. The presence and interaction of the volunteers who themselves have experienced the suffering of the patients and have done well for so long lent a strong hopeful element to the group, and encouraged imitative behavior. The intermittent attendance of recovered patients who were eager to share their positive experiences provided an additional altruistic aspect.

Information was imparted expertly by the enterostomy therapists. As reported in most writings, this is clearly a vital aspect of a medical group and often the fulcrum for later emotional expression. The correction of false and anxiety-provoking information was also valuable. The short-term nature of the group made group cohesiveness, the development of socializing techniques, existential factors, and corrective recapitulation of family of origin less frequently evident.

Although no statistical data are available to substantiate the group's value, patient feedback suggests that it was helpful. Clearly, the help afforded was limited by time restrictions. However, patients most frequently report that the group has been very useful in their adjustment to the enterostomy. Patients who returned weeks, months, or years later felt that the group was valuable to them postoperatively. It is in areas of attitude and coping that this one-session group seemed to be most beneficial.

Inclusion of Significant Others

The presence at the group of significant others has been most useful. Frequently these participants talked for a shy patient and acted as an enabler. At other times, family members demostrated how overbearing they have been in patients' lives.

Exclusion of Patients

No patient has had to be excluded from the group in the past 2 years. Many patients whose medical condition has not been favorable talk in pessimistic terms all the time. They might have been excluded from other medical groups because of a potential negative therapeutic influence. It has not been necessary to exclude them from this group.

Their expressions of hopelessness have been sufficiently offset by the optimistic voices of the patients who have made progress and the example of the volunteers.

A peculiarity of this group was the presence of both ileostomy and colostomy patients, distinct in age, diagnosis, and chronicity of illness. The ileostomy patients endured years of the most oppressive existence due to their disease process. Although anxious, conflicted, and depressed, they can now look forward to a significantly improved quality of life as the disease process has been surgically eliminated. It is relatively easy to impart a feeling of optimism and hope to them. On the other hand, the colostomy patients, older and frequently suffering from cancer, have had their illness thrust upon them suddenly with a much less optimistic future. They are usually more depressed. It has been possible to let them express their fears without too much probing.

Potential Harm

No harm deriving from the experience has been observed. While some patients (and staff) may have complained at times about emotional probing, no untoward psychological or medical effect can be contributed to this group experience.

SUMMARY

Group therapy for medically ill patients has been shown to be useful on a short- or long-term basis in a variety of illnesses. Benefits have accrued at psychological and medical levels. Many of the criteria for effectiveness in traditional group therapy have been observed to be operative in medical groups as well. But the emphasis in medical groups has been in the areas of universality, instillation of hope, altruism, imitative behavior, and imparting of information. The last-named, in particular, has been of great importance in medical groups. Thus, staff members able to impart the necessary technical information have been essential participants in these groups. At times too much emphasis on the thematic-informational approach has stifled emotional expression. A delicate balance between a structured and a more open approach would seem to provide the optimum leadership style.

REFERENCES

1. Thomas GW: Group psychotherapy — a review of the recent literature. *Psychosom Med* 1943;5:166–180.
2. Pratt JH: The class method of treating consumption in the homes of the poor. *AMA J* 1907;49:755–759.

3. Pratt JH: The principles of class treatment and their application to various chronic diseases. *Hosp Soc Serv* 1922;6:401–408.

4. Harris HI: Efficient psychotherapy for the large outpatient clinic. *N Engl J Med* 1939;221:1–5.

5. Hadden SB: Treatment of the neuroses by class technic. *Ann Intern Med* 1942;16:33–37.

6. Chappell M, Stafano J, Rogerson J, et al: Value of group psychological procedures in treatment of peptic ulcer. *Am J Dig Dis Nutr* 1937;3:813–817.

7. Pratt JH: The influence of emotions in the causation and cure of psychoneurosis. *Int Clin* 1934;4:1–16.

8. Yalom ID: *The Theory and Practice of Group Psychotherapy*. New York. Basic Books 1975, pp 3–104.

9. Stern MJ, Plionis E, Kaslow L: Group process expectations and outcome with post-myocardial infarction patients. *Gen Hosp Psychiatry* 1984;6:101–108.

10. Groen JJ, Pelser HE: Newer concepts of teaching, learning, and education and their application to the patient-doctor cooperation in the treatment of diabetes mellitus. *Pediatr Adolesc Endocrinology* 1982;10:168–177.

11. Baider L, Amikam JC, Kaplan De-Nour A: Time-limited thematic group with post-mastectomy patients. *J Psychosom Res* 1984;28:323–330.

12. Bucher J, Smith E, Gillespie C: Short-term group therapy for stroke patients in a rehabilitation center. *Br J Med Psychol* 1984;57:283–290.

13. Singler K: The stroke group, in Slegson M (ed): *Group Psychotherapy and Counseling with Special Populations*. Baltimore, University Park Press, 1981, pp 43–47.

14. Gamsa A, Braha RE, Catchlove RF: The use of structured group therapy sessions in the treatment of chronic pain patients. *Pain* 1985;22:91–96.

15. Tattersall RB, McCalloch DK, Aveline M: Group therapy in the treatment of diabetes. *Diabetes Care* 1985;8:180–188.

16. Kerstein MD: Group rehabilitation for the vascular-disease amputee. *J Am Geriatr Soc* 1980;28:40–41.

17. Lipp MR, Malone ST: Group rehabilitation of vascular surgery patients. *Arch Phys Med Rehabil* 1976;57:180–183.

18. Crawford JD, McIver GP: Group psychotherapy: benefits in multiple sclerosis. *Arch Phys Med Rehabil* 1985;66:810–813.

19. Schoenberg B, Senescu R: Group psychotherapy for patients with chronic multiple somatic complaints. *J Chron Dis* 1966;19:649–657.

20. Zakus G, Chin ML, Keown M, et al: A group behavior modification approach to adolescent obesity. *Adolescence* 1979;14:481–489.

21. Cohen MJ, Heinrich RL, Naliboff BD, et al: Group outpatient physical and behavioral therapy for chronic low back pain. *J Clin Psychol* 1983;39:326–333.

22. Basler HD, Brinkmeier U, Buser K, et al: Psychological group treatment of obese essential hypertensives by lay therapists in rural general practice settings. *J Psychosom Res* 1985;29:383–391.

23. Ebersole GO, Leiderman PH, Yalom ID: Training the non-professional group therapist. *J Nerv Ment Dis* 1969;149:294–302.

24. Spiegel D, Bloom JR, Yalom I: Group support for patients with metastatic cancer. *Arch Gen Psychiatry* 1981;38:527–533.

25. Jeffrey RW, Snell MK, Forster JL: Group composition in the treatment of

obesity: does increasing group homogeneity improve treatment results? *Behav Res Ther* 1985;23:371–373.

26. Moore ME, Berk SN, Nyparer A: Chronic pain: inpatient treatment with small group effects. *Arch Phys Med Rehabil* 1984;65:356–361.

27. Wise TN, Cooper JN, Ahmed S: The efficacy of group therapy for patients with irritable bowel syndrome. *Psychosomatics* 1982;23:465–469.

28. Rahe RH, Ward HW, Hayes V: Brief group therapy in myocardial infarction rehabilitation: three- to four-year follow-up of a controlled trial. *Psychosom Med* 1979;41:229–242.

29. Bilodeau CB, Hackett TP: Issues raised in a group setting by patients recovering from myocardial infarction. *Am J Psychiatry* 1971;128:73–78.

30. Steinglass P, Gonzales S, Dosovitz I, et al: Discussion groups for chronic hemodialysis patients and their families. *Gen Hosp Psychiatry* 1982;4:7–14.

31. Rabin, C, Amir S, Nardi R, et al: Compliance and control: issues in group training for diabetics. *Health Soc Work* 1986;11:141–151.

32. Oehler-Giarratana J, Fitzgerald RG: Group therapy with blind diabetics. *Arch Gen Psychiatry* 1980;37:463–467.

33. Bess BE, Marlin RL: A pilot study of medication and group therapy for obesity in a group of physicians. *Hillside J Clin Psychiatry* 1984;6:171–187.

34. Peled-Ney R, Silverberg DS, Rosenfeld JB: A controlled study of group therapy in essential hypertension. *Isr J Med Sci* 1984;20:12–5.

35. Deter HC, Albert G: Group therapy for asthma patients: a concept for the psychosomatic treatment of patients in a medical clinic — a controlled study. *Psychother Psychosom* 1983;40:95–105.

36. Herman E, Baptiste S: Pain control: mastery through group experience. *Pain* 1981;10:79–86.

37. Youssef FA: Crisis intervention: a group-therapy approach for hospitalized breast cancer patients. *J Adv Nurs* 1984;9:307–313.

38. Stern MJ, Gorman PA, Kaslow L: The group counseling v exercise therapy study. A controlled intervention with subjects following myocardial infarction. *Arch Intern Med* 1983;143:1719–1725.

39. Deter HC: Cost-benefit analysis of psychosomatic therapy in asthma. *J Psychosom Res* 1986;30:173–182.

40. Cunningham J, Strassberg D, Roback H: Group psychotherapy for medical patients. *Compr Psychiatry* 1978;19:135–140.

41. Maxmen JS: Group therapy as viewed by hospitalized patients. *Arch Gen Psychiatry* 1973;28:404–408.

8

Group Therapy for Patients with AIDS

Sharon Sageman

Group therapy has shown itself to be an invaluable treatment modality in helping patients cope with having acquired immunodeficiency syndrome (AIDS). AIDS, a disease which has now reached epidemic proportions on a worldwide level, is usually fatal. Its incidence is still primarily associated with certain groups, namely homosexual men and intravenous (IV) drug users, and thus it carries a social stigma which is much worse than that of other terminal illnesses. The process of coping with life after receiving a diagnosis of AIDS is a daily struggle, both physically and psychologically. For persons with AIDS, the very act of joining an AIDS therapy group is a positive statement that they want to take an active role and join with others, and have not given up. In the article "A Support Group for Dying Patients,"[1] Spiegel and Yalom write, "The very message of joining a group at this time in a patient's life conveys the idea that the person has not been put out to pasture, that she is not without importance because she is dying."

For people with AIDS, also known as PWAs, being in a group where they can share their feelings and life struggles with others is a powerful way of countering the social stigma and isolation of this illness. Since much of the psychological stress of having AIDS is due to societal scorn, shame, and the sense of feeling very alone in the world, the natural response is to encourage these people to form groups. Here they can find acceptance, and join together to support each other. Such groups were first started within the gay community itself in New

York and California, but are now being held in cities throughout the United States. This chapter includes information from many different AIDS groups, including those being held at Bellevue Hospital and the Gay Men's Health Crisis (GMHC) in New York City, at the Walter Reed Army Hospital in the Washington, DC area, at the National Institutes of Health (NIH) in Bethesda, Md, and at the Howard Brown Memorial Clinic in Chicago. To date, group therapy has been the type of psychotherapy most frequently utilized by people with AIDS in the United States. For many it continues to be a vital source of strength in coping with the isolation and despair of this illness.

Acquired immunodeficiency syndrome, or AIDS, is a disease which at the time of this writing, September 1987, has affected more than 40,000 Americans and has often been described as the most feared national epidemic known to date. Currently, about 30% of the nation's total or 12,000 adult cases of AIDS have been reported in New York City. Here approximately 60% of people with AIDS are homosexual or bisexual men, and approximately 30% are people with a history of IV drug use. The other 10% are made up of either sexual partners of infected persons, recipients of infected blood products, or those for whom the mode of transmission has not been identified. The virus which causes AIDS not only causes grave damage to the immune system, but also has a predilection to infect brain cells which can result in a serious syndrome known as AIDS encephalopathy.

This background information is vital in understanding the unique problems that come up in doing group therapy with AIDS patients. The stresses on group members are enormous — in fact, often overwhelming. They include fear of impending death, a damaged self-image (after years of being socially stigmatized for being gay or using IV drugs), and frequently an insidious deterioration of mental functioning (as well as general health) making communication and daily functioning progressively more difficult.

Group leaders are called on to maintain a sense of stability and order for the group as certain members will inevitably become sicker or more confused as time passes. Often there are conflicts over dependency for group members, arising from this as well as from forces outside of the group. In supportive group therapy, groups' intragroup dependency is generally encouraged, with group members often depending on one another as much as on group leaders. In AIDS groups, members must walk a thin line between increasing emotional involvement with one another, while at the same time defending themselves from the pain of loss over the inevitable separations and death which will occur over time.

Conflicts arising from fear of intragroup dependency surfaced early for the group described in this chapter from the GMHC.

Reulbach and Santorelli, the group leaders, had hoped that the group members would want to form friendships and exchange phone numbers. They encouraged the members to do so. This issue came up after the third weekly meeting of the AIDS group. The group members did not want to exchange phone numbers and refused, explaining "We're not ready yet." Clearly, they were apprehensive about getting too involved with one another too quickly. Their hesitation was due not only to a fear of being intruded upon at a time of immense vulnerability, but also to the fear of having to face painful losses when fellow group members died.

Conflicts over dependence vs independence come to the forefront as group members are forced to cope with increasing dependency on lovers, friends, or family members as their illness progresses. Often PWAs have no choice but to return to their families to be cared for by them, despite the fact that they have lived away from home or on their own for many years. Not only do they face issues of regression inherent in financial dependence and dependence for assistance in daily activities and care, but also the regression associated with medical illness and progressive AIDS encephalopathy which can cause confusion, communication impairment, and psychomotor retardation.

AIDS encephalopathy, a dementia which occurs as a result of the infection of brain cells by the AIDS virus, is frequently diagnosed in patients with AIDS. On postmortem examination, abnormalities of the central nervous system were found in the brains of up to 80% of AIDS patients.[2]

The psychiatric symptoms which occur with AIDS may become apparent before any physical signs of the disease develop. AIDS encephalopathy, however, is often a difficult condition to diagnose because of its subtle, insidious onset and the tendency to mistake it for depression or other functional psychiatric disorders. It is very important for the therapist working with AIDS and AIDS-related complex (ARC) groups to be knowledgeable about the mental status changes seen in AIDS-related dementia, in order to better understand both the organic and functional problems present in each member of the group.

The mental status changes which occur in these patients can range from very subtle and mild to very severe and disabling. Patients may present with neuropsychiatric symptoms with gradual onset that resemble those seen in depression or dementia. These include: dysphoric mood, apathy, extreme passivity, social withdrawal, generalized weakness, fatigue, somatic preoccupations, anxiety, loss of interest in usual activities, subtle personality change, psychomotor retardation, anorexia, hypersomnia, distractibility, and complaints of forgetfulness and impaired concentration. At times the impairments may be so subtle that these patients may remain fully oriented and not show gross cognitive deficits in everyday conversation, but they are still found to have clear-cut signs of organic brain impairment on neurometric testing. Typical impairments seen include delayed memory recall and reduced graphomotor ability. When in doubt, the group leaders should consider referring the patient for a neuropsychological test battery to accurately assess the deficits present.[3]

Another type of psychiatric disorder that is seen with patients with AIDS presents as an acute psychosis, which can mimic an affective, paranoid, or schizophrenic disorder. Symptoms can include grandiosity, suspiciousness, psychomotor agitation, rambling speech, and confusion.[3] In the author's experience with more than 150 AIDS patients, the development of an acute onset psychotic syndrome was far less common than the insidious, gradual, mental status changes of AIDS encephalopathy discussed earlier.

The importance of focusing on AIDS encephalopathy, early in this chapter, on group therapy for patients with AIDS, is underscored by the clinical experience of several of the group leaders. They reported a number of episodes in which they misinterpreted the behavior of group members. Most notable were cases where members were seen as either overly passive, resistant, or lacking in motivation. One group leader admitted to having felt a great deal of anger toward the members of the group whom he saw as deliberately uncooperative and not actively participating. He felt that their behavior was infantile, regressed, passive, and inappropriate for a psychotherapy group. With further education, he realized that most of the "inappropriately passive" behavior of group members was due to the psychomotor retardation associated with AIDS encephalopathy, not deliberate resistance to therapy. Because of the high frequency of AIDS encephalopathy, behavioral changes seen in AIDS group members ought not be attributed to a functional or interpersonal etiology until the possibility of an organic brain syndrome is considered.

Group leaders often need to take a more active role in the AIDS group to help the group deal with certain problems associated with having this disease. At times it may be necessary to protect the member(s) with encephalopathy from too much confrontation by other group members who may misinterpret their taciturn or withdrawn behavior as a resistance or deliberate rejection of the group. In this case, group leaders must walk a thin line between helping the group better understand the real nature of the problem in order to better handle it, and maintaining the confidentiality and positive self-image of the encephalopathic member.

In addition, it is extremely frightening for group members to have to helplessly watch someone in the group become increasingly confused and ill. Not only is there the identification and empathy inherent in being in the same group together, there is also the knowledge that this same deterioration may soon happen to them. Even when members are knowledgeable about the symptoms and course of AIDS encephalopathy (because often many of them have already had a great deal of experience in trying to help friends and lovers who have died from AIDS), they may fail to recognize it due to the defensive use of denial.

Experienced leaders of AIDS groups find that a certain amount of denial is important for group members to maintain a hopeful and optimistic outlook on life. In one AIDS group conducted since September 1986 at the offices of the GMHC, the two group leaders, Santorelli and Reulbach, agreed that there was little discussion about death or the terminal aspects of the illness. Instead, the philosophic orientation of the group ranged between "aggressive survival vs. acceptance of the illness" with the focus on making the most positive use of the remainder of one's life, no matter how brief.

Health care professionals who work with AIDS patients, whether in groups or individually, will often admit that they, too, use denial at times, and unconsciously want to believe that their patients can be saved. Reulbach and Santorelli described the therapists' wishes as: (1) that the patient will not die, or (2) if the patient does have to die, that he or she will not die "until all the loose ends are tied up." Both therapists expressed the view that it was very important to make sure that "loose ends are tied up" by the end of each group session. They allowed the group to run overtime by a few minutes when necessary to make sure that no member was left feeling stranded. One therapist expressed the fear that the stress of leaving a group member with unresolved feelings and frustrations could contribute to making that member physically sick. In a disease like AIDS in which patients are continually succeptible to recurrences of potentially fatal infections, this focus on reducing stress takes on added importance.

The AIDS group members themselves echoed these feelings about emotional stress resulting in physical illness. The beliefs expressed by the group were: (1) "If you feel more positive you'll be less sick," and (2), "A positive attitude could have prevented you from getting sick." These views reflect the group members' continual attempts to look for a sense of control over this devastating illness. A major focus of the group was to encourage one another to take control and not feel helpless and overwhelmed. In addition, since it is not yet known why some people carrying the AIDS virus survive for very long periods and others do not, the quest for a positive attitude as a means of prolonging life may in fact have a basis in reality. (It is the author's observation, after working with more than 200 AIDS patients over the past

7 years, that the patients who take on an active role and are the most motivated to survive *do* seem to live longer with AIDS and have longer periods of feeling relatively better and stronger between infections.)

Group members in all AIDS groups studied tended to want to spend a significant amount of time talking about medical treatments for their illness. Group leaders generally felt that it was important to allow the group to spend a certain amount of time in these medical-scientific discussions, but only to a point. It was felt that medical discussions were often used as a resistance by group members seeking to get away from emotionally charged material. In the GMHC group, the group members themselves were insightful enough to see this, and would confront those who focused on medical topics instead of talking about feelings. Earlier in the course of the group, it was necessary for the group leader to do this, so as to prevent the group from being dominated by technical and impersonal discussion. Later, group members themselves were able to take in this function and successfully limit excessive medical discussions.

Education of group members occurred in all of the AIDS groups studied. Members were usually quite eager to share their medical information with one another and to discuss health concerns. The group at NIH worked on issues about sexual activity and contagiosity. The group members at GMHC, who were already very knowledgeable about "safe sex" and how AIDS is transmitted, shared information on the newest medical treatments for AIDS and new experimental drugs. Group leaders agreed that a certain amount of sharing of medical information is helpful. The fact that much of the latest information on AIDS has yet to be published, and that many of the drug treatments are still very new and experimental, creates a real basis for the group's need to share medical knowledge. In the group at Walter Reed Hospital where members were permitted to bring family or significant others to group sessions, one group member was given permission to bring an infectious disease specialist to the group meeting to answer the group's medical questions.

In addition, it is important for group leaders to be alerted to the tendency for members to use medical discussions to distance themselves from the leader as they bond closer to each other. This phenomenon has been observed in self-help groups such as Alcoholics Anonymous. In some ways, AIDS groups resemble self-help groups. All group members share the same grave illness, and emotional bonding is promoted by virtue of the fact that they share serious problems and similar symptoms. Identification plays an important role in facilitating cohesion between group members, but also creates an interesting schism in how the group leader is viewed by members.[4] Not only is the usual transference present about the leader as a powerful authority figure, the reality is that the leader generally is much healthier and stronger than group members. He or she is the only one present who is not facing a potential death sentence in the near future.

Focusing on the medical problems of AIDS is one way for group members to point out that the group leader is very different from the members and thus to distance the leader from the group. This pattern is seen when extensive medical discussion is followed by angry complaints such as, "You are not in the same boat as we are, how can you understand us?" It may at times be helpful to point out the elements of projective identification present when a group member is trying to make the leader feel like an unwanted, useless alien because this is the way he feels about himself. The members of AIDS groups tend to be people who have suffered self-hate and isolation, and have been in the role of social outcasts for many years. The best approach is to point out how they are projecting their own anger from their frustrated need to feel loved and accepted, and at the same time provide them with kindly support and understanding.

Self-help groups carry the overt or unspoken understanding that the members can support one another in ways that are more meaningful or more effective than those which have been offered them by traditional mental health or medical professionals.[4] Here the group leader is seen in a dual role, both as supporting the self-help aspects of the group (particularly in encouraging group members' attempts at helping one another) and fostering more independent and assertive behavior among group members, and also as a representative of a traditional mental health or medical discipline.

The dynamics of the AIDS group, which involve both increased dependence and reliance on the physically healthy leader, but also suspicion and anger at the leader because he, unlike the members, is not ill and is also seen as an authority figure (and representative of the medical establishment), can set the groundwork for volatile expressions of anger. The intense, ambivalent feelings of group members toward authority figures then surface. This is an important time for exploring problems with trust, and feelings of being rejected, judged, and criticized.

In addition, the AIDS group, like other self-help groups, can be seen by its members as possessing characteristics of its own to which magical qualities of healing may be attributed. For some members there is an unconscious fantasy that as long as they continue to attend the group, they will not die. Group members may begin to express anger and frustration as other members die or get sick, and their wish to see the group as a magical protective force is not realized. Anger may be directed at the group leader as an impotent, ineffectual parent, as childhood memories of disillusionment with the fantasized omnipotent parent are rekindled in the group setting.

Not only is the therapist seen as an outsider, belonging to the traditional mental health or medical establishment, but the institution in which the group is sponsored is also suspect. Members of AIDS groups, who are usually homosexuals or drug addicts, generally see themselves as being outside of the mainstream of society. In her article about the support group for AIDS patients being held at the NIH, Deborah Newmark wrote, "The homosexual population, as a minority group, strained to assimilate into what they perceived as a 'straight' institution," the NIH.[5] This sort of transference to the institution sponsoring the group (as an intolerant authority figure) was less prevalent for groups held at the GMHC, a nonprofit community organization located in the Greenwich Village area of New York City.

Still and all, the point needs to be stressed that group therapy for persons with AIDS is a successful treatment modality in a variety of treatment settings, and with a variety of group compositions. Half of the groups discussed here consisted entirely of members who had AIDS while the other half also included persons with ARC and family members of persons with AIDS or ARC. Both types of groups were well attended and were seen as an important source of support and personal growth by their members.

Groups which included heterosexual members, such as those held at Walter Reed Hospital, reported the emergence of certain specific issues which did not occur in the homosexual groups. The female spouses of male group members with AIDS or ARC were concerned about pregnancy. A wife of a group member who was pregnant asked to attend the group. The couple sought help from the group in their struggle to decide whether to seek an abortion or risk having a child infected with the AIDS virus. The group was very sympathetic to them.

In addition, there was a different focus for groups consisting mostly of inpatients as compared to outpatient groups. For hospitalized AIDS patients, the frequently voiced concern was, "Am I ever going to get well enough to go home?" AIDS outpatients asked, "Is there anything we can do to help ourselves to stay out of the hospital?," and feared a recurrence of a serious infection.

There was a wide variety of arrangements for group leaders or facilitators, including have one male leader, one female leader, or two coleaders (either two females, two males, or one male and one female). Most group leaders interviewed seemed to prefer working with a coleader both for personal and for therapeutic reasons. Having two leaders with different personalities and styles encouraged a wider array of transferences and responses by group members and was felt by some to make for a more well-founded and therapeutically in-depth group. Cotherapists of AIDS groups expressed a great deal of appreciation for the support and assistance available by having another group leader present. This arrangement was also said to reduce staff burnout. Coleaders stated that by running the group together and discussing it fully afterward, they learned a great deal from each other, and experienced a stronger sense of personal and professional growth.

Staff burnout is a major problem for health care providers working with patients with AIDS. Dr Bertram Schaffner, a psychoanalyst on the faculty of the William Alanson White Psychoanalytic Institute in New York, wrote about the benefits of small support groups for physicians dealing with the stress of treating large numbers of patients with AIDS.[6] In the process of sharing their feelings and experiences in the group, physicians were able to gain considerable relief from realizing that other physicians also share their sense of uneasiness in treating AIDS patients, and their sense of isolation and personal failure.

This is especially important for doctors who work in separate individual practices. In the midst of a small sympathetic group of peers, doctors were able to ventilate their frustrations when working with angry or overly demanding AIDS patients and work through their feelings of guilt over neither being able to give enough to their patients nor to keep them from dying. Dr Schaffner writes that "support groups may also be used to guard members from overinvolvement professionally in a patient's welfare"[6] and help physicians achieve a better balance among caring for their patients, taking care of their own emotional well-being, and their needs to have time to be with their own families. He says that these support groups may be structured or unstructured, and run with or without a leader, but generally meet at regular intervals. He recommends that the support group be small, consisting of about four members. In addition, he writes "that an essential requirement is the strictest observance of confidentiality." Dr Schafner feels that it is important "to make sure that doctors feeling special needs for help indicate their needs clearly at the beginning of the session, to make sure that they are not left stranded and their problems undealt with at the end of the session."[6]

Bereavement issues not only affect the family and loved ones of PWAs, they are often major sources of sadness and loneliness for AIDS group members themselves. Most of the members of the AIDS groups studied had already lost close friends or lovers due to AIDS. Many were still in the process of mourning this loss at the time when they themselves were diagnosed as having AIDS. Many of the group members had already spent long periods as the caretaker for a loved one dying of AIDS. At the GMHC group, when one of the group members became very sick and weak, another group member sadly reminisced about having seen his own lover deteriorate in the same way. Thus the increasing debilitation or mental impairment of a group member not only threatens other group members who fear becoming sicker, but can trigger painful memories of loss of loved ones who died within the last year or two from AIDS.

One of the most unique aspects of AIDS groups, which sets them apart from other kinds of groups for those with life-threatening illnesses, is the fact that most of the group members are in mourning. The AIDS epidemic has had a profound effect on the gay community in New York and other major cities. This is evidenced by major changes in the sexual and social behavior of homosexual men. The grief and painful losses are now widespread and are poignantly expressed in plays, literary works (As Is,[7] The Normal Heart,[8] etc), newspapers, and artistic expressions emanating from this community. It is a community under siege, and painfully aware of this. Hence the members of AIDS groups mourn not only their own loss of health, but the recent losses of cherished friends.

"Survivor guilt" is a special issue that has been noted to arise in groups for people with AIDS. At the GMHC group members wondered, "Why am I still alive when so many of my friends have died?" The guilt felt by some of the members after one group member died paralleled the guilt they felt outside of group when they outlived their friends or lovers. In the author's experience, people with AIDS who have strong identifications or bonds with loved ones who have died of this illness often feel that they too will soon follow.

Loss of a loved one to AIDS is a deeply felt tragedy that can have profound consequences in one's life. Earlier this year, I, like thousands of others, experienced a major loss with the death of my closest friend, a brilliant young psychiatrist, with AIDS. Despite the fact that I have worked extensively with patients with AIDS for 7 years, it was not until I experienced a major personal loss that I was moved to write about this topic. The fact that my friend was a great advocate of, and enthusiastic participant in, group psychotherapy, has inspired me greatly in writing this chapter.

One of the patients in the GMHC group asked the leaders, "Why would anybody want to work with patients with AIDS?" Many mental health professionals like myself became more active in this field after experiencing their own personal losses of loved ones. Bereavement issues can be an important factor in one's decision to be a leader or facilitator of an AIDS group. One of the therapists interviewed at the GMHC said that part of his motivation to be a coleader of an AIDS group was to help him work through issues related to the loss of his own father. Other therapists made a decision to lead an AIDS group after they themselves lost close friends or lovers due to AIDS.

The tragic and fatal nature of this illness has necessitated the formation of support groups, not only for patients and health care providers but also for families and loved ones of PWAs. At the How-ard Brown Memorial Clinic, a clinic established by Chicago's gay community and involved in research in collaboration with Northwest-ern University School of Medicine, a number of different types of support groups have been started.[9] These include: (1) family support groups — for parents and siblings of PWAs. These groups consist of four to ten members, and are led by mental health professionals and mothers of PWAs, and meet twice a month; (2) "significant other" support groups — for lovers and spouses of PWAs. These groups meet for two hours weekly and are led by mental health professionals and trained peer leaders; and (3) "moving-on groups" — bereavement groups for those who have spent long periods (often between 18 months to 2 years) caring for loved ones with AIDS and now must cope with the death of the loved one. This group meets for two hours weekly.

The GMHC also sponsors these types of groups along with several other group programs. These include: (1) support groups for parents of persons with AIDS. There is one group for parents of babies and children with AIDS and another group for parents of adult PWAs. The group for parents of pediatric AIDS patients have generally been attended mostly by mothers with very few fathers participating. The parents of the adult PWAs group, which includes parents of gay men, hemophiliacs, and drug abusers, has been attended regularly by an even number of mothers and fathers; (2) a walk-in bereavement group for loved ones of PWAs; (3) a couples group consisting of eight people (four PWAs with their lovers or spouses) which meets weekly for 1½ hours per week; (4) a group specifically for PWAs who are IV drug users; and (5) two types of walk-in groups which are designed to meet the needs for support and crisis intervention for all those on the waiting list for a group program. One type of walk-in group is for PWAs; the other is for the care partners of PWAs. All persons on the waiting list for group treatment at GMHC are contacted at least once a week and invited to attend one of the walk-in groups. According to Wein, the coordinator of group services, GHMC has the largest group therapy program for AIDS in the world. There are currently about 450 people enrolled in the 42 groups being held at the GMHC, with a staff of 60 or more group leaders and facilitators.

There are also informed "drop-in" groups available for patients with ARC and AIDS sponsored by the People with AIDS Coalition in New York City. They operate a drop-in lounge called the "Living Room" where PWAs can meet and socialize with one another, and be served a light dinner. It is kept open from 1 PM to 6 PM. The GMHC offers recreational group activities for PWAs with groups for massage, knitting, films, and stress reduction. These informal groups provide a very valuable option for PWAs who wish to enjoy the support and companionship of being in a group of peers, yet are not comfortable in a more structured or psychotherapeutically oriented setting. Some patients are apprehensive about committing themselves to attending a regularly scheduled group because they may often feel too weak and ill to get to the meetings. Drop-in groups can provide an ideal alternative for these patients.

It is important to note that there are many PWAs who show great courage and dedication in striving to attend group therapy in the face of increasing weakness, confusion, and poverty. Ms Santorelli related an incident which occurred when a group at GMHC attempted to change the scheduled day for group from Saturday to a weekday evening. One of the group members protested vehemently. When asked why, he explained that he was no longer capable of remembering a change in day and hour, nor could he negotiate his way through a train station filled with rush-hour crowds without getting confused and lost. He would be too weak and slowed down to keep pace with the crowds. It was at that point that it really became clear that just getting himself to group was truly a heroic endeavor for this PWA. His mental and physical state was so fragile that he would be incapable of adjusting to any change in the group's schedule or routine. The courage and fortitude which this group member showed as he struggled to fight off his exhaustion and disorientation in order to continue attending group regularly was an inspiration to all.

In summarizing this chapter, it is important to note that group therapy is an extremely valuable treatment modality for people with AIDS and can be quite successful in a variety of settings. New groups are forming every day. Some groups consist totally of PWAs, while others are more heterogeneous and include people with ARC, spouses, or people with other diseases such as cancer. In all cases the groups were well attended and were found to be a valuable source of support for those coping with AIDS. Despite the many differences in the settings, compositions, and group leaders among the groups discussed in this chapter, there were certain features which they had in common. The group leaders whom I spoke with were all very sensitive to the fact that group members were turning to the group to provide a sense of continuity and shelter in the face of major turmoil and changes in their lives. This sense of continuity was fostered by keeping the same leaders or facilitators for as long as possible, keeping in touch with members when they were unable to attend groups, and letting the members know when there were deaths or illnesses in the group.

PWAs who attended the group at GMHC spoke about how important it was to them to be treated as people, both by the group leaders and by their peers. In joining the group, their identity as an "AIDS patient" was substituted with being a group member and a "real human being." This made for a much healthier self-image. Early in the course of the group, the damaged self-images of the members became apparent when they asked the group leaders, "Why would anyone want to work with people with AIDS?" In the months following, the group was able to build a strong sense of cohesiveness and acceptance. Gradually, there developed an atmosphere where members could feel free to discuss their feelings of inadequacy and social rejection and seek help from the group. Many of the members had been through very difficult times, struggling to survive near fatal infections and life-threatening pneumonias, before joining the group. One member had been so depressed he had taken an overdose in a suicide attempt. With the help of the group, there were no further suicidal behaviors.

In addition, four of the members began an experimental drug treatment program (AZT, and ribavirin) in an attempt to increase their life span. After they were feeling physically stronger, they turned to the group for support in their efforts to rebuild their lives. In the past few months three of the group members have begun dating again with other PWAs, and one group member was able to return to work.

Group leaders of AIDS groups reported that what their groups focused on was not issues of death and dying but rather on how to make the most of living. Now, with the advent of new treatments which may be able to extend life for some people with AIDS and help them to be more active and stronger, there is even more reason for looking toward life instead of death. The medical changes that occur in the treatment of AIDS will continue to have a major impact on group therapy for PWAs. This is the first period in which groups may have members who appear to be regaining their strength instead of getting sicker. Now, for the first time, PWAs have role models within their groups who are returning to work or starting to date again. We are on the cutting edge of major changes in the treatment of AIDS, and in the vast psychosocial impact that will result from this. The role of group therapy is being broadened as group members seek help not only in coming to terms with a grave illness but also in their attempts to rebuild their lives and find a place for themselves in the community. The strength and confidence provided in the supportive atmosphere of the AIDS group can help empower members in their quest for fuller lives. Perhaps the most powerful therapeutic benefit is in providing PWAs — people who have been struck down in the prime of life and scorned by the world — with a setting where they can truly feel accepted and valued.

Acknowledgments

The author acknowledges the assistance of Col Robert Gemmill at Walter Reed Army Hospital, Washington, DC; Virginia Lehman, Sylvia

9

Group Approaches to the
Diagnosis and Treatment
of the Premenstrual Syndromes

Leslie Hartley Gise

Group approaches offer many advantages in the diagnosis and treatment of the premenstrual syndromes (PMS). They help with compliance, which is needed to make a diagnosis of a premenstrual syndrome. They foster the study of the natural history of the premenstrual syndromes, which is needed before meaningful treatment studies can be done. They offer effective treatment, which is also economical. Since PMS patients are not psychotherapy patients, but are more psychologically minded than medical patients, the PMS group is a medical group largely involved with psychological issues.

GROUPS AND MEDICAL ILLNESS

The application of group process to medical illness represents an integration of two helping disciplines, medical care and psychotherapy.[1] In modern psychiatry this started with Pratt[2] in 1907 who treated tuberculosis patients with a group approach that stressed education, suppression of worrisome thoughts, and encouragement to go on. Group methods have subsequently been used to treat patients with a wide variety of conditions such as hypertension,[3] myocardial infarction,[4,5] parkinsonism,[6] multiple sclerosis,[7] asthma,[8] irritable bowel syndrome,[9] chronic lung disease,[10] metastatic cancer,[11] posttransplant,[12] ileostomy,[13] and terminal illness.[14]

Most groups of medical patients are homogeneous and short-term

(20 sessions or fewer). They generally stress education and support. The sessions are often described as having a clublike atmosphere with members working to help one another solve problems of daily life, particularly in relation to the condition that brought them to the group. At times, the group develops a classroom atmosphere with the leader lecturing on the condition, the treatment, and compliance. On rare occasions groups of medical patients are reported to function as a psychodynamic group.

Medical patients are often described as rigid, symptom-oriented, and unable to experience and express negative feelings, particularly aggression.[15] In therapy they may present as aloof and detached, typically avoid painful events, and have little ability or motivation for self-examination.[16]

There has been a paucity of work on groups of medical patients in the general hospital. These kinds of groups typically have limited goals.[17] They are characterized by a broad standard of inclusion in membership, brief length (ranging upward from one session), and great turnover. The goal is to build self-esteem, re-enforce ego strength, and reduce anxiety and regression for immediate (rather than long-range) improvement. Benefits of these groups are reported to include improved morale and capacity for self-care, assertiveness, and relief from depression and anxiety, as well as alleviation of physical symptoms or distress. Groups have included relatives of patients, waiting room groups, etc. Some groups have combined inpatients and outpatients with the same illness.

In terms of the expectations of the group, medical groups have been found to be more similar to women's consciousness-raising groups[18] than to psychotherapy groups. This may be because members of both medical groups and consciousness-raising groups report feeling different and distressed by their isolation[19] and because both types of groups are based on the assumption that external factors rather than intrapsychic dynamics play a major role in their difficulties. In the medical groups it is the physical condition; in the women's groups it is sexism in the environment.[20]

Most studies of group therapy with medical patients have been uncontrolled. Rahe et al[21] conducted a controlled study of postmyocardial infarction patients, and reported that brief group therapy reduced morbidity and mortality and increased the likelihood that patients would return to work. In both the experimental and the control groups life-style was the same and the educational information was forgotten. Life-style included such factors as diet (as reflected by weight and serum cholesterol) and smoking. Group therapy patients did, however, change their coronary-prone behavior (overwork, time urgency). Rahe et al concluded that it was the supportive aspects of the group therapy experience which played the most important role in the positive outcome.[21]

Another study of postmyocardial infarction patients was done by Stern et al[22] who used group counseling and exercise. These patients had so many unanswered questions about their illness and treatment that unstructured sessions resulted in lack of continuity and reversion to a dependent group with the members asking the leader questions about the illness. This led Stern et al to structure the initial sessions with education and behavioral treatment, leaving only the later sessions unstructured. Among the factors which he identified as valued by medical patients in short-term groups were advice and guidance, and learning how life style plays a role in their condition.

Wise et al[9] treated patients with irritable bowel syndrome with a method described by Buchanan[23] where each session started with a lecture that was followed by a psychologically oriented discussion period. Daily diaries were kept and discussed at each meeting, relaxation techniques were taught, and the need for behavioral modification (ie, diet) was continuously emphasized. A shift from a more external locus of control to a more internal one was reported. They actively addressed the tendency of medical patients to dichotomize their illness by separating organic factors from emotional components, an "uncoupling" of somatic symptoms from the emotional dimensions. Finally, they reported a significant reduction in dysphoric emotion despite the persistence of somatic complaints.[9]

GROUPS AND THE PREMENSTRUAL SYNDROMES

Very little has been written about the role of groups in the evaluation and treatment of the premenstrual syndromes. Walton and Youngkin[24] conducted a controlled study of the effect of a support group on the self-esteem of women with PMS and found no difference between the support group and the control group after 8 weeks. Taylor and Bledsoe[25] reported a pilot study of peer support, PMS, and stress from which they concluded that the group served to educate, to help adherence to difficult treatment regimens, and to indirectly reduce the severity of premenstrual symptoms.

Groups have many advantages in the evaluation and treatment of the premenstrual syndromes. First, they are relevant to the issues of compliance and diagnosis in this particular psychobiological problem. Second, they relate to the problem of heterogeneity in the premenstrual syndromes and facilitate a research strategy which takes this into consideration. Third, they are therapeutic. They foster peer support, offer an opportunity to blend medical and psychological treatment, and are economically efficient.

Diagnosis and Compliance

Diagnosis The diagnosis of a premenstrual syndrome is made on the basis of 2 months of daily prospective record-keeping. This requires motivation and compliance. Weekly group follow-up sessions foster compliance with daily record-keeping. The sessions are useful to make sure that the women understand precisely how they are meant to complete the daily ratings and they also foster the development of a good therapeutic alliance which is associated with increased patient compliance. The diagnosis of a premenstrual syndrome rests not on the presence of specific symptoms, but rather on the temporal association between symptoms and the luteal phase of the menstrual cycle.

The menstrual cycle By convention, the first day of bleeding is defined as the first day of the cycle. The first 14 days or so are called the follicular phase because the follicle is developing in the ovary prior to ovulation. Ovulation occurs on about day 14. The second half of the cycle (about 14 days) is called the luteal phase because, if pregnancy does not occur, the follicle degenerates into a corpus luteum. The premenstrual cycle phase is essentially the second half of the luteal phase or the week prior to menstruation. At the Premenstrual Syndromes Program at the Mount Sinai Medical Center in New York City a late luteal phase (day 21–25) serum progesterone level is done as a screening test to confirm ovulation.

Definition A premenstrual syndrome can be defined as "the cyclic occurrence of (at least 5) symptoms that are of sufficient severity to interfere with some aspects of life and which appear with consistent and predictable relationship to menses."[26] National Institutes of Mental Health (NIMH) guidelines further specify (1) a marked change of about 30% in the intensity of symptoms measured intermenstrually (from days 5–10) as compared to that premenstrually (within six days prior to menstruation), and (2) prospective documentation of these changes for at least two consecutive cycles. Essentially this means that the week before the period is quite different from the week after the period. NIMH guidelines are similar to the *Diagnostic and Statistical Manual of Mental Disorders* (DSM III-R) criteria[27] which further specify that one of the symptoms must be a mood symptom (mood swings, irritability, anxiety, or depression). Since almost all women with significant premenstrual changes have at least one mood symptom, NIMH guidelines are essentially consistent with DSM III-R criteria.

Time course Premenstrual symptoms typically start some time after ovulation and are most pronounced during the week before menstruation. Women typically look forward to getting their period because they know that within a day or two they will feel dramatically better. After menstruation, there is a symptom-free interval of at least 1 week. The duration of premenstrual symptoms may be from one day to the entire length of the luteal phase (about 14 days).

Diagnostic process There are over 150 different symptoms of PMS and these symptoms also occur in other conditions. That is, there is nothing specific about the symptoms of PMS. It is the timing, not the symptoms themselves, which is diagnostic. This means that the diagnosis of PMS is not made in the usual medical-psychiatric tradition, which is cross-sectional. The usual medical diagnostic procedure consists of taking a history, performing an examination, ordering appropriate laboratory tests, and making a diagnosis. This does not work for PMS. This traditional retrospective diagnosis greatly overdiagnoses PMS. To make a diagnosis of PMS at least 2 months of daily prospective record-keeping is required. Not only with PMS, but with other disorders as well, monitoring over time is required. For example, to diagnose some cardiac arrhythmias, a Holter monitor is necessary. For PMS the Daily Rating Form (DRF) developed by Endicott[28] is widely used and presents distinct advantages over other daily symptom record forms. It takes into account the bipolarity of changes in appetite, sleep, energy level, and interest in sex, which may be either increased or decreased, similar to the situation in depression. The DRF also rates the severity of the symptoms and monitors positive changes as well as negative ones. Fifteen percent of women actually feel better before their periods with increased libido, increased energy (eg, cleaning out the closets), and some artists have reported increased creativity premenstrually.

Acceptability of group sessions While PMS has both physical and psychological aspects, many women seeking treatment for premenstrual symptoms are not psychologically minded and find group sessions more acceptable than one-on-one contact. This is true for patients with other physical disorders as well. Many women seeking treatment for premenstrual symptoms cannot tolerate the intimacy of individual sessions and become anxious at the thought of talking about themselves to an authority figure. In general, group therapy is acceptable to medical patients who are similar in some ways to chronic psychiatric patients for whom group therapy has been widely used. Medical patients and chronic psychiatric patients are both typically regressed, narcissistic, and dependent. They are also, at times, poorly motivated.

The group and compliance The group format may also foster compliance by diluting the intensity of negative feelings brought into the treatment situation from bad experiences with medical care in the past. Women seeking treatment for premenstrual symptoms frequently report that they have had negative experiences with physicians in the past. Data from the Multidimensional Health Locus of Control Scale[37] indicate that women seeking treatment for premenstrual symptoms believe their health to be controlled by external powerful others (ie, physicians) significantly less than norms.[30] These women report that neither their gynecologists nor their psychotherapists understand their premenstrual complaints. They say that gynecologists tell them it is all in their heads and they are reassured to have contact with health professionals who are informed about these syndromes and with other women suffering with premenstrual complaints who validate their experience.

The Problem of Heterogeneity and the Development of a Research Strategy

Because the premenstrual syndromes are a heterogeneous group of disorders, a better understanding of the natural history of these phenomena is necessary before meaningful treatment studies can be conducted. Lumping together different kinds of PMS may wash out a treatment effect and explain why studies to date have not been able to demonstrate any treatment to be more effective than placebo. For example, there may be a subgroup of women who respond to progesterone, but they cannot be identified without a therapeutic trial. The research strategy in the Premenstrual Syndromes Program at the Mount Sinai Medical Center is a descriptive, epidemiologic one which requires evaluation and follow-up of large numbers of patients. This is facilitated by the group format. The goal is to identify subgroups of patients which predict outcome. For example, which women will respond without medication, which women will respond to progesterone, antidepressants, lithium, etc. At present the treatment for PMS is hit-or-miss. There is no specific rationale for treating any particular subgroup with any particular treatment.

Therapeutic Considerations

There is evidence that groups of homogeneously grouped medical patients are effective in treating a variety of disorders.[21] Furthermore, there is evidence that contact with an informed, interested, empathic clinician, as well as filling out daily rating forms, is therapeutic for women seeking treatment for premenstrual syndromes.[31] The daily ratings seem to work like a biofeedback process. Knowing what the symptoms are, and when they occur enables women to develop control over them. Education, reassurance, and support are of primary importance. Women are relieved to learn that there is a physiologic basis for their symptoms. ("It's so reassuring to know that I'm not crazy.")

Women who rely solely on medication do not seem to do as well as those who actively change their life-style. Women learn to anticipate bad days, and they can modify their activities to minimize disability. Furthermore, families can be helped to become more tolerant. Physicians must acknowledge and treat premenstrual changes, an ongoing process of care coordinating medical, gynecologic, and psychological services including consideration of life-style and stress-related factors. Patients develop a sense of mastery and control over their symptoms which either relieves the symptoms or minimizes the degree to which they interfere with functioning or cause distress. All of these aspects are aided by the group format.

Women seeking treatment for premenstrual symptoms routinely report that they feel isolated, misunderstood, and discriminated against by their friends, family, and employers. They state that they feel supported and relieved by contact with others experiencing similar difficulties. In addition, they frequently report that gynecologists and psychotherapists have not understood or helped them. Because of its psychological nature, no one discipline has taken responsibility for the premenstrual syndromes. For all the reasons above, group emotional and social support are critical in the management of women seeking treatment for premenstrual symptoms. Group social support combats the tendency for self-absorption and gives people a feeling of community, a feeling that they are among others very much like themselves, who are successfully coping with their condition.[32]

Since, to date, the treatment of the premenstrual syndromes is more of an art than a science, that is, there are no good studies proving that any particular treatment is superior for any particular subgroup, women must be informed of possible risks and benefits of treatment. Furthermore, because life-style changes and stress reduction are central to the management of these conditions, women must be actively involved, creative and resourceful, support each other, and not rely on the physician to write a prescription or to solve their problems. Although PMS is a medical condition, the evaluation and treatment involve patient participation. In acute medical situations a traditional doctor-patient relationship, a parental/authoritarian model, applies. With chronic medical problems, patient participation is often required. Just as the diabetic patient must devote a substantial effort to self-care, PMS patients must also monitor themselves. Group approaches foster these concepts.

Finally, group contact provides the opportunity to blend medical with psychological and behavioral treatment and is an economically attractive treatment modality which makes efficient use of limited medical and paramedical staff.

THE PMS GROUP FOLLOW-UP SESSION

Setting, Procedure, Membership, and Leadership

The program starts with an individual, hour-long, intake interview with the psychiatrist during which information is obtained about premenstrual symptoms as well as about medical, gynecologic, and psychiatric history. Past records are requested and appropriate medical-gynecologic examinations and laboratory tests are done. If a women is in psychotherapy, her permission is requested for the psychiatrist to speak with her psychotherapist. If she is in active treatment with or has been referred by an internist or gynecologist, the program works with the treating physician. At the end of the initial session, the woman is asked to consider one aspect of her life-style which the psychiatrist judges most likely to change during the 8-week evaluation period during which she keeps daily ratings of her symptoms and attends weekly group follow-up sessions.

The Premenstrual Syndromes Program at the Mount Sinai Medical Center is conducted by psychiatrists working with a psychiatric nurse-clinician in outpatient areas of the Department of Obstetrics, Gynecology, and Reproductive Science. The same program is available for both private and clinic patients. The membership of the group fluctuates. Some women cannot attend every week and others continue to come after the 8 weeks is up for "maintenance." The psychiatric nurse-clinician coleader provides a different perspective and runs the group when the psychiatrist is not there.

The Group Session

The PMS group starts with the patients sharing informtion and stories in the waiting room. They fill out standardized rating scales of anxiety[33] and depression[34], as well as menstrual rating forms[28,35] which they bring into the session. Patients and the nurse are asked to introduce themselves if they have not met before. The women give their forms to the leader who notes where they are in their cycle and how they are doing. The leader answers any questions about exactly how the forms are meant to be filled out.

Women who are attending for the first time are asked how they found making daily ratings. The majority state that it is helpful because they find out exactly what their symptoms are and how they are correlated with their cycle. "Now I know what to expect and I can plan for it," is a frequent comment. Women are praised for keeping records and those who have difficulty keeping records are encouraged to do so. There is no formal didactic lecture or presentation. Women ask a variety of questions each week and the leader's responses are woven into the sharing of experiences and reports on life-style changes (eg, "What is the real story about vitamin B_6, Dr Gise?").

Rating Forms

The premenstrual assessment form Two menstrual rating forms are used. The first is the Premenstrual Assessment Form (PAF),[35] a 95-item, self-rated inventory of mood, behavior, and somatic symptoms which takes about five minutes to complete and is filled out on a monthly basis on the first day of the cycle. It compares the week before the period, or the premenstrual week, to the rest of the month. That is, it asks how much change there is between that week and the rest of the month. It is a retrospective, cross-sectional assessment which rates only the last month. It is used as a measure of severity to compare one month to the next.

The daily rating form The second premenstrual rating form is the Daily Rating Form (DRF)[28] which asks the women to rate 21 symptoms on a scale from 1 to 6 each day. Since recall is inaccurate, if they forget on a given day, they are asked to leave the ratings blank. The DRF allows women to write in three additional symptoms that are not on the list. Suicidal ideation, argument with spouse, change in voice for singers (presumably due to edema of the vocal cords), or change in coordination for professional athletes or dancers are examples of added items. In addition, the DRF allows women to note if something unusual happened which might have affected their physical or mental feelings or behaviors such as a car accident or a bad cold. Obviously things other than the menstrual cycle affect how a woman feels, and these comments allow the ratings to be corrected accordingly.

Other rating forms Standard rating scales of marital adjustment[36] and beliefs about health[37] are completed on the first visit, whereas ratings of anxiety[33] and depression[34] are completed weekly.

Evaluating the Daily Ratings

When a woman has completed one or two complete months of daily ratings, the leader notes whether she had premenstrual changes by the above criteria. Sometimes there are premenstrual changes but there are also symptoms at other times of the month. In these cases, the leader says, "Yes, you do seem to have premenstrual changes, but you

148

also have symptoms at other times of the month." Some have chronic psychiatric or other adjustment problems. Many have chronic un-treated depression for which they are reluctant to take medication. In the medical group context they are often eventually able to accept treatment. Other women have a primary marital problem or a sub-stance abuse problem and the premenstrual symptoms are secondary. It may take 6 to 12 months for them to accept help for their underlying problem and to acknowledge that the premenstrual exacerbation is just that and not a primary hormonal problem with a simple drug treat-ment. This is analogous to the situation with alcoholism, which can be either primary or secondary. For primary alcoholism, alcoholism treat-ment would be recommended. For alcoholism secondary to an under-lying depression, treatment for depression would be recommended. Premenstrual symptoms may also be primary or secodary. The symp-toms of primary PMS are limited to the premenstruum, whereas the symptoms of secondary PMS occur all month with a premenstrual exacerbation.

> Miss M, a 30-year-old successful entrepreneur and businesswoman, left the program after 2 months and enrolled herself in an intensive drug rehabilitation pogram for her chronic marijuana abuse problem. She returned after 6 months and continued to report severe premenstrual mood swings. Although she did not meet criteria for major depression, she had a strong family history of bipolar illness and severe fluid reten-tion symptoms ("My hands swell so much, I have to take off my rings when I am premenstrual."). She was started on lithium and the mood swings disappeared although her chronic difficulties with relationships continued. Her social life was characterized by chaotic, turbulent affairs with unavailable men. After 6 more months she started psychotherapy and a year later she had her first meaningful, committed relationship. She continues to have premenstrual depression and irritability, but they are mild and do not interfere with her functioning.

This patient had secondary PMS. She had chronic adjustment prob-lems including substance abuse. The premenstrual component was essentially eliminated in the program with support and lithium for her probable subsyndromal major affective disorder. In addition, she may belong to a subgroup of PMS patients with a strong family history of mental illness and marked fluid retention symptoms who respond to lithium. The group approach permits the identification of such pat-terns. Recent evidence has linked premenstrual depression to seasonal depression. The group format facilitates documentation of seasonal changes and several patients have reported seasonal depression.

Prospectively Confirmed Premenstrual Syndromes

Eight out of ten women seeking treatment for premenstrual symptoms do not have a premenstrual syndrome confirmed by their own daily ratings[30] (J. Endicott, personal communication, April 1988). "I never knew I felt like this the week *after* my period," is a typical comment. Women do not deliberately lie, but looking back they remember the bad times as being premenstrual. This distorted attribution is critical in evaluating the literature on premenstrual syndromes. Most studies of PMS use samples of women "diagnosed" on the basis of retrospective ratings which grossly overestimate the incidence of PMS. Research studies[35] typically screen 100 women to find each subject between 18 and 45 years of age, with regular periods, not on medication, and without significant medical, gynecologic, or psychiatric problems. The Mount Sinai Premenstrual Syndromes Program is studying the larger group of women who are seeking treatment for premenstrual symptoms. Something is wrong with these women but it is not yet entirely clear what it is.

Of the 20% of women who have a prospectively confirmed premenstrual syndrome, 80% are sufficiently improved by the end of the 2-month evaluation period that symptoms no longer disrupt their lives. So after 2 months only 5% of the total group have significant symptoms.

Life-Style Changes

Women are asked to think about one aspect of their life-style such as diet,[39] exercise,[40] nicotine,[41] alcohol,[42] caffeine,[38] or stress[43–46] that has been associated with premenstrual symptoms. For example, if a woman is complaining of irritability and drinks 12 cups of coffee a day, she may be asked to think about her caffeine intake. If she is irritable and has been smoking 2½ packs of cigarettes a day since she was 16 years old, she may be assessed as unlikely to modify this behavior and stopping smoking would not be suggested.

Women are often asked to think about exercise. Women who have never exercised are often able to start walking for 20 minutes a day. For women who have abandoned a regular aerobic exercise program, calling their attention to this change often provides sufficient incentive for them to resume. In fact, a recent controlled study found that regular aerobic exercise reduced premenstrual symptoms.[40] A possible mechanism is changes in central beta-endorphin levels which affect mood. There are estrogen and progesterone receptors in the brain that are affected by central beta-endorphin levels.

Some women's life-styles seem under control. They do not binge on junk food premenstrually, do not use caffeine, alcohol, or nicotine, and maintain a regular aerobic exercise program. If they have an obvious source of stress in their lives, they are asked to think about it. Since 84% of women seeking treatment for premenstrual symptoms were found to have been in psychotherapy in the past,[30] they are often able to make use of previously gained self-knowledge and work on problems on their own. Others chose to start or resume psychotherapy.

When a woman decides to attend a premenstrual syndromes program, she is frequently at a point in her life when she is ready to make changes. Whereas medical patients whose doctors tell them to change their life-style often do not do so, women seeking treatment for premenstrual symptoms show remarkable ability to make these changes. Since recommendations about life-style are frequently reviewed in the media, women often take it upon themselves to make changes regardless of whether they were suggested by the physician.

> Mrs X, who had been smoking two packs a day for 20 years, and complained of irritability which got worse premenstrually, came to her first follow-up session and announced that she had stopped smoking. Because she had been smoking for so long, she had been judged by the psychiatrist to be unlikely to change this behavior, she had not been asked to think about her smoking. Needless to say she received a great deal of support from the group and continued to maintain her behavior change.

Psychological Aspects

The relationship to psychotherapy Some patients are in psychotherapy when they enter the program. Since the PMS group is not a formal psychotherapy group, it is viewed as an asset for women to be in concurrent psychotherapy. In addition, the changing membership of the group also makes depth psychotherapeutic interaction difficult. Since the majority of women seeking treatment for premenstrual symptoms at our program have been in psychotherapy in the past, they are frequently able to work on their problems on their own with the group functioning as a trigger or catalyst and the bulk of the psychological work happening outside the session. Premenstrual symptoms also can function as a resistance to psychotherapy which is worked through in the program resulting in a woman either starting or resuming psychotherapy.

Significance of premenstrual symptoms The role of premenstrual symptoms differs for different women. Some get angry and irritable premenstrually and are able to complain about things that bother them but which they suppress during the rest of the month. These women need to learn that premenstrual feelings are a window into an important part of themselves which must be attended to. These are often women with marital problems or stress-related problems which they "put up with" and "cope with" all month, but which become overwhelming premenstrually.

A 30-year-old, attractive, married, flight attendant and mother of two small children lost control and smashed her dinner plate upside down when she was premenstrual. She flew for a major airline full time, had no regular help at home, and moved frequently due to the career of her successful, executive, workaholic husband. She described a recent move when she closed on a house while she was in labor while her husband was away on a business trip. She was a compulsive housekeeper ("I never run out of milk and am never late to a PTA meeting"). Her loss of control was so foreign and distressing to her that she ran to her room and felt suicidal. It turned out that during the past few months her in-laws had been living with her and there had been major disruptive construction in her home as well. When it was suggested that she was carrying a heavy load, she said, "Do you think so? That's what I needed to hear. Maybe you are right." This woman believed, for whatever reason, that she alone was responsible for running her household. During the month after the intake interview, she asked her husband to help with some of the household responsibilities ("I just told him I needed him to make some telephone calls about the new house") and she got regular full-time live-in help. She did not come back to the program but when contacted 1 and 6 months later, she continued well, without premenstrual problems.

The woman in the example above suppressed important feelings which built up and got out of control premenstrually. Other women are too expressive of their feelings all month and when they get even more activated premenstrually, they get into trouble, saying things they regret later or causing disruption in their lives.

Miss M, a 30-year-old, single, successful businesswoman, was the youngest of five children in an enmeshed Italian family. Her parents died when she was a teenager and the siblings functioned as parents to one another. The patient blew up at her siblings when she was premenstrual and was viewed as irrational and out of control. Despite her financial success and support of her older sister, the family did not take her seriously because of her outbursts. Previous treatment with vitamin B_6, diuretics, progesterone, and psychotherapy had not helped. She continued psychotherapy while attending the Premenstrual Syndromes Program where her premenstrual symptoms were validated and she learned to modify her diet and to exercise. Miss M learned to stay in control, take more appropriate action to resolve the hateful dependency on her siblings, and separate in a more effective way. She finally had to ask her disapproving and interfering older sister to move out of her house. On entering the Premenstrual Syndromes Program, the patient had 31 severe or extreme symptoms on the PAF. Following treatment, asthma remained her only premenstrual symptom.

The problem of too little or too much feeling in PMS patients is similar to the situation with psychotherapy patients in general. Some patients do not have access to their feelings and must be helped to be more expressive. Other patients have feelings which are too strong and threaten to get out of control. These patients need to learn to identify potentially explosive situations, to control their outbursts, and to learn constructive ways to deal with things they do not like in their lives.

Linking psychosocial problems and reproductive function Women seeking treatment for premenstrual symptoms often have problems with relationships and jobs, just as women seeking psychotherapy do, but they blame their problems on PMS. In the program they learn that their problems precipitate or trigger premenstrual symptoms. They often link their marital and reproductive status to their symptoms and feel that they are single or have marital problems because of PMS. Women of different marital status' can complement and help one another.

> In one meeting, Mrs K, a married, lower-middle-class, Italian woman was complaining about the lavish Christmas presents her children received from her single, wealthier siblings. She felt humiliated since she was unable to reciprocate. The other group members were all single. They shared with her their joy in buying expensive presents for their nieces and nephews, recreating in fantasy their own childhood and indulging in the fantasy that they had children of their own. They spoke of what a treat it was to play that role. The married woman was shocked. She had never thought of it that way. Instead of being angry, she could see that her children were allowing her single siblings to indulge their fantasies and celebrate Christmas as part of a family.

Somatization What is the relation of premenstrual changes to somatization? Women present with the complaint, "Doctor, it's my hormones." This is similar to patients who present with other somatic complaints. But the typical hypochondriacal or somaticizing patient continues to talk only about somatic symptoms and resists talking about feelings. PMS patients, on the other hand, are much more easily educated and become willing to talk about their lives and feelings. Initially, they are not happy to find that they are talking to a psychiatrist, albeit in a gynecology suite. Nevertheless, they rapidly learn to connect their symptoms to the stresses in their lives.

DISCUSSION AND CONCLUSION

Group process has been helpful in approaching a variety of medical problems including the premenstrual syndromes. Significant factors include support, reassurance, validation, education, behavioral change, and learning how psychological factors play a role in producing symptoms. For the premenstrual syndromes groups are relevant to: (1) the problem of compliance with daily record-keeping and diagnosis, (2) the problem of heterogeneity of the premenstrual syndromes and the development of an appropriate research strategy, and (3) therapeutic considerations including cost-effectiveness. Most women seeking treatment for premenstrual symptoms get better when they have contact with an informed, interested, empathic clinician. Completing daily ratings is also therapeutic. Women learn exactly what their symptoms are and how they are correlated with their cycle. This seems to work like biofeedback in that the self-knowledge and awareness per se is associated with an ability to control the process.

Although controlled studies[21] have demonstrated the therapeutic effect of groups on a wide variety of medical illnesses and concluded that it was the supportive aspects of the group experience which played the most important role in the positive outcome, very little has been written about the role of groups in the evaluation and treatment of the premenstrual syndromes.

Women seeking treatment for premenstrual symptoms are often more easily educable regarding psychological issues than are typical medical patients described in the literature. Furthermore, they are striking in their ability to change their behavior and life-style. Finally, they have often had psychotherapy in the past and are able to continue to work on themselves to anticipate and control their symptoms. Initially these women do not think their problems are psychological or behavioral, but in the context of a program which provides group support, empathy, and education, they are able to work psychologically and behaviorally to alleviate their symptoms. For women who do not believe their symptoms to be related to their feelings, group sessions are often more acceptable than one-on-one contact. Aspects of group functioning that appear to be most useful with medical patients in general and PMS patients in particular include education, promotion of self-understanding, and encouraging the learning of new positively oriented behaviors as opposed to catharsis and interpersonal confrontation, which may be more beneficial in psychotherapy groups. Since most gynecologists and psychotherapists are not well-informed about the premenstrual syndromes, many patients feel misunderstood and have had negative experiences seeking help in the past. Validation and support in the group are critical in this regard.

Group process has an important role to play in the evaluation and treatment of women seeking treatment for premenstrual symptoms. A process of ongoing care emphasizing compliance and sophisticated diagnosis is fostered by the group. The group approach helps a research strategy which seeks to pursue the natural history of the premenstrual syndromes which is still poorly understood. Finally, groups are therapeutic for women seeking treatment for premenstrual symptoms and offer an economically efficient approach to these problems.

REFERENCES

1. Teplin E: Humanism in action: Hospital groups. *Contemp Psychiatry* 1984;3:44–47.
2. Pratt JH: Treatment of tuberculosis by class method. *JAMA* 1907;49:755–759.

3. Titchener JS, Sheldon MB, Ross, WD: Changes in blood pressure of hypertensive patients with and without group therapy. *J Psychosom Res* 1959;4:10–13.
4. Ibrahim MS, Feldman JG, Sultz HA, et al: Management after myocardial infarction: A controlled trial of the effect of group psychotherapy. *Int J Psychiatry Med* 1974;5:253–268.
5. Rahe RH, O'Neil T, Hagen A, et al: Brief group psychotherapy following myocardial infarction: Eighteen month follow-up of a controlled trial. *Int J Psychiatry Med* 1975;6:349–358.
6. Chafetz ME, Bernstein N, Sharpe W, et al: Short term group therapy of patients with Parkinson's disease. *N Engl J Med* 1955;253:961–964.
7. Hartings MF, Pavlov M, Davis F: Group counseling of multiple sclerosis patients in a program of comprehensive care. *J Chron Dis* 1976;29:65–73.
8. Groen JJ, Pelser HE: Experiences with and results of group psychotherapy in patients with bronchial asthma. *J Psychosom Res* 1960;4:191–205.
9. Wise TN, Cooper JN, Ahmed S: The efficacy of group therapy for patients with irritable bowel syndrome. *Psychosomatics* 1982;23:465–469.
10. Pattison EM, Rhodes RJ, Dudley DL: Responses to group treatment in patients with severe chronic lung disease. *Int J Group Psychother* 1971; 21:214–225.
11. Spiegel D, Bloom J, Yalom I: Group support for patients with metastatic cancer. *Arch Gen Psychiatry* 1981;38:527–533.
12. Buchanan DC: Group therapy for kidney transplant patients. *Int J Psychiatry Med* 1975;6:523–530.
13. Lennenberg E: QT in Boston — ileostomy group. *N Engl J Med* 1954; 251:1008–1010.
14. Yalom ID, Greaves C: Group therapy with the terminally ill. *Am J Psychiatry* 1977;134:396–400.
15. Reckless J, Fauntleroy A: Groups, spouses and hospitalization as a trial of treatment in psychosomatic illness. *Psychosomatics* 1972;13:353–357.
16. Karasu TB: Psychotherapy of the medically ill. *Am J Psychiatry* 1979; 136:1–11.
17. Lonergan EC: *Group Intervention — How to Begin and Maintain Groups in Medical and Psychiatric Settings*. New York, Jason Aronson, 1983.
18. Lieberman MA: Problems in integrating traditional group therapies with new group forms. *Int J Group Psychother* 1977;27:19–22.
19. Bird C: *Born Female: The High Cost of Keeping Women Down*. New York, McKay, 1968.
20. Brodsky AM: The consciousness-raising group as a model for therapy with women. *Psychother Theory Res Pract* 1973;10:24–29.
21. Rahe RH, Ward HW, Hayes V: Brief group therapy in myocardial infarction rehabilitation: Three- to four-year follow-up of a controlled trial. *Psychosom Med* 1979;41:229–242.
22. Stern MJ, Plionis E, Kaslow L: Group process expectations and outcome with post-myocardial infarction patients. *Gen Hosp Psychiatry* 1984;6: 101–108.
23. Buchanan DC: Group therapy for chronic physically ill patients. *Psychosomatics* 1978;19:425–431.
24. Walton J, Youngkin E: The effect of a support group on self-esteem of women with premenstrual syndrome. *J Obstet Gynecol Neonatal Nurs* 1987;16:174–178.
25. Taylor D, Bledsoe L: Peer support, PMS, and stress. *Health Care Women Int* 1986;7:159–171.

26. Workshop on Premenstrual Syndrome, co-sponsored by the Center for Studies of Affective Disorders and the Psychobiological Processes and Behavioral Medicine Section, Clinical Research Branch, National Institute on Mental Health, Rockville, Md, April 14–15, 1983.

27. American Psychiatric Association: *Diagnostic and Statistical Manual of Mental Disorders*, ed 3, revised. Washington, DC, American Psychiatric Association, 1987.

28. Halbreich U, Endicott J, Lesser J: The clinical diagnosis and classification of premenstrual changes. *Can J Psychiatry* 1985;30:489–497.

29. Harrison WM, Rabkin JG, Endicott J: Psychiatric evaluation of premenstrual changes. *Psychosomatics* 1985;26:789–799.

30. Gise LH, Lebovits AH, Paddison P, et al: Issues in the identification of premenstrual syndromes. In press.

31. Freeman EW, Sondheimer SJ, Rickels K, et al: PMS treatment approaches and progesterone therapy. *Psychosomatics* 1985;26:811–816.

32. Hackett TP: The use of groups in the rehabilitation of the post-coronary patients. *Adv Cardiol* 1978;24:127–135.

33. Spielberger CD, Gorsuch RL, Loshene RE: *STAI Manual for the State-Trait Anxiety Inventory*. Palo Alto, Calif, Consulting Psychologists Press. 1970.

34. Beck AT, Ward CH, Mendelson M, et al: An inventory for measuring depression. *Arch Gen Psychiatry* 1961;4:561–571.

35. Halbreich U, Endicott J, Nee J: The diversity of premenstrual changes as reflected in the premenstrual assessment form. *Acta Psychiatr Scand* 1982;65:46–65.

36. Locke HJ, Wallace KM: Short marital adjustment and prediction tests: Their reliability and validity. *Marriage Fam Living* 1958;21:251–255.

37. Wallston KA, Wallston BS, DeVellis R: Development of the Multidimensional Health Locus of Control (MHLC) Scales. *Health Educ Monog* 1978;6:160–171.

38. Rossignol AM: Caffeine-containing beverages and premenstrual syndrome in young women. *Am J Public Health* 1985;75:11:1335–1337.

39. Giannini AJ, Price WA, Loiselle RH, et al: Hyperphagia in premenstrual tension syndrome. *J Clin Psychiatry* 1985;46:436–438.

40. Prior G, Vigna Y, Sciarvetta D, et al: Conditioning exercise decreases premenstrual symptoms: a prospective, controlled 6-month trial. *Fertil Steril* 1987;47:402–408.

41. Wikler A: Dynamics of drug dependence: implications of a conditioning theory for research and treatment. *Arch Gen Psychiatry* 1973;28:611.

42. Mendelson JH, Mello NK (eds): *The Diagnosis and Treatment of Alcoholism*. New York, McGraw-Hill, 1979.

43. Harrison W, Sharpe L, Endicott J: Treatment of premenstrual syndrome. *Gen Hosp Psychiatry* 1985;7:54–65.

44. Harrison M: *Self-Help for Premenstrual Syndrome*. Cambridge, Mass, Matrix Press, 1984.

45. Clare AW: Premenstrual syndrome: Single or multiple causes? *Can J Psychiatry* 1985;30:474.

46. Ablanalp JM, Haskett RF, Rose PM: The premenstrual syndrome, in Sachar EJ (ed): *Advances in Psychoendocrinology*. Philadelphia, Saunders, 1980, pp 327–347.

10

Clinical Considerations in Group Psychotherapy with Cocaine Abusers

Henry I. Spitz
Susan Spitz

The value of group experiences in the comprehensive treatment of problems related to cocaine abuse is unparalleled. The focus of this chapter is clinically oriented in an attempt to delineate the central issues which confront the clinician who organizes and conducts groups composed of cocaine-dependent members.

For descriptive purposes, the most popular group formats applied to the problem of cocaine abuse fall into the categories of self-help groups and psychotherapy groups. Contemporary self-help groups incorporate elements of religious, philosophic, or encounter group experiences into a large peer group setting.[1,2] Interpersonal networking and supportive and educational functions form the matrix of many self-help group designs.

Cocaine-related self-help groups are derived from the group format originated by Alcoholics Anonymous. Evidence for these origins can be seen in current self-help group norms which insist on total abstinence from all mind- and mood-altering substances as a condition of group membership.

In addition to self-help groups composed exclusively of cocaine-abusing members, the coping and support self-help groups for families of cocaine abusers have gained popularity in recent years.[3] Cocaine-oriented variations on the theme of Al-Anon, Narc-Anon, and Adult Children of Alcoholics (ACOA) are finding an important place in the integrated treatment of cocaine-dependent individuals and their significant others.

Group psychotherapy applied to the cocaine-abusing population is a new development which blends elements of the self-help group and the psychotherapy group in order to meet the unique treatment needs of cocaine-dependent men and women. The specific clinical questions posed by composing groups which are homogeneous for the problem of cocaine abuse forms the basis for the discussion that follows.

GOALS OF THE COCAINE GROUP

Consensus exists among treatment programs with varied theoretical orientations that the initial phase of any successful program begins with a plan for achieving safe and rapid abstinence from cocaine.[4] Since abrupt cessation of cocaine use does not have the characteristic "withdrawal" syndromes associated with heroin or alcohol addiction, actual detoxification from drug effects is usually managed on an out-patient basis and precedes entry into the group.

When cocaine users cut their ties to the drug subculture they are often interpersonally isolated. Rapid entry into the psychotherapy group provides a therapeutic and constructive interpersonal network and counters excessive feelings of loneliness, alienation, and loss. The therapy group functions as an interpersonal anchor during the predictably difficult phase of initial abstinence.

Once detoxification has been accomplished, the central goal becomes one of helping the cocaine user achieve a sense of emotional equilibrium. Disabling emotional states including anxiety, panic, and depression commonly characterize the immediate emotional sequelae which follow detoxification. Group participation aids in restoring emotional balance through peer support, advice giving, and the sense of acceptance which comes from being a member of a therapeutic group.

Commonalities among group members not only form the basis for group cohesion and support but also facilitate the emergence of common life issues which form the themes at the core of the cocaine group. Group themes are chosen as they reflect areas of conflict and lack of resolution in the lives of the group members. Examples of recurrent group discussions include fears of success and failure, the appropriate expression of anger, competitive feelings, concerns about sexuality, problems with self-assertion, and the dilemma of how to incorporate pleasure and excitement into one's life without resorting to cocaine use.

Another central goal in the cocaine group resides in the effort to teach self-monitoring techniques to group members. The educational and confrontational elements present in effective cocaine groups contribute to enhanced abilities of members to prevent relapses by understanding those factors which place cocaine users at risk to resume drug use. Members are required to make a commitment to attend group for a minimum of ten sessions. Aside from providing a stable group nucleus, this initial group contract serves to help members and group leaders concretely understand the current level of motivation for change on the part of new members. In this way, denial defenses, so prominent among cocaine abusers, can be identified, assessed, and challenged when necessary.

The development of problem solving skills and new, drug-free methods of coping with life issues forms an ongoing dimension of all cocaine abuse groups. As part of the group norm of engaging with reality, members help one another with pragmatic problems as well as emotional and psychological problems. Group members with longer-term sobriety help newer members make plans to repay accumulated debts, decide when it would be most opportune to return to work, and how to engage with family and friends who have been affected as a by-product of chronic cocaine abuse.

Attitudinal shifts and life-style changes are essential for the genesis and maintenance of abstinence and the prevention of relapse. Group membership provides opportunities for learning how to delay the need for immediate satisfaction, to deromanticize the recollection of periods of excessive cocaine use, and to avoid the "people, places, and things" that facilitate the use of cocaine.

KEY DIMENSIONS OF GROUPS WITH COCAINE ABUSERS

Cocaine groups do well to begin with an emphasis on support, encouragement, and affiliative elements. The peer and leadership support vectors of the group provide the initial binding forces in the group. As the desire for acceptance among fellow group members increases, and relationships in the group deepen over time, the leader can utilize these needs to help members move toward the establishment of therapeutic group norms. Group support, while desirable, is not unconditional. Members and leaders do not support behavior such as lying, irregular attendance, poor motivation for change, and other sabotaging behaviors.

Group members often have little tolerance for those actions which run counter to the group goals. As a result, high degrees of confrontation are present in many group sessions. Group leaders must monitor and direct peer confrontation so that maximum therapeutic effect is realized and the potentially damaging effects of inappropriate confrontation are minimized. "Character assasination" and scapegoating of group members are to be actively avoided. Instead, a "caring confrontation"[5] which blends confrontation with concern allows for the maintenance of a constructive group climate and avoids the "purging" of less popular or frightening group members.

The experiential learning which ongoing group membership provides is particularly useful when working with a cocaine-abusing patient population. Learning through active group participation occurs on several levels. Members are taught how to identify, regulate, and express important feelings. On the cognitive level, members are helped to deal with fears, unrealistic expectations, and the behaviors which stem from these irrational beliefs. The psychodynamic dimension of the group provides a basis for the acquisition of insight into the motivational, familial, and environmental factors that foster cocaine use.

Insight-oriented cocaine groups value self-awareness and structure group experiences in ways which promote the attainment of insight for the membership. These groups utilize interpretation of in-group and historical material along with other psychoanalytically derived techniques in order to expand the base for self-understanding and to foster behavior change in group members.

The value of psychotherapy groups as vehicles for the expression of affect dovetails nicely with the treatment needs of most cocaine-abusing patients. Intense feelings of anger, depression, and the broad category of feelings of closeness and intimacy are three distinct forms of emotion which require work in group sessions. Through the incorporation of behavioral techniques such as role playing, assertiveness training, and communication skills training, members can develop an emotional vocabulary for identifying feelings which formerly would have propelled them toward cocaine use.

Since depression and its manifestations are so prevalent among cocaine users, the capacity of groups for countering demoralization and despair makes it an ideal milieu for recovery and rehabilitation of previously addicted individuals. Two "curative factors,"[6] universalization and countering hopelessness, are invaluable group elements. Feelings of alienation and negative self-image are rapidly offset by being a member of a functional cocaine group. Members can replace critical notions of themselves as "junkies" or addicts to more constructive attitudes of cocaine users in recovery. Group interaction and identification with others helps interfere with pessimistic preoccupations and morbid introspection commonly seen among depressed and socially isolated cocaine users.

In essence, membership in a psychotherapeutically oriented cocaine group serves to provide a new and positive subculture for the cocaine user. Groups bridge the initial gap when making the transition from active drug use to abstinence. Continued group participation facilitates the recovery process and builds strengths necessary for long-term rehabilitation and improved functional capacity in group members.

PREGROUP ISSUES

In order to effectively operationalize many of the foregoing principles, the group leader has to design a group experience in a thoughtful manner. Prior to the actual first group session, several critical functions must take place. This often underemphasized stage of the group can be called the pregroup phase. The essential goals of the pregroup phase are to carefully select, screen, and prepare prospective members for group entry so that they join with realistic goals and expectations.

The pregroup period has three central components: evaluation of potential group members; deciding on which group suits them best; and providing an orientation to group therapy for each member. Comprehensive evaluation includes psychiatric diagnostic evaluation, thorough drug history, and neuropsychological assessment when indicated. The pregroup orientation and preparation of members gives incoming members a picture of the group which they will be joining and addresses administrative details of group membership including fees, scheduling, attendance, and other group-related issues.

Pregroup preparation may take from one to several sessions. The successful completion of this phase sets the stage for the start of a therapy group experience which minimizes the likelihood of group dropouts or of untoward effects on members in the group.

STAGES OF GROUP DEVELOPMENT

The recognition of definable stages of group development yields vital information referable to the selection and timing of treatment interventions. The general stages involved in cocaine abuse groups can be categorized as follows: (1) crisis management, (2) stabilization phase, (3) induction phase, (4) establishment of group cohesion, (5) working group phase, and (6) transition and termination.

Crisis management forms the initial phase of group because many cocaine users seek treatment during or immediately following a personal crisis situation. Job loss, breakup of a romantic relationship, and escalating cocaine use to the point of possible hospitalization are recognizable crisis states requiring immediate attention. Entry into group helps decelerate escalating patterns of drug use and helps fill in for losses recently experienced by the cocaine user.

Once the crisis has passed, the group functions as a stabilizing influence in the life of the member formerly in crisis. During this phase, the leader relies on support elements in the group in an effort to engage members in the group and to construct positive group norms. Induction-stage issues relate to notions of establishing trust, affiliative ties, and jockeying for position in the group.

Group cohesion develops as a by-product of the interaction which transpires in the induction phase. Greater personal disclosure and higher levels of affect begin to emerge in the group during this stage. Cohesion forms the backdrop against which the working group phase can develop. In cocaine groups with ambitious goals, the working group phase constitutes the bulk of the group experience. It is during this phase that accumulated insights are translated into action in the safety of the group session.

Eventually, group participation concludes with a transition out of the group. Salient issues encountered during this stage include a review of past accomplishments, dealing with feelings of separation and loss of the group, and plans for aftercare following group termination.

The clinician's awareness of the stages of group development in cocaine groups provides a unique channel for the rapid differentiation between "normal" and hazardous developmental sequences observed in the group setting.

CLINICAL MANAGEMENT DECISIONS

Leaders of cocaine groups are charged with the task of considering varied dimensions of the group experience in order to tailor it to the specific needs of the cocaine-abusing population. The decisions which influence clinical management can be conceptualized as those which center around leadership factors and those which cluster in the domain of membership concerns. Many leadership issues focus on the structure, "ground rules," and leadership stance deemed most appropriate when working with cocaine-abusing patients in groups. The following discussion tries to identify and illuminate core decisions to be made by the group leader.

The issue of team or solo leadership is a basic initial question in all substance abuse groups. The workload on the single leader is large and he or she is charged with having to do support and confrontation simultaneously. This, coupled with the observation that staff burnout is high among those who work intensively with substance abusers, raises the case for a group leadership model which employs more than one leader. Team leadership is advantageous in allowing for sharing of leadership tasks in the group. The presence of more than one leader increase the opportunities for identification, interaction, and the exploration of intragroup relationships. As a result, the pace of the group experience can be accelerated.

When coleadership is utilized, leaders have to be clear on their respective roles in the group in order to function collaboratively.[7] Coleaders who can integrate their realistic differences concerning theoretical orientation, professional discipline, gender, and the like, provide the group with an excellent role model for collaborative function in adult relationships.

One specific form of coleadership involves the use of recovered cocaine addicts as special group participants. The recovered cocaine user can be considered as occupying a position midway between that of a leader and that of a member. Their memberlike qualities, including their first-hand experiences with life on cocaine, add a dimension to the group that cannot be supplied by the professional mental health staff. In order to be considered for this elder statesman role in the group, former cocaine users must have at least 1 year of documented abstinence and must consent to random urine screening for cocaine use. The professional staff and recovered cocaine counselors meet immediately following each group session to discuss group issues and to ensure that intragroup events do not pose a threat to the sobriety of the counselors themselves.

The construction of a therapeutic climate that is most conducive to positive change is of paramount importance in cocaine abuse groups. Leaders are responsible for the structure and limits of group experiences. While this is true for any psychotheraputic group, it takes on added meaning in cocaine groups since most members come from families in which limit-setting functions and boundary issues were not successfully handled.

The firm but fair rules of the group serve to model methods which members can adopt individually in an effort to gain control over their drug use and other areas of their lives where healthy self-control is required. The nonnegotiable group norm of total abstinence from all drugs provides an example of a strict but essential group norm. Experience in leading cocaine groups over time has led the authors to favor strict rather than liberal group norms. Failure to have a tight therapeutic framework for treatment of cocaine-abusing patients results in avoidable group pitfalls such as the discussion of limited or recreational drug or alcohol use. The setting of a total abstinence guideline from the outset helps keep the group on track and circumvents detours which are merely disguised resistances to the drug-free model.

Time factors are important leadership decisions. The length of each group session and the duration of the group experience over the course of time are the two major points of consideration. More debate surrounds the issue of brief vs longer-term group formats than the issue of the session length of group meetings.

Advocates of the brief group experience are enthusiastic about the capability of groups to assist in the detoxification process. Symptoms can be brought under control rapidly and a second-stage decision regarding further treatment can be made with a patient in a stable state. Longer-term groups have more ambitious goals. In order to sustain a lifelong pattern of abstinence from cocaine, patients must deal with a complex set of individual and interpersonal variables. Personality, family, biological, and environmental forces all contribute significantly to the spectrum of cocaine abuse. Ongoing psychotherapy groups provide the time and the perspective needed to learn and sustain a drug-free life-style.

Should groups be of fixed membership or open to new members along their course is another avenue of interest for cocaine group leaders. The advantages of open group membership appear to outweigh the few disadvantages of such a choice. Adding members during the course of a group experience allows for a group of sufficient size at all times. Groups consist of eight to 12 members initially. Membership turnover occurs when patients successfully complete the program and when others drop out of the group prematurely.

When a new member is added to an established group there is an inevitable pause in the flow of group patterns. In cocaine groups, new members are usually less far advanced in their recovery than their established group counterparts. This phenomenon frequently makes older members anxious insofar as it reminds them graphically of their own earlier struggles with cocaine. Newer members serve a catalytic group function, simultaneously testing the resolve of older members and providing a focal point for the altruistic needs of seasoned group members who are eager to be helpful to neophytes.

The introduction of new members mobilizes group themes of competition which are valuable for group discussion. Including new members models flexibility and openness to new experiences for the group membership. Relatively little is required from a managerial standpoint when members join the group other than helping to incorporate members into the existing group structure and deciding on the most opportune time to introduce new members.

The families of cocaine-dependent individuals are always part of the group leader's concern both for the assets they may add to treatment and for their potential for undermining treatment efforts. The family circumstances of every cocaine user should be thoroughly understood prior to group placement. Direct observation of interaction between cocaine users and their families yields critical data referable to treatment planning. Not only is the family an excellent source of historical material but the view that it affords the therapist of the patient interacting in his primary life group aids immeasurably in determining the timing and type of group therapy deemed most beneficial. Families can often be enlisted in the service of recruiting resistant cocaine users into sorely needed treatment services. Guided family interventions mobilize the powerful forces within the family network of the cocaine user to "push" the ambivalent family member into the initial phase of therapy.

The use of therapeutically prescribed medication to treat psychologically disabling symptoms may be a source of concern for therapist and patient. The judicious use of medication for depression, manic-depressive disorder, or as an adjunct to assist in the detoxification process is never presented as a solution to the cocaine problem itself. Medication is employed on a brief basis whenever possible and the consideration and monitoring of medication-related issues is discussed openly in group sessions.

A strong effort is made to differentiate between drugs with abuse potential and those designed to achieve a specific therapeutic goal. Medication themes are present in virtually all group sessions. Members are encouraged to express their feelings about medication including the fear that it is merely the substitution of one "crutch" for another and the possible confusion between being totally drug-free and yet able to take selected medications.

While the scope of the therapy group is broad, it often has limits which will necessitate the inclusion of other psychotherapeutic experiences in the overall treatment plan. Concurrent family therapy, couples therapy, and individual psychotherapy are a few examples of experiences which coexist with the primary group sessions. The group leader has to make an active effort to coordinate all therapeutic measures and to ensure that all function synergistically. The observation of the members' group behavior helps enormously in determining the combination of interventions that will be most helpful.

The group policy regarding extragroup contact among members requires serious consideration. Concerns abound in cocaine groups that members will misuse contact outside of regular sessions and thereby increase rather than reduce the likelihood of resumption of drug use. The expressed advantages for considering contact outside of group has largely to do with using the group relationships as a deterrent to impulses to use cocaine.

A viable compromise can be found in the model which requests that all group members refrain from contact outside of sessions until the group is well launched (minimally ten sessions) and until the issue of socialization outside of group has been discussed in group sessions. Once a firm sense of group cohesion has been established, it may be advisable to experiment with a telephone network among members as a test run for further contact among them. Members exchange phone numbers and are encouraged to call one another between group meetings if they feel the urge to use cocaine. Contacts among members are reported in the subsequent group session to distinguish between advantageous and improper use of the group support network.

It is naive to think that the cocaine user's contacts with other drug abusers are restricted to the cocaine therapy group. Many group members also attend Cocaine Anonymous meetings or are involved with people in their professional or personal lives who still actively use drugs. In light of these facts, it has proved more effective to adopt a clinical stance which places value on honesty and access to information concerning all dimensions of the patient's life rather than one which prohibits or sanctions specific behaviors in group members. Information concerning the extent, nature, and purpose of extramural relationships among members assists directly in evaluating progress in treatment and in identifying barriers to the process.

The management of relapses or "slips" forms a cornerstone of group treatment. Mandatory urine testing on a regular or random basis is a part of all group designs. Laboratory results are shared openly in group, allowing members to be aware of one another's state of recovery. The leader's task becomes one of translating knowledge of current cocaine use into a form from which members may learn something that promotes the rehabilitative cause.

Despite the fact that the group strives to make constructive use of slips as learning experiences, there are, on occasion, group members who are unresponsive to the group effort. Habitual drug use violates the basic principles of the group and questions the viability of group therapy alone as the treatment of choice for chronically relapsing patients. In such instances, the group leader must consider the possibility of hospitalization as a more appropriate treatment choice.

Inpatient treatment is considered when repeated attempts at outpatient treatment have failed, in cases where the familial or social circumstances of the user are highly reenforcing of drug use, and when substances other than cocaine are combined with cocaine so that the possibility of a serious withdrawal state might preclude outpatient management.

Groups can be very effective in encouraging members to enter the hospital when indicated. Group support extends to include an open invitation for the member to rejoin the group after discharge from the hospital. In settings that are close to a hospital, patients can be hospitalized directly from the group session. Hospitalization of a group member who has an escalating pattern of cocaine use serves to defuse a tense time in the life of the group and spares the member in question and the group from the additional stress of being the recipient of the collective anger born out of futile attempts to reach the deteriorating member.

The second large category of clinical management issues revolves around the membership level of the group. The composition of cocaine groups may require variation from traditional models in order to adequately meet the needs of certain subsets of the cocaine-abusing patient population. In general, cocaine groups are composed in a manner which strives to achieve a sense of balance between homogeneous and heterogeneous elements among members. There are indications for altering this design in order to reach patients with particular needs.

Age factors and gender issues are two common factors for which group composition is often modified. Adolescent substance abuse groups can be formed to simplify the leader's therapeutic mission by limiting the group exclusively to teenagers. The homogeneity permits the exploration of age-related concerns, minimizes authority anxiety, and more closely approaches the real life peer group of the members.[8]

In similar fashion, same-sex groups of male or female cocaine users have found a place in the initial phase of group treatment for many people. These groups are particularly useful in situations where anxiety related to members of the opposite sex is so intense as to inhibit group participation or to skew group behavior due to the presence of men or women in the same group. In men's cocaine groups, members frequently describe their discomfort with women, their concerns over sexual inadequacy, their demeaning attitudes toward women who use cocaine ("coke whores"), and their competitive fears concerning positions of favor with females.

Interestingly, once a same-sex group reaches a point in its development where the group has congealed, members openly express interest in and curiosity about the prospect of including members of the opposite sex. The sentiment echoes the feeling that the group would be more like "real life" if it contained both sexes. The transfer of members into mixed groups or the conversion of a same-sex group into an integrated one can take place after these issues are explored in the original groups.

Members of cocaine groups may form relationships within the group or outside of sessions. The group leader has to monitor the character of these relationships to ensure that dysfunctional subgroupings do not emerge in such a way as to cause problems in the group. The subgrouping phenomenon in cocaine groups may only result in an increase in feelings of competition or of being excluded from the "in" or elite subgroup. In its more disruptive form, the sabotaging effect of these small groups is most obvious when group members get together for purposes of using cocaine. Sociopathic group members are often the initiators of undermining experiences such as the one just noted. These members may have to be dismissed from groups in order to prevent the total demise of the group.

Confidentiality is a sine qua non of any therapeutic group experience. Members are required to preserve the anonymity of fellow group members and are instructed not to misuse information originating in group sessions. In cocaine groups the confidentiality theme takes on additional meaning since cocaine is an illegal drug. As such, data emanating from group sessions could be potentially harmful to a group member's life outside of group. Violations of confidentiality in the form of gossip about group members or in the disclosure of the identity of group participants also constitutes an unacceptable basis for continued group membership. Acceptable uses of group feedback can occur without needing to break the rules of the group. Members may discuss only the observations made by fellow group members concerning their relationship with a family member but should do so without intruding on the privacy of other people in the group by identifying the source of the observations.

Finally, membership issues surrounding attendance, promptness, and the payment of fees for the group round out the group leader's tasks. The effective leader models that which he or she wishes to become part of the ongoing group norms. Punctuality and regular attendance at all meetings are basic to any cocaine group. Although these seemingly apparent principles are espoused regularly, cocaine-abusing patients learn much from their implementation. Planning ahead, managing one's time, and accepting frustration are valuable messages which evolve from adherence to primary group standards.

In cocaine groups where a fee is charged, many group leaders prefer the billing policy of having members pay in advance for group sessions. The theoretical underpinning for this format relies in part on behavioral principles which use money in the service of enhancing motivation for treatment and more frequent attendance in circumstances where members are financially responsible for missed group sessions. Advance group payment along with commitment to undergo urine testing are two prime examples of the incorporation of contingency-contracting aspects of behavioral therapies which complement the psychotherapy group for cocaine-abusing patients.

SUMMARY

Group experiences occupy a position of prominence in the field of substance abuse. The broad applicability of diverse group formats has led to an interest in expanding traditional group models to meet the challenges presented by the increasing numbers of people seeking help with cocaine-related problems. Although the field can be viewed as being in a state of experimentation, there is a body of data emerging which suggest that groups will continue to play a central role in comprehensive treatment of coaine-dependent individuals and their families.

REFERENCES

1. Lieberman MA: Self-help groups and psychiatry, in Frances AJ, Hales RE (eds): *American Psychiatric Association Annual Review*. Washington, DC, American Psychiatric Association, 1986, vol 5, pp 744–760.
2. Vaillant GE: *The Natural History of Alcoholism*. Cambridge, Mass, Harvard University Press, 1983.
3. Galanter M, Cleaton T, Marcus CE, et al: Self-help groups for parents of young drug and alcohol abusers. *Am J Psychiatry* 1984;141:889–891.
4. Spitz HI, Rosecan JS (eds): *Cocaine Abuse: New Directions in Treatment and Research*. New York, Brunner/Mazel, 1987.
5. Rachman AW, Raboult RR: The clinical practice of group psychotherapy with adolescent substance abusers, in Bratter TE, Forrest CG (eds): *Alcoholism and Substance Abuse: Strategies for Clinical Intervention*. New York, Free Press, 1985, pp 349–375.
6. Yalom ID: *The Theory and Practice of Group Psychotherapy*, ed 3. New York, Basic Books, 1985.
7. Spitz HI, Spitz ST: Co-therapy in the treatment of marital problems. *Psychiatr Ann* 1980;10:160–168.
8. Rachman AW: *Identity Group Psychotherapy with Adolescents*. Springfield, Ill, Thomas, 1975.

11

Psychodrama and Group Therapy Approaches to Alexithymia

Peter A. Olsson

From antiquity, drama has provided mankind with cultural enrichment, emotional catharsis, growth-promoting self-awareness, and healing for the human spirit. Psychotherapists have long recognized the importance of their patients' responses to drama shared at therapy sessions. Moreno has provided the unique founding concepts for psychodrama with its therapeutic uses.[1] Byrd and Olsson, applying psychodrama techniques to the teaching of psychiatric interviewing skills, coined the term *pedagogic drama.*[2]

BASIC CONCEPTS OF PSYCHODRAMA AND PEDAGOGIC DRAMA

Psychodrama is the use of drama in a large group therapy setting. Its cornerstone concepts, as described by Moreno,[1] are creativity and spontaneity. Spontaneous enactment of mental phenomena and interpersonal situations are valued over "just talking about it." These qualities of spontaneity and creativity are combined both to see the "same old situation" in a new way as well as to see a new and perplexing situation as amenable to some old and familiar wisdom. Pedagogic drama has equivalent concepts, phases, components, and technique to psychodrama.

Psychodrama in its classic Moreno form has five components:

1. The stage is the tangible, elevated center of activity where

visual-spatial perspectives allow patient and audience-group to concentrate. Neither psychodrama nor pedagogic drama requires an elaborate stage but the action should take place in a clearly indicated area of the therapy room or classroom.

2. The director is responsible for the flow of perspectives and techniques that helps the patient discover what he needs to see and experience about himself. The director-clinician is responsible for moving the process through the various *phases*: *warm-up*, getting the audience to associate, relax, trust, and begin the group development of a theme or topic; *setting the scene*, specifying the detail of the life situation; *rising-action*, developing intensity around the key themes and conflicts presented by the patient; *declining-action*, diminishing intensity toward resolution, if possible; and *share-back*, discussion of the reactions of the audience, patient, and director. In pedagogic drama the director is the instructor and is responsible for maximizing learning through efforts to ensure that a broad array of symptoms, signs, and other psychopathologic phenomena are portrayed. The warm-up and setting of the scene are achieved by assigned readings, lectures, or films. The rising-action is a clinical interview, enacted family or group session, or other portrayal of clinical events. The share-back is the class discussion after the pedagogic drama or at stop-actions during the drama.

3. The patient-protagonist is the person who presents his life situation for exploration and therefore facilitates both his own treatment and that of every psychodrama participant-observer. In pedagogic drama the patient is a professional actor, selected student, or the instructor who portrays family, group, or individual psychopathologic phenomena.

4. Antagonists or auxiliary egos are persons from the treatment staff or audience who try to portray the patient and his significant others so that the patient can experience his life from new perspectives and attempt meaningful behavior changes. They must "put on another person's skin and walk around in it for awhile." In pedagogic drama these auxiliaries are professional actors, students, or teachers attempting their adventures in learning and clinical empathy.

5. The audience-group cements psychodrama as a true large group therapy technique. Everyone attending is involved, whether as active participant or observer. In pedagogic drama, the didactic preparation and attitude toward learning of the classroom group is analogous to the resistance or psychopathology of the patients in a clinical group therapy setting.

Of the many psychodrama techniques, I will discuss only the three basic ones:

1. Role reversal: At the initiative of the director, the patient is

asked to suddenly shift role with the person to whom he is talking. For example, a husband embroiled with his wife in heated conflict is suddenly forced to take her role. In pedagogic drama such a reversal can help an interviewer suddenly experience the impact of an unempathic question as he is forced to reverse roles with the patient. It is possible to substitute members of the student audience for the interviewer or patient at any time; this keeps the students alert and the presentation of information lively.

2. Doubling: Here a staff member or fellow patient is asked to stand close to or behind the patient to speak out the inner thoughts, feelings or perceptions of the patient. These are allegedly not heard unless the person doubled chooses to speak. Doubling is crucial at the time a role reversal is made. In pedagogic drama, this technique is effective in examining the countertransference reactions of the therapist or interviewer at such interruptions of the simulated flow of a therapy interview.

3. Soliloquy: The scene is stopped and a key person in the scene (usually the patient) delivers a lengthy monologue about his feelings, doubts, fears, or plans of action. A double can help the patient with comments from his unacknowledged thoughts and feelings. A soliloquy may also be used as a warm-up technique. The pedagogic uses are many, not the least of which is the depth exploration of issues about therapist burnout, countertransference dilemmas, and cotherapist conflicts.

PSYCHODRAMA AND ALEXITHYMIC PATIENTS

"The sorrow which has no vent in tears may make other organs weep."
Henry Maudsley

Sifneos coined the term *alexithymia* or "the absence of words for feelings."[3] He described alexithymic patients as having an impoverishment of fantasy life, a constriction of emotional functioning, and a tendency to describe endless situational details or symptoms. They prefer to use action to avoid conflicting situations, and during an interview they give the impression of being defensive. They blush or cry copiously at times or assume rigid, dull postures as if frozen into one position.[4] The recent literature indicates that alexithymic characteristics have now been reported among patients with a wide range of medical and psychiatric disorders and not just classic psychosomatic conditions. Thus careful clinical evaluation needs to be undertaken to distinguish its presence in posttraumatic states, socioculturally based operational thought, and coexistence with major psychoses or borderline states.[5] Alexithymia has even been considered to be the most important single factor diminishing the success of psychoanalysis and psychodynamic psychotherapy.[6] Taylor states:

> ...alexithymia has challenged developmental theorists to extend our understanding of how early psychological experiences and bodily sensations acquire mental representations as feelings and thoughts that eventually result in a language for expressing the emotions.[7]

This paper attempts to integrate the clinical theory of psychodrama and psychoanalytic object relations theory with experiential group therapy approaches to the alexithymic patient.

PSYCHOANALYTIC THEORY AND PSYCHODRAMA

Freud said, "The ego is first and foremost a bodily ego; it is not merely a surface entity, but is itself a projection of a surface."[8] Various residua of our bodyself and its primitive or elemental image or representations remain with us in various forms throughout our lives. The adult experience of solitude, relaxation, and quiet reflection were for the early elemental self ones of quiet sleep, physiologic quiescence, and pleasant visual gestalts. Adult anxiety and agitated depression are experiential and later analogues of sleep-disrupting dreams, early physiologic disequilibrium, and vaguely frightening visual stimulation of the primitive self. Jacobsen stated:

> In all likelihood, the limited early infantile contact with the outside world and its stimuli keeps the general level of tension in the psychic apparatus comparatively low; moreover, the cathexis of the body organs probably still outweighs that of the periphery, i.e. of the perceptive and in particular, of the motor apparatus. In this way, a continuous, "silent" discharge of small amounts of psychic energy may occur during the periods between feedings mainly through "inside" physiological channels.[9]

Jacobsen calls the simultaneous presence of libidinal and aggressive forces in the undifferentiated "psychosomatic" matrix the "primal psychophysiological self." Jacobsen continues:

> In fact, during the first infantile stages, the predominant expression of the child's emotional and fantasy life is still "psychophysiological," the so-called "affective organ language" which encompasses, however, not only the "silent" inner physiological processes emphasized above but also visible vasomotor and secretory phenomena and manifestations in the realm of oral and excretory functions. I may point out that this affective organ language survives, to some extent, even in the emotional life of normal adults in anxiety states and in other manifestations of "resomatization."[9]

I would point out that effective assertive speech and verbal expression are motor phenomena developing only after the second year of life. We can assume that the gradual developmental process that blends "affective organ language" and hallucinatory visual discharge with effective verbalization and the social use of fantasy occurs optimally in the empathic parental and family environment of "objects." Kernberg has said:

> In broadest terms, psychoanalytic object-relations theory represents the psychoanalytic study of the nature and origin of interpersonal relations, and of the nature and origin of intrapsychic structures deriving from, fixating, modifying, and reactivating past internalized relations with others in the context of present interpersonal relations.[10]

Some patients cannot make use of the psychoanalytic therapy dyad for the verbally based study and therapeutic alteration of such early distortions or deficiencies of object-relatedness. In my experience, psychodrama group therapy can be helpful with many patients who somatize or are alexithymic in dyadic verbal psychotherapy or strictly verbal groups.

The neurotic or neurotic personality disorder can verbalize derivatives of intrapsychic conflicts. The acting-out patient achieves immediate discharge of impulses by actions with an external object in reality. Sperling said, "...the psychosomatic patient tries to accomplish this by some actions with an internalized object inside his body."[11] Sperling felt that these vaguely expressed somatizations had the quality of scenic arrangements and shared with more differentiated fantasy the quality of "staging."

In psychodrama, the stage can literally be set and the body imagery and patterns of interaction can be played out in a safe, supervised setting. Over time the alexithymic patient can thus be slowly taught to visualize and verbalize his vague inner stresses and somatized conflicts. Hull has found empirically that patients with higher verbal activity or increasing verbal activity in therapy groups had fewer or decreasing physical complaints.[12]

Psychodrama is ideal for helping this process of gradually finding and using words to express feelings. Psychodrama is an active, concrete, tangible, visual-spatial, and often lively large group therapy technique. Visually and verbally assembled drama scenes from the patient's bodily or social self are combined with behavioral action, affective catharsis, and verbalization of the patient's attendant thoughts. In this sense psychodrama uses dramatization, concretization, personification, visualization, and an action orientation to playfully objectify and gradually bring vague somatizations to the patient's sphere of verbal awareness.

I hope the following vignettes speak for themselves in this regard.

"The War within: Psychodrama of a Headache"

Mr P. was a 26-year-old married, black, Vietnam war veteran who presented to a day hospital treatment setting with the primary complaint of severe headaches and difficulties in his family relationships. The conclusion by screening physicians and neurologists was that the patient's primary difficulties with headache were "functional" and not related to treatable organic causes.

Psychodrama session As the usual warm-up phase was being conducted on the day of this patient's psychodrama, he was sitting quietly in the audience, appearing attentive but tense and with a furrowed brow. The director was proceeding with a loosely structured, bantering-with-audience type of warm-up approach, where gentle probings were being made as to which life problems had been discussed in any of the small group therapy settings at the day hospital recently. One of the patient's fellow group therapy members suggested that the problem with his headaches be approached on the psychodrama stage because the group's efforts had been ineffectual toward getting him to discuss his "problems."

After very little persuasion, the patient proceeded to the psychodrama stage, where a brief soliloquy and empty-chair techniques were used to set the stage for the symptoms of his headaches. They were described as quite intense, pounding, and occurring at least 4 times a day. The patient often awoke early in the morning with a complaint of headache and would be unable to get back to sleep. Occasionally, he would awake dreaming in the middle of the night with intense headache and be unable to get back to sleep because of haunting scenes of Vietnam. When asked about the most difficult situational dilemma involving his headache, the patient immediately said that arriving home at the end of the day to his family was the most difficult situation.

The psychodrama scene was set for the patient's coming home where his wife and three children were usually awaiting. His 10-year-old daughter was particularly demanding, clinging, and almost constantly asking him to do things with her and for her as soon as he arrived at the door. His 5-year-old son was described as rather passive, serious, and always very supportive toward his father, asking the others not to bother their daddy when he had a headache. This little boy already complained of headaches himself, while the 3-year-old daughter was incessant in her demands for daddy's attention.

The first scene of the psychodrama proceeded into the patient's arrival home and a double was assigned to represent the patient's headache itself. The double pounded a chair in a loud, thumping, pulsating sound to accompany his rather harsh comments of torment toward the patient as "his headache." Finally, after confronting his family with anger, the patient received superficial support for his retiring to the bedroom to try to ease the headache. After he had left for the bedroom, the family discussed their feelings of being abandoned, not wanted, and pushed aside by daddy. The wife, in a soliloquy, delineated her ambivalent feelings about being supportive toward her husband and her resentment and anger for always having to deal both with the children and with him and his irritability during the headache episodes. These episodes had become an almost daily occurrence.

While the patient was alone in the bedroom, a fascinating dialogue took place. He was asked to reverse roles with the double who had been assigned to represent his headache. When the patient arrived in the role of his headache, he began to be sneering and tormenting in the tone of his voice. He said, "I got you under my control, baby." The headache spoke of his sadistic joy at restricting the patient's fun, marital, sexual, and family relationships. The headache reminisced about the days in Vietnam when the headaches had first begun, about the long boredom of patrols, constant anxiety about death, and the responsibility for buddies lest slip-ups in responsibility lead to immediate death. As his own headache, the patient proceeded to describe what he felt were his numerous past sins of getting numerous women pregnant and not caring for the children that ensued.

It became very clear as the "headache" proceeded in his vehement discourse, that in the current situation, the headache acted as conscience for the patient and did not allow him to "hit the street." Thus the headache seemed to curtail any possibility for the patient to go out and dance, drink, or at any time enjoy the companionship of his wife or other social relations. As an aside he remarked, "How could I chase other women anyway? I always have the headache!" The entire superego function seemed to be relegated to the headache. This seemed to come out of an apparent fear of loss of control and resulting total irresponsibility. When role reversal was done and the patient became himself again, he was asked to express his feelings to this headache that "had a spell on him." He proceeded angrily to accuse the headache and curse out the headache for its tyranny of restrictions and guilt provocations.

The director shifted attention to a dialogue between the wife and the "headache" which revealed her great frustrations at her husband's inability to have sex often enough with her because of the domination of the headache. She said, "You are like some strange and enticing mistress, you take him away to the bedroom at the very moment that I want him so much." As the "headache" (via a double) was in similar dialogue with his children, the patient learned indirectly about their anger with the headache because of the way it took their daddy away from them and particularly his son's fear that he "may get headaches like daddy when I get older some day."

At the feedback ("loveback") phase of the psychodrama, the patient was struck with the controlling, accusing, and unmercifully conscience-ridden meanings that this headache seemed to have for him. He related his intense depression at the early-morning awakenings with the headache and noted that they reminded him of the early-morning hours of his agonies in Vietnam. He was urged by his fellow group members and by the therapists to take control of more of his "conscience" and personal responsibilities, thus having less need for the "headache" to take over these functions for him. The patient admitted that in most group therapy sessions he would have a constant pounding headache, therefore accounting for his silence in group therapy. When asked by the director on the stage whether he had a headache during the psychodrama, he said, "No, at no moment did I have a headache." At the share-back, other patients in the audience spoke about similar substitute consciences they had in the forms of other somatic symptoms or overly dependent relationships with family members, "to do for me." Very supportively, the audience urged him to speak up more in group sessions as he had in the dialogue with his headache.

Comment This case serves to illustrate how elaborate detail of a patient's experiential, somatic, symptom situation can lead to helpful psychodramatic techniques directed toward elucidating the multi-layered symbolism, meaning, or defensive functions that a headache or other somatic symptom can have. The use of a double to represent a symptom or body organ itself, with the patient in subsequent dialogues with the symptom or organ, can be very helpful. Dialogue with a symptom seems helpful without insight as an obligatory companion. The dynamics that the somatic symptom has in the family constellation, social relationships, and vocational situations can be elucidated through similar techniques on the psychodrama stage.

Large Group Relaxation Techniques at the Psychodrama of a Headache, Peer Group as Biofeedback Agents

Harold, age 55, retired, mildly depressed, and in the midst of one of his daily headaches, sat looking discouraged and tense during the warm-up at our weekly psychodrama. During the unstructured warm-up he finally erupted: "I have never participated at a psychodrama here because it seems so silly! But today I just can't stand my headache! I fear I will become violent and tear up this room; I feel like this most of the time."

Harold told of his "workaholism" of many years. Now, despite comfortable retirement pay, a "beautiful, sweet wife," and all the time he could want to engage in his favorite projects, he was incapacitated by daily headaches. He felt that no one at the day hospital or anywhere really cared. He went on and on with his lonely, furrowed-brow discourse about his crippling companion of headache. He seemed impervious to the group members' expression of sympathy, gratitude for his help at small group therapy sessions, and their interpretations about his reluctance to accept help or comfort from anyone. He said that these efforts were just as futile as his wife's similar efforts at the breakfast table that very morning.

The director commenced to set the scene in the kitchen of the patient's home that morning. A fellow patient played his excessively benevolent wife. A parallel scene was set up to one side and behind the present-day breakfast situation. This ghost scene from breakfasts past contained the patient's now deceased, ultrareligious, benevolently controlling and demanding mother and father. These split-off introjects were played by two staff members who would comment abruptly, periodically, and with harsh superego attitudes that the patient had discussed at prior small group therapy sessions at the day hospital.

As the action rose in this scene the patient grabbed his head, began to tremble and cry, saying, "I can't stand the pain." The director froze the action and quickly chose two patients from the small group whom the patient trusted the most. They were placed behind and at either side of the patient. The peer patient at the right rear was instructed to place his right hand over the right forehead of the patient and his left hand at the right shoulder and neck area. The peer at the left rear was told to place his left hand at the left forehead and his right hand at the patient's left neck and shoulder muscle areas.

The whole audience group was then instructed in progressive muscle tension-relaxation starting from the feet and moving upward to calves, thighs, abdomen, chest, shoulders, neck, and forehead. The whole group and the patient did these progressively, first on the left, then on the right, and then on both sides together. Deep inspiration and slow expiration were done with each relaxation step. The only two people not participating were the two human biofeedback peer group members. They were instructed to give out a high-pitched sound if they felt tightness or tension and lower softer vocalization if they felt relaxation.

At first, the patient fought th꞉ efforts with verbal protests and muscle tensions reflected in piercing peer-produced sounds. As the exercise progressed and the parental presences were moved offstage into the audience group, lower-pitched sounds began to predominate. The patient chuckled some and at the share-back phase of the psychodrama he looked and felt more relaxed. Peers from his small group pointed out how subtly controlling and benevolently intrusive he was in much the same fashion as his parents appeared during the psychodrama. Other audience members shared similar experiences of "being just like their parents" but not realizing it until group confrontations. Although Harold was skeptical about some of these ideas, he had to admit he felt closer to the group and felt grateful for their help in helping him to relax. In subsequent weeks he seemed to be more open and expressive in his small group therapy. In fact, this type of combined psychodrama, relaxation, and "peer-contributed biofeedback" technique seems to enhance group cohesiveness in a striking way.

"Split-Brain Psychodrama" for the Alexithymic Patient

Bill was a 25-year-old Vietnam veteran who had recently entered the day hospital program complaining of stomachaches and immobilizing depression. In the hour prior to psychodrama, other hospital staff members were conducting an art therapy and educational program. Concepts of right brain vs left brain functions were presented didactically and were related to some of the patient's artwork.

As the psychodrama began, Bill expressed how difficult it was even to draw pictures, much less talk about his feelings in group therapy. In fact, he and his wife had had a confrontation the previous weekend when he could not even get out to mow the lawn. He wondered why he provoked his wife in such a manner because once he got out and "sweated, pushed, and struggled," he felt better. "Even my bellyache gets better."

In the psychodrama, the director staged the scene of conflict with his wife. As the scene was being set, the patient remarked in passing, "You known, she sounds like my sergeant in 'Nam sometimes." The patient struggled greatly to express himself, so a right brain double and a left brain double were assigned. As Bill sat in the kitchen with his wife, at first pouting and silent, then angry and confrontative, his right brain double of feelings, intuitions, and motivation beleaguered his depressed, immobilized left brain of gloomied cognition and present inaction. Finally, at prompting by the director, the left brain physically pushed Bill up out of his chair and out to the lawn. As this was occurring Bill paused and associated to his sergeant and lieutenant in Vietnam. His sergeant, like the left brain, was "all business, by the numbers, and by the book." The lieutenant was "sensitive," "caring" and "intuitive, like my mother."

A parallel scene of earlier years with his right brain mother and left brain father allowed some focus on his feelings of being caught between his parents and unsure of himself. Action pleased his father (sergeant) and reflection-feeling pleased his mother (lieutenant). Both his sergeant and lieutenant died in Vietnam as had both parents even prior to his duty in Vietnam. At subsequent small group therapy sessions, the emotional connections between the traumatic grief-loss-depression in Vietnam was explored in terms of his efforts to turn his wife into the lost objects of his military superiors and the earlier loss of his parents. So much emotional charge led her to feel tremendous frustration and him to feel immobile. His small group therapy became like his Vietnam combat unit over the next several weeks. As the group confronted, encouraged, and pushed, his situation at home improved and assertiveness toward job hunting became possible. Prior to admission he had sat around the house bemoaning and grieving about his medical-psychiatric discharge from the Army.

The concrete metaphor of right brain–left brain at psychodrama became both a cognitive and emotional means by which the patient could begin to experience his inner immobility and conflict in a tangible way. Although his insight into his intrapsychic dynamics was only modest, he and his small group used the concretized metaphors of the split-brain psychodrama session as a means to frame their efforts at mutual confrontation, support, and rehabilitation. His somatic symptoms subsided and he became more verbal.

Comment We frequently see psychodrama sessions interacting with extending ongoing small group process at the day hospital milieu, culminating in an apex at psychodrama sessions.

The split-brain psychodrama has potential to teach the patient directly about walled-off or split-off emotional states via concrete yet creative imagery. The experiential processes of dramatization, creative confrontation, and action-experience via direct assertiveness training can theoretically approach the alexithymic problem from a broader spectrum of therapeutic activity than just verbal channels. This particular patient showed modest gains in this regard.

SUMMARY

I have attempted to integrate the clinical theory of psychodrama with psychoanalytic object relations theory toward a psychodrama group therapy approach for the alexithymic patient. Psychodrama provides a playful, visual-spatial, tangible, concrete, and action-oriented experience for these patients. The therapeutic mechanisms employed are dramatization, visualization, concretization, personification, and catharsis. Occasionally, insightful verbalization is a result, but it is not crucial for therapeutic changes or personal growth in these groups.

REFERENCES

1. Moreno JL: *Psychodrama*. Beacon, NY, Beacon House, 1964, vols 1–3.
2. Byrd GJ, Olsson PA: The use of pedagogic drama in psychiatric education. *J Med Educ* 1975;50:299–300.
3. Sifneos P: The prevalence of alexithymic characteristics in psychosomatic patients. *Psychother Psychosom* 1973;22:255–262.
4. Sifneos, P. "Problems of Psychotherapy of Patients with Alexithymic Characteristics and Physical Disease." *Psychother Psychosom* 1975;26: 167–168.
5. Neill J, Sandifer M: The clinical approach to alexithymia: A review. *Psychosomatics* 1982;23:1223–1231.
6. Krystal H: Alexithymia and the effectiveness of psychoanalytic treatment. *Int J Psychoanal Psychother* 1982;9:353–378.
7. Taylor GJ: Alexithymia: Concept, measurement, and implications for treatment. *Am J Psychiatry* 1984;141:725–732.
8. Freud S (1923): The ego and the id, in *Standard Edition*, vol 19, Strachey J (trans-ed). London, Hogarth Press, 1955, p 26.
9. Jacobsen E: *The Self and the Object World*. New York, International Universities Press, 1964, pp 8–11.
10. Kernberg O: *Object Relations Theory and Clinical Psychoanalysis*. New York, Jason Aronson, 1976, p 56.
11. Sperling M: Acting out behavior and psychosomatic symptoms: Clinical and theoretical aspects. *Int J Psychoanal* 1968;49:250–253.
12. Hull D: Talking and body complaints in group therapy patients. *J Psychosom Res* 1971;15:169–177.

12

The Self-Help Group: Working with Parents of Cult Members

David A. Halperin

Self-help groups have become increasingly recognized as agents for providing significant mental health services. They enable their members to deal with problems such as alcoholism, gambling, obesity, narcotics, drug abuse, and cult affiliation. Defined as "voluntary small group structures for mutual aid and the accomplishment of special purposes,"[1] these groups are a "special form of voluntary association formed by particular populations to accomplish specific common purposes."[2] This paper examines the dynamics of self-help groups and the issues that arise when mental health professionals attempt to work with their members. In examining these issues, a group for parents of cult members is used as a paradigm. However, the issues are not specific to this population.

Self-help groups for the parents of cult members have been formed under the auspices both of the Cult Hotline and Clinic of the Jewish Board of Family and Children's Services of New York City, and of the Westchester Jewish Community Services. The author was asked to lead a group formed under the sponsorship of the latter and to supervise one formed under the auspices of the former. Both requests grew out of his professional interest in the interface between religion and psychiatry, and in the problems created by cult affiliation. The formation of such groups under the sponsorship of established mental health agencies may appear paradoxical, but it is not unique. Indeed,

51% of all self-help groups are formed or continue under agency sponsorship.[3]

The initial membership of both groups consisted primarily of self-referred individuals who had heard about programs formed by agencies to help in the task of "learning to live with our children who are cult members."[4] Participants were also referred by other members or by professionals in the community. Such groups differ significantly from traditional psychotherapy groups in the extent to which self-referral and networking and postgroup contact are encouraged.

Prior to being accepted in the self-help group, all prospective members were seen by the group leader. These were screening interviews to only a very limited degree, that is, the primary focus was informational and educational. Belonging to the self-identified community of concern was considered sufficient for membership in the absence of psychopathology sufficiently gross to prevent individuals from functioning within very broad limits in a group. Indeed, it was anticipated that the members might constitute a population whose anxiety, narcissism, and intense concerns about their children's welfare might prevent them from functioning in a more traditional group psychotherapy setting.

The parents of cult members are in fact an extraordinarily diverse group of individuals. Likewise, families vary widely in structure. In some, a degree of enmeshment was noted, but it certainly was not universal. They shared the conviction, however, that mental health professionals (like the population at large) would see them in a critical and judgmental way. Hence, their preference for the self-help group format. At the same time, they shared a sense of shame for their "failure" as parents.[5]

While the term "self-help group" conjures up the image of a group of self-selected individuals spontaneously deciding to meet at one another's homes to discuss matters of common concern, this self-help group (as is true of the majority of such groups) met under professional sponsorship, in meeting rooms provided by the sponsoring agencies, and with the support of agency staff. Group leaders/facilitators kept the boundaries of time, place, and meeting duration.

In such a self-help group, the role of the leader-facilitator is complex. In addition to being boundary keeper, she or he must be prepared to participate actively in setting forth group goals and tasks, and to share personal feelings, experiences, and attitudes. The leader-facilitator is a participant observer who can "help with the group process by virtue of...training. Of equal importance is...[being]... able to empathize with the group.[6] The degree to which actual sharing of personal data and opinions occurs obviously varies with the individual leader and group. The leader's ability to empathize is not necessarily a product of having personally undergone the experiences that led the individual members to join the group. However, in working with a self-help group, an air of analytic detachment or "objectivity" should be avoided.

The role of the leader changes during the life of the group. Initially, it is primarily one of helping the group formulate tasks and goals. For the parents-of-cult-members group, these were articulated as: (1) the examination of feelings toward children who were cult members; (2) the examination of the parents' feelings about themselves as the parents of cult members; and (3) the examination of practical steps to take to help children leave the cult. During the initial phase, the leader studiously avoided confronting group members with a reality, apparent in many instances, that either the relationship between parents and child had, for some time, been conflictual, or that the cult member had been seriously dysfunctional. Parental denial and displacement of responsibility onto the cult were accepted without further examination.

The leader's goal was to create a "holding environment" in which the members would be comfortable in discussing their feelings without fear of criticism or judgment. He recognized that the problematic relationship between group members and their children had become the focus of their lives, and that the difficulty they had previously experienced in obtaining help from mental health professionals was a function of the intensity they brought to their quest for an instant solution to their problem. Ill concealed within this quest was a nidus of dependency so intense that the limited professional-patient relationship was insufficient to provide adequate support, thus making the creation of a holding environment for this group particularly difficult. Indeed, the pervasive character of members' needs was a major factor in the formation of the self-help group, since members in effect contracted to be available to one another on a 24-hour basis. The extent to which members were in fact accessible to one another during crises was truly extraordinary. It is a characteristic of self-help groups that members develop such a degree of openness and intimacy that they do not experience this constant availability as burdensome (as mental health professionals might).

Initially, the group members seemed to welcome the leader, primarily for his professional input, although they were skeptical about his abililty to empathize with their situation. Indeed, wariness and skepticism have traditionally characterized the relationship between professionals and self-help networks. This is hardly surprising when one realizes that members of such groups are often flooded by feelings of shame, toward which they have experienced a lack of sympathy on the part of professionals.

In working with a self-help group, the leader may develop a sense that what is happening within the group is secondary to the broader activity of the national organization. The primary national self-help organization concerned with problems of cult affiliation is the Cult Awareness Network (CAN). This group organizes educational and political meetings on a regional, national, and international scale. It mobilizes its members toward political activity, for example legislation to establish "conservatorships" for members, and it provides a forum in which members can assume a more active stance in dealing with the broader problems created by cult affiliation. This feeling is exacerbated when the beginning of the meetings is devoted to a discussion of the last CAN conference. While CAN does provide a setting for the development of indigenous political leadership (as do organizations such as Gamblers Anonymous, etc), its activities cannot really meet the personal needs of individual members. Encouraging members to externalize the responsibility for their situation may, in fact, be counterproductive. The group leader must walk a fine line between, on the one hand, encouraging members to meet together and participate in the formation of indigenous leadership[7] and, on the other, demarcating clearly those areas in which professional expertise can help members meet their own goals. For these reasons, this group leader decided not to attend meetings of the CAN. Since in effect it operates as an alternative group, his attendance could infringe on the members' need for autonomy and might even be experienced as an attempt at controlling them.

The leader did not challenge members who portrayed their families as "normal." Instead, he encouraged them to talk about the burden that cult affiliation placed on any family regardless of the degree of familial pathology. In some sessions, members discussed the realistic problems created when their children might be suddenly summoned to participate in mass meditation sessions or were otherwise unable to participate in usual family rituals such as Thanksgiving dinner. These sessions proved to be particularly useful.

Even when parental responses to a child's absence clearly reflected a preexisting pattern of overinvestment (one of the possible causative factors for their child's cult affiliation), this pathologic pattern was not explored. Similarly, when parents presented material strongly suggestive of their ambivalence toward the possible return of a cult member (often because of the cult member's intense dependency strivings), this material was either not confronted, or was examined in a very supportive fashion. Members were encouraged to explore both their anger and their sense of failure as parents engendered by the actions of their children, and to accept cult affiliation realistically as being their child's attempt, however misguided, toward achieving a greater sense of independence. The members' pervasive sense of shame was often heightened by well-meaning family members who discussed a variety of panaceas or sure-fire inoculations against cult affiliation, despite the reality that there are none. As they were able to liberate themselves from this feeling, however, members were able to establish better relationships with their children.

A self-help group is not group psychotherapy under another name. The leader's basic role is to facilitate a process in which the members gather to talk about their feelings in a circumscribed problem area. It is not a forum for the exploration of underlying dynamics with the goal of conflict resolution and structural change. Even when the group leader became aware of underlying intrapsychic problems of individual group members, he restrained himself from attempting to work on them. For example, when at times, he raised the possibility or desirability of meeting more frequently than the usual once every 2 or 3 weeks, some members objected to this increased frequency primarily because of their intense defensiveness and fear of closer contact with other members. Without commenting on the cynicism and detachment that accompanied the objecting group members' schizoid style of interaction, the leader dealt with this resistance by simply observing that the work of the group would be slowed down.

On occasion, a group member's style could be destructive to the group process. The group leader would initially approach the cynical and depressed member by observing that such feelings were often the product of confusing and inconsistent relations experienced between parent and cult member, for example, cult members would obviously cultivate their parents prior to making financial demands. But when these interventions were insufficient, the group leader would ask members to leave, recognizing that:

> If a member is disruptive or so disturbed that group process and content are altered, a professional consultant might be best equipped to help the person find more appropriate help. If the disturbing force is not treated and there is no professional present, the group runs the risk of disbanding prematurely because members may feel scared and inadequate and may deal with these feelings by no longer attending meetings.[6]

In other cases, the group leader actively intervened (particularly in the early sessions) to set limits for the more anxious and bombastic members, who often seemed to use the group primarily as a forum to vent their rage at their children, the cults, and even mental health professionals for not having succeeded in rescuing their children. The leader consistently emphasized helping members see their interventions as being potentially meaningful rather than simply lapsing into a cynical state of hopelessness, like that of the bombastic propagators of "It's all a futile exercise anyhow."

The creation of a self-help group often suggests the unarticulated conviction that the status of "patient" is inherently demeaning. This was implied in the original decision to meet relatively infrequently. Professionals are viewed with profound ambivalence (1) as experts essentially lacking in empathy, but also (2) as idealized objects capable of providing magical solutions to problems. However, when one type of magic is found wanting, the intensity of their personal needs will prompt these parents to seek magical solutions from another idealized "professional," the "deprogrammer."[8]

Deprogramming is an extraordinarily controversial topic, as are the individuals called deprogrammers. Their questionable efficacy, highly questionable legal status, and unquestioned cost have been examined elsewhere.[9–11] Group members' references to this idealized "other" may reflect the need to denigrate an initially idealized leader, but it may also be an expression of the self-help group's need to invoke the spirit of a counterculture leader. Instead of confronting the group with either of these possibilities, the leader encouraged them to examine their need for "magical" solutions as a way of coping with their profound sense both of helplessness and loss.

Many members of self-help groups become extremely knowledgeable about resources available to help them with their problems. Initially, this degree of sophistication can be quite intimidating to the newly involved mental health professional. They may use it in a clearly competitive manner, often to avoid the status of patient. Interventions should address this behavior in a task-oriented way, for example, "We're all trying to work together to deal with a problem," rather than as an expression of transference. On a countertransference level, the newly involved professional must become comfortable with the reality that he has not focused his life around this issue as the group members have. While he may empathize with the members of the group, he has not single-mindedly dedicated himself to finding solutions for often insoluble problems.

Members of self-help groups are encouraged to contact one another and to regard this network as part of the holding environment. The formal beginning of the group thus often seems like an interruption in the ongoing group process. The occasional initial period of silence may be dismissed by the group members as an expression of their difficulty in talking in front of a professional.

Since members of the self-help group are almost all successful, functioning members of the community, they do not surrender their veneer of control readily. When the group begins, particularly if a new member is present, they often describe how their child was "between things," and was "unwittingly" or "deceptively" recruited into the cult group. Recognizing that new members are hesitant to participate because of a sense of shame and the expectation of criticism, members of the self-help group can often reach out to them with empathy, understanding, practical suggestions, and information about what can be done. Rather than berating them for what they ought to have done or expressing the criticism which they themselves simultaneously project on the group and anticipate in return, they can be accepting and supportive.

Emphasis is placed on helping members develop strategies to facilitate communication between parent and child rather than on past deficits in relating. During a typical session, one member brought in a letter from his son which described the life in his "new family." As he read, the father was enraged by the superficially positive tone about the cult reflected in the letter, so that he was unable to see that his son was reaching out to reestablish more reasonable social contact. The leader was able to add a significant dimension to the group's process by reframing the issues presented. This enabled the group members to listen to the actual letter rather than becoming mired in anger and self-recrimination. Even when deficits in communication represented a long-standing pattern of parent-child alienation (the more striking because of the parents' denial of its existence), the leader would encourage the member to examine whatever opportunities for communication were present in as task-oriented a fashion as possible. This would enable parents to increase their awareness of the reality that attempting to make their child either guilty or ashamed of cult affiliation could only lead to further alienation.

Working with a self-help group is a demanding and often exhausting experience. The members' demands for instant solutions and their expectation that the leader share their pain and preoccupation create a very real hazard of "leader burnout." These demands present particular problems for a leader because his relationship to such a group may blur the boundary between leader and member. For this reason the presence of a cotherapist is often helpful. Although the cotherapy relationship can create unique problems, a cotherapist can provide a needed measure of support in dealing less defensively with the group members' intense dependency strivings.

SUMMARY

The self-help movement has provided and continues to provide a source of succor and support for people who would otherwise be unable to obtain necessary care, even though it has been regarded with skepticism, and at times a certain competitive disdain by the mental health professional. The movement should be viewed more accurately as an attempt to provide assistance for people in crisis whose difficulties may be either intractable or unresolvable within the more conventional treatment framework. The professional can provide tremendous assistance in facilitating the progress of the self-help group.

188

This chapter has discussed the role of the group leader as facilitator in working with a self-help group of parents of cult members. However, the issues that arose in this group were not unique. Working with this group and responding to group issues on a here-and-now basis with group-as-a-whole interpretations, despite the limited nature of the therapeutic contract, proved to be useful, as it can be with a variety of self-help groups. Learning from the resolution of problems within this specialized context has enabled group leaders to work with other self-help groups and with other populations.

Acknowledgments

The author extends his appreciation and thanks to the Division of Group Psychotherapy of the Department of Psychiatry of the Mount Sinai Hospital, New York City, where this chapter was first presented. He also expresses his appreciation to Arnold Markowitz, ACSW, of the Cult Hotline and Clinic of the Jewish Board of Family and Community Services New York City, for his help and the staff of Westchester Jewish Community Services for their support.

REFERENCES

1. Katz A, Bender E: Self-help groups in Western society: History and prospects. *J Appl Behav Sci* 1976;12:265–282.
2. Katz A: Self-help and mutual aid: An emerging social movement? *Annu Rev Sociol* 1981;7:129–155.
3. Yoak M, Chesler M: *Self-Help Group Structures and Activities: Implications for Professional Roles.* Ann Arbor, Mich, Center for Research on Social Organization. University of Michigan, 1983.
4. Westchester Jewish Community Services: *Family Life Education Program brochure.* 1981.
5. Halperin D: Self-help groups for parents of cult members: Agenda: Issues and the role of the group leader, in Halperin DA (ed): *Psychodynamic Perspectives on Religion, Sect and Cult.* Boston, PSG, 1983, pp 333–343.
6. Coplon J, Strull J: Roles of the professional mutual aid groups. *Social Casework* 1983:259–266.
7. Toseland RW, Hacker L: Self-help groups and professional involvement. *Soc Work* 1982;27:341–346.
8. Maleson FG: Dilemmas in the management and evaluation of religious cultists. *Am J Psychiatry* 1981;136:926–929.
9. Frakt A: Legal aspects of dealing with the new religions, in Halperin DA (ed): *Psychodynamic Perspectives on Religion, Sect and Cult.* Boston, PSG, 1983, pp 369–382.
10. Halperin D: Introduction, in Halperin DA (ed): *Psychodynamic Perspectives on Religion, Sect and Cult.* Boston, PSG, 1983, pp xvii–xxii.
11. Langone M: Deprogramming: An analysis of parental questionnaires. *Cult Stud J* 1984:1:63–79.
12. Halperin D: Psychiatric approaches to cults: Therapeutic and legal parameters, in Benedek E, Schetky DH (eds): *Child Psychiatry and the Law, II.* New York, Brunner/Mazel, 1985, pp 250–266.

13

Group Therapy with the Parents of Children with Chronic Illness

Hadassah Neiman Gurfein

By the middle of the twentieth century, Americans had come to believe that chronic or terminal illness in a child defies the order of nature; it is a tampering with the existential order that all things will grow and die in the proper time. Family members are shocked when a child dies or becomes chronically ill and lack preparation for becoming survivors. In view of the shrunken size of the modern family, the death or illness of a young child has a particularly devastating impact.

Parents' reactions to the diagnosis of a severe, chronic, or life-threatening illness in a child can include anxiety, guilt, withdrawal, feelings of alienation, or somatic complaints.[1] Parental attitudes toward a child with a disease profoundly affect the child's management of the disease, the child's self-concept, response to treatment, level of emotional stress, and the response to such stress.[2] Because many serious childhood illness are now chronic, and not necessarily terminal, the developmental period during which the family lives under enormous stress is exceedingly long.

The prolonged nature of these illnesses results in prolonged periods of anxiety characterized by continual changes and decisions. Children afflicted with illness must deal not only with the effects of chemotherapy, radiation, and surgery, but also with the long-term psychological effects of the illness.[3] Nir[4] found that childhood cancer was accompanied almost without exception by posttraumatic stress disorder. And the Spinettas' study[5] indicated that the siblings suffer at least as much and probably more in unattended emotional responses to the illness. These studies underscored the earlier findings of Cairns et al[6] who found that "siblings showed even more distress than the patients in the areas of perceived social isolation, perception of their parents as overindulgent and overprotective of the sick child, fear of confronting family members with negative feelings, and concern with failure (older siblings only)." Chronic illness does not necessarily cause psychopathology but it can unleash disturbances, exacerbate difficulties, disrupt relationships, and unbalance the family system. As has been recently emphasized by the Spinettas,[5] children's anxieties are best dealt with when the parents' awareness and ability to deal with their concerns have been strengthened.

Over the years, groups have been found to be an effective form of support for individuals and families confronting illness. In 1905, Pratt,[7,8] aware of the negative effects of social isolation on physical health, organized classes for his tuberculosis patients. The improvement in their physical well-being might be attributable to "universality," which is the heightened awareness that one is not the only one facing a particular situation.[9] Groups changed from their primarily educational focus when Wender[10] introduced psychoanalytic techniques in 1951. Carl Rogers[11] described the group as a learning experience that fosters individual conflict resolution. He pointed out that members gain self-awareness and self-acceptance as a result of the feedback and responses from others.

Groups operate under the assumption that an individual's behavior cannot be isolated from his environment. Since the most significant part of one's emotional environment is the family, Kolodny[12] used groups in an attempt to change the attitudes of mothers of children under psychiatric care. Amster[13] and Durkin[14] used a group format to work with mothers of emotionally disturbed and psychoneurotic children, and Bauer and Gurevitz[15] worked with parents of schizophrenic children. Mattson and Agle[16] found that a 21-week hemophiliac parent group improved self-confidence in the parents and promoted the parent-child relationship. The meetings were conducted in a nondirective manner and parents were encouraged to reach their own answers to the questions raised in the group. Gilder et al[17] and Karta and Ertel[18] described group therapy with parents of children with leukemia. Kornfeld and Siegel[2] discussed how group therapy offered parents of children with muscular dystrophy the opportunity to explore processes in the family and helped with child-rearing difficulties.

The literature is replete with descriptions of the impact of chronic diseases on the family. But it has only been in the last several decades that widespread attention has been directed toward a model of group therapy that is supportive of the emotional needs of parents. This chapter describes the issues and goals that arose in working with a continuing therapy group involving the parents of children with cancer. The format can be used as a paradigm for parent groups with other chronic illnesses.

GOALS OF THE GROUP

An attempt was made to utilize group intervention as an effective means of working with the parents of oncology patients to help prevent psychological and emotional difficulties and to facilitate a healthy adaptation. The group tried to heighten parental sensitivity to the concerns of their children and provide guidance in child-rearing practices. The goals of the group were: (1) to alleviate current stresses and anxieties and (2) to prevent adverse behavioral and psychological sequelae in the parents and their children. In order to achieve these objectives an attempt was made to provide the parents with the following opportunities: (1) to gain educational information regarding the etiology, treatment, and prognosis of the illness; (2) to discuss their reactions, fears, and anxieties; (3) to express feelings, both negative and positive; (4) to communicate and share thoughts with other parents who are experiencing similar problems; (5) to provide interpretation, clarification, and facilitate the attainment of insight; and (6) to serve as a continuing support group throughout the prolonged period of treatment and beyond. These issues are discussed in greater detail after a presentation of the major themes brought up by the parents during the work of the group.

Support groups differ from traditional outpatient psychotherapy groups in a variety of ways. The most important differences are reflected in a differing approach to common group issues such as: (1) changing members, (2) erratic attendance, (3) lateness, (4) cancellations, (5) outside subgrouping, (6) limited contracts, (7) few rules, (8) focus on a specific issue such as illness, in contrast to focus on personality issues, and (9) the reduction of anxiety in a supportive manner. Since participants do not view themselves as patients, the group leader is expected to be more open, supportive, and participatory. While group participation does not replace individual and/or family therapy, the advantages of group work for this essentially normal population are: (1) reduction of alienation and isolation, (2) elimination of feeling different, (3) obtaining educational information, (4) strengthening defenses and the ability to cope, (5) consensual validation of thoughts and feelings, and (6) the cost-effectiveness of the process. Meetings may be regularly scheduled at a convenient time on a monthly, semimonthly, or weekly basis. Group leadership can be multidisciplinary or unidisciplinary but should always include a mental health professional since informal groups without professional leadership may increase the emotional burdens of parents and result in the inappropriate sharing of sadness.[1] Other leaders can include physicians or nurses or both. Groups may have different formats, varying from completely unstructured to a combination of unstructured with a structured educational component.

DESCRIPTION OF THE GROUP

In forming such a parent group all parents of children treated in the pediatric hematology/oncology department were invited to attend the monthly meetings. The group was based on a primary prevention model and was offered to the families as part of the overall treatment plan. It was decided that group intervention should be continuing since the reactions of parents are intensified not only during diagnosis but also during exacerbation and relapse of the illness.

The group was led by a mental health professional with the support of the pediatric oncology staff. This model was chosen because it utilized the oncologist's expertise in answering numerous questions about prognosis, protocols, and side effects of medications. In addition, it was believed that it would help facilitate an institutional transference. The average attendance was 15 parents. The number of fathers almost equaled the number of mothers. Refreshments are served before each meeting to lighten the atmosphere and set a tone of nurturance and support.

The therapist routinely met with the parents individually in an attempt to identify areas of particular concern. She maintained contact with each family between group meetings. This helped keep the staff informed about important events in the family and facilitated a positive transference to the therapist and the medical staff.

Attendance was often related to the medical condition of the child. Parents of children who approached cure felt less of a need to attend the group and many eventually terminated. Parents whose child died often found it too painful to listen to others discuss their children who were alive and doing well. They joined a bereavement group where they could more readily express their grief and mourning.

Many parents volunteered their services to the oncology department during and after treatment.

DISCUSSION

The group's major recurrent concerns have been conceptualized as falling into the categories of stress and loss. Those concerns are causation, medical issues, identification with the illness, anger and guilt, shame and embarrassment, general parenting and sibling issues, relationship with the ill child, isolation, job performance, and the ever-present threat of death.

One of the first questions that arises is that of causation. The parents often have their own private explanation of how the patient's illness was caused. Causality is a confusing concept and some parents believe that simultaneity implies cause and effect. In the group, it was apparent that thinking often contained magical links as a way of making sense of something incomprehensible and overwhelming. It is important to obtain the parent's view of causation, explore any self-references, and clarify misconceptions. Concrete explanations help clarify that simultaneity does not always imply causation. Some parents engaged in self-blame since cancer often runs in families. Parents often argued about which one of them transmitted the disease to the child.

A second concern involves medical issues. The oncology team informed parents of the diagnosis and its implications. All questions were answered in an honest, direct fashion with repeated clarification of information. Nevertheless, the parents often had many misconceptions and misunderstandings. Parents often forget important information and realistic warnings about future difficulties. This may have been due to the use of denial which minimizes the seriousness of disagreeable facts and the effects that accompany them. Denial can be dangerous if parents or patients do not heed medical advice or cautions. Parents emphasized the necessity for repeated explanations, particularly during the first few months. Questions were asked regarding blood counts, bone marrow aspirates, spinal taps, chemotherapy, and other diagnostic and therapeutic procedures. The parents related their anxieties regarding hospitalization, chemotherapy, side effects, and bone marrows and spinal taps. They conjured up images which were often worse than the actual procedures.

Most parents were encouraged to be present during medical procedures since it is important for bonding as well as for reducing the anxiety of both the parent and the child. Parents and family members often develop an extensive medical vocabulary about diagnosis, protocols, chemotherapy regimens, and medical equipment, reflecting the extent to which everyone is preoccupied with the ill child's condition. Their knowledge demonstrates the degree to which childhood cancer is indeed a family affair. Many parents used "control theory thinking," a term that was introduced by Bibring et al[19] and described by Mattson and Agle[16] in their work with parents of hemophiliacs. This mechanism of defense attempts to lessen anxiety by an anticipatory familiarization with the danger, but in contrast to intellectualization it does not eliminate affects. Many parents learn all they can about the medical and psychological aspects of their child's illness in an attempt to master their anxiety and their feelings of powerlessness. This approach gives them a sense of doing something helpful for their child's treatment.

Group participation facilitates medical management because it strengthens the formation of a positive transference to the medical team. Sometimes, of course, parents were critical of the medical profession for misdiagnosis, oversights, or lack of sensitivity to psychological issues. This often functioned as a displacement or projection of a sense of helplessness onto others, particularly physicians, nurses, and group therapists. Mattson and Agle[16] attributed this to the defensive use of denial and the adoption of a sense of superiority. Our observations were similar to theirs in noting that at the time of relapse the parents re-elevated the physicians to their former omnipotent, all-knowledgeable position.

A third concern of parents is the fear that they or their other children might become ill with cancer. The natural identification between children fosters the fear in some parents that their other children might contract a serious illness. Such thoughts evoke deep anxieties about helplessness and powerlessness. Narcissistic injury and bodily concerns about all family members are particularly acute when the illness causes disfigurement. Parental anxiety about future illness was particularly expressed with regard to the siblings that were younger than the patient and whom they feared might become ill when they reached the patient's age. They magically considered those children that were older than the patient as having passed that "dangerous age." Other parents were able to adopt a more realistic view that did not rely heavily either on identification with the illness or on denial. They maintained an attitude of guarded optimism.

Parents were reassured that the illness is not contagious and that there is little likelihood of another family member getting the same illness. Parents were discouraged from seeing the well sibling as a "replacement child." To prevent parental overinvestment in the ill child, parents were encouraged to continue to pursue their own activities and friendships. Such independent functioning balances the sense of similarity and identification extant in a parent-child relationship.

The fourth theme is anger and guilt. Many parents were aware of their anger. But they may not have been aware of its displacement onto others. They were enraged at society, God, physicians, and themselves for not having prevented the illness and protected the child. They were often disappointed in friends and relatives.

Although the presence of the medical staff may have inhibited direct expression of anger toward them, the advantages outweighed the disadvantages. Some parents accused the staff of being unable to empathize because they presumably had healthy children. Other parents freely expressed anger and disappointment. Although such emotional reactions often reflected transference responses, they were often difficult to interpret in such a large and often fluid group. Parents reported relief in being able to express anger directly and in finding the physician understanding and accepting of their feelings. It provided an opportunity for the clarification of misconceptions and miscommunications. As sessions progressed, the parents who displaced anger onto others became aware of that, so when the group talked about anger toward spouses, friends, relatives, physicians, and hospitals, these parents were able to recognize similar defenses in themselves. They were relieved to learn that it is acceptable to have appropriately channeled angry feelings.

Parents were less aware of unconscious angry feelings toward their ill child. Such thoughts were repressed, and resulted in feelings of guilt, not only about having caused the disease or not having prevented it, but also often about having escaped a similar fate. "What right do I have to lead a normal life when my child will die before she finishes first grade?" "I wish I had gotten sick instead of Danny." "I feel terrible that Tom can't play tennis anymore. I don't feel like playing if he can't — I feel...a little guilty." This "survivor guilt" can result in the curtailment of leading a full life in expiation for the sin of living while others perish. Such guilt was often repressed, and manifested itself in somatic complaints by parents or other children.

Mr K suffered severe stomachaches every time his son went into the hospital for his routine three-day treatment. After the therapist pointed out the possible connection, his stomachaches subsided.

Many of the parents felt guilty about their anger toward their ill child. After all, we live in a society which teaches us not to have hateful feelings toward people who are sick or handicapped. Some became overly concerned with keeping the child happy. Some showered their children with gifts, which only served to make the child anxious and to weaken his self-esteem.

Mrs L tearfully told the group how she sometimes wished her daughter Connie would die. Magical thinking produced feelings of guilt and anxiety, since she was convinced that if you wished hard enough wishes would come true.

Many of the parents expressed guilt over actions as well as over feelings. They felt very guilty about disciplining or punishing their ill child, and viewed it as an act of disloyalty or cruelty. Many parents inhibited the expression of anger and tried to be self-sacrificing, patient, restrained, charitable, kind, and understanding. This was a tall order! Some parents controlled direct expression of anger but manifested it in subtle ways. Such parent-child relationships were characterized by tension, and at best became drab, and devoid of humor and joie de vivre.

The often overwhelming financial difficulties brought on by the medical costs contributed to the parents' feelings of guilt. Anger and resentment about having to spend money and time on medical bills and transportation resulted in feelings of guilt. Parents also felt guilty about having fewer financial resources available for the usual activities, treats, and presents.

The peer support offered by the group appeared to expiate much of this guilt. It was a relief to learn that other parents were angry with their situation and were also impatient with their ill child, and wished that their child would die or had never been born. A distinction was made between aggressive feelings and actions; group leaders found it necessary to point out that wishes do not have magical powers and are not responsible for future events.

As the sessions progressed, the parents were able to discuss negative thoughts and actual arguments with their children with fewer excuses and rationalizations. They were encouraged not to restrict family activities just because their ill child could not participate. The continuation of normal parent-child relationships was encouraged.

A fifth issue is the shame and embarrassment of having an ill child. Parents often viewed their family as different, flawed, marked, or imperfect, and resented being the object of pity and compassion. They were embarrassed by the temporary or permanent physical disfigurement of their child, which often included hair loss, amputation, or cognitive impairment. Likewise, their other children were often embarrassed, and attributed the shame either to the patient or to themselves.

Joshua, age 13, has always tried to deny any relationship to his 15-year-old sister whose brain tumor has left her neurologically impaired. "I am embarrassed when people know that Cindy is my sister. If they ask me, I say she's not."

There is still a strong social stigma attached to many chronic illnesses. Discussing embarrassment or shame in the group helped the parents recognize the universality of these reactions. Realizing how senseless it is for the other parents in the group to feel ashamed and embarrassed appeared to help each person to come to terms with similar reactions in himself. The group experience helped them recognize that they are judged for themselves and not by the illness or impairment of their child. They were then better able to impart this to their other children. The group experience dispelled the feeling of being different, chosen, or marked.

A sixth and almost universal concern is general parenting skills — the relationship of the parents to their other children and the maintenance of family discipline. Parents reported that many of the well children were confused by the loss of parental availability and the disruption in family homeostasis. Home was often described by these children as empty, quiet, and tense, and they often felt left out. Their complaints often focused on a reduction in family activities such as trips and get-togethers. Some voiced concern about their dependence on parents who had little available time. They felt rejected, unsupported, frightened, and lonely, not only in times of crisis but also during routine hospital visits when their parents' attention was focused on the patient. After the hospital visits, the parents, physically and emotionally exhausted, often refocused on work issues, household tasks, and social obligations, once again abandoning them.

Parental absence is difficult for children of all ages, but particularly for younger ones. One can hypothesize the negative effects on infants and toddlers who are negotiating the preverbal stage or the rapprochement subphase when separation anxiety increases.[20] Separation anxiety can be inferred from behavior that is dependent, demanding, and regressive. Some of the children converted their anxieties about separation onto less threatening topics, such as boredom, isolation, and excessive freedom. Some of the younger children were reluctant to spend time away from home.

Mrs R reported that her daughter complained about boredom whenever she spent time in the hospital with her ill son. After group discussion, Mrs R realized that her daughter's experience of boredom was related to separation from her. After considerable group discussion, Mrs R began to realize that she had begun to distance herself from her well children to protect herself from future loss.

Another type of abandonment is the sudden preferential treatment of the ill child by parents, relatives, and friends. Spoiling, overindulgence, increased attention, gift giving, lax discipline, and reduced demands resulted in the intensification of normal feelings of sibling jealousy. Parents were helped to recognize that many of their well children wished that they were the patients on whom all the attention, affection, and presents were showered. Spoiling resulted when parents reduced the usual expectations because they pitied the suffering child or anticipated the child's expression of resentment. Permissiveness often led to the child's behavior becoming manipulative, provocative, and demanding. The parents often rationalized such behavior as an expression of anger caused by the illness and the side effects of medication.

Some parents began to demand more from the siblings, undoubtedly causing them to feel anger and confusion. Some parents displaced expectations onto the siblings that they had previously invested in the sick child. This most frequently occurred when a parent was narcissistically invested in the ill child and, in an attempt to deny the loss, displaced affection and expectations onto the well sibling.

Ken's illness devastated his father who had invested much of himself in Ken's athletic promise. After Ken lost his leg to Ewing's sarcoma, John, age 10, was expected to replace him as the star football player.

Parental anger was often displaced onto the well sibling who then felt anger and resentment toward the parents as well as the patient. This led to an unhealthy cycle of anger, resentment, and guilt. Some parents were caught between their own hostility and anxiety about their children's destructiveness.

Siblings often echoed their parents' self-recriminations and guilt, which overwhelmed the siblings with a sense of failure and inadequacy. Some children responded to the experience of having an ill sibling by becoming overly cautious, while others, in their striving for independence, appeared determined to prove their indestructibility. They denied their own fear and their parents' overprotectiveness by courting dangerous situations, and responded with counterphobic behavior. Parents whose children were initially misdiagnosed by the family pediatrician sometimes became insecure about their own judgment and the ability of the physicians to protect them. One parent went from physician to physician whenever any of her children became ill.

Within the group the parents were helped to recognize that the siblings felt threatened not only with the loss of a brother or sister, but with the loss of an emotionally available parent as well. It was important to allow parents to verbalize their concern and guilt about abandoning their other children. Many of them observed that silence had caused the siblings discomfort, and they gradually recognized that the entire family was caught in a game of mutual protection. They were encouraged to allow their children to verbalize abandonment fears so they could provide the necessary reassurance.

Parents were made aware of the importance of open communication among family members. They were encouraged to help the siblings share their feelings and fears in addition to keeping them abreast of the concrete day-to-day aspects of the ill child's management. The parents' sensitivity to common reactions of the well siblings was heightened; these reactions included attention-seeking behavior, somatic complaints, accident proneness, and demands for reassurance about being loved. Gilder et al[17] found not only that parents experienced relief when they realized that their children knew more about the illness than they had thought, but also that all children's adjustment to the illness was improved with greater parental responsiveness to their thoughts and feelings.

A seventh concern is the parent's relationship with their ill child which is often ambivalent and characterized by love, empathy, compassion, resentment, anger, and disappointment. Parents often handled anger by repression, denial, or displacement. Complaints about the patient's irritability, aggression, and depression, while sometimes accurate, often reflected projection of the parents' anger and depression onto their child. Often the parents assumed that the child was angry or depressed despite the fact that there was no evidence to support this conclusion.

Many parents colluded with their children's desire to avoid discussion of their illness. This was more frequently observed in families who lived with a conspiracy of silence.

David's parents were concerned about his refusal to discuss his illness. Another group member helped them realize that they had encouraged such avoidance to help ward off their own anxiety.

Parents often found it difficult to differentiate between needed care and exaggerated concern. Overprotection was evident when parental behavior in relation to the patient was exaggerated, as in the case of those parents who used the role of "super" caretaker as a defense against their own anger. One mother related that she did not leave the house during the first month after her son returned home from the hospital. She was afraid that something might happen to him if she did not watch over him constantly. She felt responsible for his safety. Such behavior was often a reaction formation to ward off awareness of anger, guilt, and depression.

The more serious the condition, the less able were parents to attend appropriately to developmental and emotional concerns. Responses to situations often reflected parents' feelings about their child's illness instead of addressing non-disease-related problems. For example, some parents underemphasized the importance of the child's relationships with the opposite sex in an attempt to protect him or her from rejection and disappointment. The parents gradually recognized that this denial was their way of handling their own anxiety, depression, and loss.[2] Parents were encouraged to give these important developmental issues appropriate attention.

Parents were helped to recognize their angry feelings and sense of guilt and to accept and understand them as common reactions. This enabled them to free themselves from obsessive concerns or exaggerated attempts at overprotection. They learned to distinguish their own reactions from the needs of the child.[2] Resumption of normal activities outside the home was encouraged. The parents were also encouraged to avoid projecting their mood onto the patient. Evidence of increased awareness of their own feelings was seen when they were able to openly share their own anger and depression. Parents reported an increase in self-awareness and self-esteem as parents. They reported more appropriate and consistent child-rearing practices and an acceptance of their own limitations.

An eighth concern is the feeling of isolation and estrangement. Many parents were disappointed and confused by reactions of withdrawal by certain friends and relatives. Many parents felt abandoned because of the unavailability of a support system. The situation was often worsened because of time-consuming hospital visits and the need to isolate the child from infection. Some parents felt ostracized because of false notions about contagion of the disease, lack of social desirability, the stigma, and the protectiveness of other parents concerned about exposing their own children to illness and death. While some friends did withdraw, these fears were often a projection by the parents onto others. Some parents avoided their friends and projected their own uncomfortableness onto them. Withdrawal from friends often appeared to be a manifestation of depression.

Many of the younger children told their parents that they were unable to talk to their friends about their sibling's illness because their friends did not understand, did not want to listen, and sometimes laughed or teased. Most of the teenagers, however, were able to turn to their friends and often did this instead of talking to their parents. They found their friends compassionate, understanding, sympathetic, and helpful. Investing libido outside the family, which is a normal adolescent development, was often a healthy desensitization — a healthy aspect of the anticipatory grieving process which eases the pain of the possible loss. It helped distance them from the illness and lessened their sense of isolation.

A ninth concern is job performance. Some parents complained about lowered motivation at work and difficulty in concentration, particularly on days of clinic visits, bone marrows, and spinal taps. If career difficulties developed, this increased the feelings of isolation. It is important to discover the reason for performance difficulties. Is it a reflection of less time available for work due to increased responsibilities at home or a manifestation of depression or unconscious guilt?

Other parents found that work was a welcome distraction, and began to immerse themselves in their jobs. They reported an improvement in work performance, and ascribed their new-found dedication to necessity. Often it became apparent that such overzealousness was a defense against depression or a need for mastery and control in some area of their lives to help them bind anxiety.

A tenth concern, the major one, is fear of death. Parents of chronically ill children seem to display the same five stages of responses that Elisabeth Kubler-Ross[21] found to be characteristic of dying patients. These are: denial, anger, bargaining, depression, and acceptance. The ever-present threat of death was often dealt with by denial, which helped many parents deal with crises and with the ongoing stress of having a child with a chronic illness.

If the parent and child had a constructive relationship, the parent was more likely to do the appropriate anticipatory mourning and grieving by testing reality, expressing positive and negative feelings, and acknowledging fears. Complications arose when the relationship was fused, overidealized, distant, or antagonistic. Antagonistic or distant relationships resulted in a great deal of guilt on the part of the parents with subsequent acting out or depressive reactions.

> Mr D expressed his fear of losing the narcissistic gratifications provided by his son's mirroring. "If my son dies, I'll miss him telling me I am the best father in the world. He is so much like me — same eyes, same color hair. . . . I'll never have another child like him. I'll feel like a part of me is gone."

Many parents found religion very helpful in dealing with illness and death. Several families traveled great distances to be blessed by religious healers. Unwavering faith offered predictability, a belief that there was a hidden purpose to the confusion, a comforting sense that their family was chosen to suffer as part of a greater plan, and, most important, a sense of protection and hope. Faith in an afterlife gave many parents assurance that their ailing child would be more comfortable after death.

Parents raised many questions about their children's anxiety regarding the threat of death. They asked for guidelines in discussing this anxiety-laden topic should the dreaded question arise. The topic of death was talked about as a part of life, in order to help the parents slowly adjust should the tragic event occur. Discussions included the death of grandparents and parents, leaving friends when moving to a new neighborhood, and other painful separations. This provided an opportunity for desensitization and anticipatory mourning. It was hoped that such straightforward discussion would serve as a model for the parents to follow at home.

When the child of a group member died, the group offered a great deal of emotional support to the bereaved, and aided the goal of making covert mourning overt. Distortions were corrected so that mourning could take place. Angry reactions and guilt were accepted and interpreted. It was often necessary to reassure the parents about the health of their other children. The parents needed to be encouraged to focus on the surviving children, prevent comparison with the dead child, and avoid using the surviving child as a replacement. It appears that the most important factor in preventing regression in their well children is helping the parents handle the death of their child by not being overprotective or demanding inappropriate independence.

While focusing on content, process should not be ignored. During the initial stages, members were more dependent and the therapist assumed a more active role to encourage discussion. Participation was encouraged in an attempt to elicit common concerns.

Since the group was also educational, explanations were given when requested. The group often secured speakers on a variety of topics for the first half of the meeting.

Initial hesitations, lack of trust, and caution about revealing feelings gave way to openness and spontaneity. Silences became less frequent and the group leaders became less active. The parents experienced a cathartic effect after sharing their innermost fears, anger, depression, and feelings of helplessness. They repeatedly recounted the details of the period of initial diagnosis and their reaction to the devastating news. There was greater ease in expressing both negative and positive feelings and a gradual reduction in inappropriate worry about illness and death. Interpretation and clarification were provided by the group leader.

In addition to the sharing of fears and problems, it was important to encourage the expression of optimism and reassurance. An attempt was made to keep group discussion somewhat balanced. If this had not been done there may have been a premature escalation of the anxiety level of newer participants which might have resulted in their reluctance to attend future group meetings.[16] Many of the newer members reported feeling particularly anxious and depressed for several days before and after meetings. The parents in the group of Gilder et al[17] reported similar feelings but found that "the stressful and painful working over of feelings and thoughts did give some relief." Some parents, particularly those using denial and avoidance, did not return after their initial session because they found the experience too painful. Newcomers sought out veteran parents for their expertise and experience. These group members provided positive role models for the new parents, and fostered the therapeutic process in an open, supportive, confrontational style.

The group discussed issues of distance and intimacy among the participants and there were proponents of each position. However, greater intimacy was restricted because of the span of time between meetings, the size of the group, and its fluid membership.

Parents gained insight into their adaptive and maladaptive use of defenses, including isolation, denial, rationalization, reaction formation, and the use of intellectual processes. Mattson and Agle[16] reported similar observations. Many parents were able to recognize when they were employing defenses to ward off painful affects and when this interfered with good parenting. They appeared to have reduced guilt about feelings of anger and resentment and their part in the causation of their child's illness. They no longer felt the need to be overly responsible or overly protective and could enjoy a more normal and relaxed relationship with their children. In those parents who denied the implication of the illness, cautious optimism was combined with a more realistic awareness of the serious nature of the illness. There was less embarrassment in discussing the subject of cancer and greater understanding of and sensitivity to the reactions of family, friends, and patient. Newer parents gradually identified with these positive attitudes and learned to take one day at a time.

In cases where children relapsed, the group helped the parents deal with their renewed anxiety. At such times the parents who were newer, less active, and more dependent became more active, and supportive of those whose children relapsed.

A unique bond formed between parents who developed a great deal of empathy and gave one another support, reassurance, and relief from isolation. As time went on there was more cheerfulness before and after the meeting (which at times was a defense against anxiety). The group became such an integral part of their lives that many parents requested more frequent meetings and no summer break.

THERAPEUTIC GOALS

The therapeutic goals for the parents were the facilitation of adaptive coping with stress and the improvement or reinforcement of parenting skills. Toward the attainment of these goals the therapeutic interventions targeted six areas: (1) to encourage open communication, (2) to establish a therapeutic alliance based on trust, (3) to encourage exploration of alternative problem-solving skills, (4) to encourage the expression of feelings, (5) to maintain an honest, realistic posture, and (6) to encourage anticipatory grief when appropriate.

The first goal is to encourage open communication. Discussion was encouraged between parents, between parents and therapists, and between parents and members of their families. The aim was to increase awareness of their attitudes toward themselves, their ill child, their healthy children, and their environment. The aim was acceptance of themselves, their children, and their feelings. Spouses often limited communication with each other because of assumptions about each other's ability to tolerate anxiety. They often spent little time alone with each other, which often magnified any previous tensions in their relationship.

Emotions were often disguised by defense mechanisms. This was often done in an attempt to hide sad, angry, or helpless feelings. For example, one parent rationalized his lack of caution by saying the physicians were overly cautious. He was not in touch with his anger toward his demanding child. His workaholic pattern allowed him to avoid getting in touch with feelings of anger, sadness, and helplessness. Sourkes[22] underscored the importance of converting the "implicit" to "explicit" in order to encourage clearer communication of feelings and needs. Thus, whenever parents minimized an important topic, it was reflected to them and given adequate weight in the hope of opening new insights and channels of communication.

The following descriptions illustrate how increased communication helped the parents cope more successfully.

> Mr and Mrs J were upset because their parents severed all ties with the family immediately following the diagnosis of their daughter's brain tumor. The therapist and the group reflected and acknowledged their sense of loss and encouraged them to initiate phone calls and conversations which eventually led to the resumption of their relationship.
>
> Mr K expressed bewilderment and anger at his wife for befriending other mothers whose children had cancer. As he began to realize that group members dealt with stress in different ways there was a noticeable reduction in his anger toward his wife.

The second goal is to foster a therapeutic alliance based on trust. This develops in part because of the supportive, nonjudgmental attitude of the therapist and the group, and because of the ongoing availability of the therapist. Parents are reassured knowing the therapist can be called on for consultation between sessions.

> Jonathan's parents called the therapist after receiving a report from the school psychologist which attributed his school problems to his reaction to his sister's illness. His parents became so anxious that they were unable to provide him with the necessary support.

The third goal is to encourage alternative problem solving methods and to evaluate adaptive and maladaptive ways of coping. Support and confrontation by group members helped parents arrive at more effective solutions. Identification and imitation among parents helped many become less anxious, more realistic, and able to adopt more effective parenting skills.

The fourth goal is to encourage the parents to express positive and negative feelings. Parents were encouraged to discuss their feelings, identify situations that caused them difficulty, and discuss alternative responses. When a parent was hesitant about admitting feelings, the therapist encouraged the expression of similar feelings by the group to normalize the feelings and reduce the guilt.

> Mrs W spent most of her time at home caring for her daughter, and restricted her outside activities. She became aware of her feelings of resentment and anger over that only after becoming aware of similar feelings in other group members. This awareness alleviated much of her guilt and she was gradually able to resume normal activities while continuing to care for her daughter.
>
> Mr J was enraged at his son's pediatrician for not having been more

available during diagnosis. After group discussion he recognized that this was a displacement of anger which he was then helped to express in subsequent sessions.

Positive feelings were often expressed, and parents shared warm, loving, proud feelings and experiences which occurred between various family members and the ill children.

The fifth goal is to maintain an honest, realistic posture in an attempt to minimize acting out and inappropriate fantasizing.[22] In order to do this, it was important to know the medical status of the patients so the parents could be helped to respond realistically.

When Mr and Mrs G discussed fears that their child would die, empty consolation and meaningless optimism would have been untruthful because her prognosis was very poor. Sharing with others who had similar fears appeared to bring some relief and lightened their burden.

The sixth goal is to encourage anticipatory grief and desensitizing discussions in order to deal with ongoing anxieties and facilitate adaptive responses in the event of the death of a child. It is important to allow repression and denial when it is useful and to discourage its use when unrealistic and maladaptive. If it was apparent that denial was being used as a defense against reality and would result in an inability to deal with feelings should the child die, then it was necessary to help parents correct unrealistic expectations.

Mr B was denying the imminent death of his daughter. Without confronting him directly about death, he was helped to express his feelings about the loss of her ability to use her right arm. Facing this reality helped prepare him for her eventual death.

It would be inappropriate, however, to dwell on death and dying with parents of patients whose prognosis is favorable, other than the extent to which this remained an underlying anxiety. With such parents we focused on the here-and-now and discussed their concerns regarding causation, side effects of medication (eg, baldness), loss of parental availability, etc.

The role of the therapist differs from the traditional role in which the aim is to uncover and interpret motivation and the source of emotional stress. The therapist was more active as an organizer, educator, and support person. The therapeutic goal for the parents was the facilitation of adaptive coping with stress. No effort was made toward reconstructive work. The group did not focus on confronting defenses, but provided support to help deal with anxiety. Because the group was a short-term experience for some parents, every effort was made to achieve closure at the end of each meeting.

The leader became a transference object and an attempt was made to use this constructively during the sessions. Unconscious feelings toward authority figures often became manifest and the leader was often tested to see if he could be trusted. Some parents attempted to create a split between the therapist and the physicians. They appeared relieved when their anger was accepted and interpreted, for this enabled them to maintain an alliance with the physician whom they still needed.

The therapist's overt reactions to the illness should include intellectual understanding, problem solving skills, consistent emotional responsiveness, and rationality. However, inappropriate countertransference reactions may occur, including unconscious anger, depression, guilt, identification, overinvolvement, overprotection, rescue fantasies, and feeling responsible for the emotional well-being of the entire family. The therapist should view these reactions as countertransference issues to be understood and worked through. The more the therapist can overcome personal defenses, the more effective he can be.

Social resistance to the subjects of chronic illness and death may affect the therapist. These are anxiety-provoking subjects and the therapist's outside world may wish to treat this resistance with various distancing responses such as teasing, joking, silence, evasiveness, and unrealistic esteem. The therapist and medical staff often become very isolated. Forming their own support group can help to improve communication, decrease isolation, and lower anxiety.

SUMMARY

The psychosocial upheavals experienced by the parents of children with chronic and terminal illnesses cannot be totally eliminated. However, parents find that psychological and emotional trauma can be minimized by preventive practices. The group therapy model appears to be an effective vehicle to help meet these needs.

The parents believed the group to be of value because it provided educational information and made them feel that their needs were important to the oncology team. It helped them realize they were not alone and that there were other parents who shared the same feelings and concerns. The curative factor of such "universality" has been pointed out by Yalom.[9] For many, the group was the only place they discussed their feelings and anxieties. They observed that better communication and open discussion regarding their child's illness reduced the anxiety and tension in their homes. The car ride to and from the group became a time and place for open discussion of problems and concerns between husband and wife. They found that open communication resulted in a stronger family bond. The discussions afforded greater understanding of the reactions and behavior of their other children, relatives, and friends, as well as a heightened appreciation of the reactions, fears, and concerns of their ailing child.

The group provides an opportunity for parents to work through the various stages of mourning, to express concerns, anxieties, and anger in a nonjudgmental atmosphere, and to gain insight into their own reactions to their unique situation. Group discussions clarify misconceptions about the disease, hospital procedures, treatment, and chemotherapy. Consensual validation reduces anxiety and minimizes guilt. Shared alternative strategies help parents act in more constructive ways. There is an increase in ego strength and an increased acceptance of the reality of their situation.

The group therapy model described here has several limitations which are similar to those reported by Gilder et al.[17] Since the group was voluntary, it was unable to help those parents who were unable or unwilling to come due to time or distance constraints. It was unable to help those who did not come because their feelings were too threatening. We were unable to deal with individual emotional problems. During the final days and hours of illness help was only available on a limited basis. Individual help was needed at such a time.

The parent group should become an integral part of a team approach to the family of the child with a chronic illness. It heightens the consciousness of the staff to emotional issues, facilitates communication between the staff and the larger family unit, and strengthens the bond between them. It provides a format in which parents can convert their fears, anxieties, and hostilities into constructive endeavors. Hopefully, instead of causing illness and stagnation, the experience can serve as an inspiration for growth and creativity. Leadership must continue from the medical and psychological community in organizing such healing opportunities if we are to enable families to free themselves, their children, and future generations of the silent but ever-present emotional burden borne by the families of children with chronic illness.

REFERENCES

1. Binger CM, Ablin AR, Feurstein RC, et al: Childhood leukemia: Emotional impact on patient and family. *N Engl J Med* 1969;280:414–415.
2. Kornfeld MS, Siegel IM: Parental group therapy management of a fatal childhood disease. *Health Soc Welfare* 1979;4:99–118.
3. Koocher G, O'Malley JG, Gogan J, et al: *The Damocles Syndrome: Psychological Consequences of Surviving Childhood Cancer*. New York, McGraw-Hill, 1980.
4. Nir Y: Post-traumatic stress disorder in children with cancer, in Spencer E, Pynoos RS (eds): *Post-traumatic Stress Disorder in Children*. Washington, American Psychiatric Press, 1985, pp 121–132.
5. Spinetta J, Spinetta PD (eds): *Living with Childhood Cancer*. St Louis, Mosby, 1981.
6. Cairns NY, Clark GM, Smith SD, et al: Adaptation of siblings to childhood malignancy. *J Pediatr* 1970;95:484–487.

7. Pratt JH: The class method of treating consumption in the homes of the poor. *AMA J* 1907;49:755–759.
8. Pratt JH: The tuberculosis class: An experiment in home treatment. *Hosp Soc Serv* 1917;4:49–68.
9. Yalom ID: *The Theory and Practice of Group Psychotherapy*. New York, Basic Books, 1970.
10. Wender L: Current trends in group psychotherapy. *Am J Psychother* 1951;3:381–404.
11. Rogers C: *On Encounter Groups*. New York, Harper & Row, 1970.
12. Kolodny E: Treatment of mothers in groups as a supplement. *Ment Hyg* 1944;437–438.
13. Amster F: Collective psychotherapy of mothers of emotionally disturbed children. *Am J Orthopsychiatry* 1944;14:44–52.
14. Durkin H: *Group Therapy for Mothers of Disturbed Children*. Springfield, Ill, Thomas, 1954.
15. Bauer I, Gurevitz S: Group therapy with parents of schizophrenic children. *Int J Group Psychother* 1952;4:344–357.
16. Mattson A, Agle DP: Group therapy with parents of hemophiliacs. *J Am Acad Child Psychiatry* 1972;11:558–571.
17. Gilder R, Bushman PR, Sitarz AL: Group therapy with parents of children with leukemia. *Am J Psychother* 1978;32:276–287.
18. Karta M, Ertel IJ: Short-term group therapy for mothers with leukemic children. *Clin Pediatr* 1976;803–806.
19. Bibring GL, Dwyer TF, Huntington DS, et al: A study of the psychological processes in pregnancy and of the earliest mother-child relationship. Appendix B: glossary of defenses. *Psychoanal Study Child* 1961;16:62–72.
20. Mahler M, Pine F, Bergmann A: *The Psychological Birth of the Human Infant*. New York, Basic Books, 1975.
21. Kubler-Ross E: *On Death and Dying*. New York, Macmillan, 1969.
22. Sourkes B: Facilitating family coping with childhood cancer. *J Pediatr Psychol* 1977;2:65–67.

14

Process Groups for the Training of Psychiatrists

Enid Lang
David A. Halperin
Hillel Swiller

For psychiatric residents the period of training during their residency forms one of the most stressful experiences of their lives. Having left the certainties of medical school, the psychiatric resident enters a field which appears to be pervaded by ambivalence and ambiguity. Indeed, psychiatry itself is a field in transition between the model of the psychiatrist as therapist and the psychiatrist as physician. During training, the psychiatric resident is forced to work with the sickest patients, a task which would elicit doubts about their competence from any professional. And the constant work with psychotic patients exerts its own regressive pull which may elicit further doubts from the residents about their own emotional stability. Finally, the psychiatric resident is forced to work with a variety of authority figures and hierarchies — each expressing its own perspective and each acting out its own competitive agenda.

During the process of training, the residents are constantly assessed by physicians (supervisors and directors of residency training) — an assessment which tries to divine not what the resident knows but who he is and how he deals with demanding and frequently hostile patients. In addition, the psychiatric residents must learn to deal effectively with nurses and other nonmedical personnel over whom they have technical authority but whose actual experience far outweighs their own. Throughout this period, the psychiatric residents must also learn to deal with the competitive professional, sexual (positive and negative), and social feelings that develop with a particular intensity during the course of work. Moreover, the psychiatric residents are at a point in their lives in which other issues such as marriage, separation, childbearing, raising children, and dealing with the agenda of adulthood come to the fore.

Because of this complex amalgam of professionally induced stress and the normative anxiety of transition, a number of training programs have instituted process groups as a means of helping residents to cope successfully with these issues. This chapter examines the formation, function, and the value of process groups for psychiatric residents. The process groups which form the subject of this chapter are led by mental health professionals as part of the training program at the Department of Psychiatry of the Mount Sinai School of Medicine.

DEFINITIONS

What is a process group? A process group is a group whose members are members by virtue of their participation in a training program. A process group exists to study its own behavior and to enable its members to learn about group dynamics and interpersonal communication. Its members will usually gain an added insight into individual dynamics, but primarily in dealing within the context of issues of professional growth and development for the residents, in which the very universality of their struggles toward professional competence are acknowledged and examined.

A process group functions as an arena in which the residents are listened to and, to some degree, nurtured. During the course of evolution of a process group, the members develop a deeper understanding of their relationship to other authority figures such as supervisors and attending physicians (and conceivably their families). As the resident psychiatrists develop a deeper understanding of group dynamics and evolution, they may learn to appreciate the value of group psychotherapy (and ultimately become group leaders themselves).

Process groups are *not* group psychotherapy. While the experience may well be therapeutic, the relationship between group members and group facilitators — their contract — is very different. Technical differences between the process group and the psychotherapy group include:

1. Time: In group psychotherapy, the time and length of the group meeting are set by the group leader. In a process group, however, the time, place, and duration of the process group meeting are set by an administration which demands conformity from members and facilitators alike. Moreover, therapy groups usually function for an

indeterminate period with members being added or leaving over time. The process group is limited in duration to the training program and terminates at its completion. New members are not added, and active members may leave for reasons of training without the question of resistance being raised. At Mount Sinai, the process group (members and facilitators) remains together throughout the duration of the training program. However, this is a particularly intensive model. At other programs, process groups may meet only at the beginning of the program as part of a process of acculturation, or near termination, in order to deal with issues around separation.

2. Membership: In therapy groups, the group leader selects the group members. He is able to choose members on the basis of ego strength, suitability for a group experience, and ability to function in an intense interpersonal context. In a process group, membership is predefined by membership in a peer/cohort group. All members of a class are invited to attend without restriction (in some programs attendance is compulsory).

3. Termination: Termination from a therapy group is an individual event which ends participation in the group but not necessarily the status of being a patient. On the other hand, termination in a process group is a group event which occurs for all members at the same time. The status of patient/member cannot be prolonged.

4. Subgrouping: In therapy groups, subgrouping is discouraged and members are told that no confidentiality exists among members of the therapy group; their reluctance to bring confidential material into the group is subject to scrutiny. In a process group, by definition, subgroups exist because the members all work together. It is understood that members will have extragroup relationships and that self-disclosure is neither indicated nor even encouraged. Indeed, one of the tasks of the process group leader-facilitator is to help the group explore the role of the subgroups in shaping the culture of the group as a whole.

5. Content: In therapy groups members are encouraged to discuss every aspect of their lives, and a reluctance to self-disclosure is an appropriate subject for examination. In a process group, many issues such as a resident's sexual preferences or activity would only rarely be explored in the group setting and then only with considerable hesitation. Rather, in a process group, the content of the sessions is directed toward the task at hand, that is, the process of becoming a psychiatrist. At the beginning of the process group, the leaders may even outline the group tasks as being: (a) our feelings about psychiatry, (b) our feelings about becoming a psychiatrist, (c) the impact of being a psychiatrist on other aspects of our life.

CREDITS AND DEBITS OF
PROCESS GROUP FORMATION

Ideally the process group should provide the members with a source of support, for it is a forum in which they have the opportunity to express their feelings with some certainty that other members have experienced comparable trauma and have had to cope with the same affect-laden environment. This experience allows the residents to face the frustrating reality of their training environment with the supportive awareness that their experiences are not unique and form part and parcel of everyone's time of transition. In more didactic terms, the process group complements the formal course work in group psychotherapy. It allows the residents to develop a heightened appreciation of the role of group dynamics, both in the formal therapeutic groups which they lead (or will lead) and in the organizational hierarchies in which they participate. And for the administration of a department of psychiatry, the existence of a process group provides residents with a forum in which they can discuss the normative discontents of training without having to "act out" the anger that develops in any such intensely competitive environment.

Coleading a process group is in many respects the most rewarding experience for a group therapist. One is given the opportunity to work with highly motivated intelligent and well-integrated (for the most part) individuals who will challenge the complacency that inevitably develops during the course of teaching and private practice.

A process group, like all intense processes, inevitably elicits concerns. The administration of residency training programs may be fearful about the impact of the process group on individual residents. While not explicitly stated, there is often expressed a muted concern that this additional stress may cause a resident to decompensate as a result of the group process. In the authors' experience, while the rare resident may decompensate during the course of a residency, the difficulties predated the process group experience and were not connected to the group process.

On another level, the administration may be fearful that the process group is a "soviet" in formation. But, as previously noted, the very formation of the process group diffuses the "everyday discontent" of residency. Of course, the administration may view the process group as interfering with the provision of services and as a further drain on service time. They may even act this out by "accidentally" scheduling other meetings during the time set aside for the process group or by stalling meetings so as to interfere with process group time. These issues should be dealt with by the group leaders who must negotiate with the administrative hierarchy to preserve the group boundaries.

The importance that the residents attach to the process groups is evident in their vocal criticism of the group leaders for acting deferentially toward the administrative hierarchy when they treat the boundaries of the process group in too cavalier a fashion.

The departmental hierarchy may not be the only group skeptical of the process group. At the formation of a process group (and usually over the course of the group), the residents themselves often express considerable objections to any demands for self-exposure. This issue — the residents' fears of self-exposure to the department and to one another — often becomes a significant leitmotif. In many ways, it is a resistance that the group leaders can cite only with reluctance and with the awareness that whatever its underlying cause, it will not be significantly resolved over the course of the group.

THE RELATIONSHIP BETWEEN GROUP LEADERS AND MEMBERS: CONTRACTS

There are significant differences between the contract of the leader of a psychotherapy group and the contract between the leader and members of a process group. An area of particular concern is the question of confidentiality. In a psychotherapeutic group, confidentiality is absolute (subject to the caveat of the Tarachoff decision). However, the group leaders of a process group form part of the hierarchical frame and context in which the group meets and under whose auspices it operates. As previously noted, it is often exceedingly difficult for the residents to accept the reality that the process group operates independently of the rest of the departmental hierarchy and that confidentiality does indeed exist. Thus process group leaders must contract with the department hierarchy not to assume any other role vis-à-vis the group members, even in so slight a function as reporting on their attendance. Indeed, if the process group is to function at all, the members should be informed during the first session that attendance is purely voluntary and that the proceedings are being conducted in total isolation from the rest of the department. The question of what role, if any, the group leaders should play in informing the department about the ongoing psychotic decompensation of a group member is obviously very complex. In the authors' experience, breaching the group's confidentiality, even if done in the service of providing additional support or obtaining treatment for a group member who is experiencing acute difficulty, would elicit so intensely negative a response from the group that the group leaders in this circumstance should trust to the multitude of other safeguards within the training program.

The group leader's role in relation to the group member in acute distress raises the question of leader countertransference in relationship to the other group members. Working with psychiatrists-in-training inevitably will elicit from the group leaders their own feelings about their own period of training. In addition, the frequent cogent complaints by the residents about the hospital/departmental hierarchy will elicit from the group leader (particularly if he is primarily involved in the private practice of psychiatry) an identification which is the more difficult to examine because of its superficial plausibility. In this context, it should be noted that while the residents' complaints may appear to be justified, their expression within the group is comparable to the expression of complaints in a group psychotherapy setting where complaints about spouses, bosses, etc usually are a covert means of expressing the members' anger at the group leader for not gratifying their dependent strivings. Group leaders should be alert to the possibility of their being seduced into fulfilling the role of the "good mother" while the group members split off their hostile affect and project it onto the denying, administrative "bad mother." The problem of splitting may be intensified for the leaders of a process group because their role is not as clearly defined as "facilitators" when compared to the clear-cut role definition of the psychotherapy group leader. In the context, the process group leader is seen and often conceptualized by the group as a role model who is working with future colleagues and is thus under a certain sense of obligation to consensually validate the group members' perception that the department is not living up to its pretensions. Finally, it should be recognized that in working with residents who are indeed alert, articulate, and intelligent, the human desire to obtain approval will operate within group leaders irrespective of their past training or sense of role.

PROCESS GROUPS: THEIR ROLE IN
TEACHING RESIDENTS ABOUT
GROUP DYNAMICS

Process groups are particularly useful in helping residents develop an appreciation about group dynamics. They function through examining with the group: (1) the obstacles that the group creates to self-study, (2) the boundary issues that arise during the course of the group, and (3) the developing of a heightened appreciation of the formation and evolution of basic assumption groups.[1] While these group tasks bear considerable resemblance to the group tasks formulated and followed within the study groups that follow the Tavistock and A.K. Rice Institute model, there are also significant differences, particularly in light of the fact that in a successful process group the group leaders are not inaccessible nor do they simply facilitate the operations of the group by acting as interpreters of group process and dynamics. Let us examine the role of the group leader in promoting the group tasks.

Throughout the course of the process group, the group leaders evaluate the group's level of self-study (which changes as the group evolves) and identify obstacles to self-study. When the group is unable to remove the obstacle, the group leaders intervene by pointing its nature so that the members may remove it and continue with their work.

The following episode is illustrative: During an early phase of the process group, the group was anxious about their performance of their ward duties. The group members would complain about unit chiefs who offered little specific instruction about how they should treat their patients — throwing the residents "to the wolves." At this early stage in the group, the group leaders silently concur about the group's limited capacity for introspection because their anxiety about their performance is too great. In succeeding sessions the group continued to focus around the inadequacy of the unit chiefs and their lack of guidance and specificity. Finally, the leaders observed that the group's constant rumination about the confusion on the wards may reflect and parallel their sense that the group leaders have been comparably obtuse and have also neglected to provide the group with specific directions to enable them to pursue the group's tasks. This intervention, which focuses on the group's use of displacement to create a resistance to self-study, may be initially ignored or meet with a resentment expressed in a "so that's what the textbook says is going on in this circumstance." Nonetheless, over time, the group did, indeed, begin to deal with its anger toward the group leaders who, it felt, were not fulfilling their dependency strivings.

Obstacles to self-study are similar to, but not necessarily identical with, resistance. Obstacles include intellectualization, displacement, silence, scapegoating. But obstacles may also include ignorance, which is, after all, not a resistance even though it represents a pseudonaiveté which does effectively block the evolution of the group. When ignorance is an obstacle of self-study it should be met with the presentation of new material. For example, in the instance cited above, there were two aspects to the leader's intervention. On one level, clarifying material was introduced to help the group deal with the obstacle to study created by ignorance. On the other level, the question of group displacement of its anger toward the group leaders onto an external environment was introduced. But it was recognized that the group might not at that time be ready to deal with this underlying obstacle to self-study, and that the formation of an alliance with the process group might entail accepting their pseudonaiveté as a full explanation of the group process.

The basic intervention employed by group leaders in helping the group to deal with obstacles to self-study is calling the group's attention to the group process as it directly unfolds. Thus the group is invited, on its own, to identify the sources of resistance. However, when an intervention on this level is not effective, the group leaders may encourage the group to consider the group process in more dynamic terms. Thus the following:

> During the course of a session, a group member announced she was exhausted that day because she had broken up with her boyfriend recently, and as a consequence had spent the previous night crying. The group initially expressed sympathy for her situation. Then, the discussion turned to the more general topic of how little sleep the members get when on call — how residents are chronically fatigued. The following week, two male group members talked about a car one had purchased — but one commented that he had purchased a car without a radio because he was afraid of vandalism and theft. The second resident then talked about how his car had been vandalized. Then the discussion turned to another resident who discussed how fearful she was of a violent patient that she had just admitted to the hospital. She expressed a wish for more security guards and protection in the emergency room. Other residents joined in the discussion, describing their experiences with dangerous patients.

When the group leader suggested that the discussion of break-ins and violations of personal security might be related to the discussion of the preceding week, the residents' initial response was a disclaimer on the grounds of reality — "You just can't imagine how dangerous it is to work in the ER." Discussion continued to revolve around this reality issue. At that point, the group leader suggested that the group was displacing its fear of intimacy within the group by expressing personal vulnerability (as had the resident the preceding week). This interpretation was again met with denial, but group activity over succeeding weeks demonstrated that by suggesting the residents deal with their underlying fears of dependency, the group process had been advanced.

The interventions of the group leaders should not be confined to an exploration of the obstacles to group process. It is often particularly valuable for the group leaders to help the group explore issues that arise around the group boundaries of time, place, and person. Indeed, in a well-functioning group, much of the most valuable process arises in exploring limit-setting involving all of these parameters. Thus the following interaction:

> The process group was scheduled to meet between one and two o'clock. However, it started late because a member of the department ran over in conducting a seminar. The residents expressed their anger on two levels: (1) The scheduled meeting time interfered with lunch, and (2) the group started late. The group members demanded that the leaders arrange for a change in meeting time.

In raising their demand, the group members were testing both the group leaders and their relationship with the administration. While they were asking for a change in meeting time, the underlying question was more basic: Did the group leaders care enough about the group members to prevent them from going hungry? That is, will the group leaders nurture the group members? This is also implicit in their questioning the extent (if any) of the group leaders' clout with the administration of the department. Would the group leaders as gatekeepers assert themselves sufficiently to ensure that the group meeting both began on time and lasted the full allotted time? Indeed, in this specific instance the group leaders initially adopted a rather deferential attitude toward their colleagues' delay which led to the formation of a group "myth" that the group leaders were "weak, hesitant, and spineless." The existence of this group myth became evident only later during the course of the group as the residents began to discuss this need to "protect" their "weak" leaders, particularly in terms of their fear that if the group members asserted themselves, the department would retaliate by "firing" the group leaders.

As this incident demonstrates, the group members both identified with the group leaders and yet projected them into the role of being mediators between the group and the department. But like many "saints," the group leaders were judged to be feeble intermediaries. This "failure" of the group leaders as keepers of the group boundaries was acted out by the group members in other ways as well. For example, a male group member assumed the role of gatekeeper by closing the door at the beginning of the meeting, thus supplanting the "emasculated" group leader. While his action might be interpreted within a psychotherapy group as reflecting his competitiveness and oedipal strivings, within the process group his actions were interpreted as reflecting the importance that the group placed on maintaining its integrity against a hostile and threatening outside world (Bion's fight-flight assumption).[1] Thus, in exploring boundary issues, the group members are given the opportunity to experience the manner in which groups organize themselves and the evolution of groups as the group strives to preserve its integrity. Eventually, the group members begin to develop a deeper appreciation of the responsibilities and parameters in which group leadership expresses itself.

The important boundary of confidentiality and the group's pervasive concern that this boundary will be breached appears continually as a metaphor for the group's sense of its own integrity and of the sense that each generation has that it, alone, will make the world anew. This sense of novelty coexists with a myth which extends between generations of residents about the process group itself. Group members have already discussed process groups with residents senior to them and these rumors become part of the received knowledge about the entire process. Group leaders should discuss these forebodings with the group in the earliest stages of process group formation, particularly because the events of prior years become embedded within the group as cautionary notes which set the limits on what can or should be discussed within the group. Thus, if a resident has been terminated from the previous year because of severe illness, the myth that he was discharged because of breaks in confidentiality may ensure that members of the succeeding process groups limit disclosure within the group and a group norm of blandness and decorum prevails. The departure from the residency program of more outspoken members of the process group may reflect their genuine disapproval of aspects of the program, but it may also reflect their fear that because of breaks in the boundary of confidentiality, that if they did not leave, then they would be discharged. In this context, the boundary of person/group composition (including the presence or absence of group leaders) is a most significant boundary to examine. The absence/presence of members, seating arrangements, sex ratio of members, and the presence/absence of members who are unstable are particularly important. During the course of the examination of this boundary condition, issues such as scapegoating or self-exclusion can be examined in a revealing and instructive manner, which provides a nonjudgmental vehicle for the examination of the charged issues that arise during the course of an intense group experience.

THE ROLE OF PROCESS GROUPS IN TEACHING GROUP PSYCHOTHERAPY

Process groups allow the group members to develop an appreciation of the manner in which obstacles to the group process develop, and demonstrate how the examination of the boundary conditions within a group allows for an examination in group-as-a-whole terms of group interaction. However, process groups afford their members the opportunity to participate in and observe the operation of basic assumption groups and thus provide their participants with a fuller appreciation of group activity both within and outside the therapeutic framework. While a didactic program should not form part of the process group, the process group itself provides a unique opportunity in which the members can learn about the role of basic assumptions in group formation and evolution. Thus, when relevant, the group leaders have pointed out to participants during the early phase of process group formation that their demands exemplify Bion's dependency assumptions.[1] Or, as the group evolves, the resident's fears of being "thrown to the administration wolves" and/or desire to deal with conflict-laden situations during the residency by transferring to another (presumably more idyllic) program can be examined as possibly exemplifying Bion's fight-flight basic assumptions. Later, during the group's evolution, as subgroups form and it becomes evident in the here-and-now of the group that certain residents relate to one another in a particularly supportive fashion, the possibility of their behavior reflecting the pairing assumption might be discussed. However, whenever these interpretations are made, it is most important that the leaders rely only on the material that presents itself in the group itself. While leaders may be aware of outside relationships between group members or between the administration and the group, their interpretive activity should be limited to utilizing material that is readily accessible to all group members. Otherwise, the members will (and rightly so) experience the group leaders as controlling and intrusive.

In the context of the pairing assumption, group subgroupings may labor and produce a group counterculture leader or "messiah." Here, a group member either nominates himself or is nominated to become a group "leader." The conflict between the group leaders and the group messiah may elicit intense countertransference on the leaders' part which may temporarily present a significant obstacle to the group's attempts to study itself. However, if the group leader deals with his intense feelings and consistently recognizes the process issues involved, a positive resolution is possible. The pairing assumption may present itself in another form: the birth of children during the course of the group. However, any interpretations of so personal a matter during the course of the group should be made cautiously. This is because while it may open the group to the discussion of sexual material, it may also be perceived by the group as being so remote from the group's tasks as to make the entire process group itself suspect ("That's just out of some old textbook") and interfere with the formation of a therapeutic alliance between the group members and leaders.

FURTHER CONSIDERATIONS ON THE PROCESS GROUP AS A SOURCE OF SUPPORT: THE ROLE OF GROUP LEADERS

The members of a process group may have agreed to participate in a program which is ultimately therapeutic, but they have not agreed to participate in group therapy. Nor have they agreed to participate in an intensive group training program. Thus, the group leaders must constantly consider walking a thin line between being didactic and nurturing on the one hand and denying, distant, and detached on the other. The regressive pull experienced as a result of the stress of training, particularly in working with severely regressed patients, should not be complemented by a lack of support and gratification in the process group. Particularly in the early phases of the process group, when the members relate to the group leaders in a dependent mode, observations such as "it must be hard for you to discuss these feelings with people you're not sure if you can trust" are helpful. During this early phase of the group's evolution, it is often helpful for the leaders to express their observations in terms of personal anecdotes, or vignettes from their own training experience in which the individual's dilemmas and the more general aspects of the situation are examined. Whatever the individual leader's personal style, the interventions must be conveyed with enough warmth to create and sustain a "holding environment."[2] The group leaders should be (in Winnicott's memorable phrase) "good-enough" leaders, who with their sense of personal confidence, security, and warmth can act as reasonable role models.

An important aspect of being a role model in this context is a capacity to tolerate aggression from group members and to be able to deal with the anger aroused by an initially unpalatable interpretation. An angry, dependent group of residents needs to be reassured that its anger will not destroy the group leader. When the group leader is able to "speak the unspeakable," even if the intervention is initially experienced as being provocative or insufficiently sensitive, his ability to tolerate the group's anger may be helpful. In this context, the ability of the group members to externalize their anger prevents the implosion, for example, the group members' inability to get angry at the group leader will lead to fighting among themselves, that would otherwise occur.[3] Indeed, when hostilities are expressed between group members in particularly virulent terms, it may be because the group members feel that they have to protect a group leader whom they feel is otherwise too fragile to tolerate aggression. Finally, it should be noted that while the group leader's use of humor and anecdote helps to establish a "holding environment" within the early phases of the group, his continuing humanity will provide the opportunity to establish a climate of collegiality and equality during the termination phase.

COLEADERSHIP AS AN ASPECT OF THE PROCESS GROUP

Leadership of a process group is an intense and emotionally involving experience. The group leader identifies with the travail experienced by the group members during their training. The intensity of the identification with group members makes it particularly difficult for the group leader to retain a sense of objectivity about the group and the group process. Thus, coleadership provides group leaders with the opportunity to validate their individual sense of the group work. Moreover, the group leaders can greatly benefit by learning about themselves and group processes by coleading a group. Coleaders for the process groups at the Mount Sinai Department of Psychiatry have usually but not always consisted of a male and female. Using leaders of different sexes may be advantageous because, on the most basic level, it replicates the parental unit. Moreover, since the resident groups consist of both men and women, this affords all residents a useful role model. However, when the coleaders are of the same sex, there usually appears to develop a splitting between the leaders in which one is labeled as the more nurturant parent. The initial splitting may be based on the perceived personality of the group leaders, but often alters during the course of the process group.

If coleaders are to work together successfully, it is important for the coleaders to basically like each other and to have a real measure of respect for each other personally and professionally. A common pairing is to join a more experienced and a less experienced group leader. This differential in experience may provide added difficulties during the course of coleadership. Above all, before the first session of the process group, the coleaders should meet to discuss their philosophies about the purpose of the process group, particularly with regard to the degree that they feel that leaders should intervene during the group process and the extent to which residents should be gratified during the course of the group. There is a broad spectrum of diversity among process group leaders over the extent to which the residents' dependency strivings should be gratified — groups have run well irrespective of the philosophic stance of the group coleaders — but if the leaders have serious disagreements and are unwilling to discuss their disagreements, the group work will be impaired. It has been the authors' combined experience that a debriefing postgroup meeting of at least a half-hour is necessary to resolve differing perceptions of the individual leader's impact on the group.

Significant benefits of coleading a process group include lending support to each other in dealing with group transference, aiding each other in observing the group process, acting as role models in the collaborative resolution of differences, helping each other in the exploration of resistances within the group, and being available to help each other appreciate countertransference issues when they arise.

The presence of a coleader permits each leader to point out group transferences when they arise, as the following illustrates:

A coleader was visibly pregnant. Yet, nobody within the process group had alluded to her pregnancy. Finally, during one session, the group members discussed plans for a Christmas party and started to "joke" about having a sex orgy with the members of the staff. The male

222

coleader commented that this "joking" related to the group members' feeling about the leader's pregnancy and the relationship between the group leaders.

While the female leader could have commented on this entire issue, the presence and intervention by her coleader enabled the group to deal with what had hitherto been a taboo area.

Coleaders can act as role models[4] as they point out to each other disagreements and settle their differences amicably in front of the group:

> At the end of the first year of residency, the members were still in a state of passive-dependency, remaining cohesive and undifferentiated within a clump filled with good feelings. During this era of good feelings, the members began to discuss their assignments for the coming year. The discussion rapidly evolved into planning for a barbecue with family members being included. One coleader commented that this discussion appeared to be the group's way of dealing with their impending separation. The coleader openly disagreed with this interpretation. He commented that the group was dealing with the barbecue and family as a means of avoiding dealing with their competitive feelings about the assignments, and that a discussion of family members was merely an extension of their competition into the realm of "who has children and who doesn't." Both issues appeared to be important to the group.

And it was after the group leaders were able to confront their disagreements, that the group members were able to confront theirs.

The group members may split the parental couple of the group leaders. One coleader will be perceived as empathic and sensitive to the residents' needs, while the other coleader will be perceived as cold, distant, and insensitive. The intensity of the transference is one aspect of all groups and supports the use of coleaders, when possible. When splitting occurs, the "preferred" leader should encourage the group to explore its anger toward the other coleader. It often emerges that the group has been unable to express its anger toward the preferred leader for a variety of transferential (as well as realistic personality) factors. Indeed, in this context the group members may be using the "disfavored" leader as a means of expressing the hostility they feel toward one another. And in postgroup sessions the leaders may discover that the favored coleader has been colluding with the group in setting up the coleader. Each coleader is in a position to help the other deal with the countertransference issues. As in individual therapy, the examination of countertransference often leads to observations of relevance within the group:

> A male coleader had commented that he envied his partner's being able to work on a limited basis so that she could be with her children. Thus, during the termination phase of a process group, when the female members (most of whom were married and had children) were uncharacteristically silent or absent from sessions in which the male members

were discussing their future plans, the male coleader observed that the male group members were actively excluding the female members from the discussion because they felt that the female members' dependency needs had already been met by their husbands. The male members acknowledged their feelings. And the female members began to discuss the myth that their needs were being met by their husbands' financial support.

Other countertransference issues that frequently arise include overgratifying residents out of a wish to be "loved" or adopting too active a stance because of the leader's difficulty in separating from the group (even including a desire to become a group member). Countertransference may even lead to a wish to abdicate the position of authority as group leader. This may occur particularly in the termination phase of the group, when a sense of basic equality has been established between group members and group leaders. Then, group leaders who desire to gratify their own dependency needs may intervene too frequently and too openly. These issues are usually readily resolved during the course of postgroup discussions.

Finally, a unique benefit which coleadership affords is the opportunity to examine in conjunction with the other group leader the parallels that arise between the group leaders' response to each other and to the group members, and to spouses and significant family members, particularly in relationship to child-parent interactions. The phases of a process group (like all groups) parallels the phases of child development. In the early phases of the group, issues centering around nurturance and intimacy are foremost; later, questions of competition and defiance of group leaders arise. And, in the termination phase, leaders like parents are forced to let go of their children and reestablish a new relationship based on equality. Thus, group leaders (if they are open with each other) may begin to appreciate how their feelings toward each other parallel feelings for their spouse. For example, a leader may resent the coleader for being seductive with the group, just as the spouse is able to win the children's affection. Later, their competitive strivings will emerge and they may appreciate how their need to be "on target" in their interpretations reflects a past in which for example, "my brother (sister) was the favorite one, so I had to be the smart one." And, finally, one coleader can tell the other that she or he "has to let the children grow up." The opportunity to experience and work through these issues is often extremely helpful and illuminating.

In this context, it should be noted that just as each child is born with its own innate disposition, so each group of residents — each generation of residents — has its own character. Some groups are timid and compliant, while other are rebellious and assertive. Some groups seem to develop an early sense of cohesion while others are always more diffuse. Coleadership provides the leaders with corroboration about the character of the group, and the presence of coleaders provides an added support to each leader as they attempt to deal with the givens of the group's personality.

PEER SUPERVISION AND PROCESS
GROUP LEADERSHIP

The complexities that occur during the course of leading a process group have led to the formation of a peer supervisory group for the process group leaders. The peer group usually meets for an hour and a half every month. It consists of the leaders of the active process groups and leaders of past groups. The existence of the supervisory group acknowledges the problems inherent in conducting process groups and serves as a souce of support to the group leaders by universalizing the issues that arise so that they can be examined in depth. It provides for the process group leaders an unusual opportunity to learn about group dynamics and particularly about the issue of leadership. Members are encouraged to present material from groups in rotation — but "emergencies" are dealt with as they arise. During the course of presentations, members are encouraged to hypothesize about the evolution of a group or to share with other group members the interventions they would make in this setting.

One of the most instructive and supportive aspects of peer group supervision is the presentation of problems that arise between coleaders. Implicit within the creation of a peer supervisory group is the assumption that any pair of coleaders will have some areas of difficulty. Coleaders are asked at the beginning of their participation to predict areas of difficulty that might arise. In a typical case, one female coleader commented that from his past performance she anticipated that her male coleader might often be late or absent — that if this occurred she would find it difficult to work with him. Her partner commented that he anticipated difficulty in working with her because he experienced her as being controlling and judgmental. That their worst fears did not come to pass is a product of the opportunity that group peer supervision affords for confronting difficulties rather than working them out in front of the group.

The peer supervision group does not function as a process group. It only examines its own behavior when the task of the group is impeded. This is particularly helpful when the meeting parallels the process between the coleaders or within the process group itself. Thus, when a group of coleaders repetitiously returned to the presentation of their difficulties with a particularly problematic resident, one of the other members of the supervisory group observed that if this paralleled the group itself, he could only anticipate a depletion of members. Ultimately, the peer supervisory group enables the group leaders to learn about their dynamics in an open, relatively consistent, and non-judgmental setting. It helps members deal with personal conflicts and differences in value but in a task-oriented and realistic fashion.

SUMMARY

The psychiatric residency is a complex and anxiety-laden period during the lives of all psychiatrists. Process groups consisting of residents and leaders are an exceedingly useful modality for dealing with the manifold professional and personal pressures that arise. This chapter examines in detail transference and countertransference issues, the course of process group evolution, supervisory schemata for dealing with potential impasses, and models for intervention and interpretation.

Acknowledgment

The authors thank all the leaders of the psychiatric resident process groups at Mount Sinai Medical Center whose ideas have contributed to the philosophy presented in this chapter.

REFERENCES

1. Bion WR: *Experiences in Groups*. London, Tavistock, 1961.
2. Winnicott DW: Primary maternal preoccupation, in Winnicott DW: *Collected Papers*. New York, Basic Books, 1958.
3. Stein A, Kibel H: A group dynamic peer interaction approach to group psychotherapy. *Int J Group Psychother* 1984;3:315–333.
4. O'Hearne, J: Comments on peer relationships, self-esteem, and the self. *Int J Group Psychother* 1987;37:519–523.

PART III
GROUP PSYCHOTHERAPY
THROUGH THE LIFE CYCLE

15

Group Therapy with Girls without Fathers: The Cult of the Woman Warrior

Theresa Aiello Gerber

This chapter discusses a latency age girls group in respect of some phenomena that emerged that may shed light on issues of identity formation and transference-related projections leading finally toward a group mythology. The significance of this material contributes to a revision of our understanding of the current sociology of latency age girls who grow up without the presence of a father in the household.

The intact nuclear family has undergone a steady erosion in the last 50 years. Single parent families have increased not only as a result of divorce and widowhood but also because increasing numbers of women have opted to become single parents by choice. This major change has demanded that children find new coping mechanisms to adjust to the new family structure. This affects not only psychic defensive strategy but has implications regarding identity formation.

Girls who watch their mothers coping alone have begun to adjust to the single mother family. In families where a father's presence is unknown in the household, girls struggle to combine the qualities of traditional femininity with the need to protect oneself (ie, the traditional role of the father). Girls of such families may fantasize less about the male-female dyadic romance and attempt to incorporate male and female selves in one person.

The issues that emerge during the course of the latency age girls groups without fathers form the subject of this chapter. However, they can be examined in particular if we use the evaluation of one particular group.

This group in question comprised eight girls between the ages of 8 through 11. The group was mixed ethnically and racially. These girls came from middle-class families and had not been deprived in financial or social terms. Seven of the eight members had lived all or most of their lives alone with their mothers. Six members were the only child in the family and only one member came from an intact nuclear family with another sibling. This group was conducted at a locally well-known neighborhood community center. Five girls were Jewish, one was a white Anglo-Saxon Catholic, and two were of mixed racial identity. Of particular importance in these girls' development is the fact that all of their mothers worked out of necessity. The girls initially had been coming to the center's afterschool program in lieu of other child care arrangements.

The majority of the patients in this group suffered from varying degrees of depression. In addition, two were socially withdrawn, one was obese, and two members had interpersonal difficulties and were considered to be "acting out" children.

THE SELF-OBJECT TRANSFERENCE,
AND THE WOMAN WARRIOR

The thematic material that forms the subject of this chapter and of this group began to emerge in the very first session: the need for an idealized self-object transference which expressed itself in the persona of the superheroines.

American popular culture has had a predilection for providing superheroes as sources of identification for latency age boys. The very concept of childhood itself has been described as a culturally derived invention. As such it follows that expectations of a normative for latency must change (or adapt) as the culture itself changes and adapts over time to changes in the structure of family life.[1,2] In Maxine Hong Kingston's book *The Woman Warrior*, the adolescent heroine periodically retreats to fantasies of empowerment in the form of the figure of a woman warrior.[3]

In recent years, there has been an emergence of corresponding superheroines for girls: Supergirl, Wonder Woman (who dates to the mid-1940s), and an assortment of pretty policewomen, etc. This latency age group (which incidentally called itself "the social club" in the Slavson tradition of children's groups) early on periodically referred to the adventures of a family of superheroines on television and in comic books under the leadership of "She-Ra."

She-Ra is really Adora (sister to He-Man, also a superhero). Adora is a beautiful and gentle young woman who, like the nymphs of Greek mythology, inhabits the woodlands of a kingdom called Etheria. Adora has discovered that with the help of her magic sword, she can, if need be, transform herself into a mighty warrior women — She-Ra.

She-Ra is the central and most powerful figure in a group of beautiful girls, each one possessing singular magical abilities. "Perfuma" can make flowers appear anywhere, "Peeka-Blue" has blue hair, is peacocklike, and is known to the group as "the watcher." The group has a wicked member too: Catra, who has black hair, rides a large cat and is jealous of She-Ra. Catra and She-Ra are the only members who look human. They appear to play out the most human emotions. All these heroines are beautiful, gentle, and playful in nature. They are notably fantastic in appearance, possessing long clouds of pink, blue, and green hair.

She-Ra is the leader of what is called "The Rebellion." The Rebellion stands against a group of men who are authoritarian, militaristic, old, and cruel. They are the ruthless rulers of the kingdom. They frequently employ robots to carry out their warfare against The Rebellion. In a sense they represent a mechanistic antinature force. (Janine Chasseguet-Smirgel[4] has suggested that men often treat themselves as machines and that dehumanization is more popular than creativity.) In terms of this fantasy, the women represent the force of creativity that conquers all.

She-Ra's family of girlish heroines parallels the historically earlier Norse mythology: that of the Valkyrie of the *Ring of the Nibelung* trilogy. Indeed, Philippe Aries[2] has suggested that Siegfried is the first adolescent cultural hero. In many respects Brünnhilde is his female counterpart — an adolescent heroine. Like The Rebellion, the Valkyrie are the virgin daughters of Wotan and they are a family of warrior women. Their task is to conduct the dead heroes to Valhalla. They eschew other contacts with men and remain dedicated to their father.

She-Ra, like her predecessor Brünnhilde, is tall, blonde, and fearless. She can be gentle and loving, motherly and severe; she is steeped in nature lore. She communicates empathically with all manner of wild beasts and monsters. Like Orpheus in the underworld, she tames them. In one episode She-Ra changes a young boy's mind — he first wishes to become "beast master" but ultimately becomes "beast protector" as a result of She-Ra's teaching. Like Brünnhilde and her winged horse Grane, she also rides a winged steed, "Swing-Wind." Just as Siegfried has "Nothung," She-Ra carries a magic sword that responds to her command "for the honor of Greyskull," the castle keep of her family. Chasseguet-Smirgel has speculated that ancient Germanic mythology "takes as its object the mother goddess rather than the father.... In this kind of group, one is witness to a real eradication of the father, and the paternal world as well as of all oedipal derivatives.[4]

When Adora transforms herself into She-Ra, she holds her sword upward. This is highly reminiscent of one of the Edwardian artist Arthur Rackham's illustrations of the *Ring*: a glorious Brünnhilde mounted on Grane with arms stretched upward leaps aloft onto Siegfried's funeral pyre surrounded by flames.

She-Ra and her friends form a sisterhood akin to that of the Valkyrie. One member, the bird-girl who is "the watcher" and who warns, is similar to Siegfried's little bird escort who accompanies him on the Rhine journey through the forests warning him of danger and providing him with her magical companionship.

The Rebellion is akin to a secret society with She-Ra as the ego ideal. Hence the group shares an identity in belonging to the society and in sharing a group ego ideal as mirrored by themselves and their leader as well.[5]

A WORLD WITHOUT MEN

In the first session of the group, one member brought her Peeka-Blue doll to the group. The group leader asked her what kind of doll it was, and all of the group members came over to tell her — that she was a member of She-Ra's family. It is of transference significance that this doll character is known as "the watcher" and guardian and can be easily associated with the therapist's role. It can also be a function of this child's need to be watched over herself in entering the group with a talisman. The group had collectively begun to point toward the emergence of transference component requirements.

The early group meetings centered on the girls' both playing and discussing plans to adorn themselves. They often like to make jewelry and would engage in cooperatively trading spangles and jewelry beads with one another. They discussed various fantasies which hinged on the future; how they planned to dress as adults, playing at being very fancy adult women, and their wishes to become like famous female performers — rock stars and models. One girl described a plan she had with her best friend: to perform on the sidewalks until they had enough money to dress like Madonna and go on the road to Hollywood.

Loewald[6] has discussed the need to envision a future for the ego: "The ego ideal represents a return to an original state of perfection of the ego not to be reached in the future but fantasied in the present... it becomes an ideal for the ego seen in a much more differentiated and elaborated form than previously in parental figures...."

Here the future is envisaged for the ego, but not yet a future of the ego."[6]

Conflict within the group initially nearly always was diverted to a return to jewelry making: a constant play that the girls would turn to throughout the group's existence. Interpersonal conflicts appeared to be temporarily resolved by a preoccupation with adornment. These periods of jewelry making and trading of beads were done in a very serious, intense style. The group leader would speculate that conflicted feelings in the lives of these girls was usually handled by avoidance in family life. Conflict was dealt with by the group as a need to be very cooperative with one another and in the beginning with the group leader as well to preserve the group as a family. A return to narcissistic concerns might have been seen as the safest route for girls whose family life was missing in siblings and one parental figure. Hence the need to enhance oneself.

A classic view of this preoccupation with jewelry and adornment (ie, the family jewels) would be to integrate the jewels as phallic genitalia. The girls would not have the fantasied phallus both in respect of their gender identity and in the lack of the father in ongoing, everyday interplay. (It has been suggested to me by David Halperin that Wonder Woman's powers came from her bracelet.) The group leader would like to suggest an additional view in the light of self-psychology: that the preoccupation with adornment (ie, narcissism) is the mode of the deprived self in retreat to self-cathexis. These girls were deprived of their most significant heterosexual relationship (the father). They suffered, consequently, the loss of an archaic grandiose self-object — that of the admiring father who can reflect back one's grandiose strivings for admiration and, ultimately, romantic love.

The group often gathered around the worktable to concentrate on games or the jewelry-making activity. At these times, one or two girls might request help with a game or involve the group leader in a discussion. While the group leader gave her attention to these girls, another girl would frequently sidle up behind her and begin to braid her hair, making suggestions as to how she — the group leader — might wear it. One child, Melissa, had already suggested that the group leader would definitely look like a teenager if she shaved it off into a Mohawk and dyed it purple. (The group thought this was a fine idea.) At these moments the group leader became to the girls more of a sister group member and hence shared in the adornment preoccupation.

The group enjoyed a dreidel game which was set up to be played (by the group) between the group leader and one member. The group took turns at playing, and the others would excitedly watch the progress of the game. As it happened the group leader often lost points but was never completely annihilated — something the group marveled at. The group leader was never completely opposed in this game — at least two or three girls would stand by to cheer her on and encourage her tenacity in the face of defeat (the encouragement of the mother who stands alone in the face of overwhelming odds). The three Jewish children of the group translated the Hebrew characters of the dreidel for her — consulting with one another when confused over the meaning of the letters and concerned that she not be cheated. Here the therapist was brought into the family of the group (ie, introduced to Judaism), made a member of the family by the group, and instructed in the mystical "language" of three members of the group.

From the first session on came speculations on the nature of their therapist. The group leader looked like a witch, some felt like Catra, the jealous member of She-Ra's group. "Was I a good witch," the leader asked? Yes, the group felt she was; that she would be "good to little children." Someone remarked that she had fuzzy hair. Two children of mixed racial identity quickly asserted, "What's wrong with that?" Some questioned, "Are you old enough to be a mother?" The answer was unanimous: "Yes." A discussion broke out as to whether or not the group leader should look like an adolescent or "a mommy." Hence, the group began to put together a composite of qualities that their therapist ought to have: the conflicting views of a "cat-woman," lusty and greedy for everything, and a "mommy" who is unselfish (self-sacrificing) and good to little children.

Catra in some respects has the fairy tale qualities of the step-mother: wicked (ie, sexual), and cruel to "little children," especially to the supplanted fairy tale daughter. Thus the conflict was set for the nature of the therapist/stepmother — supplanter of the real (good) mother and possessor of the spell-cast father.

The latency phase is a disguise for sexuality. To the latency age girl as to *Alice* "things are not always what they seem." People are not always what they appear to be but some disappointments mask enchantments too.

In *The Imaginary Companion*,[7] Nagera discussed the qualities and functions of the "imaginary companion" which to some degree parallel the projections onto the therapist's identity and the group's fantasies: As a superego auxiliary these fantasies may further development of ego and superego structures (to look like the sexualized cat-woman or her opposite, a good mother). Nagera cites S. Fraiberg who talks about the use of the imaginary companion as scapegoat, personifying the child's vices (ie, as Catra was used), as an attempt to prolong omnipotence and control, and as a primitive ego ideal. Occasionally the imaginary companion is used as a weapon for defense and provocation motivated by loneliness and neglect. Here, the mythologic family of women serves that purpose.

The group saw itself forming as an ideal family with periodic references to the ideal imaginary family of She-Ra and her friends. Even Catra, wicked as she is, is not a true villainess, but more willful, wayward, and self-indulgent, and therefore a much envied figure. She can act out the groups' fantasies and wishes by being selfish. She also serves as a means of dealing with instinctual anxiety projected not onto a father but a mother. She may serve as the mother who wishes to act on impulse and abandon the family.

In the transference the group had begun to sketch a group-idealized self-object transference. This group could be seen as hungry for idealization of a parent.[8] Masud Kahn has suggested that the two ingredients for the forming of the ego ideal are magical thinking and idealization by way of the ego functions.[9]

The group now actively had begun to discuss the wish to form a family of their own. They began expressing disappointment with their own families and wished to create a home where the group leader would be mother and they would be sisters to one another.

Melissa was very invested in the group's beginning. She had been a member of a previous group and was disappointed and impatient that the new group had taken so long to begin. In one session the girls had gathered around the table to work and talk. There was a real atmosphere of intimacy and connectedness in this interaction. Melissa reached out her arms expressively and said to the group leader, "You see, I told you that this group would be a success and it is. Look at how well everyone plays together and gets along."

The group excitedly contributed endless fantasies as to how they might become a real family. Melissa, a great romantic, suggested, "Theresa [the group leader] should search and search in the streets to find us the perfect home." Someone else suggested, "Theresa should buy us a brownstone and renovate it" to each group member's specification. Vicky, the oldest member and group cynic, scoffed, "How can Theresa possibly buy you all a brownstone and renovate it? Does she look like a millionaire to you? If she were a millionaire she wouldn't be working here." At this point, the group liked to repeat the leader's name. The group leader believes that the children felt closer to her by being able to address her by her first name, and also as a means of fantasied control of the therapist.

The group enacted building a house using large blocks and a tent. At this point the group leader remained outside of the house waiting. This activity soon transformed itself into a different one. The girls played at rolling themselves up in foam mats. While one girl was encased in the mat, another would walk or push at the mat, forcing out the girl within. The group leader commented that they were like caterpillars coming out of the cocoon to be butterflies. They seemed to have moved from creation of a family to giving birth to themselves.

Finally, the group moved into a discussion of their families and their disillusionment with them.

In one session, one child, Rachel, described disappointment with her mother and grandfather. She had returned from a disappointing visit to her grandfather whom she described as mean and abusive. She also talked of her mother's ineffectuality in dealing with him. She went on to say that her life with her mother "was not so very happy." She believed that they "were going through a phase." We talked about how adults liked to think that childhood is a happy time but that in fact it is often difficult and that when one became adult, one had somewhat more freedom of decision and choice. The group was vehement in agreement with this and one member commented that "there should be a trading post for relatives where you could trade them in for cash or a new one." This points to the intense wish in children's groups to create a fantasy family so that forging a new identity for each member seems possible.

The children occasionally alluded to visits with their fathers. The fathers were described more idyllically. Becky described her father as "very handsome" and said somewhat apologetically that he has "many girlfriends." Becky said she tried to get to know them and that some were very nice, one never liked her at all, but that her mother told her she did not have to visit that one. Becky was wistful as she listed the many women her father had been involved with. As opposed to her father, her mother had relatively few lovers.

Rachel described her father as living "in the country" with his new family. She visited him in the summer. Rachel, like the other group members, was much taken with the wildlife of the country — rabbits and deer. Like She-Ra's group, the girls described their wish to roam free in the woodlands.

All of the girls talked of their fathers in faraway voices as if the emotional (and occasionally geographic) distance made them elusive romantic figures. Vicky had recently resurrected her relationship with her father, visiting him for the first time in many years. She had a wary manner of describing her father — mistrustful, — preferring to talk of her love for her grandmother. Vicky periodically reminded everybody that she preferred her grandmother to the leader and the group. She was fond of saying, "It's nothing against you Theresa, but I'd rather be with my grandmother." Her maternal grandmother represented her link to an unconflicted past. Natalie, whose mother recently remarried, refused to discuss her stepfather (or recognize him as such at all). She frequently said she had no father. Of all the group, Natalie eventually drew closest to the therapist and remained most intensely connected.

Annie Reich speaks of the great longing of the child to become like the parent as creating an inner demand on the ego. Under certain conditions, "magic identification with the glorified parent — megalo-manic feelings — may replace the wish to be like him."[10]

Vicky, in her connectedness to her grandmother, initiated discussions in the group of the Holocaust. This topic united three members in their identity. Two of the group, Rachel and Becky, were of Sephardic paternity. Rachel, identifying strongly with her Egyptian father, would break into the Egyptian dances of a harem girl whenever the group became lively over discussions involving their future sexuality. No one described losing family to the Holocaust but rather emphasized the unification and reunion of their families here in America.

The theme of unification became apparent to the group leader in another aspect of identity. As mentioned above, all of the girls came from families with working mothers who worked out of necessity. The mothers of these girls were everything to them. They worked and arranged schools and lessons and free-time activities for their daughters. Money was a constant issue. It occurred to the therapist that the girls struggled with a central conflict: that of a need to unite traditional views of femininity (beauty, sexuality, and mothering) with a need to protect oneself (typically the role of the father). Freud has described the two types of analytic object love: the "woman who tends" and "the man who protects."[11] These girls had never known that aspect of family life because their fathers had never been there consistently. As Becky said, "You don't really miss what you never knew." She-Ra's appeal was great because she could be both beautiful and powerful (she is called the Princess of Power). In one telling episode, She-Ra escapes from prison and conquers her enemies. She meets up with her boyfriend who only knows her as Adora and thinks She-Ra is a different person. He respects She-Ra but loves Adora. He tells She-Ra that he must return to rescue Adora. She-Ra quickly flies back to prison, becomes Adora again, and allows herself to be rescued. She turns and winks to the audience as this happens, combining a phony helplessness with duplicity to keep her lover fooled as to her true identity. This would appear to be a standard characteristic of superheroes; concealment of extraordinary powers to survive and protect oneself in the ordinary world.

The girls required of their mothers that they be all things at all times. The exhausted mothers could also be transformed into superwomen. The self-object transference had the same requirement: the notion that a disappointing therapist was intolerable — she had to be superwoman. After a holiday during which the group did not meet for two weeks, at the next group meeting, the group was particulary angry with the therapist because of the two-week separation. Their anger came to a boil with everyone drawing pictures of the group leader looking like a witch, like Catra, like a monster. Finally, for one child the

Figure 15–1

conflict proved too great. She attempted to draw the group leader in a negative way as an ugly witch (see Figure 15.1), but then she gave her the blue-green hair of "the watcher," the bird-girl she had brought to the very first group meeting). She finally colored the hair over in black (the therapist's own hair color), and clothed her in the red dress of Supergirl with a large "S" on the front of her dress. The figure is walking toward the viewer, smiling with outstretched arms.

As the group identity solidified, the girls' latency age–appropriate dislike of boys came to the fore. The girls heatedly debated whether or not "the club" should admit boys. Melissa (as usual) made an impassioned speech. She said, "We wouldn't want boys; they would only disturb the peace of our group. They would fight. They would cause mayhem." Vicky described a boy at school who "was as ugly as a helch" and who pursued girls. Natalie discovered a boy under the table (incidentally, this boy was from the boys' latency group which was held at the same time and whose members periodically invaded the girls' group). She clung to the group leader's skirts but pushed her forward to make the boy leave. The boy commented that he would be back. The group leader told him that he could not come back to the group, he belonged to the boys' club right now. Natalie shrieked, "You hear that? You hear what she said? This is a girls club, no boys allowed, you hear her?" She turned to the group leader, "Right? There are no boys allowed here?" The girls had all gathered around the group leader by then (not unlike avenging warriors massing for battle). The group leader felt as if the girls had turned her into a guided missile — the role model of group protector, that is, the mother who protects (as opposed to the father).

In *The Use of an Object and Relating Through Identification*[12], Winnicott describes the object as needing to undergo several metamorphoses. The object must be related to, destroyed (by the subject), and finally survive the destruction. The object can then be further valued as having survived destruction because it now can be used in fantasy: It has survived the subject's omnipotent control.

Edith Jacobson might view this in yet another way: Identification (with the aggressor) is made out of fear but also out of love. The conditions for depression arise when loss of the ideal object is denied.

The group leader then interpreted the group's anger at her for not meeting with them for 2 weeks and their disappointment in her. The group agreed energetically that this was indeed the source of their anger. The group subsequently had great difficulty leaving the session and Rachel commented that she would like to "throw all the adults out of the building — even the nice ones — and leave it for the children for once."

Judith Marks Mishne[13] has pointed out that idealization of the self and of the object is a particular feature in children who have been abandoned by a parent as a result of divorce or psychogenic illness. This is a view of idealization as a defense against mourning: an inability to mourn as a result of severe narcissistic injury. "Abandoned children manifest inordinate idealization and mirroring of the therapist, phenomena not found in children who have lost a parent through death."[13]

Idealization of the group therapist is a defensive posture by way of identification with the aggressor (ie, the lost father): a defense against abandonment and being female. The group experienced intense narcissistic rage in response to the therapist's "abandonment" of the group by going on vacation — a replication of earlier abandonment by an idealized and lost father. The therapist's abandonment was responded to by the group as an attack on the group's collective omnipotent fantasies of control over the object, in this case the therapist.

THEORIES OF PLAY AND THE GROUP QUEST FOR IDENTITY

Freud described the two functions of play: that of trial behavior and a wish that all will turn out well. Play meets the strain of uncertainty about the child's abilities, especially as regards the future requirements of adult life. Play reflects "fragments and bits of reality." Greenacre has suggested that in play, a kind of make-believe reality testing emerges.[14]

For the girls of the social club, the test was to merge what they saw as the most desirable aspects of being female with the qualities one needs to possess in order to survive in the real world: qualities that help to utilize aggression to defend and protect and, when need be, to fight. A superadaptability and flexibility to survive is required. Waelder, in his theory of play, saw play as combining "Mastery, wish fulfillment, assimilation of overpowering experiences (repetition/compulsion), transformation from activity to passivity, leave of absence from reality and superego, and fantasies about real objects."[15] Franz Alexander viewed play as a creative source allowing for unlimited freedom of choice leading to experimentation. Greenacre has brilliantly summed up the two views of play — one is in the service of a developing neurosis (by way of repetition/compulsion), the other akin to creative activity in its spontaneity and resourcefulness.

In *Woman as Artist*, Greenacre talked of the high degree of bisexuality required of the artist: "the empathic capacity of the artist to move between primary and secondary thought processes."[16] She suggests that the gifted girl child is susceptible to the fantasied phallus (ie, the family jewels). This certainly could be one view of the group's periodic identification of themselves as warrior women. Given the lack of fathering in this group, the need for such a fantasy might even be intensified.

Chasseguet-Smirgel, in discussing Anzieu's work on groups, describes the group as self-generated.

> ...it is itself an omnipotent mother. It is not organized around a central person (the leader) but around the group itself. The group illusion is then a realization of the wish to heal one's narcissistic injuries and to identify oneself with the good breast (or with the omnipotent mother...the father figure is chased away...it is as if the group information represented the hallucinatory realization of the wish to take possession of the mother by the subship, through a very regressive mode, that of primary fusion.[4]

A deeper view is one that is intrinsic to a core identity that must respond to the reality that the mothers of these children know. The old values of women did not help them to survive or to support a child at the same time. There had been too much disappointment and failure with regard to men. It is no wonder that the girls turned (as boys do) to identification with a more powerful same-sex object, not just as identification with the aggressor, but because the mother represents the whole of security from the adult world. The family becomes a matriarchy and one's sisters become true allies. Even though the need for protection (and love) for the future is still intense, it is the new task of identity to absorb the quality of wishing for protection within oneself.

Acknowledgment

For Gerda Schulman.

REFERENCES

1. Sarnoff R: *Latency*. New York, Jason Aronson, 1976.
2. Aries P: *Centuries of Childhood*. New York, Vintage Books, 1962.
3. Kingston MH: *The Woman Warrior*. New York, Vintage Books, 1977.
4. Gedo J, Wolf E, Terman D: The transformation of the self in adolescence. *J Youth Adolesc* 1, 3.
5. Loewald HW, quoted by Kahn M: Ego ideal, excitement and the threat of annihilation, in Kahn M (ed): *The Privacy of the Self*. New York, International Universities Press, 1974, pp 193–194.
6. Nagera H: The imaginary companion, in Eissler R, Freud A, Hartmann H, et al (eds): *The Psychoanalytic Study of the Child*, vol XXIV. New York, International Universities Press, 1969, p 165.
7. Kohut H, Wolf E: The disorders of the self and their treatment, in Morrison A (ed): *Essential Papers on Narcissism*. New York, New York University Press, 1986.
8. Kahn M: Ego ideal, excitement and the threat of annihilation, in *The Privacy of the Self*. New York, International Universities Press, 1975.
9. Reich A: Narcissistic object choice in women, in *Psychoanalytic Contributions*. New York, International Universities Press, 1973.
10. Winnicott DWW: The use of an object and relating through identification, in *Playing and Reality*. New York, Penguin Books, 1975.
11. Mishne J: Trauma of parent loss through divorce, death and illness. *Child Adolesc Social Work* 1984;1:1.
12. Freud S: On narcissism, in Rickman J (ed): *A General Selection from the Works of Sigmund Freud*. New York, Doubleday Anchor, 1957, p 104.
13. Greenacre P: Play in relation to the creative imagination, in *Emotional Growth*, vol 2. New York, International Universities Press, 1971.
14. Waelder R, as quoted by Greenacre P: Woman as artist, in *Emotional Growth*, vol 2. New York, International Universities Press, 1971.
15. Chasseguet-Smirgel J: *The Ego Ideal*. New York, WW Norton, 1985.
16. Greenacre P: Woman as artist, in *Emotional Growth*, vol 2. New York, International Universities Press, 1971.

16

Group Psychotherapy with Adolescents: Clinical Perspectives

John I. Dintenfass

Working with adolescents, as difficult as it is, can be a challenging and rewarding experience. Scheidlinger[1] has noted a number of basic goals that almost all adolescents strive for:

1. Loosening dependent ties on parents and achieving separation-individuation from them
2. Coping with anxiety about trying to manage on one's own and finding security in oneself and with extrafamilial objects
3. Permitting oneself socially acceptable gratifications of aggressive and sexual drives
4. Resolving sexual identity

To these might be added a fifth: establishing career goals.

The adolescent needs time and room to grow, to think for himself, and to reach his own conclusions about the "big questions": Who is he? Where is he going? What is life really about? Many of us continue to grapple with these same issues as adults. Peers often provide the milieu where he can struggle with such issues while receiving empathy and emotional support.

In responding to normal adolescent development, the therapist must exercise restraint and "let it happen" at its normal pace, not "make it happen." It is important not to interfere with adolescents' deidealization of adults, which naturally occurs during midadolescence, when the adolescent develops an adult body image which leads to a more mature ego ideal. In order to achieve successful development, he has to free himself from attachment to archaic objects, achieve ego and superego reorganization, and begin functioning as an adult in terms of the freudian mandate of "working and loving."

A BRIEF LITERATURE REVIEW

As early as 1914, Freud[2] paid attention to the benefit of group psychotherapy for adolescents in discussing narcissism and idealization in "schoolboy psychology." He recognized that the group provides a natural forum for expression by adolescents, particularly during the early and middle years of this developmental period.[3] Here, the adolescent can best express the polarities of his changing moods and behavior: progression/regression, success/failure, happiness/depression, love/hate, acceptance/rejection, independence/dependence, and expression/withdrawal.

In part, the group is effective for the same reason that individual treatment works with adolescents: the key role of idealization in establishing a therapist-patient bond. By making a hero of the leader and by idealizing peer group standards, the adolescent facilitates group psychotherapy. Freud[3] (and, later, Aichorn[4] and Gitelson[5]) emphasized that the leader, consciously and unconsciously, helps create group cohesion via his role and his interventions.

Reich,[6] Laufer,[7] and Kohut[8] further elucidated the importance of the ego ideal in early adolescence, when one sees a repetition of the oedipal process. Shapiro et al[9] elaborated on identity formation by exploring three interrelated aspects of individual delineation in group adolescent experience:

1. The group's communication to the adolescent of its perceptions and attitudes toward him, and how this relates to his self-definition
2. The adolescent's "defensive" use of the group via projective identification, including projection of conflictual aspects of himself onto others with whom he identifies
3. His relationships to authority figures, including integration of such figures' new delineations of him and his modification of projections onto them

Vann Sprueill[10] notes that the young adolescent relates to the therapist in four distinct but convergent ways:

1. More or less realistic perceptions of the relationship, consonant with the individual's age and experience
2. Impulses, wishes, defenses, fantasies, and experiences transferred from past relationships with parents

3. Displacements from present relationships with parents and other significant objects
4. Narcissistically, that is, dealing with the therapist as if he were a hero who possessed idealized qualities which the adolescent has not yet internalized in his own ego ideal, and/or dealing with the therapist as though he played the parental role of responding to the patient's wonderful inner qualities

Depending on his awareness of these dynamics, the therapist responds to them consciously or unconsciously. For his part, the adolescent gradually achieves an integration and maturation of ego drives relating to self-definition, what has been called the extensive reorganization of the personality structure of childhood.[3,11-17]

Bion[18-20] basically agreed with Freud that the group provides a repetition of family patterns. In terms of group dynamics, Kurt Lewin[21] was concerned with interpersonal relationships among group members. A change in one component of the group leads to changes in the group or in individual members. He was concerned with the "social field" where interrelatedness exists between the person and the environment.[21] Powdermacher and Frank,[22] and Yalom[23] further elucidated Sullivan's[24] theories of groups by focusing on interpersonal relationships as the primary factors in personality development and in pathogenesis. Scheidlinger[1,25] emphasizes other aspects: "(1) meaning of behavior; (2) development of social attitudes and capacity for group ties; (3) group emotional process; (4) role of the leader, and (5) interaction between individual personality and group factors."[25]

Redl,[26] Bion,[18] and Freud[3] linked group formation to types of leadership. Redl was concerned with primary and secondary emotions and "emotional contagion." He and Bion also shared the view of the leader as a central person. Freud felt that the leader's personality and ideas influence a group. Bion differed in viewing the leader and group members alike as being at the mercy of "basic assumption" forces.[20]

Bion's experience in groups is generally recognized as the classic theoretical work in this treatment modality. He focuses on basic family assumptions, myths, and roles, that is, the parents' personality organization and long-term interactions with their children often determine adolescents' unconscious belief systems and dynamics. Thus, therapeutic work can be undercut by the mobilization of unconscious family-based impulses, for example, when the adolescent tries to avoid external reality tasks without taking responsibility for his feelings and behavior. Family and individual assumptions also may reflect powerful unconscious group themes, for example, satisfaction of dependency needs or fight-flight aggression toward external reality.

Bion dealt with these basic assumptions or unconscious fantasies in adolescent therapy by asking the adolescent to take responsibility for his feelings, which he felt was necessary for successful treatment. By avoiding all acting out within the group and by only giving interpretations, the therapist ensures that the group first "stews" in its own anxiety and then moves forward as its members are forced to seek and find their own answers to emerging problems.

The literature demonstrates that for many adolescents, individual psychotherapy has been of much benefit in working with their psychopathologies. The same can be said for group and family work, for many adolescents are neither ready nor sufficiently developed emotionally to benefit fully from an individual psychodynamic, psychoanalytic approach. At times, group therapy may be the only available treatment mode. For more seriously disturbed adolescents, a combination of therapeutic approaches (individual, family, group) usually will provide optimum treatment results.

ON BECOMING A GROUP THERAPIST
FOR ADOLESCENTS

Prior to undertaking group treatment with children or adolescents, the therapist will benefit from participating in an adult group, both as a leader and as a member (the latter could be via a T-group or process group). This provides him with important exposure to small-group process formation. In group therapy with adults, one usually encounters a more stable and mature, more understanding and compassionate, and less acting-out population than is the case with adolescents. In turn, the therapist has less need to exert structure and control. He experiences group transferences and resistances and gains a clearer understanding of interpersonal psychodynamics and psychopathologies than when working with children or adolescents.

Viewing videotapes of an experienced therapist conducting group and family therapy will benefit the trainee. The visual depiction of dynamic processes, for example, verbal and nonverbal communication, peer relationships, power struggles, transferences, and resistances, helps prepare him for group work with adolescents. The trainee's style and technique will also be honed by the invaluable experience of working with an experienced cotherapist.

THE SCREENING PROCESS

A good screening process is key to the adolescent's effective evaluation and treatment. Many therapists find it necessary to see the adolescent for four to six sessions to understand individual and family dynamics clearly, and to assess whether the adolescent's pathology makes him appropriate for group and, if so, for what group.

In the initial meeting, one allies oneself to the adolescent, hearing his needs and empathizing with the material he presents. At the same time, it helps to be realistic about the adolescent's situation, which is not easy to assess because he tends to be guarded and defensive, and often to develop a negative transference based on a parental image. It is important to assure the adolescent that the interview and all treatment material is strictly confidential, although, initially, he may not believe this. However, the therapist must also make clear that confidentiality may be broken in case of danger to the adolescent or a potential victim.

The adolescent needs to feel that the therapist is "for real," someone who understands his ever-changing needs, who can listen to his problems and concerns, even if he does not agree with his desires or values. Such a therapist will be aware of current adolescent trends and concerns in family life, peer relationships, popular culture, and fashion. Conveying such understanding helps the adolescent to be more open about his hopes and dilemmas. Adolescents, at all stages of development, frequently feel that the world around them "does not understand." The sense that "no one listen to me" is re-enforced when adolescents, who tend to be acutely sensitive to injustice of any kind, sound overidealistic or self-righteous.

Following the diagnostic interview, it is helpful for the therapist to meet with each adolescent accepted for the group to orient him to rules and guidelines for group interaction. It is essential to help the adolescent feel comfortable for the group experience, which can be presented as educational as well as therapeutic. Usually, he will wonder whether he will be put on the spot and whether the therapist will introduce confidential material. Repeated assurance about this helps the adolescent deal with the basic eriksonian developmental issues of trust vs mistrust. *Good preparation for group therapy is as important as the therapy itself.*

COORDINATING GROUP AND INDIVIDUAL TREATMENT

If possible, the same therapist should see the adolescent in individual treatment as well as in group. When more than one therapist is involved, the adolescent is likely to play off one therapist against another or otherwise to engage in splitting. The frequency of treatment depends on the nature of the pathology as well as the therapist's availability. If group therapy is the primary treatment modality, the therapist might see the adolescent weekly or biweekly for individual sessions. Such sessions are key in helping the therapist keep abreast of intrapsychic dynamics and deal with personal issues not addressed in the group.

PARENTAL INVOLVEMENT

It generally is beneficial to have a positive parental support system. If possible, the therapist might meet with the prospective member's parents to obtain a detailed developmental history, and to gain a better understanding of the adolescent's role within the family and family dynamics. The therapist also might clarify the cost of treatment and the responsibility for payment. If he does not do so, he can expect acting-out behavior from the parent or the adolescent or from both.

Periodically, the family may be involved in treatment, especially with acting-out adolescents. Although the group usually can deal with such behavior, the therapist may feel it advisable to engage in family treatment in addition to, or instead of, a group approach. The adolescent and the family usually are seeking, explicitly and implicitly, guidance in such situations and so welcome one or more family sessions.

PRINCIPLES OF GROUP COMPOSITION

Some basic principles the therapist might follow in forming groups of adolescents are:

1. Compose groups according to the age of the adolescent (early, 12–14 years old; middle, 15–17; and late, 18+).
2. For insight-oriented groups, keep neurotic and adjustment disorders together. However, an exception can be made to include one or two psychotic adolescents, depending on degree of pathology.
3. Drug and alcohol abuse problems belong in special groups.
4. Group together adolescents of similar class backgrounds, for significant tensions can arise when this is not done. For example, an adolescent from an upper-class background often arouses jealousy and envy from a lower-class peer. Upper- and lower-class ways of functioning tend to differ in terms of family and other support systems.
5. Adolescents with physical or cognitive disabilities (eg, eating or learning disorders) do well in groups whose members have similar problems, for they gain support and insight from their peers.
6. Carefully evaluate what kind of group is most suitable for a particular conduct disorder adolescent. Given the acting-out potential of individuals with this pathology, limit the group to the same sex.

248

GOAL SETTING

It is important to determine the adolescent's developmental stage in order to establish realistic treatment goals. Considerable damage can be done when unrealistic goals, and criteria for meeting them, are determined by the therapist, the adolescent himself, his family, peers, or societal influences (eg, the mythology of popular culture). The therapist and the group help the adolescent to realize that he is part of an interdependent world and that he therefore must adapt to societal norms.

THE INITIAL SESSION

It is important to begin groups as early as possible in the school year, and certainly no later than midyear. (One exception is a short-term group with specific goal-oriented activities.)

At its first session, the group members sit in a circle wherever they want and the two therapists sit opposite each other. This gives the group a balanced feeling while providing the cotherapists with direct eye contact. At the initial meeting and at all meetings involving new members, each member introduces himself and states why he is in the group. If possible, this is done spontaneously after one of the therapists has explained the desirability of members getting to know one another. Following this, the therapists or a group member state(s) the guidelines for group goals and functioning.

The therapists impress upon the members that they will be responsible for the group agenda. Some practical issues which can be mentioned at the beginning are the duration of each session and length of treatment. Many early adolescent groups (for 13–14-year-olds) meet for one hour; middle- and late-adolescent groups can last a half-hour longer. Members should take care of their basic needs prior to the session.

It usually is best to deal with medical disabilities, competing activities, and medications on an individual basis. Depending on the maturity of the group and the discretion of the therapist(s), members can and should discuss such intimate issues as drug use and sexual behavior and pregnancy, although sometimes these sensitive subjects might better be reserved for individual sessions.

TREATMENT ISSUES

Therapeutic orientation will vary according to the nature of the group. For example, a psychoeducational model usually is preferred for a learning disability group or for a conduct disorder group, which is more interpersonally than intrapsychically oriented. Conversely, it is difficult to treat a group of borderline and narcissistic patients because of intense transference issues, which often lead to acting-out behavior.*

Conduct disorder adolescents tend to be prone to alcohol and drug involvement and, particularly if from an urban ghetto, delinquent behavior. Such teenagers have narcissistic disorders marked by low self-esteem and lack of superego formation (eg, the capacity for guilt). They may manifest low tolerance for intrapsychic exploration and little empathy for others. Their therapy focuses on their acting-out behavior and its effect on themselves and their environment. Group treatment may help such adolescents develop the capacity for remorse and guilt. To encourage this development, the therapist might provide participants with opportunities to engage in role playing, for example, expressing how it feels to be the victim of a crime.

When acting-out behavior becomes out of control, the therapist might conduct one or more individual sessions, possibly involving a parent or other family member. Yet the therapist can try to deter such behavior from happening in the first place by making it very clear that no physical disruption will be permitted during group sessions. (Any limits the therapist sets for group behavior must, however, be understandable to, and accepted by, group members.) Of course, it is desirable that adolescents express strong feelings and conflicts over violent impulses in group sessions so that members can struggle with them.

It is important for the therapist to evaluate any organic disorders (eg, a learning disability or epilepsy) that may accompany conduct disorders. Groups that are well structured, with a focus on interpersonal experiences in the family and school, generally prove most beneficial.

Psychotic early adolescents do well in groups where their own or similar pathologies can be found, such as in day treatment schools. Treatment revolves around self and body image, particularly pubertal changes. These adolescents need help with basic relating and tend to be sensitive in interacting with their peers and the surrounding environment. Educating them to cope with their feelings and the nature of the world around them is central to treatment.

---

* An example of acting-out behavior occurred in a group of early adolescent sons of military personnel, most of whom had adjustment disorders. A 14-year-old white male with a conduct disorder and poor, largely hostile communication with his parents became very provocative in group sessions. This encouraged acting-out behavior by other members. When confronted by the therapists and his parents with the disruptive effects of his behavior, he took off a shoe and threw it through a window, breaking it, and ending the group session. Subsequently, the adolescent was seen individually and in family treatment.

THE GROUP ROLE OF THE THERAPIST

The therapist of an adolescent group has to be keenly aware of both individual dynamics and group process. An individual adolescent's transferences are directed to peers as well as to the therapist(s). While peer-oriented transferences relate primarily to sibling relationships, parent- or peer-oriented transferences to the therapist also occur frequently.

The therapist does not attempt to achieve in-depth, intrapsychic reorganization. Rather, groups benefit adolescents largely in terms of social experience, self-image, peer and sibling relationships, and furthering normal maturation. In addition, group therapy serves as an arena for the re-creation and reconstruction of family processes.

The therapist serves as an "encourager" rather than as an explainer. As a leader, he often illustrates rather than directs, models rather than coerces. The adolescent comes to accept what he is and not what he does. It is important for him to come to terms with his own narcissistic needs, recognize his immaturities, and know when to call for help. Group therapy affords him, like other participants, an opportunity to reduce interpersonal blocks and to move toward more warm, honest, nonexploitative relationships with others. It also is usually helpful for the group for him to reveal some aspect of his private world and to model an observing, appropriately self-critical ego.

The therapist needs his "third ear" in listening for a basic theme, which usually is set within the first 10 to 15 minutes and usually continues throughout the session. Because adolescents develop this theme via their self-reflections and interactions, the therapist need not articulate it.

The personality of the group leader is particularly important to successful treatment. Adolescents are drawn to an individual who is warm and interesting. Groups also function best when the therapist takes care not to dominate them, and to tolerate regression as well as defiance of authority in adolescents' struggle for separation and individuation.

STAGES OF TREATMENT

Groups evolve in terms of three discernible stages:

1. *Early*, when issues of trusting the leader and other group members are primary. This period often is characterized by hostility and contempt toward parents and other authority figures.

2. *Middle*, when the main struggle for independence takes place. The adolescent turns inward, examining his wants and needs in order that his sources of gratification will be self-determined rather than by

a parent serving as his ego. This sudden sense of freedom can be both heady and very anxiety-provoking. Will the adolescent follow his own impulses or parental demands? Will he heed more his own needs or the norms of the group?

3. *Final*, when key issues are consolidating treatment, separating from the group, consolidating one's identity, and planning postgroup treatment.

ISSUES OF SPECIFIC AGE GROUPS

Early Adolescence

It is essential that the therapist keep in mind an adolescent's developmental stage and not expect more of him, verbally and emotionally, than he can produce. Early adolescents tend to be particularly interested in physical and sexual developmental issues, and in identifying with "idol figures." Their social and interpersonal interactions usually are with the same-sex peer group. As the early adolescent achieves increased self-awareness and self-image, he experiences renewed, and increased, sexual drives.

Many adolescents experiment with alcohol, drugs, homosexual relationships, and rebellious behavior as they come to grips with who they are and how their bodies work. At the same time, they realize that they must become aware of their environment, particularly home and school and the role they will play in each. Uncertain what that role should be, adolescents often manifest insecurity in same-age relationships, as well as in ties to older teenagers.

Role models for ego ideals frequently shift from mass media heroes (eg, beauty queens or sports and entertainment stars) to more accessible nonfamily figures. The early adolescent gradually becomes more curious about the real, rather than the mythical, dimensions of the surrounding society; concomitantly, he becomes less prone to fantasy and social withdrawal. Boys often focus on sports, where personal prowess and competition matter.

Early adolescent boys undergo pubertal changes, including the development of secondary sexual characteristics. They become more aware of male-female differences and explore their sexuality via masturbation. Boys also tend to be concerned with their reputation among peers on macho issues (from athletic prowess to penis size). The element of self-discovery becomes as important as that of self-awareness. For girls too, early adolescence involves sudden physical self-development, which in turn may spark a long-term struggle with gender identity. Their bodies are changing with the onset of puberty and menstruation, and the new sexual and generative possibilities these changes bring. More than their male counterparts, early-adolescent females tend to relate changing body image and peer relationships to their immediate envionment. Girls become aware of being viewed by their parents and male peers in a different light because of their new physical presence and the impact it has. Some become flirtatious and coquettish.

For early-adolescent girls, treatment can be a sensitive issue, particularly with a male therapist. Similarly, early-adolescent boys can be discomfited by a female therapist. Thus, smaller (four to six members), same-sex groups work best for this age group.

With some guidance from the therapist(s), the group will tend to find its own direction, usually focusing on such concrete subjects as self-image, as opposed to interpersonal issues. Early adolescents of both sexes generally wish to identify with an adult authority figure, usually of the same sex, preferably a parent or caretaker. In time, as they struggle for greater individuation, autonomy, and self-realization, they look to peers for authority figures.

Successful treatment of early-adolescent groups depends on a focus on group process, particularly in terms of helping members define and move toward achievable goals. Early adolescents sometimes engage in sexual acting out when issues around authority, and personal drives and anxiety become too charged. When this occurs, the cotherapists provide a supportive balance for group interaction, while the kind of projected techniques and use of noncathected objects (eg, a blackboard) discussed below can help refocus the discussion.

Middle Adolescence

The middle-adolescent group (aged 15–17 years) tends to be more positively motivated toward treatment than the early adolescents. For example, they tend to respond to the presence of refreshments with more sharing and less acting out than is the case with their younger peers. One can do therapy with same sex or opposite-sex groups, depending on one's orientation, members' pathologies, and the setting. The adolescents themselves seem to prefer, and often request, the presence of girls. Cotherapists of the opposite sex can be particularly effective in dealing with male-female issues while also replicating parental images.

For the midadolescent, the optimal treatment modality is individual therapy in conjunction with a group. In individual work (one or two sessions per week, or biweekly at a minimum) the therapist and the adolescent can explore intrapsychic dynamics while re-enforcing group themes.

LATE ADOLESCENCE

This stage usually begins at age 17 and sometimes extends into the early 20s (or later if pathology is not dealt with). By now, the adolescent is working hard at resolving issues of gender identity and separation-individuation. These issues can be brought into sharp focus when an adolescent becomes involved with drugs or alcohol, delinquent behavior, acting out in the family, or learning difficulties.

While the younger adolescent may not be emotionally mature enough or receptive to individual, insight-oriented psychotherapy, so that group treatment becomes the primary treatment modality, the older adolescent may be ready for and may desire individual psychotherapy, for which group treatment may be an important complement.

For late adolescents, who are more mature in terms of self-image and interpersonal relationships, therapy is more intrapsychically oriented. Process is emphasized, as participants tend to be supportive of one another. Peer relationships are less focused on gender identity, while interpersonal interactions in group revolve more around present life situations, for example, career aspirations, heterosexual (or homosexual) relationships, and possible crises in these areas, than around family matters.

Late adolescents face the difficult task of beginning to "put their lives together." For most late adolescents, group therapy will prove of considerable benefit in this process.

A PERSONAL EXPERIENCE

This therapist began in 1969 with two, midadolescent groups of both sexes led by himself and a cotherapist. A mental health professional saw each adolescent once for a diagnostic evaluation, his or her suitability for group therapy, and orientation to the group therapeutic experience. The primary criteria used for selection were diagnostic appropriateness, motivation, and degree of acting-out behavior.

Each adolescent was informed about, and discussed with the therapist, certain basic principles concerning therapy, including duration, attendance, commitment, confidentiality, parental involvement, and rules against sexual acting-out behavior with group members and drug involvement.

One core group included the two therapists and eight adolescents, about the ideal size. The therapists served as a fulcrum for group stability, and also were transferential figures for group members. The groups met weekly after school for 7 months, with sessions lasting 1½ hours. No violent or other physical acting-out behavior was permitted — and none took place.

The cotherapists involved parents only in an emergency, with the understanding that the concerned adolescents would be present for these sessions. Each adolescent was seen individually only for crisis intervention around medication.

The groups sat in a circle in the warm, comfortable environment of a large treatment room in an outpatient clinic. Soft drinks and cookies provided nurturance for the adolescents and the cotherapists; such oral gratification helped decrease the anxiety level and helped stimulate interaction.

Treatment focused on interpersonal relationships. When group members raised dynamic issues, the cotherapists encouraged their exploration while offering little if any direct interpretation. At the end of each session, the group set aside five to ten minutes to reflect on the session's basic theme(s). This proved helpful and constructive for some adolescents in terms of facilitating insight and understanding of the basic issues raised. Presenting problems centered around such general themes as separation-individuation and gender identity. Also central were family dynamics (in terms of parental figures and siblings), peer relationships (from friendships to intimate relationships, self-concept to responsibility for others), self-worth and self-esteem, current school performance, and future career goals.

Role playing and the use of a blackboard helped the adolescents discuss such charged material as physical attraction and sexual behavior. While projective, both of these techniques were useful in exploring in depth otherwise difficult material in a nonconfrontational manner. For example, one of the group members brought a radio to a session. The therapist drew on the blackboard a stick figure walking down the street with a radio. Group members engaged in a lively, spontaneous discussion about what kind of signals this radio's antennas send out and what responses they receive. The symbolic blackboard figure helped the whole group discuss issues of self-image, peer relationships, and sexual attraction relevant to their own friendships, and made it easier for some of the more withdrawn members (as well as a borderline and a schizophrenic participant) to become part of the discussion.

Therapy was exploratory, with a strong emphasis on members' empathy and support for one another. This process encouraged adolescents to clarify for themselves and to educate one another about their feelings. Group bonding, as well as therapeutic alliances, usually took place within four to six sessions; thereafter, subgrouping and, eventually, dyadic formation occurred.

The cotherapists held a half-hour postsession meeting to discuss the group's psychodynamics, individual dynamics, interpersonal interactions, transference-countertransference issues, and potential research possibilities. In addition to self-supervision, they participated in a weekly one-hour supervision with an experienced group therapist.

Since it was known from the outset how long the group would last, the cotherapists discussed from the first session termination issues, focusing increasingly on them as the group neared its end. For adolescents, termination is a charged process, for it is closely related to separation and rejection.

At the conclusion of the second group, the members gave themselves a party, providing their own music and refreshments. The party both reflected and served as a model for improved self-confidence and esteem, motivation, self-expression, and taking responsibility. Group members also invited friends, which signified that core participants had become cohesive and confident enough to allow others in.

Approximately 50% of the adolescents involved requested further treatment, that is continuation of the group or individual treatment, with some requesting participation in both simultaneously.

HANDLING ABRUPT TERMINATIONS

One member of each group (both males) terminated treatment suddenly following a group discussion of sensitive material. In the first group, the dropout was a 16-year-old black male (A), who was in treatment for a school phobia. His mother had died of a drug overdose and his father's whereabouts were unknown. The boy was living with his maternal grandmother and, although a good student and varsity swimmer, was often too depressed and withdrawn to attend school. He also was an engaged, contributing member of the group until one session when he mentioned that he had a problem with soiling and then hiding his underpants from his grandmother. This revelation was embarrassing to him as well as to other group members. Although supportive and empathic, they were unable to deal with it in any depth. He did not come back the following week and his grandmother reported that he did not wish to continue in treatment.

In the second group, C, a 17½-year-old white male, entered group therapy following suspension from school for verbally abusing his teacher. For 4 months, he attended group regularly and was an oral and supportive member. During one session, C recalled that, while visiting his relatives in Ohio the previous summer, he decided to "pick up" a girl and have sex with her in the back seat of his car. After she left, he had five more experiences the same afternoon. Another group member commented: "That was quite an accomplishment." After this session, C did not return to the group, although the cotherapists attempted to reach out to him. Several months later, a group member reported hearing that C had joined the Marines.

In both cases, the result might have been different had each been seen in individual as well as in group psychotherapy. It also might have made a difference if, during the diagnostic and follow-up interviews, the adolescent had been better oriented on how to discuss charged, embarrassing, or otherwise highly intimate material. Monthly follow-up by the therapist for 3 months with each boy revealed that A continued to attend school regularly and was asymptomatic while C had indeed joined the Marines. Although the two boys terminated abruptly, both benefited from the experience of group therapy.

SUMMARY

This chapter provides a general overview of adolescent group psychotherapy and touches on several key diagnostic and treatment issues. Primary among these are proper selection and preparation prior to treatment. As Slavson[27,28] has clearly stated, it is important to make a careful selection and grouping according to the general level of psychosexual development and pathology and the need for "group balance," for example, between "talkers" and "silent" members. Of particular importance is the role of the therapist as a facilitator of ego development. The leader must provide the particular qualities that are helpful in motivating group process. These include an empathic approach to the needs and sensitivities of adolescents and the capacity to differentiate between normal adolescent turmoil and conflict, and psychopathology.

REFERENCES

1. Scheidlinger S: *Focus on Group Psychotherapy*. New York, International Universities Press, 1982.
2. Freud S (1914): Some reflections on schoolboy psychology, in *Standard Edition*, vol 13, Strachey J (trans-ed): London, Hogarth Press, 1961, pp 241–244.
3. Freud S (1921): Group psychology and the analysis of the ego, in *Standard Edition*, vol 18, Strachey J (trans-ed). London, Hogarth Press, 1955, pp 67–145.
4. Aichorn A: *Wayward Youth*. New York, Viking Press, 1935.
5. Gitelson M: Character synthesis: The psychotherapeutic problem of adolescence. *Am J Orthopsychiatry* 1948;18:422–431.
6. Reich A: Pathologic forms of self-esteem regulation. *Psychoanal Study Child* 1960;15:215–232.
7. Laufer M: Ego ideal and pseudo ego ideal in adolescence. *Psychoanal Study Child* 1964;19:196–221.
8. Kohut H: *The Analysis of the Self*. New York, International Universities Press, 1971.
9. Shapiro R, Zinner J, Berkowitz M, et al: The impact of group experiences

on adolescent development, in Sugar M (ed): *The Adolescent in Group and Family Therapy*. Chicago, University of Chicago, 1986, pp 87–103.

10. Spruiell V: Adolescent narcissism and group psychotherapy, in Sugar M (ed): *The Adolescent in Group and Family Therapy*. Chicago, University of Chicago, 1968, pp 27–40.

11. Erikson EH: *Identity and the Life Cycle*. New York, International Universities Press, 1959.

12. Erikson EH: *Identity, Youth and Crisis*. New York, Norton, 1968.

13. Blos P: *On Adolescence: A Psychoanalytic Interpretation*. New York, The Free Press, 1962.

14. Inhelder B, Piaget J: *The Growth of Logical Thinking from Childhood to Adolescence*. New York, Basic Books, 1958.

15. Freud A: *The Ego and the Mechanisms of Defense*. New York, International Universities Press, 1936.

16. Freud A: Adolescence. *Psychoanal Study Child* 1958;13:255–278.

17. Jacobson E: *The Self and the Object World*. New York, International Universities Press, 1964.

18. Bion WR: Group dynamics — A review. *Int J Psychoanal* 1952;33:235–247.

19. Bion WR: Group dynamics — A review, in Klein M, Heimann P, Money-Kyrle R (eds): *New Directions in Psychoanalysis*. New York, Basic Books, 1955.

20. Bion WR: *Experiences in Groups*. London, Tavistock, 1961.

21. Lewin K: Group decision and social change, in Newcomb T, Hartley E (eds): *Readings in Social Psychology*. New York, Holt, 1947, pp 330–344.

22. Powdermarker FB, Frank JD: *Group Psychotherapy: Studies in Methodology of Research and Therapy*. Cambridge, Mass, Harvard, 1953.

23. Yalom I: *The Theory of Practice of Group Psychotherapy*, ed 2. New York, Basic Books, 1975.

24. Sullivan HS: *The Interpersonal Theory of Psychiatry*. New York, Norton, 1953.

25. Scheidlinger S: *Psychoanalytic Group Dynamics — Basic Readings*. New York, International Universities Press, 1980.

26. Redl F: Diagnostic group work. *Am J Orthopsychiatry* 1944;14:53–67.

27. Slavson SR: *An Introduction to Group Therapy*. New York, International Universities Press, 1943.

28. Slavson SR: *A Textbook in Analytic Group Psychotherapy*. New York, International Universities Press, 1964.

SUGGESTED READINGS

Ackerman NW: Group psychotherapy with a mixed group of adolescents. *Int J Group Psychother* 1957;2:249–260.

Anthony EJ: Age and syndrome in group psychotherapy. *Top Problems Psychother* 1965;5:80–99.

Arsenian J, Semrad EV, Shapiro D: An analysis of integral functions in small groups. *Int J Group Psychother* 1962;12:421–434.

Beck AP, Peters L: The research evidence for distributed leadership in therapy groups. *Int J Group Psychother* 1981;31:43–71.

Berkovitz IH: On growing a group: Some thoughts on structure, process, and setting, in Berkovitz IH (ed): *Adolescents Grow in Groups*. New York, Brunner/Mazel, 1972, pp 6–28.

258

Brandes NS: *Group Therapy for the Adolescent.* New York, Jason Aronson, 1973.

Epstein N: A comparison in observation and techniques utilized in group therapy with male adolescent character disorders from varying socio-economic backgrounds. Read before the American Group Psychotherapy Association, Chicago, 1967.

Epstein N, Slavson SR: Further observations on group psychotherapy with adolescent delinquent boys. *Int J Psychother* 1962;2:199–210.

Ezriel, H: A psychoanalytic approach to group treatment. *Br J Med Psychol* 1950;23:59–74.

Foulkes SH; Psychodynamic processes in the light of psychoanalysis and group analysis, in Scheidlinger S (ed): *Psychoanalytic Group Dynamics — Basic Readings.* New York, International Universities Press, 1980, pp 147–162.

Fried E: Ego emancipation of adolescents through group psychotherapy. *Int J Group Psychother* 1956;6:358–373.

Grotjahn M: Aspects of countertransference in analytic group psychotherapy. *Int J Group Psychother* 1953;3:407–416.

Hurst AG, Gladieux JD: Guidelines for leading an adolescent therapy group, in Aronson M, Wolberg LR (eds): *Group and Family Therapy.* New York, Brunner/Mazel, 1980, 151–165.

Josselyn IM: *The Adolescent and His World.* New York, Family Services Association of America, 1952.

Josselyn IM: Adolescent group therapy: Why, when, and a caution, in Berkovitz IH (ed): *Adolescents Grow in Groups.* New York, Brunner/Mazel, 1972, p 105.

Kaplan SR, Roman M: Phases of development in adult therapy groups. *Int J Group Psychother* 1963;13:10–26.

Kraft IA: An overview of group therapy with adolescents. *Int J Group Psychother* 1968;4:461–480.

MacLennan BW, Felsenfeld N: *Group Counseling and Psychotherapy with Adolescents.* New York, Columbia, 1968.

Munzer J: Acting out, communicating or resistance? *Int J Group Psychother* 1956;16:434–441.

Munzer J, Greenwald H: Interaction process analysis of a therapy group. *Int J Group Psychother* 1957;7:175–190.

Rabin HH: Preparing patients for group psychotherapy. *Int J Group Psychother* 1970;20:135–145.

Rachman AW: *Identity Group Psychotherapy with Adolescents.* Springfield, Ill, Thomas, 1975.

Redl F: Group emotions and leadership. *Psychiatry* 1942;5:573–596.

Rioch MJ: Group relations conferences: Rationale and technique. *Int J Group Psychother* 1970;20:340–355.

Rioch M: The work of Wilfred Bion on groups. *Psychiatry* 1970;33:255–278.

Scheidlinger S: *Psychoanalysis and Group Behavior.* New York, Norton, 1952.

Scheidlinger S: Freudian group psychology and group psychotherapy. *Am J Orthopsychiatry* 1952;22:710–717.

Shapiro R: Adolescence and the psychology of the ego. *Psychiatry* 1963;26:77–87.

Torda C: A therapeutic procedure for adolescents with emotional disorders, in *Pathways in Child Guidance.* New York, Bureau of Child Guidance, 1970.

17

A Group Dynamics Perspective on the Residential Treatment Center for Adolescents

David A. Halperin

The long-term residential treatment center for adolescents is a complex environment utilizing individual, family, and group approaches in the rehabilitation of severely damaged adolescents. Of primary importance is the creation of a therapeutic milieu which fosters the development within the adolescent of those skills which will enable him to become an autonomous, socially functional adult. This chapter examines the role of group process in the creation of a therapeutic milieu and the use of group modalities in working with these deprived and dysfunctional adolescents. These issues are examined with reference to the treatment contexts provided by such facilities as the Stuyvesant Residence Club of the Jewish Board of Family and Children's Services of New York, and the Gramercy Residence of the Green Chimneys School. The issues presented in these residences placed within an urban context are not restricted to the residential treatment center dealing with adolescents from inner-city, primarily minority, environments.

THE RESIDENTIAL TREATMENT CENTER AND ITS RESIDENTS

By locating a residential treatment within an urban context, the treatment center reflects the transitional nature of its task, that is, to provide a holding environment in which the troubled, dysfunctional adolescent can begin to explore more socially productive options. Unlike the residents of treatment centers placed in more sylvan settings, the residents are exposed to the creative, the faddish, and the truly malignant within the space of a single city block. Moreover, a location within an urban context precludes the use of restrictions and curfews which would be more meaningful in more isolated settings (although efforts are sporadically made to ground residents who have been particularly provocative).

The residents of the residential treatment center clearly form part of that group of "difficult patients" whom Pines[1] has poetically characterized as follows:

> They do not seem to be able to share the more basic assumption of the group that the enterprise (in this case the residence) is worth pursuing persistently and patiently and the self-understanding arrived at from emotional involvement with other persons is a process that can give one a sense of worth and competence through having gotten nearer to the truth about oneself and about human nature.[1]

Beyond a shared alienation, the residents share little but a common history of deprivation and a sense that their world has offered little continuity other than a continuity of institutional placement and institutionalized detachment. Thus, a primary task for the residential treatment center is to enable the residents to develop both a meaningful community and a sense of continuity — a sense that a world exists in which individuals offer more than a superficial façade of concern.

With rare exceptions, the residents of the residential treatment center come from families in which one or both parents are absent. The reasons for their absence range from the prosaic ("he just left") to the melodramatic ("I saw my mother being shot"). For many, their last memory of their father is an idealized screen memory of a figure who disappeared before their fifth birthday, and whose current whereabouts (or even existence) is unknown. In many cases, even if the parents are available, their pathology and/or the family's pathology are so profound that contact with them on any level is problematic and potentially countertherapeutic. Indeed, in many cases, the residence has assumed the role of parenting figure and actually has legal custody. The overwhelming majority of residents are either black or Hispanic though on occasion youths from other backgrounds are represented.

While a wide variety of disorders are represented diagnostically, the predominant diagnoses are conduct disorders. However, superimposed on this underlying disorder, many residents have dysthymic or anxiety disorders. Some residents are more fragile, and have been referred after hospitalization for either a schizophrenic or (very occasionally) an affective disorder. However, it must be emphasized that the loose structure of the transitional residential treatment center is ill-equipped to cope with the acutely psychotic resident and that if an individual requires consistent medication, placement in a residential treatment center whose primary task is transitional preparation for independent living is an exceedingly dubious proposition. Ultimately, the residence acts as an alumni club for the residents in their transition from an institutionalized placement to the noninstitutional world. Its task is to catalyze within a brief time a sufficient sense of identity and autonomy which will enable the resident to enter an adult, noninstitutionalized world.

THE RESIDENTIAL TREATMENT CENTER AND ITS STAFF

The staff of the residence usually consists of a director (an overseer of the total operation of the facility), a psychiatrist, social worker(s), and a cadre of child care workers (paraprofessionals with some experience of college). In addition, there are the usual ancillary personnel such as maintenance staff, cooks, and secretarial help. These latter often function as significant members of the staff in therapeutic terms as well as maintaining the physical substrate of the residence. Indeed, they may even help the residents develop practical skills which will be of use vocationally or in living.

The task of the residence is to create a community of activity in which a degree of group cohesiveness can develop that will foster a process of appropriate socialization (most residents have previously been connected to groups whose cohesiveness was harnessed to antisocial pursuits). It is felt that this process can be accelerated through the formation for the residents of a "second-chance" family which will replace the frequently absent or dysfunctional family of origin. Indeed, at times, the residence is too successful in creating this sense of identification so that termination becomes an extremely difficult and traumatic issue. It is, after all, not surprising that the resident who has never had any prior experience of a positive family environment will be extremely loath to give it up when it has been experienced.[2] In recognition of this reality, residents are encouraged to maintain their contact with the residence after discharge, particularly if the discharge was a planned and appropriate culmination of the therapeutic process (residents who were discharged prematurely may often have a secondary, antisocial agenda in socializing with current residents).

In a sense, the residential treatment center often functions as an extended family (and therapeutic community) in which former members feel comfortable in visiting unannounced to discuss their experience postdischarge. Staff members are encouraged to meet with these former residents and to utilize these contacts to support the current residents who may doubt the possibility of their being able to have an adequate adaptation postdischarge.

THE DIRECTOR'S ROLE

There has been an increasing recognition of the role of the staff in residential treatment settings in fostering group processes. Since the pioneering studies of Maxwell Jones and Stanton and Schwartz, there has been an increasing appreciation of the extent to which the leader or director of the residential treatment center fosters the development of the therapeutic environment. Kernberg[3] has defined the ideal group leader as an individual who:

> ...utilizes solid ego synthetic capacity and a firm sense of ego identity both to select a particular constant (or even shifting) style of intervention and to tolerate the dissonance and conflict created by the complex variety of hierarchically structured strategies available.[3]

Kissen has amplified this by his emphasis on the group leader's flexibility and his developing an awareness of his own countertransference needs so that "the leader's ego strength should be associated with a freedom from undue countertransference distortions such as the need to be a charismatic figure and to obtain narcissistic gratifications from interactions with the group members."[4]

The residential treatment center is vulnerable to this species of malignant regression because the director may over time begin to accept unquestioningly the resident's overvaluation and idealization. Moreover, because the task imposed on the staff members is so monumental, there is a real tendency on the part of staff to gather around the charismatic figure of the director with the fantasy that he, at least, can provide definitive answers to their problems. In this context, it is extremely important to make every effort to ensure the existence of staff meetings at which all staff members are encouraged to share their observations about the state of the residence.

Kissen[4] has emphasized the importance of the director in encouraging contact between the different hierarchically organized subsystems that develop within a residential treatment setting and of his exercise of an active role in facilitating communication across the subsystem boundaries. It is an exceedingly sensitive task to mediate between the professional and paraprofessional members of the hierarchy of the residential treatment center. Their differences in background and training provide ample opportunity for splitting. But if the director adopts a pragmatic, nonconfrontational approach without recourse to cant or jargon, when he avoids the temptation to act out his own competitive strivings with other staff members by using overly theoretical or "psychoanalytic" formulations, he aids in the process of providing a supportive professional environment in which staff can meaningfully operate.

In task-oriented terms, the goal of the residential treatment center is the creation of a holding environment in which the residents are given the opportunity to explore options for the future in a relatively unpressured setting. Even though the residents may present themselves as seeing the residential treatment center simply as an inexpensive hotel — as little more than a relatively secure, cheap base of operations (or depredation) — this superficial message should not be accepted at face value. The staff should cooperate with the resident to help him confront his disengagement and consider the residence as a place for protection and reflection.

The creation of a holding environment fosters the operation of the residential treatment center as a second-chance family in which the residents are given the opportunity to work through the dysfunctional experiences of their youth. The presence of consistent and competent staff figures provides the possibility for identification and for modeling. The staff are viewed as figures who are idealized (the siblings who *were* successful), mirrored, and, on occasion, devalued. The staff's presence is particularly important in that they do act as self-objects who provide for the residents a sustenance which their absent parenting figures abnegated.

The introduction of significant female figures is an intrinsic aspect of the creation of a second-chance family. Indeed, it is particularly important for the residents to have the experience of significant female figures who play a nontraditional and assertive role in order to challenge the residents' stereotypes about the relationship of men and women outside the residential treatment center. For many residents, significant female figures elicit intense transferences which are compounded out of dependency (they were often the only available parenting figure) and rage (they may have performed their tasks with incompetence and in settings pervaded by a sense of real or fantasied transience). Moreover, their experience of other important female figures may have been such as to confirm the received street wisdom that portrays women either as manipulative, controlling "spider women" or as passive, helpless creatures who are the appropriate prey of any male who chooses to exploit them.

The absence of a father and the experience of an incompetent mother may stimulate within residents the desire to form a family. Here, the resident both identifies with his children and reenacts with them the experience of competent parenting. Considerable attention has been paid to the role of the teenage mother, but the role of the teenage father has been relatively ignored. Given the current pandemic of teenage parenting, it is important not to accept on an unqualified basis the folk wisdom which portrays the teenage father as an unreactive, irresponsible, or detached youth residing within a residential treatment center or on the street. Experience shows these youth to be unrealistic, perhaps, but often concerned and involved in the growth and development of their children. The fantasy of being an adequate father figure is certainly operative within the negotiations they conduct with their girlfriends to whom (in many cases) they give significant parts of their income. The presence of adequate figures for identification adds significantly to their skills during the process of negotiation.

The actual role that female figures play within the residential treatment center is less important than their assumption of a position of real responsibility. Woman may act as directors, office managers, nurses, or therapists. Whatever their activity, their presence as significant figures who can relate on a plane of equality to males is most important.

While the female authority figure is readily seen as the "mother," the role of other staff members is more complex. If the director is the "old man," then the other staff members (professional or paraprofessional) are often seen as the wiser, older siblings or occasionally as younger "with it" parents. This perception transforms the therapist from a traditional figure who exercises "therapeutic" detachment to an advocate who works on behalf of his patients.

The role of the therapist-advocate entails a flexibility on the part of the staff member. Rather than acting simply as a case manager, the therapist is called on to represent the resident in his dealings with other staff members (particularly during staff meetings and with the outside world). The value of this role cannot be overstated, particularly in terms of its fostering the formation of a therapeutic alliance between the resident and the staff member. However, inherent within the role of a therapist-advocate is the danger of overidentification with the resident. An important task of the staff meeting is to help the staff member to appreciate this potential source of difficulty when and if it appears to arise.

Within the extended group qua family that constitutes the residential treatment center, the child care (paraprofessional) staff members are often perceived as siblings who have been able to organize their lives. The residents' ability to identify with the paraprofessional because of ethnic or religious similarities often fosters the formation of particularly strong bonds between the resident and the child care staff.[5] The fact that both resident and child care staff often come from similar backgrounds also provides the resident, whose outlook may be pervaded by cynicism and suspicion, with appropriate role models. It re-emphasizes to the resident that realistic change in his life circumstances is possible. The ability of the child care staff to relate to the residents around realistic issues and provide pragmatic solutions often provides the residents with a sense that their personal problems are solvable without their resorting to inappropriate and often dyssocial activities which seductively promise instant gratification.

It should be noted, however, that because the child care staff have been able to adapt to the broader society, they may be intolerant and even punitive toward residents who have difficulty during the period of adaptation. Moreover, because the adaptation of the child care workers themselves may be fragile, the potential exists that as they work around residents who pursue immediate gratification, the child care staff may be encouraged in regressive behavior. In this context, the staff meeting is a particularly valuable tool is preventing this self-destructive behavior.

GROUP PROCESSES WITHIN THE STAFF

The most visible forum in which group processes operate within the residential treatment center is the staff meeting. It is important to involve all professional and paraprofessional staff members. Ancillary personnel should be encouraged to attend because they can often offer valuable insights into resident behavior and information about the actual level at which the residents are operating, as well as the functioning of the residential treatment center as a whole. Because of their position outside of the formal therapeutic and administrative hierarchy, ancillary personnel are often adopted by (or, on occasion, may adopt) residents as role models and advocates. It is at the staff meeting that limits are set around such issues as visitation, curfews, and antisocial and dyssocial behavior among the residents. If at all possible, limits should be set in a manner which encourages the residents to act as a group. In making all the residents responsible for the actions of every resident, the cohesiveness among the residents is enhanced and a sense of civic responsibility is created. Without the cooperation of the residents as a whole, the process of setting limits degenerates into an exercise in punishment for its own sake, which is ultimately self-defeating.

In setting limits, there is a continuing tension between the need to meet the demands of the individual resident and the requirement to maintain a group-as-a-whole approach. In this context, issues such as overidentification with the residents should be explored and hopefully resolved. The staff meeting should not be conducted in a judgmental manner. Above all, it should not be a forum in which the director feels free to "therapize" other staff members by explaining away their observations simply as a product of their inner pathology. It should be characterized by a sense of respect for the opinions and attitudes of all participants. However, issues such as overidentification may require examination in a more intimate setting. Even here, the emphasis should be on the creation of an atmosphere of mutual respect. Open communication must be fostered while therapist and concerned child care workers discuss all aspects of the resident's growth and development and the role that the residential treatment center should play in fostering autonomy. By using the larger staff meeting and the more intimate working group, the possibility of splitting among the staff is decreased. At times, group-centered interpretations about the actual process within the group and its parallels with the group process within the residential treatment center may be extremely fruitful.

GROUP ISSUES IN WORKING WITH
THE RESIDENTS: GENERAL CONCERNS

Adolescence is a period in which group activities play a particularly significant role in enabling the individual to develop a sense of self.[6] The very pervasiveness of group activities which accompany the process of identity formation among adolescents make their parents wonder if they are the parents of individual children or group leaders in a group time-limited only by their children's maturation. Within the residential treatment center, group activities should be used to foster the development of an individual's sense of self and of his cohesion with other members.

Residents should be required to attend a general weekly community meeting. However, this general community meeting should not be considered to be the only therapeutically significant group within the residential treatment center. Subgroups naturally form around issues such as ethnicity, sexual orientation, economic status, educational status, the time of entry into the residential treatment center, and the time remaining before discharge. The multiplicity of roles which staff and residents assume is most fully displayed within the community meeting. On one level, it provides a place and time in which members can express their concerns about general issues, for example, curfews, food, room assignments, etc. On another level, it provides a forum in which members express their concern about other residents to the staff. Finally, it provides a setting in which residents can express their feelings about the staff.

Whatever the actual realistic issue that is raised, it is important for the staff to recognize that much of the substance that is discussed at the community meeting reflects the degree of connectedness between the stated tasks of the residential treatment center and the realities present at the residence. Thus, complaints about staff or the lack of amenities often reflect the status of group processes within the residential treatment center rather than actual concrete difficulties. In this context, after the departure of a long-term, highly regarded director, the residents formed a counterculture group — "the Federation." They formed a group because of their accurate perception that the professional staff was not providing a significant sense of continuity. Comparably, in a residential treatment center with a rapid turnover among the professional staff, the residents would not attend community meetings consistently but focused instead on developing strong ties with the paraprofessionals who provided a greater sense of continuity.

The optimal functioning of a group is dependent on the creation and development of appropriate and realistic group tasks. Within small groups, it is particularly important for the staff members to set realistic goals for the residents and to deal with them in an appropriate fashion when these expectations are not met. When leadership of a small group includes paraprofessional as well as professional staff members, the possibility of having realistic expectations is enhanced. When a professional staff member has an unrealistically high expectation of a resident's potential, the resident may respond to these unrealistic demands with acting-out behavior directed at the staff member, who is experienced as an overdemanding parent.[7] This possibility was averted in a recent group where the psychiatrist was present as a consultant participant, as the following interchange illustrates:

"What are your goals, now that you're at the residence?"
"Well, they keep telling me that I have to go to college."
"What would you like to do?"
"Well, frankly I've always liked electricity. I'd like to be an electrician."
"Good, then you'll make more money than both of us."

The sense of relief within the room was palpable. No longer did the resident have to live up to or act out his therapist's fantasies of academic success. In other cases, the paraprofessional small group leader performs a valuable service by introducing a note of reality into often abstract discussions of the goals and expectations of treatment.

Small groups are helpful to those residents awaiting discharge. And the paraprofessional group leader who shares a community of background with the resident is often able to give the resident a more realistic and practical approach to the problems he will experience in matters of housing, employment, and the myriad of other details that arise in trying to survive in as complex and discouraging an urban environment as New York City. Likewise, small groups help residents to negotiate relationships with their friends outside the residential treatment center. Matters such as dress, decorum, etc can be discussed by female small group leaders in a manner that is neither competitive nor judgmental but which conveys how women relate to men.

Group processes afford a means of intervention in other circumstances as well. When residents require hospitalization or when the possibility of serious medical illness is present, group approaches have allowed a discussion of the implications of hospitalization, the importance of medication, the implications of substance abuse, the dangers of AIDS, and have even encouraged residents to visit residents who required hospitalization for either psychiatric or medical reasons. More recently, group approaches have facilitated the discussion of contraception, the importance of prudence in sexual encounters, and the relationship to sexual partners. The residential treatment center for adolescents is uniquely vulnerable to AIDS because the life-style of some residents and adolescent experimentation place many residents within the groups most at risk. By using group approaches to discuss AIDS, its implications, and measures of avoidance, it may be possible to protect some residents who would otherwise succumb.

In more positive terms, small groups have been formed to meet the positive and creative interests of the residents and to interest them in socially productive activities. While participation in sports, photography clubs, or visits to other culturally stimulating activities is often sporadic, such efforts at least signal to the residents those activities which they may pursue after discharge. Ultimately, if the residents are to function within the community after termination, they must develop the skills that will enable them to utilize group contexts in the outside world in a positive fashion.

SUMMARY

The residential treatment center for adolescents functions as a transitional setting in which the residents increase their ability to function autonomously, both socially and vocationally. This chapter examines this process from the vantage point of group dynamics and the role of group-centered interventions in facilitating change. Particular emphasis is laid on the residential treatment center as a means of providing for the vulnerable, deprived adolescent a "second-chance" family as an aid in the process of developing a sense of self-esteem and continuity. In addition, the role of group psychotherapy in creating a holding environment that aids in the exploration and examination of feelings is highlighted.

Acknowledgments

The author expresses his appreciation to the staff members of the Stuyvesant Residence Club of the Jewish Board of Family and Children's Services of New York City and to its former director, Larry Schwartz, MSW, and to the staff of the Gramercy Residence of the Green Chimneys School for their support and helpful suggestions. An earlier version of this paper was presented at the Annual Meeting of the American Association of Children's Residential Centers in October 1984.

REFERENCES

1. Pines M: Group therapy with "difficult patients," in Wolberg LR, Aronson ML (eds): *Group Therapy*. New York, Stratton International Medical Book, 1975.
2. Halperin DA: Termination: Its therapeutic and legal dimensions in the long-term residential treatment center. *Residential Group Care Treatment* 1986;3:3–17.
3. Kernberg O: A systems approach to priority setting of intervention in groups. *Int J Group Psychotherapy* 1975;25:251–275.
4. Kissen M: General systems theory: Practical and theoretical implications for group intervention. *Group* 1980;4:1:29–40
5. Halperin DA: Psychiatric consultation with mental health paraprofessionals: Challenges and rewards, in Nash K, Smith S (eds): *Paraprofessionals*. New Haven, Yale, 1978, pp 163–174.
6. Blos P: *The Adolescent Passage*. New York, International Universities Press, 1967.
7. Goldberg C: The functions of the therapist's affect in therapeutic conflict. *Group* 1983;7:3–19.

18

Multiple Group Therapy with Hospitalized Adolescents

Paul Kymissis

Adolescence represents one of the most sensitive, delicate, ambiguous, difficult, and decisive states of human development. Psychiatric diagnosis and treatment during this stage is a great challenge for modern psychiatry. Many of the treatment modalities that have been widely used with adults and children have not been easily applied to adolescents. For example, psychoanalysis initially was very skeptical of the possibility of treating adolescents because of "the fluidity of the ego" and it was suggested that psychoanalytic therapy be postponed for a later stage of life. Even in the field of pharmacologic therapies there have not been well-controlled double blind studies which prove the effectiveness of antidepressant therapy with adolescents.

Under these circumstances, adolescent psychiatry has been looking for new ideas and techniques to expand its armamentarium. Beyond the outpatient office therapy of the adolescent, the inpatient psychiatric care often represents the only realistic choice of action. However, adolescent inpatient psychiatric care has been a controversial issue over the last four decades.

There are only a few hospitals in the country which have special adolescent psychiatric units. Some services treat adolescents up to the ages of 14 or 15 on their children's units whereas others treat adolescents on adult units. The reasons for the latter preference may be economical or therapeutic, especially since a separate adolescent psychiatric unit is a difficult and expensive operation. Besides the appropriate physical facility, it is essential to have well-trained and skilled personnel who are capable of working with adolescents.

Many of the inpatient units for adolescents formerly offered treatment for up to 6 months or 1 year. However, today adolescents usually stay on an inpatient unit only for a shorter period of time, due to financial (insurance) and even therapeutic considerations. Out of these developments, the short-term adolescent psychiatric unit has emerged, with an average stay of 20–30 days. The short-term adolescent unit is a relatively new development (mostly after the 1960s) and represents a new challenge to adolescent psychiatry in terms of adopting techniques and searching for new ideas as to how to utilize this short time in the best possible therapeutic way. We attempt to avoid the development of gangs and group disruptions which some authors[1] have anticipated as a potential product of the adolescent propensity to form gangs. In an effort to maximize the effectiveness of the short-term inpatient treatment of the adolescent on a unit of a municipal hospital, we have developed a special program in which we use systems theory, group process, and psychodynamic principles. We attempt to integrate into the total treatment plan of the patient, participation in different groups led by different therapists. Since adolescence represents a second chance for individuation,[2] peer relationships become very important in this process and can provide significant support to the adolescent in proceeding toward individuation and development of his own identity. In this we not only have a group of patients but we require a group of therapists. The treatment of the individual by various therapists, which has been called "the team approach," is not a totally new concept in medicine. In one of the temples of ancient Greece that were used as healing and counseling centers, an interesting team approach was used.

The person who came for counseling would start walking along a corridor lined with many windows. Behind each window was a priest-counselor. The counselee would start early in the morning with the first window and he would proceed to the other windows, where would discuss with each priest various aspects of his question. By evening he would reach the last window and the last priest would give him the answer, after all the priests had conferred and discussed the issue. In order to deal with this multiplicity of variables, and conceptualize this highly complex process in a holistic way, we found that general systems theory provides a useful theoretical framework.

General systems theory is not a new technique, but a way of thinking, in which genetic, biological, intrapsychic, interpersonal, and social phenomena are conceptualized simultaneously in their complexity. In general systems theory the person is viewed as a living system, which is in transaction and interdependence with other systems, such as his peers, his family, his social groups, and his environment. If we see hospitalization in the context of this framework, then any meaningful treatment plan should represent an attempt to integrate, in a comprehensive way, modalities and techniques that will deal with the medical, psychological, social, educational, and vocational needs of our patients.

When a patient is admitted he or she is first seen in the emergency room, where the decision for admission is made. The following day at a team meeting an initial diagnostic formulation will be made and a treatment plan discussed. The concept of the treatment plan has been redefined in recent years. It is a goal-oriented, problem-oriented plan, where each member of the psychiatric team will undertake a specific role within a time frame.

It may be easy to talk about treatment plans and describe them on paper, but often it is extremely difficult to implement them in a responsible way. Close coordination is imperative and open communication among staff members is essential. In order to meet the needs of a comprehensive treatment plan in a very difficult adolescent unit we have included the multiple group psychotherapy approach. One of the criticisms of the all-adolescent psychiatric unit has been that adolescents group together in a disruptive way. We have decided to use exactly the same power the group process provides and channel it in a constructive and therapeutic way. Adolescents on an acute care inpatient service represent an area where the leader has to be familiar with the principles of the small group process, the developmental tasks of adolescents, and the clinical psychopathology of adolescence, and he also has to be ready to deal with the frustrations, the problems, and the challenges of adolescent psychotherapy. After the patient is assigned to his doctor and the treatment plan is formulated, the doctor will see the patient at least twice a week in individual therapy sessions and once a week in group. In the multiple group psychotherapy approach we use the following groups: (1) the doctor group, (2) the morning group, (3) the art group, (4) the placement group, and (5) the prevocational group.

THE DOCTOR'S GROUP

This is a 45-minute, open-ended group which meets once a week. New admissions become part of the group immediately and patients stay in the group until they leave. The composition of the group varies and is composed of all adolescents excluding those ward members who cannot participate because they are violent, bizarre, or overtly psychotic; patients who refuse to participate; and the severely retarded. The usual themes are related to the medical aspect of their treatment (medication, physical problems), discussion about therapeutic passes, plans for discharge, etc.

The therapist takes an active role, sets limits, is a source of information, encourages group participation, and offers himself as a model for identification. Patients are encouraged to improve their communication skills, learn to listen to one another, and externalize their problems by recognizing them in one another. It has been our experience that some patients who have been too anxious or disorganized to participate in individual therapy feel more secure in the group. Anthony and Foulkes, after observing psychotic children in group therapy, concluded that the development of group ego sustained the defective ego of the individual in the group.[3]

Some of Yalom's descriptions of curative factors in group psychotherapy could be observed in this group although its life in terms of duration is very limited: acceptance, universalization, reality testing, ventilation, interpersonal learning.

Another group experience in the adolescent boys unit is the morning group which meets 3 times a week for 20 minutes. In this group all ward staff and patients participate. This type of group is often called the community meeting. This is a very important experience and has diagnostic and therapeutic value, as it represents the beginning of the day. In the nonpsychiatric wards of a general hospital, the physician with his team will make rounds in the morning and see every patient in his bed, review the laboratory tests, examine the patient physically, etc. In the old-fashioned mental hospital, the patients used to be lined up in front of their beds and the physician would walk across the huge dormitory like an army officer inspecting his troops. In the morning group all staff and patients sit in a circle for 20 minutes. During this experience, the doctor could observe the patient functioning in his natural environment: the peer group. Patients who seem withdrawn, depressed, hallucinating, or agitated will be easily identified in the morning group. The staff shares the leadership and the usual themes are related to the whole ward in general. Patients are directed to bring up personal issues in their other individual and group sessions.

Some common themes include: talking about ward events; outside trips; sexual acting out on the unit; patients losing items like shoes, etc; discussions of certain ward rules; complaints about the temperature, the food, and the staff; lack of adequate number of chairs; ward activities; how to deal with certain difficult psychotic, aggressive patients, etc. Quite often themes from this morning group become the focus of other therapy sessions which take place later during the day. Nonverbal communication in adolescent groups is as important as verbal communication. For adolescents who have difficulty verbalizing their feelings, but who are willing to use nonverbal means of communication, we developed a special art group.[5] The therapist for this group is the psychologist of the unit and the technique we use is called "synallactic group image therapy."[6]

Synallactic group image therapy (SGIT) was developed by G. Vassiliou and is based on a systems understanding of the grouping process. In order to facilitate this process, G. Vassiliou introduced a catalytic-regulatory (CA-RE) system called the "collective image." The collective image is a product of the group. All patients prior to the group session are asked to draw or paint freely anything they want and bring it to the session. In the beginning of the session they vote for the drawing or painting they want to discuss. The selected artwork is placed on an easel and the artist is asked to explain what he did, give it a title, say what it reminds him of, and describe his feelings before, during, and after the creative process and also his feelings in the here-and-now. Then the other members of the group are asked to described what they see, what memories the art brings up, etc. This process provides a smooth takeoff for the session and the group is able, through the nonverbal channel of the drawing or painting, to start relating to one another and thus the verbal channel starts opening up. To the extent of the resulting overlapping of the projections of the group members to the artwork, a common theme starts emerging which is the collective image. The collective image facilitates the transition from the nonverbal channel of communication to the verbal one and provides a CA-RE system to ensure that anxiety is kept at levels which enable the group process to continue developing.

The therapist also uses the collective image to bring the discussion to the here-and-now, by asking, for example, "How does this painting or theme relate to us here?" When the anxiety of dealing with here-and-now issues becomes overwhelming the group always has the choice of going back and discussing the painting. Also, the painting could become a substitute for direct verbal expressions, which could become disruptive and threatening of the grouping process. For example, one patient, instead of saying "I don't like you," can tell the painter, "I don't like your painting." The themes which are discussed in each session with the graphic symbols of the paintings and the collective image remain very vivid in the memory of the group members and slowly the group develops its own culture and language. Some of these themes keep coming back again and again but usually at a higher level of organization and complexity leading the group to a spiral process of development and higher functioning. For example, early group sessions may start with inanimate objects and later animate objects and persons interacting could follow.

A few clinical examples will further understanding of the SGIT. In one session the chosen painting depicted the hospital, and the members of the group talked about their feelings of asking for help and "being locked up." In another session a patient drew the earth as a cone in the middle of the universe. The subsequent discussion focused on the group's fear of being lost, abandoned, etc. One patient, Ralph, who was diagnosed as borderline, drew a picture of a bomb but called it "The Magic Match." He tried to deny his feelings of anger and explosiveness but the group was able through the drawing to help him see that the match is ready to set off an explosion. Adolescents quite often have difficulty seeing consequences in a symbolic way, and realize that what "you initiate" will have consequences.

A common theme in an adolescent group is drugs. At the next session Ralph presented a painting entitled "What Will You See If You Look Through Blue Glass Pointed at the Sun." Behind the pseudosophistication of his title, the painting provided a smooth takeoff of a discussion on "grass," drugs, etc. Kevin, a black, paranoid schizophrenic, created a painting which he said represented, "knowledge, wisdom, and understanding." The discussion focused on racial feelings, being black, and provided a nonthreatening symbolic way to exchange ideas on a sensitive subject. A very common issue in the adolescent groups is anxiety related to the conflict around identity. Through the drawing "Who Is It" the group talked about a man with three different personalities. Then they came to the here-and-now to talk, how they felt, at times, different, as though changing their personalities. The theme of anger is recurrent, but recurs each time in a different way. A patient named Adrian drew a marijuana joint, consuming almost the whole body, which was inside the joint. Another patient, Neil, in another session, brought up the issue of different drugs and how they could affect the user.

The art also provided a useful tool for expressing transferential feelings toward the therapist. A patient, Jeff, in a group session, created the painting "The Invasion of the Mind Snatchers," and discussed his feelings toward the psychiatrists, who "try to take over your mind." A similar theme was depicted in a drawing by a patient named Victor entitled "Jail Hospital." On the left side of the drawing a bird is flying away. The group talked how they sometimes equated hospitals with jails. They talked about "dealing with the system establishment." The central theme was: "You are never right, they control you like they control slaves." Aggression and depression at times was able to be expressed through the drawing. A patient, Neil, produced the drawing "Inside a Volcano." The group was able to see that the volcano was surrounded by blackness and depression. Depression was also depicted in an open way, as in a painting by Ralph entitled

"Freedom or Death." The group talked about death and Ralph finally suggested that the outcome will be death. Frequently, internal conflicts related to aggression could be projected and externalized through art, as in Victor's drawing entitled "The Atomic War with Russia." The group talked about the possibility of a nuclear war. They discussed their feelings and concluded that "everybody will be gone."

John was a borderline patient. He created a painting entitled "Dazed and Confused." The group was divided in the discussion about the red dot in the painting, whether it is walking out of the darkness or getting deeper into it. Sex is another popular theme in adolescent groups. Jeff, a boy who was struggling to prove his masculinity, created the painting, "Ecstasy." He talked about his plans to have sex with his girlfriend during his pass ("me and my chick in bed"). On Valentine's Day the group selected a drawing depicting flowers and hearts. They talked about sex and drugs.

Another group was developed to assist patients on the ward who are waiting for placement and in the interim cannot return to their homes. These patients have to stay on the unit usually longer than a month. They could stay 2 to 3 or even 4 months, waiting, going for interviews, etc. For this special group we developed the placement group. The therapist is the social worker of the unit and the number of members varies from 3 to 8. In case there are not enough boys, we add girls from the girls ward who are waiting for placement too. This group focuses primarily on issues related to feelings of rejection, abandonment, separation, information about residential centers, group homes, etc.[7]

One adolescent, A.L., was told that he would not be able to go home when he was ready to be discharged because his family was not ready for him to return. He was disappointed and started regressing and withdrawing. He was referred to and participated willingly in the placement group (initially he refused to participate in other therapeutic activities). After several weeks, when he was leaving for a group home, he asked to say a few words. He took a deep breath, cleared his throat, and said, "I wanna thank you guys and Mrs Z too. I never would have made it without you. I am gonna really miss you but I know that you can't stay in one place forever." After he left he still kept in touch with the leader, "to check up on the group," and to let them know "he's making it" in his new place.

The group role playing and interview practice was also often used to prepare youngsters for placement interviewing. Some patients even used poetry. An adolescent boy, B.N., during his last group session wrote a poem entitled, "What This Group Means." It will be useful to share this poem with the reader.

Group means talking about stuff that hurts.
Group means Mrs. Z. saying, "I can't hear you if you
all talk at once."
Group means crying because you can't go home.
Group sometimes means feeling better and sometimes
feeling worse.
But, group means feeling that your feelings are O.K.

Another group on the ward is the prevocational group. This is for adolescents 15 years and older who are struggling with conflicts related to their vocational orientation and are trying to develop realistic plans and goals for their life. The therapist is the vocational counselor of the unit and this group consists of about 6 to 8 members (boys and girls) who meet once a week for one hour. The main goal of the group is to assist the patients to develop a sense of purpose and goal in their lives. Topics include career choices, plans for the future, types of occupations, training qualifications, etc. Occasionally the group leader invites guests to the group such as a police officer, or an officer from the Navy who discuss their own experiences. Another relevant subject frequently discussed is applying for a job and going for an interview. Role playing is used for this. The therapist brought different pictures of the same girl, how she could have presented herself at an interview — sexy, sophisticated, sloppy, refined, etc — and asked the group to discuss her chances to be accepted.

Since this is one of the groups made up of both boys and girls, issues like sex frequently came up. In one session the girls complained that they are used and the boys feel that the girls tease them in order to manipulate them. The boy often takes the girl out, and she does not want to have sex. The boys said that there are two types of girls, "the girls that do and those who don't." The subsequent discussion focused on issues of respect, sex, values, etc. A girl pointed out that she wants to know where a boy stands and suggested that honesty in that sense is the best way to start a relationship. Since this group was dealing with future possibilities and plans, issues like getting married, having children, parenting, came up frequently for discussion. On these issues the group members, although confused about themselves, were able to confront one another in a realistic way.

Since adolescents accept more easily ideas coming horizontally than vertically, this group experience has been exceptionally rewarding. Besides the described groups, we have a parent group in the evening and we have a media group, where adolescents participate in making films, animations, etc.

SUMMARY

This chapter has been a brief description of the group therapy process on the male adolescent psychiatric unit. We still have to research and study in a systematic way the impact this experience has on our patients and be ready to modify it according to their needs. Certain general observations and concepts may be mentioned as a conclusion:

1. Since inpatient treatment of adolescents is becoming shorter and goal-oriented, we have to modify our techniques to deal with this challenge. Adolescents could use group therapy as an adjunct to individual therapy, pharmacotherapy, etc as long as it becomes integrated in the total treatment plan. In multiple group therapy, well-trained therapists should participate in a coordinated effort. Supervision and coordination should not be seen as interference. Interstaff conflict, competition, and countertransference issues have to be discussed early in frequent meetings. In the described program all the therapists meet 3 times a week to discuss their work with the patients, exchange ideas, and coordinate their efforts. Group therapy with adolescents should be structured in a nonimposing way, which will give the patient freedom of expression within a therapeutic atmosphere.

2. The approach of multiple group therapy has been useful in stimulating the interest of different staff members in their participation on the unit. Their role was clearly defined and their feelings of frustration have been discussed. The patients have the opportunity to relate to different therapists, and express different aspects of their transferential relations.

3. Working with adolescents in groups can be a frustrating, disappointing, and emotionally painful experience. Some therapists although they see the usefulness of group therapy, give up the idea of leading adolescent groups themselves. Quite often what one reads about group therapy with adolescents is very different from what he experiences in an adolescent group. Despite the often chaotic atmosphere, serious treatment can take place. The patients will feel protected by a therapist who "can manage group turbulence."

4. Creative techniques like art, painting, poetry, role playing, and making films provide additional channels of communication besides the verbal one. It is important to keep in mind that these groups are short in duration and in-depth explorations or dramatic structural changes cannot be expected. Their usefulness lies in the fact that they help to transform the hospital ward from a detention center or holding place to a therapeutic community. Short-term hospitalization of adolescents cannot be very ambitious in terms of expectations and results. But still it remains a powerful experience, which has the potential of becoming a new beginning in the life of the adolescent. If the adolescent's

movement toward self-destruction can be reversed and a new constructive process begins, then we can say that hospitalization has played a successful role and a new beginning in the life of the patient has commenced.

REFERENCES

1. Beskind H: Psychiatric in-patient treatment of adolescents: A review of clinical experience. *Compre Psychiatry* 1962;3:354–369.
2. Blos P: *On Adolescence.* New York, The Free Press, 1962.
3. Foulkes S, Anthony J: *Group Psychotherapy.* London, Penguin Books, 1971.
4. Yalom I: *The Theory and Practice of Group Psychotherapy.* New York, Basic Books, 1970.
5. Kymissis P: The use of paintings in analytic group therapy, in Wolberg L, Aronson M (eds): *Group Therapy.* New York, Stratton Intercontinental Medical Book, 1977, pp 129–136.
6. Vassiliou G, Vassiliou V: On the synallactic aspects of the grouping process, in Wolberg L, Aronson, M (eds): *Group Therapy: An Overview.* New York, Stratton Intercontinental Medical Books, 1974, pp 158–174.
7. Zabusky G, Kymissis P: Identity group therapy: A transitional group for hospitalized adolescents. *Int J Group Psychother* 1983;33:99–109.

19

Short-Term Intensive Group Psychotherapy: A New Approach to the Functionally Ill

Edward K. Rynearson
Stephen J. Melson

Medical patients who present with "functional" complaints* constitute a major subgroup in most physicians' practices. Studies of the prevalence of depression in medical patients[1-3] and epidemiologic studies utilizing strict criteria for psychiatric disorders indicate a level of psychiatric morbidity among medical patients of 10%–20% or more.[4-5].

For the majority of the functionally ill, a negative workup for "organic" disease followed by reassurance and brief pharmacologic treatments aimed at symptom relief are appropriate and sufficient interventions. A significant proportion of functional patients are plagued with symptoms of greater duration and severity so that, paradoxically, in everyday activities they are largely *nonfunctional*. Most members of this group do *not* attribute their troublesome symptoms to a "cause" as abstract as "psychological conflict" or "stress" and so persistently seek relief in the medical system; unnumbered others turn to a plethora of "alternative" nonmedical treatments. Though both physical and psychological symptoms are present, it is the *physical* distress that has legitimacy in the eyes of the patient. Once diagnosed as functional this legitimacy is threatened; the patient feels

---

* *Functional illness*: A colloquial medical term for a wide range of symptoms (autonomic instability in various systems, pain, physical manifestations of anxiety, altered mood states) that are usually chronic or recurrent, attributed to a biomedical sickness, and for which relief is sought from physicians or paramedical caregivers.

stigmatized, his symptoms a betrayal of some mysterious inner weakness. In this climate of dismay and diminished self-esteem, psychiatric consultation is accepted but rarely welcomed.

Internists and generalists who repeatedly come into contact with functional patients may recognize the futility and needless expense of repeated negative workups and reassurances but are as frustrated as their patients in changing the course of this syndrome. Psychiatrists who work in medical settings are therefore uniquely placed to bridge the mind-body dichotomy that leads to functional disability and inappropriate use of medical facilities. As in all medical-surgical centers, we see large numbers of psychologically resistant, functionally disabled patients. We have devised a treatment approach that utilizes an intensive group format to overcome resistance, restore self-esteem, and promote change.

Our treatment program was established in 1975. To date, over 1200 patients have undergone treatment. Prospective outcome studies on consecutively treated patients have been completed over two time intervals (1978–1979 and 1983–1984). This chapter describes our treatment approach, cites representative case illustrations, and suggests the effectiveness of short-term intensive group psychotherapy (SIGP) from the findings of a prospective 2-year follow-up study.

PATIENT POPULATION AND TREATMENT CRITERIA

Patient Population

The 50 patients on which we have 2-year follow-up data are a subset of 60 patients who completed the original 6-month outcome study from a total of 120 consecutive admissions. Demographically, the 50 do not differ appreciably from the original study group; they are predominantly white (47 of 50 patients, or 94%), middle-aged (mean 36.3 years) women (39/50, or 78%) who had presented at our medical center with refractory physical complaints (41/50, or 82%, mean duration 25 months). Most were married (32/50, or 64%) or divorced (9/50, or 18%) and well-educated (45/50, or 90% had a high school diploma or above). Nearly half (23/50, or 46%) had undergone previous psychiatric evaluation, and 20 of the 50 patients (40%) had had previous psychiatric treatment; nine patients (18%) had previously attempted suicide.

Since most of our patients are referred from internists or surgeons within our medical center, 39 patients (78%) had received medical evaluation and treatment for their complaints; 11 patients (22%) had been hospitalized in the year prior to admission.

Table 19-1
Principal Diagnoses

Affective disorders	
Dysthymic disorder (depressive neurosis)	21
Major depression, single episode	2
Major depression, recurrent	1
Atypical depression	1
Anxiety disorders	
Generalized anxiety disorder	11
Agoraphobia with panic attacks	2
Panic disorder	2
Personality disorders	
Borderline	7
Histrionic	1
Passive-aggressive	1
Mixed	1
Adjustment disorders	
With depressed mood	2
With mixed emotional features	2
Somatoform disorders	
Conversion disorder	1
Hypochondriasis	1
Atypical	1
Psychological factors affecting physical condition	2
Eating disorders	
Bulimia	1
Total	60

Diagnostic criteria per *Diagnostic and Statistical Manval of Mental Disorders* (DSM-III-R).[6]

Admission Criteria

Our criteria for short-term intensive group psychotherapy are much less specific than the inclusion criteria of other investigators of short-term therapy. Highly resistant, physically distressed patients present with a *wide* range of DSM-III-R diagnoses[6] (depressive, anxiety, and/or personality disorders are the most common underlying diagnostic entities) (Tables 19-1). We specifically *exclude* from SIGP any patient with a high suicide risk, active psychosis, organic mentation, and active alcohol or drug dependence.

TREATMENT PROTOCOL, STAFFING, AND SETTING

A small group (six to eight patients) undergoes an intensive time-limited (3 or 4 weeks) treatment. Figure 19-1 outlines the weekly

	MONDAY	TUESDAY	WEDNESDAY	THURSDAY	FRIDAY
8:30	Introductory Monologs Produced	Videotape Review	Videotape Review	Videotape Review	Friday Tapes Produced
9:00	Psychodynamic Group	Psychodynamic Group	Psychodynamic Group	Psychodynamic Group	Psychodynamic Group
10:30	Break	Break	Break	Break	Break
11:00	Art Therapy	Art Therapy	Art Therapy	Art Therapy	Lunch Prepared by Group - Guests & Families Visit the Unit
12:30	Lunch	Lunch and Staff Meeting	Lunch	Lunch	
1:30	Psychodynamic Group	Psychodynamic Group	Psychodynamic Group Art Review Group	Psychodynamic Group	Psychodynamic Group
2:45	Break	Break	Break	Break	
3:00	Discussion of Program & Videotape Review	Behavioral Group	Videotape Review	Behavioral Group	Weekend
4:00					

Figure 19-1   Weekly treatment format.

treatment format which remains constant from week to week. Our staff is small and consistent; a full-time MSW cotherapist and half-time psychiatrist are the major staff members. The art therapist and psychologist are adjunctive members of the therapy staff helping to provide nonverbal and behavioral dimension to the psychodynamic focus of treatment. The psychotherapy unit is housed in a nearby apartment building separate from the medical-surgical ambience of the clinic and hospital. The unit remains strongly identified with the medical center where continued consultation and support may be requested.

THERAPEUTIC PRINCIPLES AND PRACTICES

Support and Self-Inquiry

In working with this distressed and resistant population, we have designed a treatment program which offers a high degree of *support* and empathy to ease distress while demanding intense *self-inquiry* to overcome psychological resistance. We have found it effective to offer therapy on a daily basis to provide the requisite support and psychodynamic focus. We have selected group therapy as the primary mode of treatment because of its enriched opportunities for interchange and support. The group becomes a lively, dynamic embodiment of now-shared distress, conflict, and resolution. The process of resolution comprises more than symptom relief; with our psychodynamic model applied in a group setting, our goal includes insightful mastery of psychological conflict.

Our approach to the new patient is one of support and optimism. The patient has frustrated the supportive efforts of familiar surrounding figures. Each new patient will have visited the psychotherapy unit before admission, allowing a limited familiarity with the therapeutic program. One or two new patients begin treatment each Monday morning, replacing the one or two patients who left the unit the Friday before. The patients who make up the existing group are in different stages of treatment. This weekly turnover of group members and heterogeneity of therapeutic experience within the group creates a psychosocial climate of fermentation.

CONFLICT RESOLUTION

There is a persistent psychodynamic focus on present conflicts, often reenacted within the group, and their association to past conflicts with primary family members. The process of resolution cannot begin until the patient becomes aware of present and past conflicts. The intensive daily format of psychodynamic group therapy permits a thorough *inventory* of salient conflicts and a solid beginning for resolution. This resolution is viewed as an ongoing, adaptive capacity to master conflict. The conflict will not necessarily be reduced (and certainly never obliterated) with short-term therapy, but the skills now acquired will promote further mastery of internal and external conflict in the coming months and years.

New members witness other members presenting current and past conflicts. Within 2 or 3 days, new patients are sufficiently trusting of the group and acculturated to the process of therapy so they can begin to explore and share their own conflicts. The resistant patient has long been handicapped by a limited capacity for self-observation and analysis. For many patients, this is the first time the existence of suppressed conflicts, often accompanied by strong affects, has been recognized. This early phase of therapy is psychologically confusing and disruptive for the resistant patient. Short-term intensive *group* therapy appears to have several unique therapeutic elements at this time of confusion and disruption which are not offered by individual therapy:

1. The direct observation of therapeutic change in others offers *hope*. Witnessing the pain and confusion of other group members leading to mastery and relief allows heightened tolerance to newly perceived distress. The daily validation of therapeutic change in others strengthens the resolve to continue therapy.

2. Group members are able to directly and openly *care for* one another. The plurality of caregivers that group therapy offers the distressed, resistant patient provides an available, diversified substratum of care. This can be sustaining for the present, and later there will be an opportunity to care for another distressed group member.

To not only receive but to *give* care is a therapeutic windfall of group therapy.

3. *Group cohesion* (the spirit of therapeutic camaraderie) encourages commitment to one another and the process of getting better. One member's difficulty becomes a problem for the entire group and the *affiliative* pressure to remain and resolve the difficulty can be catalytic for the resistant patient.

4. Resistant patients are often handicapped by their inability to express or share affects. This inability may be a manifestation of underlying defective perceptions. These misperceptions serve a defensive purpose — protecting the patient from painful and unacceptable affective experiences. Daily immersion in the intensive interchanges of affects with other group members stimulates and *resonates affects* previously isolated and repressed.

5. With each successive week of therapy, each member is obliged to acquaint new members with their own present and past conflicts. With continued treatment, these *repeated self-presentations* are changed by more detailed perception and changed again by the reaction and interpretation of other members.

Separation and Termination

With time-limited therapy, separation and termination become issues from the moment therapy begins. New patients anticipate leaving the unit 3 weeks after initiation of treatment. This limitation may be extended by a week allowing some adjustment to consolidate therapeutic changes and/or more time for resolution of separation conflicts. Termination is not absolute. A 1-month follow-up visit is routinely scheduled, and the patients are encouraged to call if they need help. In dealing with the resistant patient, it is important to remain available and to encourage future contact for continued support.

The new patient witnesses and experiences *separation* reactions at the end of each week as patients leave. This reaction often stirs unrecognized separation conflicts which serve as important experiences in therapy. The weekly separations also permit a rehearsal enactment and mastery for eventual separation from the group and for future separations.

Therapeutic Coordination of Staff

The staff meets weekly to formulate an individual treatment plan for each patient. Different methods of intervention (art therapy and behavioral therapy) are simultaneously applied and coordinated by the treatment team:

1. Art therapy: Adjunctive to the psychodynamic groups, art therapy provides patients an opportunity for the direct expression of personal experience, dreams, fantasies, and expressions of self with the emphasis on images rather than language. Routine assignments in art therapy include initial self-descriptions, childhood history and family diagrams, personal masks,[7] abstract depictions of affect and fantasies of an ideal situation, and group projects to facilitate group process.

2. Behavioral therapy: Adjunctive to the psychodynamic groups, a psychologist leads a "problem-focused" group. Problems are defined as maladaptive, repetitive cognitive, emotional, behavioral, and interactional patterns. Emphasis is on the here-and-now problems of the individual and their interactions within and without the group. Therapeutic interventions (role replay, cognitive, behavioral, paradoxical, and strategic techniques) and adjusted to the adaptive capacities of each member.

3. Audiovisual aids: Videotaping of individuals and groups provides yet another view of self-presentations, and a record of group interactions.[8] Televised replay of daily psychodynamic groups allows the patient a view of self while interacting with others. Weekly monologue tapes[9] made as a personal diary by each patient allow self-reflection and the opportunity to observe week-to-week changes. Short, emotionally provocative movies are viewed by the therapist and the group together each week. This provides a rich opportunity for the clarification and discussion of the mechanisms of psychological distortion. While everyone has watched and heard an identical series of images, there is invariably a broad spectrum of perceptions.

Role of the Therapist

Some of the familiar duties of group leadership are diminished with intensive daily group therapy. There is little need for formal rules for attendance and involvement. Patients become quickly committed to the therapy program. Exceedingly few (less than 2%) drop out of treatment. The leader is not left with the group task of coping with the disruptive aftermath of unexpected dropouts. Group silence is also a rarity, for the group resumes the therapeutic focus still fresh and unforgotten from the last therapy group. The active clarification of group inertia, inquisitorial questioning, scapegoating, blaming, gossiping, and group narcissism is a necessity, but the intensive pace of therapy allows these clarifications to be more directive than confrontative.

In short-term intensive group therapy, the group leader's role is *protective* as well as facilitative. In the intensive fast-paced group interchange, the frightened, unadaptable patient may display a façade of protective anger, paranoia, or narcissism. It is important for the group leader to protect the group and its now alienated member from enacting the defensive rejection that will follow. Group cohesion and individual trust are important to establish and maintain in short-term therapy. If alienating interaction threatens group cohesion and individual trust, the leader must clarify its defensive purpose and encourage return to more productive interchange.

CLINICAL STUDIES

Case Illustrations

Psychotherapy outcome studies in a clinical setting present complex practical and methodologic challenges to the clinician/researcher. The risk of overinvolvement in computer-generated "numbers" is reduced by continuing study of individuals as they actually live following psychotherapeutic intervention. Three case histories were selected from 50 patients followed for 2 years after treatment to illustrate some common presentations and therapy experiences in our work with the functionally ill. The first two were chosen by the staff as having common presenting symptoms and as having reported change as a result of treatment. The third was chosen as an example of an unsuccessful treatment effort as reported by the patient.

Case 1

Sandra, a 44-year-old married grocery checker from a small coastal city three hours' drive from our medical center, had not worked for several months when she was referred for gastroenterologic consultation by her family physician after a 6-month exacerbation of her chronic symptoms. Presenting complaints included difficulty swallowing solid foods, postprandial epigastric distress, headaches, fatigue, episodic breathlessness with chest tightness, and multiple phobias with severe social withdrawal. Neither she nor any family member had ever received psychiatric care.

After a thorough medical evaluation indicated that her complaints were "functional," the patient was referred for psychiatric evaluation. We learned that her recent exacerbation of symptoms occurred immediately following the accidental death of her only sibling, a 33-year-old half-brother. It was also noted during evaluation that she had a congenital deformity of her left forearm and hand; she had been hospitalized numerous times from age 2 to 12 for corrective surgical procedures.

Her initial week in the unit was marked by considerable resistance to psychological interpretations, apprehension, and tearful withdrawal. With consistent group support, she began to talk about her lonely, isolated childhood marked by her father's abandonment of the family when she was one year old, her terrifying experiences with hospitalization (forced separation from her mother and physical constraints to control her panic), and her subsequent caregiving attachment to her half-brother born after her mother's second marriage when she was 11.

With the uncritical acceptance of her painful recollections came a new sense of alliance and security that enabled her to pursue further self-inquiry. She discovered patterns of anxious attachment or separation followed by physical symptoms leading to prolonged efforts at medical intervention — a recurrent experience in her adult life. Finally, she was able to grieve for her half-brother with the group, giving others the opportunity to explore their losses.

Sandra's husband attended the unit during her final week so that the focus of her treatment on attachment and separation issues could be examined in the context of the marriage.

Case comment This woman's clinical presentation suggested the need for immediate intervention away from her usual environment. The historical evidence for a well-developed capacity for alliance, a specific focus of treatment, and persistence of misguided efforts to overcome disabling symptoms predicted a positive treatment outcome.

Two years after treatment, she is working and socially active. She periodically experiences her old symptoms but says, "Now I know what they mean." Her medical office visits have dropped from 21 the year before treatment to 2 per year since leaving the unit.

Case 2

Mike, a 34-year-old unmarried aeronautical engineer, was referred by his internist for psychiatric evaluation. For the preceding 2½ years he had suffered from progressive symptoms of hyperventilation and marked fatigue. His job was in jeopardy because of prolonged medical absences.

Mike had never been in therapy; he was cynical, even fatalistic about the prospect. His mother, a chronically depressed woman whose therapy had spanned most of his life, had committed suicide 4 years before. She had locked herself in the bathroom and shot herself. He never wept or mourned her death, nor did he weep during that initial interview, explaining through a cryptic smile that he had always considered himself a "survivor." He stoically confessed that for the past year his panic and shortness of breath had led to the dissolution of his engagement, followed by near-paranoid rages against his boss who had threatened to fire him.

Initially, he was a shy, frightened participant in the group who was able to care more for other group members than for himself. Most of his early interactions were to comfort and support others, which he began to appreciate was his long-assumed role within his family. By his second week in therapy he was able to cry for himself and he began to unravel the long-suppressed feelings toward his mother. After 4 weeks of group therapy he made a tearful separation from the group, feeling much improved. He maintained contact with several group members and scheduled several supportive visits to help him through a series of frustrating romances.

Case comment The severity of this patient's symptoms and their calamitous effect on his work indicated immediate intensive psychotherapy. The patient was able to define and begin to work through several recent stresses and to appreciate his constricted maladaptive response to real or threatened loss. He was committed and empathic in his relationships without and within the group.

Two years after treatment, he returned to school for an advanced degree in engineering, allowing advancement at work, and was about to marry. In retrospect, he felt that the short-term group psychotherapy treatments had catalyzed lasting changes in his image of himself and others — changes that he continued to modify and refine.

Case 3

Karen, a 21-year-old woman, presented with a 3-month history of psychogenic vomiting. She anticipated psychotherapy with tested cynicism. Not only had her chronically depressed mother undergone many years of treatment, but Karen herself had skipped from one source of therapy to the next. Her parents had divorced 10 years before, and it was during that year that she began to vomit — and began counseling.

She had a difficult time compressing her history of 21 years, for it was filled with a chain of seemingly unrelated self-images in relationships that she oscillated among — committing herself to becoming a nun, then a professional dancer, then a journalist, then a preschool teacher, and most recently a secretary. Her relationships reflected the same inconsistency, except with her family to whom she would return between careers and affairs.

There was a desperate capriciousness in her interactions and insights while in short-term group psychotherapy. During her first week there was an uncomfortable immediacy to the release of her perceptions of herself and others, including the group members. The second week she became withdrawn, distrustful, and was as confused and bewildered by this change as the group members who had known her the week before. She was gently confronted but would not respond until someone in the group suggested that she had not focused on her unresolved feelings about her parents. At that point, her eyes widened, she assumed a fetal position in her chair, began to rock back and forth, and icily said, "Get away from me, don't touch me." Half an hour later she was less paranoid, tearfully said that she had hated herself and her parents, and could never love herself or accept love from anyone. She could not respond to the supportive efforts of the group or, more precisely, could not feel their support. The group respected her need for distance.

During the last week of treatment, she reattached herself to one of her former boyfriends who wanted to marry her. She could not remain focused on herself or therapy and impulsively terminated treatment without follow-up. She was satisfied with the external changes she had arranged, and she stopped vomiting.

Case comment This young woman's inability to adapt to her chaotic percepts had manifested itself a decade before and had not been modified by considerable psychotherapy. Unable to remain focused or insightful with herself or others, group psychotherapy served to objectify rather than resolve her difficulties. She was so impulsive

290

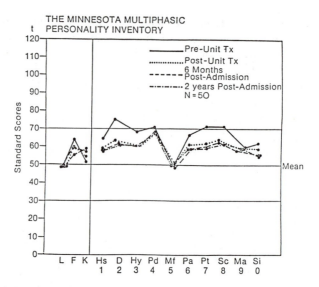

THE MINNESOTA MULTIPHASIC PERSONALITY INVENTORY

Pre-Unit Tx
Post-Unit Tx
6 Months Post-Admission
2 years Post-Admission
N = 50

L F K Hs D Hy Pd Mf Pa Pt Sc Ma Si
1 2 3 4 5 6 7 8 9 0

Figure 19-2   Individual serial MMPI.

and impatient that Karen's vector with time was pendular, characterized by wide opposing swings. Short-term therapy became enmeshed in this desperate rush (Figure 19-2).

Two years after therapy she did not feel that the short-term intensive psychotherapy had been helpful. "I was so confused and in such a fantasy world that I think it just stirred me up." She felt that her father had been more helpful with his approach of being critical and directive. She felt that pragmatic individual counseling would have been more helpful. She continued to have serious questions about her future career and independence from her family. She still panicked when she found herself in an intimate relationship; she had been engaged 3 times during the intervening 2 years. Her psychogenic vomiting recurred intermittently.

Clinical Follow-up

Our preliminary 6-month and 2-year follow-up study assessed the effectiveness of short-term intensive group therapy and whether effects were maintained following treatment. Utilizing standardized therapist and patient-rated psychological tests (see Appendix), patients were assessed on multiple levels of functioning before treatment, posttreatment, at 6 months, and at 2 years. A semistructured 25-minute interview was conducted with each of the subjects at 6 months and 2 years after treatment. Inquiry was made into current physical and psychological functioning, the development and resolution of stressors, and the ability to work.

The obvious difficulty with this effort to study outcome lies in controlling the numerous variables, from arbitrary patient selection through a very complex, multimodal treatment process to the effects of subsequent treatment and life events. Our preliminary efforts have been directed toward characterizing our patient population and seeking test instruments that might measure some of the changes that we hypothesize are a result of treatment. That these efforts produce data that must be highly qualified and interpreted with caution is acknowledged.

The results of such instruments as the serial Minnesota Multiphasic Personality Inventory (MMPI) can be very misleading, as illustrated in case 3. The possible effects of additional treatment on successful or unsuccessful outcome needs further study. Our preliminary study utilized patients as their own controls and did not have a comparison group such as a waiting list control or a different treatment approach. We have attempted to remedy this in a study nearing completion; in the meantime we cannot claim that the changes measured could not have occurred with a simpler treatment program, or no treatment at all.

Data generated during the four testing intervals were subjected to both linear and quadratic trend analysis[10] to establish significant differences in mean values over time and significant rates of improvement or deterioration over time. These analyses were carried out on the group as a whole (6-month N = 60; 2-year N = 50) and on the DSM-III-R diagnostic subgroups dysthymic disorder (N = 25), anxiety disorder (N = 9), and borderline personality (N = 0).

Findings

Measurements following short-term intensive group treatment for a mean of 3 weeks showed the following:

1. Significant decrease in psychopathology
2. Significant increase in positive social attitudes
3. Maintenance of most treatment effects over 6-month and 2-year intervals.

Results among evaluation procedures and instruments were consistent. Therapist ratings and patient self-rating were very similar.

An example of our preliminary findings for the diagnostic subgroup *dysthymic disorder* (N = 25) is seen in the composite MMPI (Figure 19-3). Statistically significant changes were present in all scales except L, MF, and MA, in the direction of less psychopathology, and

292

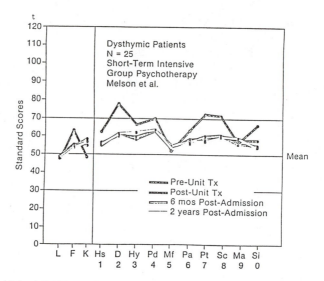

Figure 19-3   MMPI dysthmic disorders. (Reproduced with permission from Melson et al.[11])

were maintained over a 2-year period. The composite MMPI can, of course, conceal individual changes that might be different.

Further Therapy

All patients completing short-term intensive group psychotherapy are scheduled for a 1-month review session; any other recommendations for extended group, couple, or individual psychotherapy sessions are decided on in staff conferences during each patient's final week in the unit. Of the 50 patients followed for 2 years, 22 (44%) had 5 or more hours of psychotherapy after short-term intensive group psychotherapy.

Medical Expenses and Working Days Lost

For the 42 patients for whom annual medical expenditures were available, major reductions from the year before treatment to the second year after treatment were recorded (Figure 19-4). The mean medical expense figure for the second year following treatment approximates the national average for adults aged 20–40 years. The figure includes the mean cost of intensive group psychotherapy at the time of the study. For the 31 patients employed during the year prior to therapy, mean working days lost due to illness declined tenfold in the year after treatment (Figure 19-5).

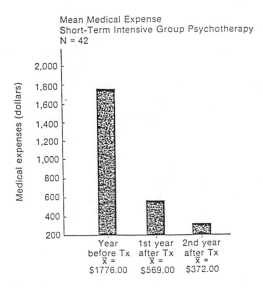

Figure 19-4　Medical expenses.

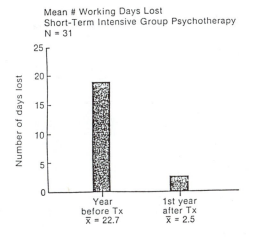

Figure 19-5　Working days lost.

SUMMARY

Functional illness is a colloquial medical term used by internists and generalists to define a large group of physiologically and psychologically symptomatic patients who repeatedly seek medical treatment for symptom relief. In our multispecialty medical center, we have devised a new (1975) psychotherapeutic format for these chronically disabled, psychologically resistant patients.

Short-term intensive group psychotherapy provides removal from the discouraging isolation of the home environment for a time-limited period of 3 or 4 weeks while avoiding the expense and stigma of psychiatric hospitalization. *Support* is coupled with *intensive self-inquiry* in daily psychodynamic groups, art therapy, behavioral groups, and the creative use of audiovisual techniques. This immersion in a variety of therapeutic modalities helps overcome resistance and fosters new adaptations to past and present psychological conflicts.

Our preliminary clinical studies suggest significant therapeutic change and maintenance of changes following treatment. Major reductions in medical care expenditures and time lost from work are important benefits. Current research compares an evaluated but untreated control group and stress management group with short-term intensive group psychotherapy.

REFERENCES

1. Zung W, Magill M, Moore JT, et al: Recognition and treatment of depression in a family medical practice. *J Clin Psychiatry* 1983;44:3–6.
2. Nielsen AC, Williams TA: Depression in ambulatory medical patients. *Arch Gen Psychiatry* 1980;37:999–1004.
3. Wright JH, Bell RA, et al: Depression in family practice patients. *South Med J* 1980;73:1031–1034.
4. *Use of Health and Mental Health Outpatient Services in Four Organized Health Care Settings.* Mental Health Service Systems Report, series DN No. 1, US Dept of Health and Human Services (NIH), 1974.
5. Barsky AJ III: Hidden reasons some patients visit doctors. *Ann Intern Med* 1981;94:492–498.
6. American Psychiatric Association: *Diagnostic and Statistical Manual of Mental Disorders*, ed 3, revised [DSM-III-R]. Washington, DC, American Psychiatric Association, 1987.
7. Melson SJ, Thurman W: The making of masks in psychotherapy. *Psychiatr Ann* 1982;12:1086–1089.
8. Rynearson EK, Flanagan P: Distortions of self-image and audio-visual therapy. *Psychiatr Ann* 1982;12:1082–1085.
9. Wilmer HA: Use of the television monologue with adolescent psychiatric patients. *Am J Psychiatry* 1970;126:1760–1766.
10. Meunch GA: The assessment of counselling and psychotherapy: Some problems and trends, in McReynolds P (ed): *Advances in Psychological Assessment.* Palo Alto, Calif, Science & Behavior Books, 1968, vol 1.
11. Melson SJ, Rynearson EK, et al: Short-term intensive group psychotherapy for patients with "functional" complaints. *Psychosomatics* 1982; 23:197–205.

The therapist and patient completed the Global Pathology Index (GPI). The GPI is the last item of the Hopkins Brief Psychiatric Rating Scale, a standard sensitive instrument for the measurement of psychopathology and treatment-related change. The major advantage of this test is its simplicity (rating on a 0-to-8, absent-to-extreme continuum), providing a single score.

The Minnesota Multiphasic Personality Inventory (MMPI) was administered to assess the type and degree of maladjustment. Well-controlled studies show that MMPI changes correspond to clinically relevant alterations in patients involved in successful and unsuccessful treatments.

The 18 scales of the patient-answered 480-item California Psychological Inventory (CPI) measure the presence of positive psychological attributes.

The Nowicki-Strickland Locus of Control Scale measures an individual's perceived mastery of his or her world. Relatively *internalized* persons see the self as in control; *externalized* persons see the control reenforcements as external to the self. In previous studies, *high externals* obtained higher scores on neuroticism and anxiety than did those with a more internal orientation.

The Cornell Medical Index (CMI) (see Table) assessed the frequency and duration of physical complaints before and after therapy. Medically significant emotional disturbance has been associated with 30 or more *yes* responses and with various configurations on this 195-item index.

Cornell Medical Index (N = 48): 2-Year Follow-up

Symptom	Significance*	Linear Trend*	Quadratic*
Eye and ear complaints	.4345	.5473	.3604
Respiratory	.0001	.0343	.0001
Cardiovascular	.0000	.0017	.0001
Digestive	.0000	.0103	.0000
Musculokskeletal	.0000	.0000	.0000
Skin	.0001	.0003	.0030
Nervous	.0004	.0169	.0018
Genitourinary	.0002	.0958	.0005
Fatigability	.0089	.0000	.2653
Frequency of illness	.0007	.0003	.0331
Miscellaneous	.0314	.5103	.0255
Habits	.0000	.0004	.0009
Mood and Feeling Patterns			
Inadequacy	.0000	.0000	.0000
Depression	.0000	.0000	.0000
Anxiety	.0019	.0528	.0034
Sensitivity	.0001	.0002	.0218
Anger	.0000	.0000	.0000
Tension	.0000	.0000	.0000

P = 5.05.

Usually from one to four psychosocial stressors (listed in the *Diagnostic and Statistical Manual of Mental Disoders* [DSM-III-R][6] under Axis IV) were judged etiologically significant by the clinician as having contributed to the disorder. They were rated on a seven-point severity scale from 0 (unspecified) through 1 (none) and on up to 6 (extreme), providing a total cumulative score.

The adaptive function level (DSM-III-R, Axis V) was rated on a six-point scale from 6 (very poor) to 1 (superior). A poor score reflects marked impairment in either social relations or occupational functioning (or moderate impairment in both). A superior score indicates unusually effective functioning in social relations, occupation, and use of leisure time.

20

Group Therapy with Geriatric Patients

RoseMarie Perez Foster
Jeffrey R. Foster

The geriatric patient has been heavily burdened by both social and clinical stereotyping. The erroneous assumption that severe organic deterioration is normative to the aging process, or that all elderly persons inevitably disengage from life, has frightened both patients and clinicians alike and created a vicious cycle of inappropriate pessimism in the therapeutic setting.[1]

Contrary to these biases, however, a significant body of literature has begun to emerge pointing to the responsiveness of the elderly to both individual and group psychotherapies.[2-4] Group therapy as a primary treatment modality for older patients began in the 1950s with the pioneering work of Silver[5] and Linden,[6,7] both of whom worked with the severely impaired elderly in institutional settings. Seen as both cost-effective and counteractive to the social isolation and withdrawal common to this patient population, group therapy also challenged the assumption that the elderly were not responsive to therapeutic intervention or emotional change.

More recent work with the elderly has integrated the thinking of self-psychology and the pivotal importance of self-object relations occurring throughout the life cycle.[8,9] Frequently isolated or devoid of significant others, many lonely elderly persons lack a sustaining self-object matrix which can adequately fuel ego activity.[10] The interpersonal interaction, empathic support, and consensual validation offered by a group indeed provides a context where the isolated older person's ego can be emotionally refueled or replenished with necessary narcissistic supplies.[11,12]

The published literature on group therapy with the elderly includes work with both inpatient and outpatient populations. Clinical groups span the healthy, intact older persons; those with the respective spectrum of functional disorders (ie, depressions, paranoid states, character disorders, etc); and those elderly with significant organic impairment. This chapter presents a selected overview of the literature on group therapy work with the elderly, highlighting technique, patient composition, and process variables. It should be noted that there are very few empirical studies which experimentally assess treatment efficacy. Most outcome data emerge from geriatric patients in mixed diagnostic groups and use posttreatment measures whose reliability is difficult to assess. Findings generated from experimental designs as opposed to more common analogue studies or incidental reporting are so noted.

GROUP TECHNIQUES FOR THE COGNITIVELY IMPAIRED GERIATRIC INPATIENT

There are several task-focused group modalities specifically designed for the organically compromised hospitalized older patient. These approaches have arisen, in part, in response to the frequently reported phenomenon that institutionalization accelerates social isolation and a general trend toward personality disintegration.[13,14] *Sensory retraining* is a group therapy technique for severely regressed older patients who have deficits in motoric and cognitive abilities and are thus handicapped in discriminating basic sensory stimuli. The goal of sensory retraining is to engage the regressed older patient in an array of multisensory stimulation so as to increase sensitivity of the remaining senses and hopefully enhance environmental functions.[15] Conducted in small groups of five to six, patients in a planned fashion name objects, feel textures, clang instruments, etc. The group format provides the context for peer feedback and social re-engagement, as well as consistent positive re-enforcement for sensory retraining strides. Some authors have emphasized the benefits of more than one session per day to maintain continuity and sustain a high stimulatory level.[15,16]

Reality orientation (RO) is a group technique which deals directly with the classic symptoms of confusion, disorientation, and memory deficits through intensive cognitive and memorial stimulation. This treatment was originally developed by Folsom,[17] who contends that no patient is totally confused; it is the job of the staff person to find the areas of "wellness" in the patient and try to expand its boundaries.

Reality orientation was originally designed for institutionalized older patients but the technique is also practiced in day care settings. In the RO process every contact by the patient with the staff member is used to improve the patient's awareness of time, place and person. All activities in which the person is engaged are continuously verbally labeled. Repetition of information and re-enforcing the patient for correct responses is essential. Environmental aids such as large clocks, calendars, and boards depicting date, year, and weather are also used. Reality orientation group or classroom RO is a supplementary, more intensive form of RO for more confused patients. Small groups of optimally four patients are usually seen daily. As with milieu RO, patients are taught basic time, place, person, and object information. However, the group setting provides personal and interpersonal attention in which treatment objectives can be prescribed, attained, and practiced in a firm, supportive environment.

The literature offers predominantly good reports on the efficacy of RO. Anecdotal evidence in the form of case reports and staff observations indicate that RO is an effective therapeutic technique.[17–20] In one of the few controlled experimental designs Harris and Ivory[21] report that 5 months of RO treatment significantly changed both the verbal orientation behaviors and the overall clinical impression of female geriatric mental patients. No such changes were found in a control group who received traditional hospital care. Barnes[22] found no significant changes in patients' overt behavior or informational ability after 6 weeks of classroom group RO treatment. This finding suggests that group RO treatment alone is not potent enough to produce cognitive-therapeutic changes, and that group RO must be used in conjunction with the sustained re-enforcement effects of the environmental milieu RO approach.

Remotivation therapy is a structured group program used with institutionalized elderly individuals who can function on a verbal cognitive level. It aims to reach the intact interests of the patient in group discussions about everyday life (eg, grooming, dining in public, current events, plant care, etc). This group technique is an effort to resocialize the individual and arouse his interests in the environment by helping him learn or relearn a wide variety of informational knowledge.[23] Remotivation was originally developed for administration by hospital aides. Groups range in number from 8 to 15 and typically meet once or twice a week.[24] Traditionally, this therapy follows a formalized plan of five steps which evolves from establishing a climate of acceptance, to introduction and discussion of a relevant topic of discussion geared to the group's interests, needs, and level of functioning. The group members are helped by the leader to explore the subject matter, to use their own available intellectual resources, and to apply the knowledge of their own immediate life circumstances.[25] The results of Bovey's experimental study[26] show that remotivation therapy significantly enhances the self-concept of geriatric patients.

A remotivation group can be organized around the accomplishment of specific tasks. Patients with poor personal appearance respond well to a grooming remotivation group. Previously apathetic elderly female patients can be successfully motivated to plan and prepare ward social events.[27] Lyon[23] reports, however, that short-term task-oriented remotivation groups do not produce long-term motivation effects; they generate, instead, islands of active participation which quickly disappear after task completion. Remotivation groups must be ongoing, Lyon adds, for higher-level changes in behavior and attitudes to occur.[23] Various offspring of the original remotivation therapy procedure are reported.[28] Wallen[29] describes a successful motivation therapy program for medically improved elderly veterans who were unmotivated to leave the hospital. The main goal was to develop more personal and social responsibility on the part of each patient so that eventual courses of action could be taken for placement in the community. In an experimental design, Nevruz and Hrushka[30] compared the effects of a "motivation" group specifically focused on leaving the hospital, vs a nondirective verbal group, on the discharge rate of geriatric psychiatric patients. Both groups were equally and significantly effective in producing an increase in the discharge rate. This finding suggests that the factors producing change in even the highly focused motivation and remotivation groups are based on certain emotional dynamics common to all types of group process.

VERBAL, PSYCHODYNAMIC GROUP TECHNIQUES WITH THE GERIATRIC INPATIENT

Unlike the specified group techniques described above, the psychodynamic group therapies include a complexity of therapeutic styles, goals, and diagnostic qualifying criteria which are difficult to classify. Nevertheless, since 1950 when Silver[5] first reported that geriatric inpatients are amenable to group psychotherapy, the unsteady stream of literature indicates positive therapeutic effects.

Authors consistently report that verbal group work with the institutionalized functionally disturbed or organic older patient is presented with the major difficulties of short attention span, persistence of ideas, variable confusion, and vacillating memory function.[5-7] These specialized problems have been met by reports of higher therapist activity levels, frequent group sessions for serial continuity,[31] and dual group leadership for increased support and arousal of sharper transference phenomena.[7] Conversely, despite the mentioned difficulties and more advanced levels of pathology, inpatient geriatric groups are noted to achieve group cohesiveness faster than outpatient groups given patients' enhanced daily contact and interaction.[32]

Positive criteria for verbal group participation include personal approachability, a relative degree of reality orientation, and verbal coherence.[5,33] Several authors, however, report that verbal group therapy with severely withdrawn and disoriented patients can be achieved with the aid of specialized approaches. Feil[34] states that severely regressed nursing home patients can participate in emotionally expressive group process only if the group worker can form an individual relationship with the patient outside the group in which he or she demonstrates sincere, empathic concern for the patient's suffering. Manaster[35] reports successful expressive group work with severely confused hospital patients where all sessions are first initiated by basic RO techniques. Using controlled experimental designs, both Gugel[36] and Wolk and Goldfarb[37] found that verbal group therapy was effective with organic brain syndrome patients in improving cognitive symptoms. Both authors interpret this as an amelioration of the depressive aspect in these patients' "organicity."

Verbal group styles with the geriatric inpatient are highly varied. Lichtenberg[38] regularly convened a "tea party" of refreshments, games, and conversation with psychotic geriatric patients. Although psychotic content remained unchanged, patients showed striking improvement in mood, physical appearance, and hygiene, thus decreasing the earlier tendency toward general deterioration. This was similarly reported by Corcoran,[39] and Ross[40] in a review of inpatient geriatric group therapies. Wolff[41] describes an "understanding brother" approach in group work with state hospital elderly. In an ambience of social refreshments and open discussion, the therapist encourages criticism of hospital staff, clinical methods, food, etc. Wolff states that organic patients will show some improvement in reality orientation and interest in themselves and surroundings.[41] The same author[42] compared, through clinical reports, the efficacy of group vs individual therapy with functionally disturbed and organic elderly, and found the group approach to be more useful in its more specified focus on interpersonal skills and resocialization.

Linden[6,7,43] reported detailed descriptive data of the group therapy process with his population of "senile" institutionalized women. He described long silences and unspontaneous interactions in the initial phases of his groups with patients looking toward the male doctor for valuable statements and emotional reactions. Though no group cohesiveness or process seemed apparent during the initial months, verbal inactivity during session time belied significant changes taking place in the patients' ward behavior which now was more cheerful and optimistic. Likewise, in later phases of the group, active participation in group session did not necessarily correlate with positive therapeutic gain as passive members also showed significant signs of therapeutically generated change outside the group setting.

For those institutionalized geriatric patients in hospital and nursing home settings whose verbal ability is intact and who can maintain a relatively long attention span, a typical group process is frequently reported: initial preoccupation with somatic ailments; active responsivity to therapists' encouragement to reminisce about life events in earlier years; and ultimate expression of conflicts and inner feelings about current life circumstances where life in the institution becomes the matrix for group discussions.[44–46] These reports consistently show positive therapeutic change in the areas of increased self-esteem and socialization skills, as well as the generally enhanced "motivation to live."[44] In a process report of an interactive inpatient group, Leszcz et al[1] describe the clinical and apparently dynamic changes in a group of elderly depressed men, who in the face of personal and physical losses had disengaged from the environment. The authors attribute therapeutic effectiveness to the group's dual process of providing narcissistic supplies and offering empathic understanding of the members' narcissistic losses to the self.[1]

Butler[47] has described the developmental importance of life review and reminiscing for the aged. He described it as a normative process characterized by a progressive return to consciousness of past experiences, and particularly the resurgence of unresolved conflicts. Recent years have yielded numerous reports of "life review" group therapy[48] and "reminiscence groups" with geriatric patients.[49–51] Authors consistently report that reminiscing tends to facilitate cohesiveness within the group, as members are able to share and validate common experiences. The life review process stimulated within the group setting can also lead to constructive integration of old conflicts, as well as the acceptance of previously troublesome life experiences through adaptive rationalization.[47]

VERBAL PSYCHODYNAMIC GROUPS
WITH ELDERLY OUTPATIENTS

Group process descriptions of outpatient verbal groups with elderly people who suffer from mood or neurotic characterologic difficulties significantly resemble phenomena seen with younger age groups.[52–54] Patients use interpretation and make therapeutic gains in enhanced interpersonal functioning and a decrease in depression. However, an often reported phenomenon unique to elderly outpatient groups, is that group cohesiveness and positive group process will often not occur unless the older persons' age-related feelings of emotional deprivation are first met through concrete gratification. This is well described by Levine and Poston,[54] whose groups were unsuccessful and never reached cohesion until a casual coffee lounge period preceded the actual group session. Here patients were nurtured by both oral gratification and the presence of group leaders who made themselves directly available in a warm social manner. It is interesting to note the commonality of this age-related need in both emotionally healthier geriatric outpatients and the previously described institutionalized elderly who likewise responded to oral gratification from the staff. This phenomenon is consistent with the report by the present authors from a 1982 survey of geriatric groups in the New York metropolitan area.[32] Therapists of both inpatient and outpatient geriatric groups cited loss and deprivation as the top ranking content theme. These reports highlight the obvious narcissistic needs of the elderly, as well as the function of the therapeutic context to potentially refuel them.[32]

There are several reports of outpatient groups where the normative, age-related aspects of physical dysfunction are the focus of the group process. The purpose of these groups is to help elders accept the physical changes of the life cycle and substitute new behaviors that will result in increased feelings of self-worth. Using this modality, Deutsch and Kramer[55] anecdotally described therapeutic improvement in patients' general dealing with life stresses. Liederman et al[56] used posttherapeutic projective testing and found that these group patients showed a strengthening in higher-order neurotic defenses and a decrease in the more regressive defensive mechanisms. In an experimental design Paradis[57] showed a significant decrease in the depression of geriatric outpatients whose group focused on better modes of coping with age-related physical problems. Several authors have reported the use of cognitive therapy approaches in groups of physically compromised elderly. Focusing on the role of attitudinal beliefs surrounding physical disability and its influence on mood, these authors consistently found positive therapeutic change in their cognitive telephone group therapy with homebound disabled elders.[58,59]

Conversely, Stever et al[60] did not find cognitive-behaviorial group therapy for depressed elders superior to psychodynamic group therapy in relieving depression and anxiety. In a controlled experimental design using rigorously defined diagnostic populations, these authors found both treatments to be equally successful in producing significant therapeutic effects.[60] This finding, they conjecture, may support the seminal findings of Luborsky et al,[61] that most comparative psychotherapy studies do not show substantial differences among treatment types. However, it may be further hypothesized that for the lonely geriatric patient, therapeutic effectiveness, regardless of modality, lies in the group's ability to rekindle the self-object matrices so necessary in sustaining adaptive ego activity.

Several authors report on patient homogeneity and its effects on geriatric group therapy. Levine and Schild[62] treated a homogeneous group of depressed patients with group therapy. The authors viewed this as a positive therapeutic factor, as the universality of depressive feelings in the patients led to basic empathy and acceptance rather than alienation and fears of rejection. In treating several homogeneous groups of elderly outpatients (ethnic, obese, character disorders) Franklin (personal communication, May 1981) attributes his consistently successful outcomes to diagnostic homogeneity in group composition.

Berger and Berger[63] and Berger[64] described a holistic group therapy approach with geriatric outpatients who had been previously institutionalized for severe functional or organic disorders. Using a mixture of verbal, music, movement, and gestalt therapies, the authors report relief in "group members' anxiety, self-hate, and depression."[63,64]

Several group therapy modalities are reported within the geriatric day care setting. Folsom (personal communication, July 1981) describes great success with RO milieu accompanied by intensive RO groups. Rathbone-McCuan and Levenson[65] use socialization therapy with day care clients, attempting to compensate for the role losses suffered as a result of the aging process. Group work is directed toward creating new social roles for the client, for example, friend or helper; or reestablishing aspects of former roles, for example, parent, worker, etc. Striking therapeutic changes were noted in previously unspontaneous clients who now participated in active peer and heterosexual relationships. Kubie[66] and Turbow[67] both view verbal groups as basic elements of the day care setting. Turbow finds this technique especially helpful on the death of a group or family member.[67]

SOME PRACTICAL ISSUES IN
CONDUCTING GROUP THERAPY
WITH THE ELDERLY

The collective clinical experience discussed previously is certainly encouraging as to the suitability and efficacy of group therapy for this chronologically older patient population. However, there remain a number of practical questions for which guidance is helpful concerning the start-up of a geriatric group and its subsequent evolution. A recent survey was made by Foster and Foster[32] in which 20 group therapists who were experienced with geriatric groups in both inpatient and ambulatory settings were interviewed concerning the logistics and distinctive features of conducting these groups that affected both patients and therapists.

Group Composition and Logistics

Not all patients are suitable for group therapy. In particular, patients with severe psychopathology or potentially reversible organic brain disorders should first be engaged and evaluated on an individual basis. Patients with strong hostilities to either the group setting or toward the therapists are usually not personally helped and are often disruptive to the group process. Sometimes several individual sessions with potential members are helpful to promote initial rapport with the therapists. Group composition should avoid, where possible, "cultural rifts" between members that may inhibit group cohesiveness. The average group size is often in the range of 6 to 12 patients where the larger sizes are intended to accommodate a subgroup of patients who do not come regularly but rather episodically (eg, due to poor health, to transportation difficulties, or inclement weather, or to psychologic preferences to remain marginally involved). The groups usually meet weekly for sessions lasting from 60 to 90 minutes.

Initial Patient Rejection Rates

Approximately 15%–25% of patients for whom group therapy is recommended reject the offer. The characteristics of the rejectors are varied but do not seem to reflect factors concerning age, marital or socioeconomic status, or prior exposure to group therapy.

Attendance and Attrition Rates

Typical attendance rates at sessions are in the vicinity of 75%–90% with the most frequent reason for absence being related to illness (self or family). Other reasons include inclement weather, episodes of increased emotional resistance, and vacation traveling. Once the group is started, its size is fairly stable after the first month during which some attrition occurs due to the growing ambivalence of a few members. Over the remainder of the initial year of the group there is further dropout of members, typically due to illness or death, that ranges from 22% for ambulatory groups to 66% for inpatient groups. The attrition rate is replenished by new member who are added to the group as it evolves. These dropout rates are not fundamentally different from those found in many younger-aged psychodynamically oriented psychotherapy groups where cumulative attrition rates may rise from

13% to 29% by the 12th session up to 27% to 63% by the end of the next 12–20 months.[68]

Group Cohesion

Most geriatric groups become cohesive although the time course may be quite variable. The most usual time frame to reach cohesiveness is approximately 2 to 3 months. However, some outpatient groups may take anywhere from 6 to 12 months to become cohesive.

Distinctive Group Features

Older patients may be particularly ambivalent about engaging in group processes due to a complex interweaving of issues concerning losses and their sense of time. The time sense includes the dual perceptions of both their own longevity combined with an awareness of a growing imminence of death. These themes may leave an older patient hesitant to invest in the group with the fear that meaningful new relationships may soon be lost. These factors may contribute to the extended time that it may take some geriatric groups to become cohesive.

Other distinctive features of many geriatric groups concern modifications of therapist techniques that often occur. Generally, the therapists often show increased activity and heightened flexibility in running geriatric groups than they would demonstrate in conducting younger-aged groups. The increased activity varies from the sharing of more personal feelings or giving personal concrete examples during the group to the taking on of an "advocacy" role to directly encourage patients to deal with health, landlord, and political issues that may affect them. The increased flexibility of therapists includes serving food at sessions, including important patient caretakers in the group, encouraging group members to have social contact outside the group meetings, having telephone contact with members to facilitate their attendance, and the frequent use of cotherapists in conducting the groups.

CONCLUSION

The published literature supports group therapy as a clinically effective intervention with elderly patients at varying levels of cognitive and emotional adjustment. There are many basic similarities to group work with younger populations with respect to cohesiveness, interpersonal learning, and consensual validation of common experiences. However, the most unique feature that emerges in doing work with the elderly population is that regardless of therapeutic modality, narcissistic loss and deprivation reign dominant in both manifest and latent group process. This is noted in reports of overt and articulated preoccupation with losses, as well as in unconscious, but determined expression of needs for narcissistic supplies.

The general gerontologic literature repeatedly points to the normative developmental tasks and ensuing adaptive stresses that characterize the senescent years. The present literature constructively presents therapeutic modalities which can alleviate some of these stresses.

REFERENCES

1. Leszcz M, Feigenbaum E, Sadavoy J, et al: A men's group: Psychotherapy of elderly men. *Int J Group Psychother* 1985;35:177–195.
2. Gotestam KG: Behavioral and dynamic psychotherapy with elderly, in Birren JE, Sloane RB (eds): *Handbook of Mental Health and Aging*. Englewood Cliffs, NJ, Prentice-Hall, 1980, pp 775–805.
3. Stever J: Psychotherapy with the elderly. *Psychiatr Clin North Am* 1982;5:199–213.
4. Gallagher DE, Thompson LW: Effectiveness of psychotherapy for both endogenous and nonendogenous depression in older adult outpatients. *J Gerontol* 1983;38:707–712.
5. Silver A: Group psychotherapy with senile psychotic patients. *Geriatrics* 1950;5:147–150.
6. Linden ME: Group psychotherapy with institutionalized senile women: study in gerontologic human relations. *Int J Group Psychother* 1953;3:150–170.
7. Linden ME: Transference in gerontologic group psychotherapy: studies in gerontologic human relations IV. *Int J Group Psychother* 1955;15:61–79.
8. Kohut H: *The Restoration of the Self*. New York, International Universities Press, 1977.
9. Orenstein A: Self-psychology in childhood: Developmental and clinical considerations. *Psychiatr Clin North Am* 1981;4:435–453.
10. Chessick RD: *Psychology of the Self and the Treatment of Narcissism*. Northvale, NJ, Jason Aronson, 1985.
11. Cath SH: A testing of faith in self and object constancy. *J Geriatr Psychiatry* 1976;9:19–40.
12. Modell AM: Normal psychology of the aging process. *J Geriatr Psychiatry* 1977;10:47–52.
13. Euster: A system of groups in institutions for the aged. *Soc Casework* 1971;52:523–529.
14. Bolin R: Sensory deprivation; an overview. *Nurs Forum* 1974;13:240–259.
15. Folsom JC, Boies BL, Pommerenck K: Life adjustment techniques for use with the dysfunctional elderly. *Aged Care Servi Rev* 1978;1:1–11.
16. Huber R: Sensory training for a fuller life. *Nurs Homes* 1973;7:14–15.
17. Folsom JC: Reality orientation for the elderly mental patient. *J Geriatr Psychiatry* 1968;1:291–307.
18. Taulbee EE, Folsom JC: Reality orientation for geriatric patients. *Gerontologist* 1975;15:508–510.

308

19. Ireland MJ: Starting reality orientation and remotivation. *Nurs Homes* 1972;21:19–20.
20. Letcher P, Peterson L, Scarbrough D: Reality orientation: A historical study of patient progress. *Hosp Community Psychiatry* 1974;25:801–803.
21. Harris CS, Ivory PB: An outcome evaluation of reality orientation therapy with geriatric patients in a state mental hospital. *Gerontologist* 1976;16:496–503.
22. Barnes J: Effects of reality orientation classroom on memory loss, confusion, and disorientation in geriatric patients. *Gerontologist* 1974;14: 138–142.
23. Lyon GG: Stimulation through remotivation. *Am J Nurs* 1971;71:982–992.
24. Pullinger WF: Remotivation. *Am J Nurs* 1960;60:682–685.
25. Robinson AM: *Remotivation Techniques; a Manual for Use in Nursing Homes.* Philadelphia, Smith, Kline & French, 1966.
26. Bovey JA: The effect of intensive remotivation techniques on institutional geriatric mental patients in a state hospital. *Diss Abstr Int* 1971;32:4201–B.
27. Sink SM: Remotivation: Toward reality for the aged. *Nurs Outlook* 1966;14:26–28.
28. Carini EM, Coskey SA, Michlewski J, et al: Remotivation groups: Too structured for current needs? *Hosp Community Psychiatry* 1971;22:37–38.
29. Wallen V: Motivation therapy with the aging geriatric veteran patient. *Milit Medi* 1970;135:1007–1010.
30. Nevruz N, Hrushka M: The influence of unstructured and structured group psychotherapy with geriatric patients on their decision to leave the hospital. *Int J Group Psychother* 1970:19:72–78
31. Yalom ID, and Terrazas F: Group therapy for psychotic elderly patients. *Am J Nursing* 1968;68:1690–1694.
32. Foster JR, Foster RP: Group psychotherapy with the old and aged, in Kaplan HI, Sadock BJ (eds): *Comprehensive Group Psychotherapy*, ed 2. Baltimore, Williams & Wilkins, 1983, pp 269–278.
33. Burnside IM: Group work with the aged: Selected literature. *Gerontologist* 1970;10:241–246.
34. Feil NW: Group psychotherapy in a home for the aged. *Gerontologist* 1967;7:192–195.
35. Manaster A: Therapy with the "senile" geriatric patient. *Int J Group Psychother* 1971;22:250–257.
36. Gugel RN: The effects of group psychotherapy on orientation, memory, reasoning ability, social involvement, and depression of brain damaged and non-brain damaged aged patients exhibiting senile behavior. *Diss Abst Int* 1979;40:2365-B.
37. Wolk RL, Goldfarb AI: The response to group psychotherapy of aged recent admissions compared with long-term mental hospital patients. *Am J Psychiatry* 1967;123:1251–1257.
38. Lichtenberg JD: A study of the changing role of the psychiatrist in the state hospital. *Psychiatr Q* 1954;28:428–441.
39. Corcoran D, cited by Geller JA: Proposal for institutionalized group psychotherapy. *Psychiatr Q Suppl* 1950;24:270–277.
40. Ross M: A review of some recent group psychotherapy methods for elderly psychiatric patients, in Rosenbaum M, Berger M (eds): *Group*

Psychotherapy and Group Function. New York, Basic Books, 1963, pp 105–121.
41. Wolff K: Group psychotherapy with geriatric patients in a mental hospital. *J Am Geriatr Soc* 1957;5:13–19.
42. Wolff K: Comparison of group and individual psychotherapy with geriatric patients. *Dis Nerv System* 1967;28:384–386.
43. Linden ME: The significance of dual leadership in gerontologic group psychotherapy: studies in gerontologic human relations III. *Int J Group Psychother* 1954;4:262–273.
44. Saul SR, Saul S: Group psychotherapy in a proprietary nursing home. *Gerontologist* 1974;14:446–449.
45. Lazarus LW: A program for the elderly at a private psychiatric hospital. *Gerontologist* 1976;16:125–131.
46. Burnside IM: Long-term group work with hospitalized aged. *Gerontologist* 1971;11:213–218.
47. Butler RN: The life review: An interpretation of reminiscence in the aged. *Psychiatry* 1963;26:65–76.
48. Sable L: Life review therapy: An occupational therapy treatment technique with geriatric clients. *Phys Occup Ther Geriat* 1984;3:49–54.
49. Baker NJ: Reminiscing in group therapy for self-worth. *J Gerontol Nurs* 1985;11:21–24.
50. Gardella LG: The neighborhood group: A reminiscence group for the disoriented old. *Soc Work Groups* 1985;8:43–53.
51. Schafer DE: Reminiscence groups and the institutionalized elderly: An experiment. *Diss Abstr Int* 1985;46:1060.
52. Johnson HF: The effects of encounter groups on selected age related variables in a volunteer geriatric population. *Diss Abstr Int* 1970;32:739-A.
53. Berland DI, Poggi R: Expressive group psychotherapy with the aging. *Int J Group Psychother* 1979;29:87–108.
54. Levine BE, Poston M: A modified group treatment for elderly narcissistic patients. *Int J Group Psychother* 1980;30:153–167.
55. Deutsch CB, Kramer N: Outpatient group psychotherapy for the elderly: an alternative to institutionalization. *Hosp Community Psychiatry* 1977;28:440–442.
56. Liederman CP, Green R, Liederman VR: *Geriatrics* 1967;22:148–153.
57. Paradis AP: Brief outpatient group psychotherapy with older patients in the treatment of age-related problems. *Diss Abstr Int* 1973;34:2947-B.
58. Evans RL, Halar, EM, Smith KM: Cognitive therapy to achieve personal goals: Results of telephone group counseling with disabled adults. *Arch Phys Med Rehabil* 1985;66:693–696.
59. Evans RL: Cognitive telephone group therapy with physically disabled persons. *Gerontologist* 1986;26:8–11.
60. Stever JL, Mintz J, Hammen CL, et al: Cognitive-behavioral and psychodynamic group psychotherapy in treatment of geriatric depression. *J Consult Clini Psychol* 1984;52:180–189.
61. Luborsky L, Singer B, Luborsky L: Comparative studies of psychotherapies. Is it true everyone has won and all must have prizes? *Arch Gen Psychiatry* 1975;32:995–1008.
62. Levine B, Schild J: Group psychotherapy of depression. *Soc Work* 1969;14:46–52.

63. Berger LF, Berger MM: A holistic approach to psychogeriatric outpatients. *Int J Group Psychother* 1971;23:432–444.
64. Berger LF: Activating a psychogeriatric group. *Psychiatr Q* 1978;50:63–74
65. Rathbone-McCuan E, Levenson J: Impact of socialization therapy in a geriatric day-care setting. *Gerontologist* 1975;15:338–342.
66. Kubie, SH: *Group Work with the Aged.* New York, Greenwood Press, 1953.
67. Turbow SR: Geriatric group day care and its effect on independent living. *Gerontologist* 1975;15:508–513.
68. Roback HB, Smith M: Patient attrition in dynamically oriented treatment groups. *Am J Psychiatry* 1987;144:426–431.

21

Group Psychotherapy with Soviet Immigrants

Anna Halberstadt
Lena Mandel

Despite the individualistic bias of modern society in the United States, working with patients in group psychotherapy is, nonetheless, a significant form of treatment. Working with patients in a group setting is perceived as going against the prevalent thrust of a society which presumably fosters alienation and isolation. This chapter examines group psychotherapeutic approaches to people who reside in the United States but who come from a very different society, a society which self-consciously exalts group norms, and, by implication, devalues individuality and individual eccentricity. This chapter describes the experience of group work with Soviet Russian immigrants, a population that, despite its considerable ethnic, geographic, cultural, and professional diversity, displays a certain commonality which has profound implications for their integration into a working group.

PERSPECTIVES ON DIFFERING SOCIETIES

Soviet immigrants are all (albeit to different degress) members of a category, the self-proclaimed "Homo sovieticus," and thus products of a totalitarian society. Seventy years of total political repression have created the psychological and behavorial patterns that are necessary to ensure survival in a pervasively hostile environment. Some of these survival strategies conflict directly with the tenets of all treatment models of psychotherapy. Indeed, the very concept of psychotherapy is radically new to these patients. Psychotherapy and the provision for psychotherapy do not exist in the Soviet Union. Moreover, the very existence of an unconscious has been considered essentially anti-Marxist. Freud is considered to be a nonperson in the Soviet Union.

The idea of looking for help in any way is profoundly alien to the ex-members of a society which worships strength and brands both compassion and introspection as bourgeois qualities not fit to survive in the "new world." Still more alien is the process of "baring one's soul" to a perfect stranger, particularly one attached to an institution. This is something absolutely unthinkable in the Soviet Union, where such a luxury would almost automatically be punishable. The mental health field, in particular, is too rich in innuendos for a Soviet immigrant who comes from a country where psychiatry has been notoriously misused as a means of political coercion. In addition, anyone who has ever seen a psychiatrist in an outpatient clinic or hospital in the Soviet Union is registered in their files. This registration may prove to be a major obstacle in finding a job, getting promoted, going abroad as a tourist, or even obtaining a driver's license.

Past experiences of Soviet immigrants have consisted of dealing only with government owned and operated services where any functionary's allegiance is always presumed to be exclusively to his agency, that is, to the government. Therefore, the relationship between the functionary and the client is one characterized by disrespect and a mutual lack of trust. The functionary is universally seen as an adversary whom the client, through discreet subterfuge, must manipulate at all costs.

Segal[1] considers ambivalence toward authority to be one of the central characteristics of the Soviet Russian people. This ambivalence is manifested through a combination of hostility and dependency. The dependency is exacerbated by the obverse side of the oppressiveness and intrusiveness of the Soviet society, that is, its paternalistic quality. For those who do not question authority's existence, it can be seen as the omnipotent good mother who provides cradle-to-grave security. It is the source of all sustenance, information, and caretaking. The system encourages dependency and compliance and discourages personal responsibility. Thus, "adaptation to freedom," as Goldstein[2] noted, becomes a major problem for immigrants:

> Each Soviet immigrant carries within himself a totalitarian state, a system of inner dictates. This internal map is the product of all his past experiences and struggles. It creates the conflict between his dependency and his quest for freedom. It reflects a central aspect in the psychological structure of the *Homo Sovieticus*, which is the emphasis on collectivism.[2]

This spirit of collectivism is both the result of Marxist propaganda and a remnant of the patriarchal traditions of the peasant communities of prerevolutionary Russia.[1] The prerevolutionary collective responsibility of the peasants has been transmuted into an all-pervasive underground barter system of "counter economics." As Hedrick Smith[3] has noted, this underground "collectivism" is absolutely necessary for survival in a society with massive and systemic shortages of goods and services. Thus, one's relationship to the group — the way one is evaluated by this group, "the others," for example, the collective, the neighbors — is a matter of paramount importance for survival.[1]

Goldstein[4] has examined the values that govern the relationships between the individual and the group within the Soviet society: They include a strong family orientation, interdependence, a social orientation, group identification, and commitment to the long-term goals of the group. Living in a highly ideologized society, *Homo sovieticus* is a kind of compound identity that represents a collective idealized image, which to a great extent has become internalized by the individual and which is represented intrapsychically as a feeling of belonging to Soviet society. This sense of belonging is valued much more highly than the individual freedom or autonomy so important for Americans.

Thus, Phyllis Hullewat,[5] in a study conducted on displaced Soviet citizens in 1968 by the Harvard Project on the Soviet Social System, reported that a battery of psychological tests that were administered to 51 Soviet young men (all of whom were raised in the Soviet Union) and to a control group of American men, revealed that the strongest needs of the Soviets were (1) need for affiliation; (2) need for dependence; and (3) oral needs (preoccupation with getting and consuming food). The contrasting needs of the Americans were (1) need for achievement; (2) need for approval; and (3) need for autonomy. The study found the central conflicts of the Soviets to be (1) trust vs mistrust; (2) optimism vs pessimism, with a tendency toward hopelessness and helplessness; (3) activity vs passivity — becoming passive-aggressive or manipulative. This was in sharp contrast with the central conflicts of Americans which they identified as (1) intimacy vs isolation; and (2) autonomy vs belongingness. Hullewat outlines the dynamics of the Soviet immigrant family as characterized by "family enmeshment and lack of autonomous functioning accompanied by incomplete object constancy and difficulty in managing ambivalent feelings.... A family structure that is adaptive in the Soviet system can become maladaptive in the American system where autonomy and competitiveness are highly valued."[5]

An important characteristic of the *Homo sovieticus* is his narcissism. Segal[1] has contrasted the narcissism expressed in Soviet society with the narcissism that is commonly considered a typical American trait. He has criticized Kernberg's implication[8] that narcissism is not typical for societies where there is no competition and people are encouraged to be "mutually supportive." Segal believes rather that the realities of Soviet life stimulate the development of narcissism that is caused by feelings of insecurity and inadequacy and which manifests itself in a constant seeking of admiration. Accordingly, he sees Soviet reality as not being able to provide an individual with emotional support, while at the same time stimulating ambitiousness, overbearing demands, and a pathologic desire to succeed.[1] The Soviet society gratifies its members' narcissism by the creation of innumerable awards and by its hierarchical structure. Thus, it is not surprising that a popular hobby within the Soviet Union is the collecting of lapel pins of rank. The narcissism extends to an inability to examine Soviet history; while Americans may assume inevitability, they do not claim infallibility. The Soviet Union rests on just that claim of an unfailingly correct "general line."[6]

Erikson has identified "pseudo-species" as a group of people who adhere consciously, or unconsciously to a particular doctrine, ideology, or religion.[9] Their adherence is so stringent that they place everyone who believes differently in the position of the "other," as if they were members of a different species. Each pseudospecies assumes its purity, its moral rightness, and professes a fear that a connection with the "other" will contaminate it and take away from it the qualities that make it special, chosen, even immortal. Howells and Galperin, in an unpublished discussion (1984) of pseudospeciation and the Soviet Jewish immigrant, point out that, despite their emigration, the Soviet immigrants adhere to a prevailing faith that the Soviet Russian people are better, smarter, more altruistic, more self-sacrificing, and generally morally superior to, other people:

> The distortions born from this world view have emigrated with our population, some of whom will tell you that the light bulb was invented by a man called Yablochkov, the radio — by Alexey Popov, and the steam engine — by two serf brothers from the Ural mountains. Lenin is often quoted as saying that the Russian language is the richest, most powerful tongue in the world.

Another distinctive characteristic of the Soviet immigrant population is their highly conflicted sense of ethnic identity. The absolute majority of immigrants are Jewish — simply because Jews are the largest of the three groups of Soviet population allowed to even apply for emigration (the other two being Armenians and Germans). In the Soviet Union Jewishness is considered a nationality, not a religion (as it is, for example, in the United States). One's nationality is marked in one's internal passport. Therefore, regardless of one's religious belief, one is identified as a member of a persecuted minority.

The actual motivation to leave the USSR varies widely from economic and political reasons to a quest for creative and religious freedom. Indeed, the desire to leave may reflect curiosity about the "free world," or even a neurotic sense that an escape to the West will allow one to escape from personal problems. Whatever the secondary motivation, the principal reason why these people emigrate from the Soviet Union is the existence of a very real state-sponsored system of anti-Semitism. Therefore, while on the one hand these people seek to leave the Soviet Union because they are Jewish, on the other hand they lack a real sense of Judaism as a religion, because Judaism, like all other religions, has been persecuted and virtually outlawed in the Soviet Union for the past 70 years and there has been practically no Jewish education or Jewish observance possible in that country for several generations. The Soviet Jewish emigrés have almost no notion of what it means to be Jewish, with the few exceptions being Jews from the formerly independent Baltic republics of Estonia, Latvia, and Lithuania, where Jewish religion and culture flourished between the two world wars, and certain groups of Sephardic Jews from relatively isolated communities in the Caucasus and central Asia, who preserved some of their traditions.

Thus, most Jews within the Soviet Union have a primarily negative Jewish identification. For them being Jewish is almost like being possessed by a hereditary disease over which they have no choice or control, but which follows a family from generation to generation and which constitutes a considerable social and professional handicap, effectively relegating the person to the status of a second-class citizen. Thus, many Soviet Jews seek to emigrate in order to shed an identity that they experience as a cumbersome burden. As Goldstein noted: "The sense of identity that most Jews develop in the powerful and hostile Soviet environment is highly conflicted and neurotic. Emigration for them is very often prompted by a very powerful internal quest for a healthier identity."[4]

CHARACTERISTICS OF PSYCHOTHERAPY GROUPS WITH SOVIET IMMIGRANTS

In view of the pervasively different Soviet environment and the distinctive experiences of Soviet Jews, it is not surprising that the psychotherapy groups in which they participate will have distinctive characteristics. These distinctive characteristics can best be examined in the context of a representative group of Soviet emigrés. The group under examination consisted of five widows all of whom had initially entered individual psychotherapy for treatment of depression. These women, aged 48 to 68 years, were all Jewish, with the exception of one ethnic Russian, and resided in the Washington Heights area of Manhattan. The group members came from different parts of the

Soviet Union: Moscow, Kiev, Sochi, and Odessa. The initial focus of the group was that of a bereavement group with an agenda of helping these women to adapt to widowhood, a loss which compounded the preexisting multiple losses which had accompanied their uprooting and emigration.

One might consider group therapy to be an ideal treatment modality for this relatively homogeneous group of patients precisely because these people have lived within a collectivist regime and in a society which values the need to "belong." Such was not the case for several reasons. As mentioned previously, psychotherapy is an unfamiliar concept for people from the Soviet Union. Being accustomed to the psychopharmacologic approaches prevalent within the Soviet Union, Soviet immigrants are very skeptical of the value of "just talking." While in time Soviet immigrants can accept the concept of individual psychotherapy, since it has a certain congruence to the medical model of treatment and feeds into their innate sense of respect for the authority of an expert, group therapy poses additional issues. Specifically, group therapy entails talking to fellow patients, in this case fellow immigrants, who are not accepted as "experts" and who, as fellow immigrants, are objects of suspicion. Thus, even the process of group formation, which necessarily involves "recruitment" and "selling" group therapy to patients who are already in individual therapy, provided major obstacles and proved to be a major undertaking: Out of a pool of 12 potential group candidates, only five were finally persuaded to at least try group therapy. And of these five, all clearly gave their consent only out of their respect for the therapist and out of their desire to please her, continuing all the while to express suspiciousness and even hostility toward their prospective fellow group members.

Suspiciousness and hostility toward fellow immigrants is very characteristic of the emigré community. It should be noted that the emigré community in New York City is relatively small (approximately 75,000 immigrants), closed, and quasi-incestuous, since everybody in it either has had some direct contact with or has heard about almost everyone else. Relationships among immigrants are often highly ambivalent. On the one hand, they seek out one another and identify with one another, but as Segal[1] has pointed out, they often seem to be ashamed to belong to a group of people whom they perceive as reflecting all their own shortcomings and problems. This projection results in hostility and suspiciousness, where fellow immigrants are blamed for whatever problems the individual might have experienced in adjusting to American society. The stress and frustration of this adaptation further exacerbate communication problems among immigrants, leading to the formation of a society in which arguments, gossip, and jealousy become rampant. The claustrophobic character of emigré society creates a very real stumbling block in the efforts of recruitment during the formative period of a psychotherapy group. All prospective members expressed the fear that whatever they might reveal to the other group members would immediately become grist for the gossip mills of the Russian emigré communities. Assurances of confidentiality were scarcely effective because the concept of confidentiality in any sort of official context is inconceivable to a former Soviet citizen (indeed, "privacy" does not exist as a word in the Russian language).

Certain common themes arose during the course of group therapy. These included feelings around the multiple losses, the difficulty in adjusting to a radically different society, intergenerational problems, loneliness, and isolation. But, despite the fact that these common themes could be readily identified, little actual working through occurred in the homogeneous group because of the lack of basic trust. No matter how depressed and unhappy these patients revealed themselves to be during the course of individual therapy, all of the group members were extremely resistant to even identifying these feelings during the course of group therapy and the members characteristically competed with one another under the pretense that things could not be better either for themselves or their children.

The example of Mrs M is illustrative. During individual therapy Mrs M dealt with her impotent rage against her younger daughter for using and exploiting her, and with her increasing guilt for having induced her older daughter and her grandson to join the family in the United States where they were now experiencing problems in finding employment and in adjusting. Yet, here is Mrs M talking to the group:

> I am so happy to be here. You know, I never even suspected that people could live so well. It is simply wonderful to have the whole family together, and you should see what a beautiful house my daughter just bought. My kids are doing so well! There is nothing else in the world that I want, just to see them doing so well.

The discrepancy between their productions in group and in individual therapy are due to several factors. As Yalom[7] has pointed out, a candidate's potential for group work is affected by his previous history of belonging to various formal and informal groups. As a former Soviet citizen, each member of this group had experienced forced affiliation with a host of various groups from early childhood. Participation in such groups is invariably marked by a high degree of cynicism and "as if" behavior in which participants play certain roles that are totally unrelated to their actual inner selves.

Another issue is raised by Mrs T. Mrs T is a lonely and intensely depressed woman who fancies herself to be more worldly and sophisticated than her fellow immigrants. Thus, she agreed to participate in group therapy primarily because she anticipated that the group would afford her a stage on which she could demonstrate her innate superiority. Her comments during the group were in this vein, as the following illustrates:

> You should all learn to look at the bright side. The way you mope and groan is thoroughly Soviet, there is no place for that kind of attitude in America. Now, look at me: Nobody could tell my age because I take care of myself. I am still very attractive to men, it's me who is not interested. I do not need anybody and am perfectly happy by myself.

Mrs T illustrates how anger at the multiple losses of Soviet immigrants often never get worked through to any significant degree because they experience the mourning process as being discouraged both by the host American community, and, to a far greater degree, within their own subculture. It is as if by mentioning the loss of one's multiplicity of ties of one's native country, the emigré grants recognition to the loathed political system.

The emigré's inability to mourn is further exacerbated by "survivor's guilt" which has been described primarily in the literature referring to the Holocaust.[8]

While the experiences of Soviet immigrants cannot be compared to those of the Holocaust survivors, members of both groups have left behind family and friends who may face the consequences of their choice. This guilt may express itself in an obtuse manner, such as in the depression experienced by one group member who was convinced that the murder of her son during a street robbery in Russia was in retribution for her emigration. This survivor's guilt makes it extremely stressful for the group members to question the validity of their decision to emigrate or to examine the consequences of their having left the Soviet Union.

The group members were raised in a society which, arguably, is more involved with the myth of its creation than is any other society. Moreover, it is a society in which appearance is always esteemed over substance and in which nuances provide the only indication of status and position. It is a society which maintains appearances at all costs, creating a Potemkin village of socialist progress, because if appearances are destroyed, then the myth of its creation and the discrepancies between mythology and reality would have to be investigated. Thus, the risk taking and the degree of interpersonal trust, which are essential qualities for successful participation in a therapeutic group, are lacking in this group of patients. Their departure from the qualities which lend themselves to successful participation in group therapy is illustrated in the following dialogue:

> Mrs I: It must be tough for you having both your daughters in England. My daughter is only in New Jersey and still I don't see her nearly as

often as I would like, for instance, like my neighbor's kids: they live down the block. . . .

Mrs T: Oh, it's nonsense. I much prefer having my daughters on another continent. This way we can have our own space and do not intrude into one another's lives. It's so provincial and so Russian to want to have your kids near you at all times. . . .

The members of this group were extraordinarily dependent, by American standards, in a wide variety of ways. For example, the members would never arrange the chairs themselves or suggest that refreshments be served. They would ask the therapist's permission to open or close the door, or even to change seats. When the therapist came back after vacationing in Israel, none of the group asked any questions about it. This kind of dependent posture has generally been cited as a significant factor impeding the success of a group.[7] Indeed, this group's dependency illustrates Yalom's perception that: "There appears to be a general clinical sentiment that heterogeneous groups have advantages over homogeneous groups for long-term intensive group therapy. . . . Clinicians widely believe that the homogeneous group tends to remain at a superficial level."[7]

Whitaker and Lieberman[9] clarify the question of heterogeneity vs homogeneity by suggesting that within heterogeneous groups the therapist can work with the patient around the areas of conflict and reworking patterns of coping, while homogeneous groups are suggested in re-enforcing areas of ego strengths. Thus, Pollock notes that "homogeneous groups of individuals with the same attitudes toward dominance produce less change than do groups that are heterogeneously composed for the same variable."[10]

Hence, it is not surprising that the pressures the Soviet society exerts on the individual are so intense, that, irrespective of the individual's strength or psychopathology or even the differences in coping style, the products of the Soviet society are too similar to create sufficient dissonance or incongruity for changes to occur within a homogeneous group. The restrictive culture created within this homogeneous group of Russians mirrors in miniature the restrictive culture in which they achieved maturity. Thus, their group experience exhibits cultural norms of restriction, dogmatism, and a search for similarities, which include the submergence of individuality and the discouragement of self-disclosure or even of personal honesty in confrontation.

There has been a tendency to assume that a "homogeneous" group of individuals should be treated within homogeneous groups. However, when the group's homogeneity is the product of a procrustean uniformity of style and a rigidly imposed pattern of coping with conflict, as in the homogeneous group of Soviet immigrants who have come to the United States as adults, having formed their mature personalities under the totalitarian regime of the Soviet Union, then the potential for this group to perceive a therapeutic group as a re-creation of the familiar collectivist society must be strongly considered. In this context, the possibility that a therapeutic group may evoke feelings of suspicion and mistrust, an exaggerated competition for favored status, and ultimately intensify group resistances, reflects the authors' clinical experience.

Paradoxically, it appears that the Soviet immigrants' feelings of loss of motherland and their isolation within their new country can be worked through more fruitfully within heterogeneous groups that include both new immigrants and "native" Americans. Indeed, exposure to the conflicts and patterns of behavior — of conflict resolution and coping with the issues of everyday existence — adopted by native Americans appears to be more therapeutic because it leads the new American to an enhanced sense of acceptance within the prevaling society. Working within heterogeneous groups leads the immigrant to successfully mourn his losses and ultimately toward a final acceptance of the reality of immigration, as well as the realistic problems that arise for anyone living within the United States. Thus, the heterogeneous group serves as a corrective experience for those who saw their emigration as a panacea for a host of personal problems that were unresolved within the Soviet Union, for example, the physician who finally obtains his medical degree in the United States is forced to confront the reality of medical practice, or the husband who seeks a separation from his spouse is forced to deal with the issue of divorce, etc.

GROUP PSYCHOTHERAPY WITH SOVIET ADOLESCENTS

Group psychotherapy with Soviet adolescents presents a distinct range of issues. Soviet adolescents are usually much more assimilated than their parents to the host American culture. With the incorrigible avidity of adolescence, Soviet adolescents are often fluent in English and rapidly adopt new models of dressing and socializing. In addition to the usual conflicts of adolescence, the Soviet adolescents struggle with a similar confusion and conflict between their adaptation to American society and the parental value systems rooted in the Soviet past. Their homogeneous agenda lends itself to the incorporation of Soviet adolescents into homogeneous groups. The clinical work discussed in this chapter is the product of the clinical experience gained from leading several groups of Soviet adolescents in high schools in New York City. These boys and girls lived in Brooklyn, in an area densely populated by recent emigrés from the Soviet Union. Most of the immigrant families were from the southern Ukraine (hence the area's name, "Little Odessa"), but some were from other parts of the USSR.

Initially, the groups were referred to as "discussion groups." Their primary focus was to facilitate the adjustment of emigré adolescents to living in the United States. Groups were scheduled to meet weekly at the school building and to run for about an hour. While the group rapidly developed a core membership of six to eight members, individuals were allowed to attend meetings on an "interested-but-uncertain" basis. The members often socialized (with the leader's sanction) outside the group. Indeed, since the members went to the same school, lived in the same neighborhood, and sometimes were related, it was expected that there would be extramural contact. Of particular importance in facilitating the formation of the groups was the leader's reassurance to the group members that all material discussed within the group would be confidential, and that the content of the group sessions would be discussed with teachers, student counselors, or parents *only* with the group members' permission. As a result, the groups were attended regularly. In several cases members requested referrals for individual therapy, and after the initial group leader discontinued leading the groups, other groups have been successfully conducted under the same agency auspices.

Certain issues arose consistently during the course of the groups:

1. A stronger sense of isolation and separation was observed as compared to their peers of different ethnic background. In general, most group members seemed to have little in common with their American-born peers. Indeed, some group members identified with Caribbean blacks because they, unlike American blacks, were immigrants. In general, the group members felt isolated from and disappointed with their American schoolmates. Indeed, their sense of isolation resulted on occasion in fights between Soviet and Puerto Rican gangs.

2. Adolescents identified with their parents' values in such important areas as politics, education, marriage, etc. They also adopted their parents' view of Americans as cold, materialistic, unfeeling, and "primitive." Some expressed criticism of American families as being detached and distant, and contrasted these families with the warmth and closeness that prevailed in their own homes. Like their parents, they were skeptical of Americans who, while married, had separate bank accounts, and they questioned the practice of unmarried couples living together.

3. The presence of intergenerational conflict was exacerbated because the group members had become much more fluent in English than their parents and superficially had adopted many of the indicia of American culture more rapidly than their parents. Thus, many

group members reported that their parents were extremely over-protective and fearful of the "bad" influence of American freedom on their children. One male group member (who dressed à la mode in a jacket adorned with 30 buttons, each having a picture of a rock star) reported:

> When I get up in the morning, mother calls me from work: "Don't forget to lock the doors and to turn off the lights when you leave. Be careful when crossing streets, don't stay out late, etc." Then father calls me: "Don't forget to call and tell me what time you are coming home. Don't go out with your friend X in his car, he is a bad driver and he looks weird." Then the grandmother calls me and starts from the beginning with: "What did you eat?"

Thus, group members were called on to deal with their parents' somewhat exaggerated fears of street crime, blacks, and strange fashions. Yet, despite this infantilization, they were also called on to serve as interpreters and mediators with the outside world for both parents and grandparents.

4. Confusion over values was expressed in increased anxiety, depression, and a variety of asocial activities, such as truancy. From 70% to 80% of group members were female. They were characteristically uninvolved in their studies, a surprisingly high percentage were engaged, and many married early, dropping out of school. Perhaps their concentration on Russian nightclubs and discos represents both a reaction to the traditional Russian and Jewish emphasis on scholastic achievement and a species of Americanization.

However, by the leader's focusing on letting the group members ventilate their feelings without resort to using psychoanalytic jargon or a detached psychoanalytic stance, these adolescents were able increasingly to integrate themselves into their schools.

GROUP PSYCHOTHERAPY WITH
SOVIET IMMIGRANTS
IN HETEROGENEOUS GROUPS

While group psychotherapy in homogeneous groups is useful for Soviet adolescents, group psychotherapy for Soviet adults in homogeneous groups intensifies group resistances. Efforts to work with Soviet immigrants in heterogeneous groups have been more successful. Let us examine the issues that arise in working with Soviet adults in the context of a homogeneous group that was formed to deal with work-related issues and the complexities of forming relationships. The group initially consisted of seven members, all of whom were bright, reasonably well-functioning individuals without severe pathology. Two group members were Soviet immigrants, the other members were ethnically mixed: one was Hispanic, one was Italian, and the rest were American Jews.

As has been previously noted, Soviet adults find it exceedingly difficult to trust to the bona fides of other group members. Thus, one of the Soviet members dropped out after two sessions. The dropout had previously been in individual therapy and had derived great benefit from her therapeutic experience. Nonetheless, she felt "uncomfortable in sharing her problems with 'Americans' and 'strangers.'" She continued in individual psychotherapy because only in individual therapy did she feel that she retained enough contact with her therapist. Not surprisingly, the issues that formed the focus of her therapy related to her inability to mourn the loss of her mother, sisters, and other close friends who had remained in Moscow. Her sense of separation and isolation had also been exacerbated by her recent move to a prosperous suburb where there were few, if any, Soviet emigrés, and by her daughter's increasing involvement in school activities. In a sense, her being in a heterogeneous group exacerbated the sense of isolation she was experiencing within her life in a non-Russian suburb.

Many of the issues that Soviet immigrants bring to the group psychotherapy setting are exemplified by the progress of Alyosha. Alyosha arrived in the United States at the age of 16. He entered individual and family therapy at 18 because of multiple somatic complaints and phobias related to heights, subways, and driving. During the course of therapy, his symptoms had greatly diminished and he was able to drive, albeit with some anxiety about using the tunnels and bridges which link New York City to New Jersey. Nonetheless, at 23 he still lived in a one-bedroom apartment with his family of origin and had job-related difficulties. Group therapy was suggested because of his continuing enmeshment with his family. It should be noted that, despite the family's fluency in English (Alyosha's mother had been an English teacher in the Soviet Union), the entire family felt lonely and isolated among Americans and among their fellow Soviet emigrés. Every family member described difficulties in forming relationships of any depth in the United States. Alyosha had, however, taken steps toward forming a satisfying relationship with a woman. Alyosha, like other members of his family, mourned and idealized his past in Leningrad. He regarded other Soviet emigrés, especially if they did not originate in either Moscow or Leningrad, as being primitive, vulgar, and pushy. On the other hand, Alyosha perceived Americans as cold, materialistic, and unsophisticated, or in the case of his only American girlfriend, as too independent and "masculine."

Within the group, Alyosha began to form meaningful and significant relationships with the other group members. Of particular importance was the relationship he formed with Nina, the Puerto Rican member of the group. Nina was preoccupied with having moved from Puerto Rico to New York. Because of their shared history of immigration, she and Alyosha formed a bond which focused on both the need to adjust to American society and the difficulties this entailed. Both of them were able to ventilate their feelings of anger at their loss of homeland, to mourn this loss, and to move on.

The formation of relationships with other group members has significantly enriched the group experience for Alyosha. He formed relationships with older women whom he perceived as "little sisters" despite their being significantly older. The presence of two older men within the group enabled Alyosha to reexamine his relationship with his father. In more general terms, the group offered Alyosha an opportunity to relate to adults without the burden of overprotection and enmeshment, which is the product of coming of age in Soviet society and which fosters the sense of individual powerlessness. Alyosha's ability to utilize group psychotherapy may also reflect his having arrived in the United States as an adolescent. For the older Soviet immigrants, the pattern of helplessness and dependency may be so much a part of their style of coping with external difficulties, that working within groups becomes exceedingly frustrating.

In this context it is ironic to note that in the era of *glasnost*, the Soviet Union has begun to show an increased interest in the use of self-help groups on the order of Alcoholics Anonymous to deal with its pervasive alcoholism. However, it is questionable whether these efforts are going to be successful. In the Soviet society, which infantilizes the individual and promotes dependency and which has abused the group process through a wearying round of youth group/union/party meetings, it would seem that a therapeutically focused group would be experienced as simply yet another attempt to rob the individual of his freedom to choose his intoxicants. The freedom to participate constructively in groups is not divisible from the freedom to participate as an individual within the society.

SUMMARY

This chapter discusses the issues that arise in atempting to utilize group psychotherapy in working with Soviet Russian emigrés. These immigrants are a product of a society that has consciously attempted to create a new human ethos in which the collectivistic is exalted over the individual. Thus it is exceedingly difficult to work with adult Soviet immigrants who perceive the group approach with a skeptical, cynical, and dependent stance. However, when efforts are made to integrate them into heterogeneous groups, or when group members are Soviet immigrant adolescents rather than adults, group therapy is useful in helping the individual to successfully mourn his country of origin and to adapt to a more open society.

REFERENCES

1. Segal B: *Vstrecha Sovetskogo Cheloveka s Amerikoi* (The meeting of the Soviet man with America). *Noviy Zhurnal* 1983;3:50–65.
2. Goldstein E: Psychological adaptations of Soviet immigrants. *Am J Psychoanal* 1979;39:257–263.
3. Smith H: *The Russians*. New York, Ballantine Books, 1976.
4. Goldstein E: Homo Sovieticus in transition: Psychoanalysis and problems of social adjustment. *J Am Acad Psychoanal* 1984;12:115–126.
5. Hullewat P, cited in Smith H: *The Russians*. New York, Ballantine Books, 1976, pp 56–57.
6. Pfaff W: *New Yorker*, Dec 6, 1987.
7. Yalom I: *The Theory and Practice of Group Psychotherapy*. New York, Basic Books, 1979.
8. Kinsles F: Second generation effects of the Holocaust: The effectiveness of group therapy in the resolution of the transmission of parental trauma. *J Psychol Judaism* 1981;61:53–67.
9. Whitaker and Lieberman, cited by Melnick J, Rose G: Expectance and risk taking propensity: Predictors of group performance. *Small Group Behav* 1979;10:389–401.
10. Pollack H: *Change in Homogeneous and Heterogeneous Sensitivity Training Groups*, dissertation, University of California, Berkeley, 1966.

INDEX